THE TWO
REVOLUTIONS

Antonio Gramsci and the Dilemmas of Western Marxism

by Carl Boggs

SOUTH END PRESS   BOSTON, MA

Copyrights are required for book production in the United States.
However, in our case, it is a disliked necessity. Thus, any properly
footnoted quotation of up to five hundred sequential words may be
footnoted without permission, so long as the total number of words
quoted does not exceed two thousand. For longer continuous quotations
or for a greater number of total words, authors should write for
permission to South End Press.

Library of Congress Cataloging in Publication Data

Boggs, Carl.
    The two revolutions.

    Bibliography: p.
    1. Gramsci, Antonio, 1891-1937. 2. Communists--
Italy--Biography. 3. Communism--History. I. Title.
HX289.7.G73B63 1984   335.4'092'4 [B] 84-13871
ISBN 0-89608-226-1
ISBN 0-89608-225-3 (pbk.)

Cover by Bonnie Acker
Typeset by Diane Bushee and the South End Press collective
Design and Paste-up by the South End Press collective
Printed in Great Britain at The Pitman Press, Bath

Dedication:

*For my mother,
Harriet Boggs*

Table of Contents

Preface

Anyone familiar with Antonio Gramsci's writings will know that the inspiration for the title of this book came from one of Gramsci's most important early essays, "Two Revolutions," which appeared in the journal *Ordine Nuovo* in July 1920. The message of this brief article was that the transition to socialism must occur on two distinct but interwoven terrains—the state and the economy. Gramsci's point was that a good part of what we call revolution actually *precedes* the conquest of political power, and it is this prefigurative dimension of politics that shapes the conflict of regimes, armies, organizations, and leaders. It is not enough for movements to simply overthrow the existing state machinery, or destroy the old institutions, or even to bring into power leaders calling themselves "communists." Beneath the level of insurrection and statecraft there must be a gradual conquest of social power, initiated by popular subversive forces emerging from within the very heart of capitalist society.

Yet if "Two Revolutions" presented a vision of change rooted in the dialectic of politics and economics, it further anticipated a much broader and more novel dualism in the *Prison Notebooks*, where the conquest of social power came to signify more than transforming the means of production: it meant a general reconstruction of civil society, extending beyond the factory into every sphere of community life. Socialist politics, in other words, would have to be completely redefined to meet the new challenges of advanced capitalism: it would have to pass through the multilayered reality of daily existence, through the realms of culture, social relations, and the family as well as work—into the deepest recesses of popular consciousness. The theoretical and political implications for Marxism of such an innovative framework were and still are enormous. Above all, it pointed to a complex strategy grounded in a consensual, democratic process in which the great mass of people actively participate in overturning the multiple structures of domination. These ideas represented a bold departure within Marxism insofar as they affirmed the principle of a non-economistic, non-vanguardist mode of socialist transformation. As a kind of metaphor for Gramsci's theory, then, the phrase "Two Revolutions" can be seen as the unifying thread of this study.

The present volume is the culmination of several earlier projects on the topics of Gramsci, European Communism, and Western Marxism in general. A previous book, *Gramsci's Marxism* (Pluto Press, 1976), was written essentially as a brief introduction to Gramsci's ideas at a time when concise, sympathetic English-language accounts were still virtually nonexistent. While that book was more than a simple introduction to Gramsci, it was limited both by its brevity and by its scope—that is, by the emphasis I placed on clarifying Gramsci's main concepts and situating them within the Marxist tradition. The considerable interest shown in that book, along with the growing popularity of Gramscian theory, convinced me that a second, but far more comprehensive and critical, treatment would be a useful addition to the expanding body of neo-Marxist or "Western" Marxist literature.

Readers of *Gramsci's Marxism* will find in *The Two Revolutions* a number of fundamental departures as well as an overall shift of emphasis. First, the tremendous output of Gramsci commentary during the past decade has given rise to a variety of interpretations which naturally entered into the preparation of this book, and permitted an intervention into the debates around the meaning of Gramsci's work that simply was not possible earlier. To seriously assess the contributions of any major theorist requires the passage of time, a certain historical (and perhaps even spatial) distance. Thus the bulk of Marx's writings has been accessible for nearly a century, and of course the secondary literature over that time span has been immense. For the succeeding generation of Marxist thinkers—Kautsky, Bernstein, Lenin, Luxemburg, to name some—the time frame has been 50 to 70 years, more than enough time in most instances for the debates around their theories to have settled. In the case of Gramsci, however, we confront a body of writings that (for a variety of reasons) has been available to a wide public only since the 1960s, and even later than that outside of Western Europe. (The *Prison Notebooks*, for example, were not translated into English until 1971, and Gramsci's earlier publications did not appear as collected volumes until 1977 and 1978.) Consequently, only now are we in a position to systematically evaluate the work of a Sardinian intellectual who some observers contend is the most important Marxist theorist of the twentieth century. And the great amount of scholarly and political attention devoted to Gramsci in recent years has already helped to clarify the value of that work, although it is true that many interpretations have had just the opposite effect. In any event, this book sets out to accomplish what probably could not have been accomplished just a decade ago.

Whereas my earlier book stressed the basic thematic unity and continuity in Gramsci—organized largely around a picture of him as a "democratic" variant of Lenin—*The Two Revolutions* emphasizes a more multi-dimensional and changing Gramsci. Here I explore the three sides or "faces" of Gramsci's thought (revolutionary or council democracy, Leninism, and Western Marxism) which intersect, overlap, and indeed at times contradict each other, accounting for what I have called the "conflicted legacy." This approach situates Gramsci in a transitional and ambiguous historical setting which made it impossible for him, or any other European theorist of his period, to arrive at the sort of theoretical consistency suggested in *Gramsci's Marxism*. In trying to impose upon Gramsci a more or less singular vision relevant to the capitalist West, I overlooked the sources of ambivalence and tension, the contradictory pushes and pulls at work in a theory which, after all, was formed in the course of rapidly-changing historical conditions. I had assumed a much too simple relationship between theory and politics, as if the former could be uniformly translated into the latter; in reality, the linkage in Gramsci's case has turned out to be infinitely more refracted than I was willing to believe. Indeed, a closer investigation reveals in Gramsci a clash at times between theoretical directions and political imperatives—the inevitable result of strong historical pressures. For this reason *The Two Revolutions* is more critical of Gramsci than the earlier volume, although in general I have retained the same degree of enthusiasm for the guiding concepts and sensibilities of his work.

To the extent that the Gramsci who emerged from *Gramsci's Marxism* was a Lenin who, in the context of Italy, was simply more attuned to the issues of democracy and cultural transformation than the Russian Lenin, I understood this as a positive new synthesis. In *The Two Revolutions*, on the other hand, the Leninist or Jacobin side of Gramsci is viewed quite differently: it is defined as a residue of the Bolshevik model, which tends to *block* those democratic and culturally subversive tendencies that, as Gramsci himself insisted, were indispensable to revolutionary change in the West. It is now possible to see more clearly what Gramsci apparently did not see at all: that Leninist vanguard strategies, which naturally give rise to bureaucratic centralism where they are successful—that is, to more rather than less repression—can furnish no solutions to the intricate tasks facing socialists in advanced capitalism. And "reconstitutions" or "extensions" of Leninism, however attractive, merely end up as efforts to save what is no longer salvageable.

I have also taken greater pains in *The Two Revolutions* to situate Gramsci historically. This entails more than simply incorporating additional historical material bearing on Gramsci's intellectual and political formation, though I have done this. Nor is this a matter of identifying Gramsci as a uniquely *Italian* theorist even if, like Machiavelli and Croce before him, he did symbolize a particular "national" tradition which transcended his role as a Marxist or Communist intellectual. At issue is the dialectic between theory and history—or, in Gramscian terms, the very historicity of concepts and themes which allows us to locate them within a developmental process (for example, a specific phase of capitalist expansion). Hence the aforementioned contradictions in Gramsci can be understood precisely with reference to a certain historical specificity: the general stage of European capitalist development, the unique social forces (e.g., Catholicism) operative in Italy, the Bolshevik Revolution and subsequent Comintern hegemony within world Communism, and so forth. From this viewpoint, *Gramsci's Marxism* was more strictly an intellectual portrait in the sense that the theory was approached on its own terms, somewhat independent of its unique historicity—a fault that Gramsci himself would no doubt have been the first to detect.

At the same time, Gramsci's work (like Marx's) cannot be reduced to the status of historical relic. The concepts which illuminate his theory (ideological hegemony, social bloc, war of position, organic intellectuals) have a "universal" significance beyond the Italian setting of the 1920s and 1930s. The critical theme running through all of these concepts was the profoundly *ideological* or *cultural* dimension of class and political struggle in the West, which of course coincides with the premise of "Two Revolutions." For Gramsci the primary focus was not the objective determinants of crisis but rather the subjective responses to it; not simply a structural analysis of political economy but comprehension of the dynamics of mass consciousness; not the institutional engineering required for the conquest and management of state power, but the ideological-cultural preparation for a new type of society. Since the overriding issue today in the industrialized countries is the absence of a mass-based radical opposition even in the midst of ongoing economic crises—the legacy of a depoliticized public sphere which itself is an expression of bourgeois hegemony—Gramsci's ideological thematic remains more relevant than ever. Within such a thematic Gramsci originally posed a range of questions that retain their urgency in the 1980s. How can the deep and multifaceted consensus underlying bourgeois institutions be effectively challenged? How does "common sense" become transformed into critical consciousness on a large scale? What are the mechanisms through which a new stratum of organic intellectuals can be generated? Quite clearly our capacity to imaginatively pose such problems, even if definitive answers are not always forthcoming, will be decisive to the success of any future strategy.

It is worth noting that this type of ideological thematic has theoretical implications which Gramsci himself could not have fully understood or confronted. The powerful critique of positivism and economism that necessarily accompanied his emphasis on hegemony (and its reverse side, the project of cultural transformation) sets the guideposts for what in contemporary parlance is referred to as a post-industrial vision: the alternative to a growth-oriented industrialism which fetishizes science and technology in the service of material values. While Gramsci's philosophy of praxis never questioned the integrity of Marxism as the only viable critical-dialectical theory for its period, insofar as his goal was to restore a Marxist totality destroyed by orthodox social democracy, the ultimate thrust of his critique runs counter to the productivist logic in Marxism. The very assumptions underlying the metaphor "Two Revolutions" would seem to indicate as much.

A final note on theoretical interpretation: since Gramsci produced some of his most important work under the harsh conditions of prison life, his writings (or "notes") were not systematically organized in conventional fashion. The result is that many of the concepts, terms, and premises he employed were exceedingly vague or lacking in clear definition or application, so that they are especially open to widely-divergent explanations. Gramsci's isolation from politics during the final decade of his life only compounded this problem. Here I have chosen to explore and measure his theoretical discourse, as much as possible, according to the overall "Leitmotifs" (or unifying themes) of the work just as Gramsci himself counseled in the *Notebooks*. Admittedly this is not easy, but it does allow the observer to draw out conclusions and otherwise fill gaps necessitated by the fragmentary and incomplete nature of Gramsci's work. For example, I have taken the liberty of establishing certain linkages between the philosophy of praxis, hegemony, and war of position even though such linkages are nowhere explicitly made in the *Notebooks*. I have further used the concepts "prefigurative" and "counter-hegemonic" to capture the essence of Gramscian politics despite the fact that Gramsci himself never adopted such terms. These examples could be multiplied. Naturally this method involves a degree of projection and even speculation about Gramsci's intentions and motivations, which of course gives the interpreter some added license. If there are dangers in this kind of thematic approach, they are nonetheless to be preferred over a more literal translation which perhaps loses sight of the larger political context. And they are to be preferred to the official and semi-official interpretations which completely reformulate the concepts to fit the needs of the current party line. Still, I have sought to avoid any extreme bias or distorted imposition of a narrow evaluative schema by including a more balanced discussion of the "three Gramscis."

This book is the outgrowth of a long process, dating back to my first attraction to Gramsci and Marxist theory as a graduate student at the University of California, Berkeley in the 1960s, and has been shaped by more intellectual forces, political experiences, and even social involvements than I can begin to list or even remember. I would like to express my gratitude once again to those persons who were so helpful at the time of my earlier Gramsci project, although many will probably find *The Two Revolutions* virtually unrecognizable as a extension of that study. In addition I would like to thank several others who more recently contributed their support and assistance in one form or another: Michael Albert and Carl Conetta of South End Press, Peter W. Hunt, Mark Kann, Russell Jacoby, David Plotke, Raymond B. Pratt, Michele Prichard, and Ken Richard. Finally, I wish to acknowledge my debt to the late Alvin W. Gouldner, whose lively critical spirit—all too rare in the upper echelons of American academic life—was more influential in my development than he probably realized.

—Los Angeles, Calif.   October, 1984

1 Gramsci and the Marxist Tradition

The most appropriate method for evaluating the work of any theorist, as Antonio Gramsci once observed, is to first identify the thematic unity which permeates that theorist's entire range of contributions. To do this it is necessary to locate the point where historical context, intellectual vision, and political commitment intersect. If we apply this logic to Gramsci himself, the necessary point of departure is the familiar crisis of European Marxism in the 1920s and 1930s. An Italian revolutionary whose epic struggles spanned the critical period 1915-1935, and whose most mature years were spent in fascist prisons, Gramsci in many ways came to symbolize and personify that crisis. His involvement took shape at a vital historical juncture—the collapse of social democracy, the Bolshevik Revolution, the later rise of fascism and Stalinism, and the decline of socialist prospects in the West—which initially eroded the preeminent status of Marxism within the working-class movement and then challenged the core premises of the theory itself. It was an involvement that, despite its long periods of terrible frustration, defeat, and pain, inspired a body of theoretical work characterized by an originality and influence scarcely duplicated in the twentieth century. At the same time, like his contemporaries Rosa Luxemburg, Georg Lukacs, and Karl Korsch, Gramsci produced a legacy that was as ambiguous as it was imaginative; a bold effort to confront the predicament of Marxism, it also ended up *reflecting* that predicament.

The disintegration of a stifling and fatalistic Marxist orthodoxy after World War I, though associated with political failure at the time, immediately gave rise to new radical perspectives and

1

visions in which Gramsci's theoretical contributions were to play a major role. Clearly the paralysis of the Second International was not a result of contingent historical factors, incompetent leaderships, or incorrect political lines so much as it was the outgrowth of *internal* limitations and contradictions of Marxist theory before 1917. The crisis was not therefore simply a matter of poor translation of theory into practice nor the misappropriation of Marx's presumably valid ideas by his successors within the various Socialist parties and trade-union movements. On the contrary, it derived from perhaps the single most important premise of classical Marxism: aspiring to a scientific status. The theory sought to project history and politics as an expression of the laws of motion of capitalist development, as a matter of objective necessity. As scientific determinism gave way to what might be called a "critical-revolutionary" mode of response, three sometimes overlapping and sometimes conflicting alternatives presented themselves: council communism, Leninism, and Western Marxism. One of the most fascinating and most unique characteristics of Gramsci is the manner in which these alternatives to orthodoxy converge, in whatever tense and contradictory fashion, throughout the complex totality of his social and political thought.

Marxism: Scientific and Revolutionary

The Marxist tradition has from the outset given expression to two distinct and competing theoretical currents—one best described as scientific or rationalizing, the other critical or emancipatory.[1] Each gained ascendancy during specific historical periods. The scientific side emphasizes the primacy of material forces, the base-superstructure model, structural determinancy, laws of capitalist development; in the sphere of economics it places strong faith in technological progress and industrial growth, whereas in politics it looks to large-scale organization (parties, party-states, unions) as the prime-movers of change. Against this the critical side focuses upon the role of subjective agents, social totality, the power of human will over institutions, and the openness of history; in economics it stresses human over material forces, while in politics it is oriented toward collective voluntarism and popular self-activity. The analytic and detached spirit of the scientific outlook, which often coexists with an apocalyptic vision of capitalist breakdown in the distant future, corresponds to the logic of social stability and political quietism. In contrast, the critical-revolutionary outlook is more impatient and activist, often given to the extremes of romanticism and quixotic adventurism, and thus tends to gain strength at times of popular upsurge. If scientific-rationalizing Marxism represents a theory which seeks to comprehend the boundaries to human subjectivity, critical Marxism looks to a transformative politics that can overcome the limits of nature.

From the standpoint of social movements, scientific Marxism distinguished clearly between "true" and "false" consciousness, "correct" and "incorrect" theory in a way that generated a hierarchical division of labor between leaders and followers, elites and masses. Its very minimal concern for issues related to democracy and mass participation, along with its insensitivity to the problems of bureaucracy and hierarchial social relations, is therefore hardly surprising. Moreover, the reliance of scientific Marxism upon a simple and one-sided materialism, which anticipated that conditions of revolutionary change would flow naturally out of the economic contradictions of capitalism, meant that the whole sphere of social or "human" activity (e.g., culture, popular consciousness, authority relations) could justifiably be sidestepped insofar as it was viewed as having no dynamic life of its own. At both levels, the critical dimension affirmed precisely what was absent from scientific determinism: proletarian self-activity, egalitarian social relations, the Hegelian preoccupation with subjectivity, consciousness and ideology.

These two tendencies coexisted as part of an often conflicting relationship in Marx's own work, and to a lesser extent in Engels and other late-nineteenth century Marxists. In opposition to those themes which analyzed consciousness as an expression of material conditions could be found those which stressed the power of human subjective intervention to prevail over structural barriers. As is well known, the critical side predominated in the writings of the early Marx, where the concern for the dialectic, alienation, and praxis corresponded to a political optimism which typified European radicalism in the 1840s. While Marx never abandoned the critical-revolutionary spirit, his later works (notably *Capital*) shift their emphasis toward scientism and contain what Wellmer calls a "latent positivism."[2] It was this determinist component of Marx that Engels seized upon and articulated in the years following Marx's death, and it was this legacy which Engels bequeathed to the Second International.

The two currents of Marxism could inhabit the same intellectual edifice so long as the theory had not yet attached itself to political movements. Once the application of theory to practice became a burning issue, as it did with the emergence of German

Social Democracy and the Second International, pressures favoring an Engelsian scientific materialism were irresistible. By the 1890s few Marxists questioned the "scientific" character of their enterprise. This new "synthesis," which lasted until the crisis of World War I, embraced above all the idea of a single Marxist theory rooted in historical necessity and understood as the most advanced expression of industrial progress. One consequence of this for the European social-democratic parties was a marked dogmatism and formalism of theoretical discourse and political style. Another result was the tendency to see in the trajectory of capitalist development itself the conditions for eventual socialist transformation; industrial growth and technological change would furnish the requisite infrastructure for human emancipation. Scientific Marxism during this period thus adhered to a rigid unilinear view of Marx's historical schema, which for socialists encouraged a passive waiting stance until the capitalist mode of production had exhausted its potential and finally collapsed. In the meantime, huge party and union bureaucracies—committed to mass mobilization around essentially reformist goals and parliamentarist strategies—evolved to manage the ebb and flow of class conflict.[3]

It is therefore easy to see how classical social democracy before 1914 could embellish a bizarre mixture of Darwinian evolutionism and messianic catastrophism, reformist pragmatism and revolutionary vision, since where capitalist expansion was viewed as stable (with immediate socialist prospects correspondingly dim) it could be understood as a necessary prelude to future revolutionary cataclysm. Hence both Kautsky in Germany and Plekhanov in Russia looked to immutable laws of social development—laws which in time would doom capitalism to breakdown, ensuring a degree of ideological certainty and optimism where the left was either nonrevolutionary (Germany) or weak (Russia). The crisis of bourgeois society was imminent because, while the system could generate increased economic abundance and technological capacity, the growing concentration of capital and the inability of commodity production to meet social needs would inevitably give rise to class polarization.

The long struggle to develop a scientific Marxism ultimately floundered in the midst of the very global crisis it had so confidently predicted. As the war produced economic chaos and the erosion of political authority in one European country after another, social-democratic parties could not rise above the fatalism, passivity, and national chauvinism into which they had fallen; European Marxism revealed itself less as a guide to revolutionary action than as a theoretical apology for retreat. The breakdown of capitalism was accompanied by the breakdown of Marxism.

But while the crisis of Marxist orthodoxy meant paralysis and defeat for social democracy, it simultaneously signaled a rebirth of the critical-revolutionary tradition. Actually, there were already stirrings in this direction at the turn of century with the spread of anarchism and syndicalism in southern Europe, the theoretical work of Labriola and Croce in Italy, Sorel in France, Luxemburg and Landauer in Germany, Pannekoek and Gorter in Holland—to name the most influential. Insofar as Marxism was no longer the hegemonic expression of a single organizational center, diverse currents now took hold and, during the revolutionary decade 1914-1923, influenced the political landscape of many countries. In central Europe and Italy council communism introduced the theme of revolutionary democracy; in Russia—and in the member parties of the Comintern—Leninism sought to put insurrectionary politics on the agenda; and throughout Europe (but especially in Germany) what later came to be known as Western Marxism fixed its attention on previously ignored "superstructural" issues such as philosophy, culture, ideology and consciousness.

Interestingly, those currents owed much of their theoretical and political dynamism to influences *outside* of the pre-1914 Marxist tradition. Thus the council movement drew upon elements of anarchism and syndicalism; Leninism owed much to the 19th century contributions of the Russian radical intelligentsia; and Western Marxism, aside from its return to themes in the "early" Marx, found inspiration in Hegelian philosophy, the sociology of Simmel and Weber, and the *Lebensphilosophie* associated with Husserl and Bergson. Nevertheless, each expressed an ambivalent or compromised attitude in certain ways toward this revitalized critical thrust—that is, each carried forward some important aspect of scientific Marxism even as it overturned the orthodoxy. For example, council communism attacked the bureaucratic party and trade-union leaderships in the name of direct proletarian democracy but still embellished a narrow productivism and worker-ism that fetishized the factory. The Bolshevik party engineered a seizure of state power in a largely pre-capitalist setting—an event that dramatically affirmed the Leninist "actuality of revolution" against orthodox political fatalism, rudely discarding Marx's evolutionary historical schema in the process. Yet Lenin himself subscribed to a crude philosophical materialism (which he later reconsidered) and he came to define the vanguard party as a repository of scientific theory, elite control, and economic modernization. Finally, whereas Western Marxism undertook the ambitious task of renovating the entire philosophical foundation, this project was often marred by a stubborn attachment to Leninist organizational forms and (in its later phase) a drift toward apolitical pessimism that increasingly lost touch with its critical origins.

Antonio Gramsci's Marxism can best be situated within the historical juncture of orthodox decline and critical counter-response. In theoretical terms Gramsci never adhered to scientific materialism; he had no patience for the base-superstructure framework from the very beginning. Politically, the young Gramsci broke decisively with Italian social democracy by the end of World War I. His subsequent development was shaped at different points, and in different ways, by each of the three emergent tendencies mentioned above. This helps to explain both Gramsci's unique originality and many of the ambiguities and dilemmas left by his legacy.

The Convergence of Theory and Politics

The man who was to become one of the most influential Marxist theorists in the twentieth century spent his early life in modest surroundings, on the margins of Italian society. Antonio Gramsci was born in Ales, Sardinia on January 23, 1881. Although his mother had belonged to a landowning family, his father was a low-level civil servant who lost his job upon being jailed in the context of a political feud. Injured from a fall at the age of four, Gramsci developed a hunchback condition and apparently experienced great physical and emotional difficulty throughout his youth. He was an excellent student, however, and after finishing secondary school in Cagliari went to the University of Turin on a limited scholarship in 1911. Gramsci's first years in Turin were characterized by hard study, social withdrawal, and recurrent illness. He took courses in history, philosophy, and linguistics but, despite encouragement from his professors, decided to leave the university before completing his degree in 1915. From all accounts, the young Gramsci was powerfully attracted to Hegelian thought, which in pre-war Italy was identified with the work of Benedetto Croce.

If Gramsci's early political outlook was that of a Sardinian nationalist sensitive to the plight of the underdeveloped south and the islands, his subsequent contact with the industrial milieu of Turin (the home of Fiat) rapidly transformed him into a socialist. In

1913 he joined the Italian Socialist Party (PSI) and soon emerged as a leading intellectual figure in the Turin section of the PSI. By the end of 1914 he was writing for various Socialist periodicals, and in 1916 he began work as co-editor of the Piedmont edition of *Avanti!* (the major PSI newspaper). It was during this period that Gramsci first developed his talents as a political commentator and critic of the Italian cultural scene. He became deeply radicalized toward the end of the war and, influenced by the syndicalist movement and the ideas of Sorel, grew more and more disenchanted with the moderate and indecisive PSI leadership. By 1917, with the popular upsurges in Turin gathering momentum, Gramsci was recognized as a highly-respected PSI journalist and activist whose sympathies clearly rested with the party's left wing.

From this point on, Gramsci's intellectual and political life—brief when compared with the long productive spans typical of Marxist theorists like Kautsky, Lukacs, and Korsch—can be traced through four rather distinct stages. The initial one, which covers the period 1916 to 1919, encompassed the formative years of Gramsci's overall development: his involvement in the Turin working-class movement, his active membership in the PSI, his exposure to Crocean idealism, his first attempts to come to grips with the failure of traditional Marxism. This was also a critical period in the early history of the Italian left, since it included the participation of Italy in the war, the economic breakdown and crisis of authority that followed the war, the spread of revolutionary ferment, and the strategic collapse of the PSI as internal factionalism and political timidity led to paralysis just as new revolutionary opportunities presented themselves. It was this paralysis which drove Gramsci to oppose the dominant (orthodox, reformist) leadership groupings in the PSI, and which further led him to question its theoretical premises.

Gramsci's prolific writings during these years (most of which appeared in *Avanti!* and *Il Grido del Popolo*) touched upon immediate events and developments: the war, the immobilism of the liberal regime, the activities of the PSI and the trade-union movement, and of course the Bolshevik Revolution. His commentary was shaped by a distinctively Piedmontese, or more specifically Turinese, viewpoint. Turin at this time was known as the "Red Capital" of Italy, the Mediterranean Petrograd, because of its advanced and concentrated industry (autos, iron, steel, textiles) and its militant working-class struggles. At the same time, Gramsci wrote about a broader range of topics that went beyond the political moment—most notably philosophy, culture, and Italian history—but their journalistic format inevitably worked against any elaborate theorization.[4]

The second period spans the dramatic postwar insurgency—the *Biennio Rosso*, or "Red Two Years"—of the *Ordine Nuovo* (New Order) movement in 1919-1920, when mass strikes, factory occupations, and the rapid expansion of the factory council movement in Turin seemed to promise what Gramsci envisioned as a "new era in the history of humanity." Gramsci was part of a small nucleus of Piedmont Marxist intellectuals (called the *Ordinovisti*) which established editorial control over the journal *L'Ordine Nuovo* in May 1919 with the aim of giving theoretical expression and political direction to the massive spontaneous struggles of Turinese workers after the war. Gramsci during this period was probably more intimately involved in the everyday life of workers than at any other time in his political experience, and most of his *Ordine Nuovo* writings reflect this. Despite the failure of this upsurge to push beyond the provincial boundaries of Turin, and its eventual isolation from the rest of the Italian left, the *Ordinovisti* provided a rich theoretical legacy which paralleled the rise of council communism in other European countries and gave inspiration to later working-class struggles in Italy. It is worth noting here that Gramsci, as main editor of *L'Ordine Nuovo*, was identified by Lenin as the Italian revolutionary figure who came closest to the Bolshevik orientation—an assessment that was surely based upon distorted information concerning the Turin council movement.

Though brief, the *Biennio Rosso* phase had a vital and lasting impact on Gramsci's thought; in certain respects it was the most intense and productive period of his life, even if in the end it turned out to be extremely frustrating both for Gramsci personally (it precipitated one of his several emotional crises) and for the movement that failed. The contributions Gramsci made in 1919-1920, while once again of the short-essay variety, were many: his penetrating critique of the PSI and the Marxism of the Second International, his analysis of political parties and trade unions in the evolution of capitalism, his articulation of the theme of factory councils (*consigli di fabbrica*) and soviets as new forms of socialist democracy, his elaboration of the concepts of "dual power" and "prefigurative struggle" as crucial elements in the transition to socialism.[5]

The years 1921 to 1926, from the founding of the Italian Communist Party (PCI) to his arrest and imprisonment by the fascist regime, mark the third stage of Gramsci's intellectual-political development. With the entrance of most of the *Ordinovisti*

into the PCI, which was formed at Livorno in January 1921 along
Leninist lines, Gramsci began to move into national politics in Italy
and was soon to emerge as a dominant force within the PCI
leadership. During this period a good deal of Gramsci's energy
was consumed by the ongoing and bitter factional struggles in the
party around questions of political strategy, which was usually
connected to the rivalry between Gramsci and Amadeo Bordiga.
While both Gramsci and Bordiga agreed that social democracy was
the "left wing of the bourgeoisie" and that a Leninist insurrectionary party should replace the outmoded PSI, their disagreements were many. Thus Gramsci supported and Bordiga opposed
the Comintern's united front policy; Gramsci believed that electoral politics was at least tactically necessary, whereas Bordiga tended
toward abstentionism; and Gramsci adhered to a much less
centralist view of the party than Bordiga who was always
suspicious of the councils and other mass organizations that
Gramsci saw as counterweights to party bureacracy. In May
1922 Gramsci went to Moscow, where for 18 months he acted as the
PCI representative to the Executive Committee of the Comintern
and where in late 1923 he participated in the Fourth Comintern
Congress. After a brief stay in Vienna, Gramsci returned to Italy
just as fascism was consolidating its power, and was elected to
parliament in May 1924. With Bordiga in prison and increasingly
isolated, Gramsci presided over a weak and disorganized Communist party during 1924-1926, and at the important Lyons'
Congress in January 1926 Gramsci managed to win majority
support for his broad-based strategy. But Gramsci's stewardship
was extrememly short-lived, for he would himself be arrested in
November 1926, with the party leadership being driven underground or into exile shortly thereafter.

Throughout much of his active PCI years Gramsci was able to
continue as editor of *L'Ordine Nuovo*, which after 1921 shifted its
emphasis from the factory councils to the revolutionary party.
However, many of his writings also appeared in the PCI daily
L'Unita and in the party's theoretical journal *Stato Operaio*,
(*Workers' State*). Understandably, these articles and essays centered around the concrete exigencies of party strategy and tactics in a
political context of urgent demands and rapid change. The famous
"Lyons' Theses" (authored jointly by Gramsci and Palmiro Togliatti) was surely the most comprehensive statement of PCI theory
and strategy during these formative years—a statement which
brilliantly outlined the party's role in Italian history. But Gramsci's party-oriented writings also included his analysis of fascism,

the Leninist party, early Soviet development and related international issues, and the "Southern Question" (to which he devoted an important article not long before his arrest).[6]

And finally, there is the period of prison confinement, isolation, and physical torment that spans the years 1926 to 1937, representing the culmination of Gramsci's theoretical work at the very time of his greatest depression and impotence. Gramsci was arrested in November 1926 during a fascist crackdown on left opposition in the wake of a reported assassination attempt against Mussolini. The PCI had made plans for Gramsci's escape to Switzerland, but as the party's General Secretary and a parliamentary deputy he decided to remain in Italy. Along with other PCI leaders, he was put on trial in 1928 for "organizing armed insurrection" and, after sham proceedings, he was sentenced to jail for 20 years. Throughout his imprisonment he remained a member of the PCI, but he was increasingly cut off from the flow of events and quickly lost his political influence. Gramsci's prison experience involved one horror after another: cut off from his party contacts and (except for visits from his sister-in-law Tatiana) his family, and transferred from prison to prison, he spent a decade in virtual isolation, bad health, and constant uncertainty about when he would be released. His intellectual work was further hampered by fascist censorship (which was fortunately lax at times) and inaccessibility of reading materials. By the end of 1933, with rapidly failing health, Gramsci was permitted to move to a private clinic under police supervision and then in 1935 he was sent to the Quisisana Clinic in Rome. An international campaign for his release, led by Gramsci's close friend Piero Sraffa, achieved belated success but Gramsci by this time was too ill to be moved and died five days after his official pardon, on April 27, 1937.

The pain and despair of the prison years was accompanied by intense, if necessarily sporadic, bursts of theoretical creativity. No longer engaged in immediate political activity, he could now adopt a much more contemplative or "theoretical" viewpoint which enabled him to reflect more clearly and with greater depth upon his previous experiences. As Gramsci put it in one of his letters from prison, "... it is possible to find serenity even in the face of the most absurd contradictions and under the pressure of the most implacable necessity, if one succeeds in thinking 'historically' and dialectically and in identifying one's own defined and limited task with intellectual sobriety."[7]

Gramsci began writing his "notes" (the *Quaderni del Carcere*, or *Prison Notebooks*) in the prison at Turin in February 1929 and continued work on them intermittently until 1935 when his deteriorating health made sustained concentration impossible. In all there were 32 notebooks consisting of 2,848 pages (about 4,000 when typewritten), which covered a vast range of topics—Italian history, education, culture, philosophy, the role of intellectuals, theory of the state, the rationalization of capitalist production, Catholicism, the family and sexuality. But the central and guiding theme of the *Notebooks*, which combine fragmentary notes and observations with systematic analysis, is the development of a new Marxist theory adequate to the requirements of socialist transformation in the advanced capitalist countries. Though unfinished and unpolished, they still bear all the marks of Gramsci's brilliant and penetrating mind; it is also clear that, unlike the pre-prison writings, the *Notebooks* were viewed as something for posterity, or *"fur ewig"* (as Gramsci expressed it.) In 1931, Gramsci complained that he "no longer [had] a real program of study and work. This was inevitable. I wanted to think about a particular set of problems, but at some point research would have to be done in important libraries. Without this, it was impossible to revise my ideas and expand upon them."[8] It is all the more remarkable, therefore, that the *Prison Notebooks* would later be generally regarded as one of the most important contributions to twentieth century Marxism.[9]

The significance of the *Notebooks* for Gramsci's personal ordeals in prison can hardly be emphasized enough. On the one hand, such difficult work was a way of sustaining political commitment. Thus a little more than a year after his incarceration Gramsci wrote: "for her [his mother], my being in prison represents a terrible disaster, one link in a chain of mysterious causes and effects. For me, it represents one episode of a political battle that was being fought and will continue to be fought, not only in Italy but in the whole world, for who knows how long a time."[10] At the same time, writing served to establish precious linkages with the outside world. As Giuseppe Fiori observes in his biography of Gramsci: "For Gramsci, this work became life itself: these memoranda and brief notes, these sketches of the first germ of ideas, these tentative ideas left open for endless development and elaboration, were all his way of continuing the revolutionary struggle, his way of remaining related to the world and active in the society of men."[11]

These four phases of Gramsci's thought and politics, as will become evident in subsequent chapters, represent quite different sets of priorities, theoretical emphases, and responses to particular historical situations; they vary not only with changing events and issues but with the gradual transformation of Gramsci's ideas over time. The shift in thematic emphasis from his pre-prison to prison contributions is pronounced in certain areas (e.g., on the role of the party). Until late 1926, virtually all of Gramsci's intellectual work was closely tied to everyday political struggles—first in the PSI, then in the *Ordine Nuovo* group, and finally in the PCI and the Comintern. For this reason the writings of the first three stages were directed more concretely to activities, issues, and personalities of the moment, and therefore often assumed the character of political statements, brief essays, and journalistic commentary. The *Prison Notebooks*, as mentioned above, were formulated under circumstances of isolation and distance from the factional debates taking place within the PCI and Comintern, and inevitably expressed a greater sense of detachment. For this reason, and owing to the obvious limitations imposed by censorship, Gramsci's prison work was generally more *conceptual*, more sweeping in its historical scope, and sometimes also more fragmentary and difficult to follow. No longer preoccupied with leadership obligations or journalistic duties, Gramsci was now able to step back and draw theoretical lessons from his years of political involvement and from the dramatic changes which swept Europe during the tumultuous 1914-1926 period. If one finds in the *Notebooks* little of the sense of urgency typical of Gramsci's earlier writings, and perhaps even less in the way of a direct strategic or tactical focus, they do possess greater substantive depth and stylistic openness.

Yet, despite these historical variations, there is an overall continuity to Gramsci's Marxism through all four stages. What the *Prison Notebooks* most often reflect is a theoretical elaboration (and in some cases redefinition) of key concepts, insights, and observations contained in his pre-prison work. The image of two or more historically distinct Gramscis, each occupying different theoretical paradigms, is a false one because the various dimensions of his commitment—councilist, Leninist, and Western Marxist—overlap and converge in changing fashion throughout the four phases. What bears emphasizing is that there is nothing resembling a sharp philosophical discontinuity or "epistemological break" in Gramsci; from his initial exploratory articles in *Avanti!* to the imposing theoretical reflections of the *Notebooks*, it is possible to detect an underlying thematic unity to Gramsci's work.

One of the most persistent and visible themes in Gramsci was the effort to merge the spheres of radical intellectual activity and ongoing political struggles—that is, to politicize or "democratize" the theoretical function which in orthodox Marxism had become divorced from what Gramsci called the "popular element." For Gramsci, this uniting of theory and practice, thought and action, subject and object was not merely a guiding methodological principle but was also the driving spirit of his own personal and political life. Revolution demanded not only the application of rational-cognitive thought, but a passionate, emotional commitment and an intense partisanship on the part of the theorist—a commitment and partisanship rooted in the politics of everyday life. Of the leading Marxist figures during this period, surely only Lenin devoted as much attention to matters of political *strategy*; for both, the study of history, philosophy, and even culture was meaningful primarily as a guide to *specific forms* of revolutionary action. And like Lenin, Gramsci was able to combine in a single personality the skills of political leadership and the capacity for creative theoretical work as few others were able to do. But what distinguished Gramsci even further among important European Marxist intellectuals (Lenin included), was his relatively humble social background and the close contact he maintained with working-class politics and culture throughout his adult life.

This spirit of engagement dominated every phase of Gramsci's intellectual output, as a passage from one of his prison letters to his sister-in-law Tatiana Schucht clearly revealed: "My entire intellectual formation was of a polemical nature, so that it is impossible for me to think 'disinterestedly' or to study for the sake of studying. Only rarely do I lose myself in a particular strain of thought and analyze something for its own inherent interest. Usually I have to engage in a dialogue, be dialectical, to arrive at some intellectual stimulation. I once told you how I hate tossing stones in the dark. I need an interlocutor, a concrete adversary, even in the family situation."[12] Insofar as Gramsci always remained a *partisan* observer of events, theorist of history, cultural critic, and philosopher, what made his contributions in these areas so alive was their intimate connection to the world of political action.

The Three Faces of Gramsci

To speak of an underlying continuity or thematic unity in Gramsci's thought does not imply the development of a single, one-dimensional Gramsci whose entire range of contributions can be neatly fitted into one mold. The absence of an abrupt philosophical "break" merely indicates the persistence of a critical-revolutionary direction through the four phases of theoretical formation just outlined. As I have suggested, it was a basic direction that Gramsci pursued along three distinct but sometimes crisscrossing paths—council democracy, Leninism, and Western Marxism—which do not strictly correspond to particular chronological stages. The common tendency to view Gramsci as a singular theorist with one overriding project in mind, whether "Leninist" or "humanist" or "Hegelian," obscures too much; it conceals not only the originality but the irresolvable tensions in the complex theoretical structure. In situating Gramsci it is necessary to emphasize, first, the tremendous variety of intellectual influences upon him both within and *outside* of Marxism, and, second, his involvement in a world virtually defined by political crises, cataclysmic events and rapid change.

Gramsci's early commitment to the factory council movement in Turin and to the general aim of workers' self-management, reflected most vividly in the *Ordine Nuovo* period, represented a broad vision of *revolutionary democracy* which he carried forward into his later writings.[13] Perhaps more than any other Marxist theorist of his time, Gramsci set out to understand the conditions under which a democratic transition to socialism might be realized—the necessary organizational forms, approaches to the state, political strategy and tactics, leadership styles, and so forth. Gramsci's Marxism was at its core a democratic theory embracing an active, participatory, popular spirit, an orientation no doubt encouraged by his fixation on the political dimension of revolutionary change. While it is true that other theorists and movements proclaimed democratic goals, Gramsci's viewpoint was rather distinct. In contrast to Bernstein, Kautsky, and other theoreticians in the Second International, he refused to equate the notion of democracy with the prevailing institutions and practices of bourgeois democracy; he departed from Lenin's "Jacobin" conception, which simply assigned democratic content to the dictatorship of the proletariat; and he found the Sorelian and syndicalist emphasis on spontaneous mass activity lacking in political concreteness. What each of these conceptions failed to provide, from Gramsci's perspective, was a theory of *popular* democracy grounded in new forms of authority.

The democratic component of Gramsci's Marxism is expressed in his philosophy, beginning with the earliest critiques of PSI orthodoxy. As previously mentioned, Gramsci counterposed his *critical* approach to the generally accepted scientific materialism even before the mass upheavals of the *Biennio Rosso*, and he never abandoned it in any of his writings. For Gramsci, a critical philosophy had democratic implications since it necessarily stressed the active, "voluntarist," and *collective* side of historical change whereas the scientific viewpoint, with its fatalistic reliance upon objective forces and rigorous "laws" interpreted by a special leadership, had elitist consequences. Gramsci was convinced, after witnessing the immobilism of the PSI, that revolution would not occur mechanically with the breakdown of capitalism but would have to be consciously *built* through purposive human action within a variety of settings. The transition to socialism could not be expected to follow a unilinear or pre-established pattern. Following the groundwork laid by Antonio Labriola, Gramsci came to understand history as an indeterminate process that could never be fitted into rigid schemas. Thinking along much the same lines as Rosa Luxemburg, he assumed that the initiative for revolutionary politics would have to grow out of popular self-activity, with leaders being no more than the "chorus" of the masses. And like Karl Korsch, he argued that such a realization demanded a new (reconstituted) Marxist philosophy which would restore the subjective dimension to socialist movements and place human actors at the center of history.

During the council period of 1919-1920, Gramsci sought to articulate a concept of social transformation that could give concrete, institutional meaning to these general popular-democratic impulses. The actual widespread emergence of factory councils in Turin suggested to Gramsci the real possibility of a system of workers' control and (at a later stage) community self-management; the councils, as precursors to soviets, would ultimately constitute the nucleus of a new kind of state. The strategic imperative therefore was not to *conquer* the existing state apparatus but to create new popular organs of authority *before* the overthrow of the bourgeois state. Neither the Kautskian social-democratic (parliamentary-electoral) nor the "Jacobin" centralist models could furnish the basis of democratic politics; each was too bureaucratic, too removed from civil society. Gramsci's powerful critique of the PSI and CGIL (as organizations confined to the "terrain of bourgeois democracy"), which he first spelled out at the time of the *Biennio Rosso* and developed further in the 1920s, was motivated by such an outlook. So too was his later argument for a mass party with close ties to everyday social reality and linked to a network of workers' and peasants' committees, in opposition to Amadeo Bordiga's ultra-Leninist conception of a tightly organized vanguard party designed mainly for the purpose of seizing state power. What Gramsci had in mind, especially before 1921 but even after, was an organic process of popular struggle that could prefigure the new communist society by gradually extending the domain of egalitarian, non-bureaucratic social and authority relations. This "prefigurative" dimension suggests certain parallels with the Dutch Council Communists (Pannekoek, Gorter) of the same period.

If in the *Prison Notebooks* Gramsci seems to depart from the council thematic while shifting to a more Jacobin emphasis, at the same time his main concepts—"hegemony," "social bloc," "war of position," and above all "organic intellectuals"—are anchored to still unmistakable (if more vague) democratic commitments. Here a good deal of attention is devoted to reconciling historical antagonisms within the Marxist tradition: party and class, intellectuals and masses, centralized leadership and democracy. The language of the *Notebooks* (e.g., "consent," "integrated culture," "organic," "*ensemble* of relations") reveals a sensitivity to the dangers of authoritarian politics, or what he sometimes labels "bureaucratic centralism." And Gramsci's frequent references to a future "national-popular" movement in Italy were strategically tied to the necessary transformation of civil society (involving the gradual construction of egalitarian social relations and democratic political forms) in a way that was meant to undercut an elitist instrumentalism—with its imposing threat of "Bonapartism" or "Caesarism"—generally characteristic of the struggle for state power. The role Gramsci assigned to intellectuals in the revolutionary process best exemplifies this larger theoretical perspective.

Gramsci's considered dismissal of scientific Marxism led him to question the elitist premises of both Kautsky and Lenin, for whom the intellectuals were bearers of a highly specialized body of knowledge and theory ("science") which is superior to the partial and mystifying ideology of the popular strata. At the same time, Gramsci refused to follow a tempting alternative—the cult of mass spontaneity and the denial of any significant intellectual function typical of both the anarchists and Sorelian syndicalism. The result was a kind of synthesis contained in his theory of the organic intellectuals, which he sketched in only the broadest outlines in the *Notebooks*. Thus Gramsci tried to articulate, not altogether successfully, the conditions under which a subordinate or rising class could generate its *own* intellectual stratum on the basis of its own self-activity. At the very least this allowed for a more dynamic, open-ended, and *democratic* understanding of theory and the intellectual function than had prevailed earlier. Gramsci insisted that what distinguished Marxism from past philosophical systems was its expression of an authentically *popular* system of beliefs; from this point of departure it was possible to view all thinking human beings as in some sense philosophers and intellectuals, and to conclude that the subordinate classes might eventually produce their own revolutionary theory and consciousness without elite intervention. Probably more than any other Marxist thinker, Gramsci sought to "democratize" theory by incorporating its traditional concerns into a new popular language, thereby concretely actualizing a novel convergence of politics and philosophy.

In presenting Gramsci as a theorist of revolutionary democracy I do not wish to suggest that he was able to resolve critical issues which had somehow mystified all other Marxists. On the contrary, his genius consisted mainly in the ability to *pose* questions in new, insightful, and suggestive ways; for various reasons he rarely elaborated his arguments in a sustained and coherent fashion. Hence in the *Notebooks* he fails to directly address many vital political and organizational problems, and it is no secret that his ideas on the state, bureaucracy, new forms of authority, and the role of intellectuals were never fully developed. One result is that the ambivalence surrounding the dualism Jacobinism vs. popular self-activity, which so thoroughly shapes Gramsci's work, remains unresolved.

This leads to a consideration of the second dimension of Gramsci's Marxism—his Leninism. From certain angles, the case for a predominantly "Leninist" Gramsci (at least from 1921 on) would appear to be strong.[14] After all, he expressed nothing but glowing praise of Lenin and the Bolshevik Revolution; he was a founder of the Italian Communist Party in 1921 and a Comintern delegate in 1922-1923; he became the party's General Secretary during 1924-26 and presided over the "Bolshevization" of the PCI; he was quite reserved in his criticisms of the Soviet Union; he made numerous references to the "dictatorship of the proletariat" in his third-stage writings; and the *Prison Notebooks* embellished at certain points a pronounced Jacobinism. There is no denying

Gramsci's vanguardist side nor his consistent loyalty to the international Communist movement during the 1920s and 1930s. Yet matters are not so simple: there are many cracks and strains in Gramsci's Leninism and, more significantly, his theoretical understanding of it had little in common with what would later be labeled "Marxism-Leninism."

In the midst of the Turin working-class upheavals of 1918-1920, Gramsci looked to the Russian revolution for inspiration and, like many other socialists frustrated with the political inertia of Second International parties, found in Leninist strategy a source of theoretical and strategic rejuvenation. But for the Gramsci who was caught up in the excitement of the *Biennio Rosso*, this inspiration was hardly the Lenin of the vanguard party and centralized state power. What he saw was a revolutionary theorist and leader whose imaginative politics broke decisively with the historical "laws" of Marx's *Capital*; Lenin's entire *modus operandi* upheld the "actuality of revolution" in a setting which "textbook" Marxists had not considered ripe for socialist advances. *This* Lenin was congruent with Gramsci's own spirit of voluntarism, his commitment to an insurrectionary strategy, his desire to restore the political element to a Marxism that had fetishized the sphere of production, material forces, and the economic base. To the degree that Leninism meant a critique of "economism" at this juncture, Gramsci completely shared the premises of such a critique—the idea of rescuing politics from its submergence in the "base" and raising it to the level of a creative, positive historical force. Thus, from Gramsci's standpoint, Lenin (in practice if not in theory) moved away from the strictures of positivism and economism precisely in his quest for a new transformative synthesis.

It should be recalled, too, that Gramsci's *council* experience of this period must have distorted his perception of the Bolshevik Revolution, which he interpreted as a process grounded above all in the soviets (popular assemblies) and factory committees, with the centralized party carrying out only supportive and coordinating functions. This view may have been reinforced by inadequate or one-sided information reaching Italy from Russia, as well as by a certain misguided optimism on Gramsci's part. Whatever the case, the soviets did of course play a vital role in the Russian events and it would have been natural for Gramsci to see in them the concrete embodiment of Lenin's participatory theory outlined in *State and Revolution*. But this side of Lenin rapidly yielded to the "other" Lenin of *What Is To Be Done?*, for already by 1921 the soviets and other popular organizations were either destroyed or assimilated into the Bolshevik party as "transmission belts". Quite clearly, this was not the vision of Leninism that Gramsci had in mind. With the failure of the council movement and the rise of fascism, however, Gramsci's position shifted and his earlier critique of Jacobinism gave way to a more party-centered orientation by late 1920. As a leading figure in the nascent PCI, Gramsci endorsed the Comintern's binding principles (hierarchical command, tight discipline, closed membership, etc.) and looked to the party as a highly-flexible combat organization. Thus from 1921 to 1926, while deeply-involved in PCI politics and immersed in the struggle against fascism, Gramsci's outlook moved closer to the vanguardist Lenin of *What is To Be Done?*[15] As in the case of Luxemburg, Korsch, and Lukacs, all of whom diverged theoretically from Bolshevism but ended up accepting it in practice, Gramsci apparently saw in Comintern politics the only viable hope for preserving socialist identity while simultaneously combatting fascism. Still, Gramsci's Leninism in the 1920s was always a qualified and even tenuous version that departed in many ways from the Bolshevik ideal. His critique of Bordiga's ultra-centralist view of the party has already been mentioned. In the recurrent debates with Bordiga, Gramsci consistently favored a *mass* party rather than a strictly *cadre* organization; he pushed for internal democratization at a time when Lenin was imposing a ban on factions within the Soviet party; and, above all, he encouraged growth of the workers' and peasants' committees as a check on bureaucratization —a preference clearly shaped by the *Ordine Nuovo* years. The "Lyon's Theses" of early 1926 reflected the most significant pre-prison attempt to articulate for the PCI this neo-Leninism.

Gramsci's evolving Jacobinism carried over into the *Prison Notebooks*, especially in those sections of the "Modern Prince" where he invoked the legacy of Machiavelli as the "first Jacobin" who fully grasped the transformative potential of politics. Lenin appears as the contemporary parallel to Machiavelli, a bold and innovative thinker who affirms the primacy of political action on behalf of a unifying objective. The *Notebooks* were filled with references to the leading role of the revolutionary party, which for Gramsci embodied the universalizing interests of the working class and was indispensable for taking the movement beyond its parochial, spontaneous, corporatist phase.

If in his prison writings Gramsci set out to furnish a *theoretical* basis of Leninism, he also modified it and even countered it at many points. For example, he argued that the socio-political differences between Russia and the West were so fundamental as to call for entirely different strategies; thus Gramsci's "Leninism" could be expected to depart radically from the Bolshevik model. Here Gramsci introduced a new concept ("ideological hegemony") and a new strategic dimension ("war of position") that would lead to new ways of thinking about politics and the role of the party. Gramsci introduced a *language* that was in certain respects foreign to Lenin. The revolutionary party Gramsci envisaged was less a combat apparatus geared to the seizure of state power than a "collective intellectual" designed to carry out ideological-pedagogical functions within civil society as part of the "war of position." While Gramsci's ideal party was conceived to do both, its *initial* preoccupation would be mainly ideological, or counter-hegemonic. Following this line of thought, it might be argued that Gramsci's consuming aim in the *Notebooks* was to broaden, enrich, and "democratize" Lenin's theory of revolution—that is, to make it applicable to the more developed Western nations. Probably a more accurate interpretation is that Gramsci found himself suspended between two conflicting sympathies—Jacobinism and revolutionary democracy—and was ultimately unable to arrive at a synthesis or a non-Leninist resolution of this tension.

In either case, efforts to present Gramsci as a conventional Leninist do more to distort than to illuminate his theoretical contribution. If the Jacobin strain persists, it has little in common with either the politics of the Bolshevik Revolution or the extreme vanguardism (and bureaucratic centralism) that characterized later Soviet development. Yet the very presence of this Jacobinism must be acknowledged insofar as it ran counter to the other currents in his work—councilism and Western Marxism —and no doubt imposed limits upon how far he could theoretically develop them.

The appearance of Gramsci's "Western Marxist" side must be understood in this context. Probably even more than these other responses to the breakdown of scientific orthodoxy, it was associated with an evolving critical tradition in Europe (especially after 1925).[16] It is possible to identify at least two rather distinct stages in the early life of Western Marxism. The first (roughly 1917 to 1923) was marked by a spirit of revolutionary optimism at a time when popular insurgency—triggered in part by the Russian Revolution— swept across the European continent. With social democracy in disarray, Marxism suddenly yielded to an open, decentralized and thus more creative definition. The second phase (after 1923) came in the aftermath of the crisis, with the eclipse of revolutionary hopes, the initial stirrings of fascism, and the rise of Stalin in the USSR ushering in a period of retreat and pessimism. In theoretical terms, both phases brought about serious efforts to reconstruct Marxism on neo-Hegelian foundations: the return to an emphasis on subjectivity, consciousness, and ideology which had been missing from determinist materialism, the rediscovery of philosophy and the dialectic which prewar Marxism had buried and left for dead. Gramsci can be located at the center of this neo-Hegelian revival in the 1920s and 1930s—indeed he epitomized both its most advanced expressions and the new contradictions which accompanied them.[17]

Gramsci entered the Italian political scene at a time when Labriola's critical Marxism had already been making inroads into PSI orthodoxy for some time. And he was reaching intellectual maturity just as the powerful national influence of Croce's Hegelianism was reaching its peak. Owing to a tradition of philosophical idealism extending back well into the nineteenth century, the reaction against the scientific materialism of the Second International occurred earlier in Italy than elsewhere in Europe. It was this influence which shaped Gramsci's thinking during his student years at the University of Turin and later when he joined the PSI. Between 1915 and 1919 his essays articulated its central themes—a Crocean preoccupation with the "ethico-political," a non-determinist view of history derived from Labriola, a critique of positivism and economism adopted from both. To do this the young Gramsci added his conception of a gradually unfolding proletarian culture as the basis of socialist transformation. All of these concerns would occupy an important place in the later development of Western Marxism, and they would remain a permanent feature of Gramsci's philosophical outlook through the *Prison Notebooks*.

The *Biennio Rosso* period created an opportunity for new expressions of this critical tradition, as well as for its political translation within the Turin council movement. Gramsci viewed the councils not merely as instruments for gaining economic reforms or even political power; they were the nucleus of new forms of authority—a new state—where the proletariat would gradually recover its collective subjectivity, establish a sense of its historical mission, and take over management of the economy despite the bureaucratic obstacles imposed by the parties and unions. Like the Council Communists, Gramsci understood the soviet phenomenon as a break with the old forms of bourgeois power, as a reconstituted public sphere rooted in the factories (and to a lesser extent community life in general), where workers for the first time could become self-determining producers. And like Sorel, he appealed to a myth of proletarian solidarity at the point of production, incorporating it into a less apocalyptic, more organic and structural conception of revolutionary politics than what was envisioned by the French syndicalists. Despite a certain productivism here, the council phase (elsewhere in Europe as well as Italy) inspired an explosive convergence of themes: neo-Hegelian philosophy, ideological-cultural struggle, working class self-activity. Thus it was no accident that other Western Marxists like Korsch and Lukacs were similarly attracted to the council experiments of the postwar years.

With the formation of the PCI, Gramsci's new loyalties soon forced him to move on to a new set of priorities. In the first place, organizational and time pressures took him away from his earlier philosophical and cultural concerns; his writings in the 1920s, while still revealing in many respects, were devoted largely to internal party debates, immediate tactical discussions, and issues related to Comintern politics. Secondly, the party's very precarious struggle for survival (in the context of fascism) necessarily gave rise to an instrumental outlook—and Gramsci, as a PCI leader, could hardly have been immune to this influence. The inevitable result was a subordination of Gramsci's neo-Hegelian inclinations to the requirements of a party-centered tacticism more compatible with Leninism. Yet even here Gramsci's emergent Western Marxism does not vanish but reappears in a different (and quite attenuated) form through his conception of the mass party, a definition of united front, worker-peasant alliance, and the Southern question which took into account ideological factors, and his vision of a distinctly "national" strategy for the PCI.

Once in prison, Gramsci began to explore his neo-Hegelian assumptions for the first time; indeed, the *Prison Notebooks* (especially the lengthy philosophical sections) stand as one of the great contributions to Western Marxism. If the *Notebooks* retain much of Gramsci's earlier sense of political optimism, they are equally a product of the *second* phase in Western Marxism and thus reflect a kind of theoretical retrenchment born of political defeat. Paralleling the work of Lukacs in *History and Class Consciousness* and the early Frankfurt School, Gramsci's prison writings were motivated by a desire to understand why the working class had generally suffered political defeat. Like these theorists, Gramsci also believed that a project of this magnitude demanded a complete philosophical reworking of Marxism, which in turn meant a rediscovery of Hegel. But Gramsci was virtually alone in turning this reassessment around and seizing the opportunity it furnished for conceptualizing a new revolutionary strategy for the West.

If any single theme can be said to have decisively shaped the *Prison Notebooks*, it would have to be the problem of *ideology*: ideological domination, cultural struggle, popular consciousness. Every component of Gramscian theory—state and civil society, the role of intellectuals, social bloc, concept of the party and political strategy—ultimately revolves around this theme. Thus Gramsci's famous notion of "ideological hegemony" is the most far-reaching and probably the most original construct in his work. In contrast with Lenin's more narrowly political definition of hegemony, Gramsci introduced it to analyze the multidimensional nature of class rule; he insisted that bourgeois domination is exercised as much through popular "consensus" achieved in civil society as through physical coercion (or the threat of it) by the state apparatus, especially in Western capitalist societies where education, mass media, culture, and the legal system can so powerfully shape consciousness. The strength of bourgeois forms of hegemony in European countries could be invoked to explain the drift of working-class politics toward moderate reformism and even conservatism. From this viewpoint, the absence of revolutionary consciousness could be attributed not to fortuitous historical events or proletarian "immaturity" but to certain immanent processes within capitalist development itself whereby the majority of people tend to internalize the dominant ideological and cultural values.[18] Insofar as the *Notebooks* attached great significance to the role of "superstructural" factors (cultural traditions, political myths, the "common sense" outlook of everyday life) in reproducing popular support for bourgeois institutions, it follows that the imperatives of marxist strategy would have to change accordingly. Here Gramsci theorized the possibility of an alternative hegemony, or emergent "integrated culture," that would lay the basis of a counter-hegemonic movement broad enough to initiate the transition to socialism. Consistent with the overall premises of Western Marxism, this "war of position" schema contains two major implications: first, that the transformation of civil society takes on an importance even greater that the contestation for state power and, second, that the new state system must be built upon non-authoritarian foundations.

Gramsci's conceptualization of the state-civil society relationship opened up new areas of theoretical inquiry and political action previously closed off by conventional Marxism. In philosophical terms, it was grounded in the neo-Hegelian themes of totality, the dialectic, praxis. Widespread use of the term *"ensemble* of relations" in the *Prison Notebooks* reflected an effort to transcend the old base-superstructure model, even if Gramsci sometimes slipped back into old language patterns with his references to a "reciprocity" between the two spheres. Whereas the scientific tradition dwelled upon the material forces, Gramscian theory incorporated other components of the totality as well—politics, culture, social relations—none of which assumed universal primacy. And the logical implications of this philosophy for political strategy were clear: no dimension of human existence (however "subjective") was to be ignored. Each aspect, moreover, was closely interwoven with all others, so that a change in one was necessarily linked to multiple changes in the totality.

There is no simple formula to determine the relative weight of the three critical traditions—revolutionary democracy, Leninism, and Western Marxism—for Gramsci's general theory. Still, two generalizations do seem appropriate. First, each of the currents is stressed at different moments throughout Gramsci's mature work and coexists with the other currents in a sometimes uneasy and conflicted relationship (e.g., Leninism and Western Marxism in the *Prison Notebooks*). If revolutionary democracy is most fully emphasized in the council period, it nonetheless persists throughout the 1920s and, while it does not figure prominently in the *Prison Notebooks*, nowhere does Gramsci ever explicitly abandon his earlier council ideals. Leninism is most clearly visible in the party writings but, as I have argued, unmistakable traces of it can be found in both his earlier and later work. The Western Marxist thrust does not completely surface until the *Notebooks*, yet its origins in Crocean philosophy go back to Gramsci's initial formative stages. None of these tendencies has dominated sufficiently to constitute the basis of a single unified outlook; nor do they neatly correspond to any chronological pattern. Interpretations which have tried to force Gramsci's multi-layered thought into such crude frameworks inevitably produce more confusion than clarity.

The second point is that Gramsci, whatever his inclinations toward Jacobinism, seemed in his more theoretical moments to be struggling for a new kind of political discourse compatible with a non-bureaucratic, non-statist transition to socialism. Quite clearly, this approach would mean transcending the limits of both social democracy and Leninism—even if Gramsci's own political life was very much shaped by the dictates of Leninist organizational priorities. The new Gramscian political language also implied a critique of Soviet bureaucratic centralism (and of course Soviet Marxism itself), although once again the immediate political situation was a restraining factor. From this standpoint, both the councilist and Western Marxist sides of Gramsci's thought share a good deal in common: rejection of the old hierarchical social and authority relations, commitment to popular self-activity, a vision of cultural transformation. Their essentially *democratizing* impulse conflicts with the authoritarian ethos of Leninism, ruling out any effective "synthesis" of all three tendencies in Gramsci. Hence, while Gramsci emerges as the only Western Marxist who did not retreat from politics, his effort to outline a new strategy could in the end have only mixed success. The general *theoretical* implications of council communism and Western Marxism were decisively blocked by the *political* reality of the period: Comintern hegemony and the privileged status of the Russian experience, the struggle against fascism, the rise of Stalinism.[19] In this context, Leninism was generally seen as the most concretely viable alternative. Not surprisingly, then, Gramsci's full theoretical impact would not be felt or appreciated until much later—nearly a generation after his death.

This raises the possibility of a "fourth dimension" in Gramsci—namely, that he was a precursor to the famous "Eurocommunist" model adopted by various Communist parties in the advanced countries. Such is the official view of the PCI, theorists and leaders of other parties (e.g., Santiago Carrillo in Spain), as well as some independent observers who see in Gramsci a certain combination of Leninist orthodoxy and modern structural reformism.[20] The historical fact that Gramsci was a founding father of Italian Communism—and one of the party's early leaders and martyrs—is often taken as proof of this intimate linkage.

But a close examination of Gramsci's theoretical and political commitments reveals that the image of a "Eurocommunist" Gramsci, however loosely constructed, is an illusory one. None of the main currents in Gramsci's work—council democracy, Leninism, and Western Marxism—can be said to anticipate the PCI's *via Italiana* strategy originated by Togliatti in the 1940s and later revised by the Eurocommunists in the 1970s. In actuality, *each* of these currents took shape precisely *in opposition* to the social-democratic tradition which in Gramsci's Italy most approximated what Eurocommunism later came to represent. Ironically, much of what Gramsci found anachronistic and politically debilitating in the old PSI would be championed within the PCI in his name fifty years later: scientific Marxism, the parliamentary road to socialism, primary emphasis on electoral politics and trade unionism, the notion of internally reconstructing the bourgeois state. Official

Eurocommunist ideology notwithstanding, the Gramscian vision of a fully revitalized and democratized civil society has never been incorporated into Eurocommunist theory at any level. For example, Gramsci's unrestrained hostility to the Italian state, his critique of party and trade-union bureaucracy, and his effort to define the constituent elements of socialist democracy, however rudimentary they might have been, find no echo in Eurocommunism, which has been defined through many years of institutionalized attachment to *pluralist* democracy. A dialectic of class struggle and social transformation rooted in mass insurgency has been confounded with a politics of non-confrontational, peaceful change and institutional management.[21]

Eurocommunist parties have appropriated the stature and memory (but not the *theory*) of Gramsci in order to legitimate their political claims just as the Soviet leaders use the images of Marx and Lenin to justify their managerial rule. In the process these parties have manipulated central Gramscian ideas—hegemony, social bloc, war of position, organic intellectuals, even the factory councils—within a narrow electoral-parliamentary enclosure that has distorted their original meaning. Thus the war of position ends up as the internal modification of existing state structures rather than a comprehensive transformation of civil society. As I have argued elsewhere, Eurocommunist structural reformism has far more in common with Bernstein's political evolutionism than with Gramscian theory in any of its dimensions.[22] It should be emphasized that such a political translation of Gramsci does not simply involve redefinition of old categories to meet new historical conditions; the categories themselves have been emptied of all dialectical and transformative content. Yet the very impact of such translations, or misappropriations, cannot be overlooked insofar as it too is part of Gramsci's ambiguous legacy.

Elements of a Theoretical Style

Like many other theories, Marxism involves much more than a body of concepts and generalizations, or a methodology, or even a vision of the future. Insofar as theory itself is part of an unfolding social and historical process, and therefore varies greatly according to the specificity of time and place, it is possible to speak of a particular theoretical language, spirit, or *style* that goes beyond explicit substance. This emphatically applies to Gramsci's Marxism, which was the product not only of a turbulent Europe between 1917 and 1935 but of an Italy in the midst of perpetual crisis and transition.

In rebelling against the passivity of orthodox Marxism, Gramsci injected a spirit of activism, impatience, and optimism into his work. To some extent this corresponded to his well-known preoccupation with "superstructural" concerns: politics, philosophy, culture. Despite his abundant references to totality, Gramsci actually devoted little attention to matters of political economy in his writings, especially in the *Prison Notebooks*; in devaluing the material "base," his work was essentially silent regarding the presumed laws of capitalist development. For Gramsci, dwelling on the economic sphere meant steering theory in the direction of descriptive, static categories confined to the prevailing (capitalist) logic. This is why he spoke enthusiastically of Leninism and the Bolshevik Revolution as a "revolution against *Capital*." In contrast, his voluntarist sensibilities generated a different kind of language—that of change, transformation, the "actuality of the revolution." It is possible to go even further and argue that Gramsci was above all a distinctly *political* theorist who, like Lenin, saw in politics the real lever of class struggle, social renewal, and, ultimately, community. If Gramsci wrote as a *theorist of revolution*, driven by a passion for social renewal, it took the form of political inspiration and vision derived first from Lenin and then later, in the *Notebooks*, from his rediscovery of Machiavelli.[23] Yet, while Gramsci's near obsession with the political sphere distinguished him from other Western Marxists—indeed it even conflicted with some of his own neo-Hegelian premises—his particular orientation differed markedly from Lenin's. With the partial exception of the later PCI period, Gramsci's style of political discourse avoided the instrumentalism and tacticism characteristic of Lenin's more party-centered and power-focused theory.

A further stylistic component of Gramsci's Marxism derived from the uniquely *national* role of both theory and theorist. First, one of Gramsci's overriding goals was the creation of a specifically Italian Marxism that would be the indigenous expression of a truly "national-popular" movement. Such a world-view would have to take into account the unique aspects of Italian history and culture, offer a unifying perspective, and develop a language that spoke to the immediate concerns of ordinary Italian people. While a dedicated internationalist, Gramsci turned away from a mechanical borrowing of strategic models from abroad and even more from the attempt (for example, by Stalin) to impose a universal model from a single center. Gramsci's extensive study of Italian history and culture—including his work on Machiavelli, the Risorgimento, the "Southern Question," Pirandello—can be understood in terms of this commitment. Second, Gramsci in his personal life emerged as a profoundly "national" political and intellectual figure whose contributions could be respected by Marxists of all stripes, as well as some liberals and Catholics. Following Croce, and employing a Gramscian schema, Gramsci the theorist could be described as an "intellectual of a new type" who articulated themes reflective of the mood for change in an Italy where both liberalism and Catholicism were in crisis.

Finally, Gramsci's work is conspicuous for both its non-systematic and non-sectarian quality—rather unique among Marxists at the time. In part this was an imposed style, first because of the journalistic format typical of his earlier writings and then because of the difficult prison conditions he was forced to endure. In greater part, however, it grew out of his life-long hostility to all forms of scholasticism; for if theory were to have a *revolutionary* meaning it would have to go beyond the self-contained philosophical systems of the past and become a manifestly "popular" force. Consistent with the critical side of Marxism, Gramsci understood theoretical activity as a changing, dialectical component of mass struggles, sensitive to novel ideas and discoveries of whatever origins and never contemptuous of the spontaneous of "primitive" stirrings of popular revolt. The *Prison Notebooks* were unique in their effort to unravel the political language of everyday ideology, or "common sense." What often set Gramsci's theoretical approach apart from that of his contemporaries was its searching, probing, tentative character. He scarcely gave the impression of a theorist setting out to construct a closed system of thought based upon rigorous scientific principles, formal abstractions,or conclusive truths. And he seemed even less concerned with presenting his ideas as the necessary or "correct" extension of Marxist (or Leninist) orthodoxy.

Yet these positive virtues—openness, eclecticism, breadth of theoretical sweep—contained their reverse side. One problem was that Gramsci's intellectual output, while voluminous, was generally lacking in clear organization and sustained, logical argumentation. His writing style, which at its best was rich and even poetic, was more often abstruse, fragmentary, and difficult to understand. Many readers of Gramsci complain that it is often impossible to find a unifying thread in his particular writings much less a theoretical coherence in the whole of his work. Surely this is a major reason why Gramsci has been subjected to such diversity of interpretations. At the same time, Gramsci would no doubt have responded that the theoretical enterprise itself, much like politics, is necessarily shaped by ambiguity, unevenness, and indeterminacy. What does emerge from a repeated and empathetic reading of Gramsci, however, is one of the most original and compelling social theories of the twentieth century. It is a theory which, in each of its three dimensions, embodied a rare synthesis of intellectual imagination, political refusal, and critical spirit—a synthesis that indeed pointed to a new language of politics, and which contributed immensely to the revitalization of Marxist and radical thinking in the 1960s and 1970s.

Footnotes

1. The most recent, and most comprehensive, elaboration of this dual tradition within Marxism can be found in Alvin W. Gouldner, *The Two Marxisms* (New York: Seabury Press, 1980), especially chapter 2. In place of Gouldner's term "critical," with its heavily pedagogical implication, I have occasionally substituted "critical-revolutionary" because of its more clearly *political* definition.

2. Albrecht Wellmer, *Critical Theory of Society* (New York: Seabury Press, 1974), chapter 2.

3. This conception of a routinized Marxism, transformed into an official legitimating ideology of bureaucratic parties and unions, shares much in common with the classic analyses of German Social Democracy developed by Michels and Schorske. See Robert Michels, *Political Parties* (New York: Collier, 1962) and Carl Schorske, *German Social Democracy, 1905-1917* (New York: John Wiley and sons, 1955), chs 4,5 and conclusion. It differs, however, from the interpretation offered by Korsch, who argued that it was precisely the sustained *independence* of Marxist theory from ongoing political movements that precipitated its disintegration into a formalized scientific system. See Karl Korsch, *Marxism and Philosophy* (New York: Monthly Review, 1970), pp. 64-71.

4. The bulk of these writings is contained in Paolo Spriano, ed., *Antonio Gramsci: Scritti Politici* (Roma: Editori Riuniti, 1967)—and exhaustive collection that includes most of Gramsci's pre-prison articles in *Avanti!, Il Grido del Popolo, L'Ordine Nuovo, L'Unita*, and *Stato Operaio*, as well as his contributions to official party (mainly Communist Party) literature. The early period (before 1917) is covered by the volume *Scritti Giovanili* (Turin: Einaudi, 1958). The best English translations of this material can be found in Quintin Hoare, ed., *Antonio Gramsci: Selections from Political Writings 1910-1920* (New York: International Publishers, 1977), and Paul Piccone and Pedro Cavalcanti, eds., *History, Philosophy, and Culture in the Young Gramsci* (St. Louis: Telos Press, 1975).

5. Gramsci's work during the *Biennio Rosso* was published almost exclusively in the pages of *L'Ordine Nuovo*. It is contained in two of the previously-mentioned collections—*Scritti Politici* and *Selections from Political Writings 1910-1920*.

6. Gramsci's most significant party writings have been assembled in *Scritti Politici*. Their English translation is contained in Quintin Hoare, ed., *Antonio Gramsci: Selections from Political Writings 1921-1926* (New York: International Publishers, 1978). This volume also includes a number of important letters between Gramsci and his comrades in the PCI leadership.

7. "Letter to Tatiana," March 7, 1932 in Lynne Lawner, ed., *Antonio Gramsci: Letters from Prison* (New York: Harper and Row, 1973), p. 227.

8. "Letter to Tatiana," July 3, 1931, in Lawner, *op. cit.*, p. 200.

9. The initial Italian publications of the *Quaderni del Carcere* were assembled by Einaudi in six volumes between 1948 and 1951. An anthology of Gramsci's writings, edited by Mario Spinella and Carlo Salinari, was published by Editori Riuniti in 1963. It was not until the early 1970s, however, that the most significant of Gramsci's writings on politics and philosophy were translated into English and brought together in a single volume: Quintin Hoare and Geoffrey Nowell Smith, eds., *Selections from the Prison Notebooks of Antonio Gramsci* (London: Lawrence and Wishart, 1971). Gramsci's revealing prison letters, as indicated above, are contained in the Lawner volume. The earlier and more comprehensive Italian anthology of the letters is Sergio Caprioglio and Elsa Fubini, eds., *Letters dal carcere* (Turin: Einaudi, 1965).

10. "Letter to Teresina," February 20, 1928, in Lawner, *op. cit.*, p. 120.

11. Giuseppe Fiori, *Antonio Gramsci: Life of a Revolutionary* (London: New Left Books, 1970), p. 237.

12. "Letter to Tatiana", December 15, 1930, in Lawner, *op.cit.*, p. 193.

13. Oddly enough, efforts to explore this democratic component of Gramsci's thought have been rare. Such a gap is all the more surprising given that Gramsci was one of the very few Marxists to even *pose* the issue of revolutionary democracy. In part this can be attributed to the influence of official PCI interpretations of Gramsci, which present him as a theorist concerned essentially with *pluralist* democracy. The only systematic attempt to confront this problem is John Cammett's "Socialism and Participatory Democracy," in George Fischer, ed., *The Revival of American Socialism* (New York: Oxford University press, 1971), pp. 41-60. Unfortunately, this brief but excellent article scarcely mentions the council theme and never really explores the significance of democratic participation for Gramsci's overall theory. Jerome Karabell's "Revolutionary Contradictions: Antonio Gramsci and

the Problem of Intellectuals," in *Politics and Society*, vol. 6, no. 2, 1976, also takes up the question of democracy, but its main focus is on the role of intellectuals. There is a brief discussion of this theme in Walter Adamson, *Hegemony and Revolution* (Berkeley: University of California Press, 1980), pp. 209-213, but the problem of democratic socialism is never addressed. A good theoretical treatment of the state and democracy in Gramsci—but one that is schematic and confined to the *Prison Notebooks*—is Norberto Bobbio's "Gramsci and the Conception of Civil Society," in Chantal Mouffe, ed., *Gramsci and Marxist Theory* (London: Routledge and Kegan Paul, 1979), pp. 32-43. On the *Ordine Nuovo* period and the council movement, there are some excellent sources which provide and abundance of historical detail but they too generally fall short in the area of democratic theory. Those most sensitive to this issue include: Paolo Spriano, *Gramsci e l'Ordine Nuovo* (Rome: Editori Riuniti, 1965), chs. 3-5; Gwynn Williams, *Proletarian Order* (London: Pluto Press, 1975), pp. 103-120; and John Cammett, *Antonio Gramsci and the Origins of Italian Communism* (Stanford, Calif.: Stanford University Press, 1967), ch. 4.

14. Those who see only the Leninist side of Gramsci, or who present him as a conventional Leninist, are consistent with Palmiro Togliatti's seminal interpretation of the late 1950s. Of course Togliatti, as leader of a still nominally Leninist PCI, had political reasons for trying to ideologically appropriate Gramsci in this way. See Togliatti, *Gramsci* (Rome: Editori Riuniti, 1967), pp. 161-207. This along with related essays is contained in the English translation *On Gramsci and Other Writings* (London: Lawrence and Wishart, 1979), pp. 161-207. In the contemporary literature on Gramsci, Leninist versions are plentiful. Examples include: Luciano Gruppi, *Il concetto di egemonia in Gramsci* (Rome: Editori Riuniti, 1972); Christine Buci-Glucksmann, *Gramsci and the State* (London: Lawrence and Wishart, 1980), esp. pp. 3-16, 119-127, and 174-185; M.A. Macchiocchi, *Pour Gramsci* (Paris: Editions du Seuil, 1974); and Bagio de Giovanni, "Lenin and Gramsci: State, Politics, and Party," in Mouffe, *op. cit.*, pp. 259-286. The Gruppi volume is one of many "official" efforts which, following Togliatti, presents Gramsci as simultaneously a Leninist and a precursor to the postwar PCI. For a critique of this interpretation, see Paul Piccone, "Gramsci's Marxism: Beyond Lenin and Togliatti", *Theory and Society*, no. 3, winter 1976, pp. 485-512, and Carl Boggs, *The Impasse of European Communism* (Boulder, Colo.: Westview Press, 1982), pp. 119-137.

15. By 1926, as Davidson observes, Gramsci had attained a

good knowledge of Lenin's work—and of course there was much less ambiguity at that point about the political course of the Bolshevik Revolution. See Alastair Davidson, *Antonio Gramsci: Towards and Intellectual Biography* (London: Merlin Press, 1977), p. 233.

16. In presenting Western Marxism as an extension of the *critical* tradition I am departing radically from Perry Anderson's schema in *Considerations on Western Marxism* (London: New Left Books, 1976). Anderson defines Western Marxism in a way that permits him to conflate both the critical and scientific traditions; his list includes not only Lukacs, Gramsci, Marcuse, and Sartre, for example, but also Bauer, Della Volpe, Colletti, and Althusser the latter four all hostile to Hegelianism. The result is that Anderson obscures the crucial distinctions between these two groups, making it impossible to specify the unique theoretical contributions of either. For an exploration of Western Marxism which does not suffer from this flaw—that is, which sees it as an expression of the critical tendency—see Russell Jacoby, *Dialectic of Defeat* (Cambridge, England: Cambridge University Press, 1981).

17. Not until the 1970s did Gramsci receive even minimal attention as a "critical" or Western Marxist. The explanation, once again, lies mainly in earlier PCI efforts to identify Gramsci as a Leninist for purposes of party legitimation; these interpretations typically conceded the Hegelian influence upon the young Gramsci through Labriola and Croce, but maintained—incorrectly—that he outgrew or abandoned it in his later writings. Anderson's desire (in *Considerations*) to correct this only further complicates the matter since his defining motif —Western Marxism as the theoretical expression of intellectuals detached from working-class politics— quite obviously does not apply to Gramsci. Anderson's negative critique parallels an earlier hostile treatment by Neil McInnes, *The Western Marxists* (New York: Library Press, 1972). One of the first *sympathetic* efforts to locate Gramsci squarely within the critical tradition is Karl Klare's introduction to Dick Howard and Klare, eds., *The Unknown Dimension: European Marxism since Lenin* (New York: Basic Books, 1972), pp. 3-33. In a similar vein, but more explicitly focused on Gramsci, is the earlier contribution of Mihailo Markovic, "L'unita di filosofia e politica nel Gramsci," in Pietro Rossi, ed., *Gramsci e la cultura contemporanea* (Rome: Editori Riuniti, 1967), pp. 19-27. See also Giacomo Marramao, *Marxismo e revisionismo in Italia* (Bari: De Donato, 1971). Still, perhaps the only commentator to draw out the full implications of Gramsci's Western Marxism has been Paul Piccone. See his "Phenomeno-

logical Marxism," *Telos* no. 9, fall 1971, pp. 3-31; "Gramsci's Hegelian Marxism", Political Theory, February 1974, pp. 32-45; and "From Spaventa to Gramsci," *Telos* no. 31, spring 1977, pp. 35-65. The difficulty with Piccone's interpretation is that it exaggerates the Hegelian dimension of Gramsci to such a degree that the conflicting strains and tensions in his thought are suppressed. More recent discussions of Gramsci in the context of Western Marxism include Tom Long, "Marx and Western Marxism in the 1970s," *Berkeley Journal of Sociology*, vol. XXV, 1980, pp. 13-66, and Jacoby, *Dialectic of Defeat*, esp. pp. 105-108.

18. The notion that the failure of European radicalism in the 1920s should in part be attributed to *internal* dynamics of working-class development was hardly unique to Gramsci. It was also shared by early Frankfurt School theorists, by Wilhelm Reich, and notably by Lukacs in *History and Class Consciousness*. There are crucial similarities (and some contrasts) between Gramsci's concept of ideological hegemony and Lukacs' idea of "reification," which I will spell out further in Chapter 5. On Lukacs, see Andrew Arato and Paul Breines, *The Young Lukacs and the Origins of Western Marxism* (New York: Seabury Press, 1979), chs. 8 and 9.

19. For an excellent discussion of the stifling impact that Soviet-Comintern hegemony had on an emergent Western Marxism in the 1920s and 1930s, see Jacoby, *Dialectic of Defeat*, ch. 3.

20. As might be expected, efforts to demonstrate a continuity from Gramsci to Eurocommunism actually begin with Togliatti, The PCI held its first conference on Gramsci in Rome in 1958, inspired partly by the theoretical ferment linked to the debates around structural reformism at the Eighth PCI Congress in 1956. Togliatti's contribution at the conference was an attempt to show a theoretical convergence between Lenin, Gramsci, and the *via Italiana*. See his *Gramsci*, pp. 135-182. Probably Togliatti's most ambitious effort to establish a bridge between Gramsci and his own concept of structural reforms is his "Nel quarantesimo anniversario del partito comunista Italiana," in *Il partito* (Rome: Editori Riuniti, 1964). This laid the groundwork for the standard PCI interpretation since the early 1960s; see, for example, Luciano Gruppi's *Socialismo e democrazia* (Milan: Edizioni del Calendario, 1969), which is one of the most comprehensive attempts to develop a Gramscian basis of PCI strategy since the early 1960s. By the mid 1970s, with the appearance of "Eurocommunism," Gramsci became even more fashionable and his influence on party development was now more or less taken for granted. See Giorgio Napolitano, *Intervista sul PCI* (Bari: laterza, 1976), p. 46 and

Gruppi, *Il concetto di egemonia in Gramsci* (Rome: Editori Riuniti, 1975). Pietro Ingrao's *Masse e potere* (Rome: Editori Riuniti, 1975) also contains many positive references to Gramsci. Among non-Italian commentators, those who have emphasized the Gramsci-Eurocommunism connection include: Santiago Carrillo, *Eurocommunism and the State* (London: Lawrence and Wishart, 1977), pp. 44, 102; Fernando Claudin, *Eurocommunism and Socialism* (London: New left Books, 1978), p. 85; and Carl Marzani, *The Promise of Eurocommunism* (Westport, Conn.: Lawrence Hill and Co., 1980), pp. 35-38, 289.

21. There is now a growing literature which departs from the conventional PCI thesis of a structural reformist Gramsci. See, for example, Lucio Magri, "Italian Communism in the Sixties,' *New Left Review* no. 66, March-April, 1971, pp. 37-52; Mario Telo, "L'interpretazione togliattiana,". in Il Manifesto, *Da Togliatti alla nuova sinistra* (Rome: Alfani Editore, 1975); Paul Piccone, "Beyond Lenin and Togliatti: Gramsci's Marxism", *Theory and Society*, vol. 4, no. 1, winter 1976; Jonas Pontusson, "Gramsci and Eurocommunism," *Berkeley Journal of Sociology*, vol. 25, 1980; and Carl Boggs, *The Impasse of European Communism*, pp. 119-137.

22. Boggs, *The Impasse of European Communism*, pp. 134-137.

23. Many commentators have duly noted the centrality of political themes in Gramsci, but few have discussed the non-Leninist uniqueness of his political theory within the Marxist tradition. Those few include: Ralph Miliband, *Marxism and Politics* (London: Oxford University Press, 1977), introduction; Mark E. Kann, "Antonio Gramsci and Modern Marxism," *Studies in Comparative Communism*, summer-autumn, 1980; and Matthew F. Stolz, "Gramsci's Machiavelli,". *Humanities in Society* vol. 4, no. 1, winter 1981. See also Anderson, *Considerations on Western Marxism*, p. 45, for a slightly more conventional Leninist interpretation of Gramsci's "political" Marxism.

24. On the role of Gramsci as a Crocean-style "national" theorist, see Nicola Auciello, *Socialismo ed egemonia in Gramsci e Togliatti* (Bari: De Donato, 1974), pp. 175-76.

2 The Making of a Revolutionary Theorist

The theoretical and political outlook of the young Gramsci was nurtured in the idealist setting that had dominated Italian intellectual life before World War I. There was of course the omnipresent figure of Benedetto Croce, whose philosophy had a powerful impact on the development of Marxists (as well as non-Marxists) of Gramsci's generation. While Croce himself only briefly flirted with Marxism, the Neapolitan theorist was the main conduit of Hegelianism in Italy and also the most visible proponent of a new cultural renaissance.[1] At least equally important was the work of Antonio Labriola, who virtually alone in Italy before the turn of the century sought to rediscover the unity of theory and practice that had been the core element of Marx's own project. As a student at the University of Turin Gramsci became attracted to the Hegelianism shared by Croce and Labriola, so that by the time he joined the Italian Socialist Party (in 1913) he instinctively opposed the scientific materialism that was equated with authentic Marxism by PSI leaders and theoreticians. Already in these early formative years Gramsci seemed to exhibit an impatient voluntarism—a strong preoccupation with the concerns of collective will, consciousness, and culture—which produced what must have been some unsettling tensions in his organizational commitment to the PSI. Indeed, as an activist in the Turin federation of the party, he emerged very quickly as one of the leaders in the assault on theoretical orthodoxy.

During his initial phase of political involvement (1915-1918), Gramsci gravitated toward journalism, at which he was very competent and on occasion brilliant, and his intellectual influence within the local PSI organization rapidly conferred on him a leadership role which he accepted only ambivalently. His leadership duties, however, did not prevent him from being critical of the official PSI line or fueling new, oppositional tendencies among Turinese workers—both of which he did in his *Il Grido del Popolo* and *Avanti!* articles. Gramsci was quite modest about his topical contributions to party publications, not only for his early period but later: "In ten years of journalism I wrote enough words to fill up fifteen to twenty volumes of 4,000 pages apiece, but it was stuff written for the very day it appeared and I always thought it would be dead the day after..."[2] Though possibly true at one level, this negative self-assessment would in effect relegate the early Gramsci to theoretical oblivion when his work of this period actually furnished many insights into his understanding of Italian history, the nature of his own political commitments, and the thematic evolution of his later work.

Gramsci's early writings covered a rich variety of topics—philosophy, culture, Italian history, the socialist Party, the Bolshevik Revolution—from a viewpoint that is surprisingly consistent although not yet theoretically grounded.[3] Something of the political and intellectual flavor of the immediate pre-*Biennio Rosso* years, above all the sense of crisis and imminent upheaval that characterized this period, was captured here. So too was the philosophical presence of Croce, the political influence of Sorel, and the historical analysis of Gaetano Salvemini, though curiously one detects little of the impact of Antonio Labriola that many Gramsci scholars have seen as crucial to his early development. Moreover, aside from references to Lenin in the context of the Russian Revolution, there was scarcely any mention of the major figures in European Marxism—Kautsky, Bernstein, Luxemburg, Plekhanov, Bauer, *et. al.* This conspicuous detachment from the Marxism of the Second International reflects not only his hostility to scientific determinism but also his initially suspicious (or insecure?) attitude towards Marxism *tout court*. Here Gramsci's spirit of independence, which served to remove him from the epic Marxist debates of the time, became a source of strength insofar as it enabled him to utilize new ideas and fresh insights from a diversity of traditions. It further helps to illuminate the peculiar originality and eclecticism that characterized Gramsci's later Marxism.

It is possible to identify in the early Gramsci a preoccupation, however unshaped and fragmentary, with four broad themes. The first, and probably most central, was the adoption of a critical or "creative" theoretical posture stressing subjective "will" over objective forces and linked to an anti-positivism grounded in Hegelian-Crocean philosophy. The second involved the goal of building an integrated and autonomous proletarian *culture* that would transform the working masses from oppressed and dehumanized victims of capitalism into revitalized collective architects of a classless society. Thirdly, there was a conception of the Italian bourgeoisie as an enfeebled class incapable of bringing about a modern, secular, liberal order and thus more vulnerable to the incursions of popular upheaval than was the case in other European capitalist societies. Finally came Gramsci's analysis of the Bolshevik Revolution as both a momentous political event for the European left and a decisive theoretical rupture with orthodox Marxism.

Croce and the Philosophical Origins

The theoretical degeneration of pre-World War I Marxism into different manifestations of scientism and economic determinism coincided with two related political developments: the decline of revolutionary prospects in Europe by the turn of the century and the integration of electorally successful socialist parties (notably German Social Democracy) into the political system of advanced capitalism. A key methodological feature of this process was the growing obsession of Marxists with the internal mechanics of capitalist political economy. Concepts were locked into, and ultimately mirrored, the very premises of bourgeois development—e.g., productivism, linear economic growth, capital accumulation, fetishism of science and technology. As the actual historical gains of the proletariat failed to validate the more optimistic expectations of nineteenth century Marxism, many socialists looked for a kind of fatalistic deliverance in "scientific truth"; science itself therefore became a religious faith in the dominant (Kautskian) tendency of the Second International. Theory degenerated into a scholastic project, remote from the everyday political activity. Immobilized by such a mechanical theory, the social-democratic parties uniformly failed to take advantage of the opportunities afforded by the long-awaited crisis which swept Europe in the period 1914-1923. Only the Bolsheviks in Russia, who had long since overturned what Lenin called "legal" or "textbook" Marxism, were able to carry out a successful revolution at the moment when the established order was in shambles.

For the young Gramsci, positivist Marxism generated no interest, and he instinctively gravitated toward the "critical" theory which he found in neo-Hegelianism. Already as a newly-enrolled PSI activist he concluded that, in submerging both the "philosophical" and "political" dimensions of theory, orthodox Marxism would inevitably give rise to a mood of quietism and passivity; he was convinced that for Marxist intellectuals it was a natural response to the sagging spirit of working-class struggles. Scientific materialism could be a source of certainty and comfort at a time of political retreat and despair, for in adopting this theory it was possible to feel that "I have been defeated for the moment, but the tide of history is working for me in the long run." Or, as Gramsci later added: "When you don't have the initiative in the struggle and the struggle itself comes eventually to be identified with a series of defeats, mechanical determinism becomes a tremendous force of moral resistance, of cohesion, and of patient and obstinate perseverance."[4]

Having begun to explore Hegelian philosophy as a student in Turin, Gramsci readily accepted the intimate Hegel-Marx connection; the result was a profound radicalization which led to his enlistment in the PSI. Much as Marx's theory of history evolved out of the (left) Hegelian synthesis in the 1840s, Gramsci found his point of departure in Croce and in the broader Italian idealist tradition. Years later, Gramsci would comment: "In a short introduction to the extract of Croce's *Religione e serenita* I wrote that just as Hegelianism had been the premise of Marxism in the nineteenth century, so the philosophy of Croce might be the premise of a renewed, contemporary Marxism for our generation."[5] Persuaded that Croce was the most important Italian thinker of the prewar period—a truly "national" intellectual whose influence, like Hegel's, extended in a number of political directions—Gramsci referred often to the Neopolitan in both his early and *later* writings. It was through Croce's neo-Hegelianism that Gramsci first developed an appreciation for dialectical philosophy as an answer to the one-dimensional determinism in vogue within the PSI. Croce wrote extensively about the tasks of philosophical renewal and cultural transformation, themes more or less forgotten within orthodox Marxism. Gamsci assimilated these concerns into his own more modest but also more *radical* theoretical efforts, which immediately suggested a greater emphasis on the ideological over the material sphere which he derived from Croce's notion of the "ethico-political". Gramsci's thought here was decisively shaped by two

Crocean assumptions, which remained with him until the end: the historical specificity of Italian development, and a view to change based in a free-flowing dialectic in which human beings are able to control their own destinies.[6]

The influence of Antonio Labriola's Marxism on Gramsci's formative years was more complex and indirect. In certain respects the parallels between these two theorists were rather striking—for example, in their attempt to forge a unity between philosophy and politics—but in fact Gramsci rarely cited Labriola in his early articles and did not seem to take serious notice of him until 1916-17.[7] It was Labriola, after all, who first introduced the term "philosophy of praxis" (Gramsci's euphemism for Marxism in the *Notebooks*) and who, even more than Croce, appropriated philosophical idealism for the sustenance of Italian Marxism. Labriola, moreover, was one of the few pre-1900 European Marxists who challenged the economistic reductionism of the base-superstructure model. The irony in all this is that Labriola's theoretical impact on Gramsci was actually mediated through Croce.[8]

For Gramsci, following Croce and Labriola, historical process followed an open, more of less indeterminate logic shaped more by collective human "will" than by the external power of natural laws. He argued that Marx "was not a messiah who left a file of parables pregnant with categorical imperatives, of absolute indisputable norms independent of time and space." Thus Marx did not approach the study of history as a "metaphysical positivist" but as an investigator and interpreter of the past whose only imperatives were *political*—e.g., "Workers of the world unite." When understood from a critical standpoint, the concept of will (*volonta*) simply implies a consciousness of political ends and the means necessary to achieve them.[9] Positivism had to be comprehended for what it was—a "scientific superstition" created out or "blind faith" by an intellectual stratum seeking a form of "deliverance" through divine laws. In a revealing essay written in 1918, "Mysteries of Poetry and Culture," Gramsci stated the case further:

> Critical communism has nothing in common with positivist philosophy, the metaphysics and mysticism of Evolution and Nature. Marxism is based on philosophical idealism which, however, has nothing in common with what is ordinarily meant by the word 'idealism' i.e. the abandonment to dreams, cherished chimeras and feel-

ings, the state of always having one's head in the clouds without concern for the necessities and needs of practical life. Philosophical idealism is a doctrine of being and knowledge, according to which reality is known theoretically...[10]

In Gramsci's view, the idea of a linear, material, necessary progress toward socialism downplays the task of transforming popular consciousness. He observed that the economic determinism of PSI and CGL (General Confederation of Labor) theoreticians became "the doctrine of the proletariat's inertia," typified by the manner in which CGL theorist Claudio Treves "reduced Marx's doctrine to an external scheme or a natural law that inexorably takes place outside of human will, outside of active human associations and the social forces developed by this activity which itself becomes the determinant of progress: the necessary cause of new forms of production." Gramsci suggested that there are historical moments when human collective will-power can acquire "an importance which it normally did not have," leading to new conditions which are themselves "economic facts."[11] This formulation, which so clearly opposes the power of subjective intervention to the restraints of "natural laws," could easily have come from the philosophical sections of the *Prison Notebooks*.

If Gramsci saw in positivism the philosophical viewpoint most compatible with political reformism, then neo-Hegelianism was associated with the development of a "critical" or "revolutionary" communism. Croce's focus on the "ethico-political" realm, while clearly too one-sided in the autonomy it assigned to ideology, was nonetheless consistent with an activist stance that foresaw purposive human beings seizing hold of their own historical opportunities. In contrast with the Russian Bolsheviks, the reformists emerged as the classic dogmatists and "utopians," for "they are those who mortgage the future and seek to imprison it in their pre-established shapes." Hence the reformist adaptation to the rules of the bourgeois state and the orthodox tendency to conceive of history as a "natural organism that goes through fixed stages of predictable development" actually converge in the twin expressions of scientism and utopianism.[12] Gramsci continued:

> They (the reformists) do not understand history as free development of freely born and integrated energies, as something unlike natural evolution, in the same way that man and human associations are different from molecules and aggregates of molecules. They have not learned

that freedom is the force immanent in history which blows up all pre-established schemes. The philistine of socialism have reduced the finely-woven cloth of socialist doctrine to a rag, have dirtied it and then ridiculed those who they think do not respect it.[13]

The Italian reformists, according to Gramsci, were much too obsessed with the world of "facts," with given reality—an outlook of those who want to *preserve* bourgeois institutions. To move beyond this framework would require an altogether different set of assumptions grounded in dialectical philosophy. Hence to change the world meant elaborating a system of "moral principles," a "sense of political direction, that could order facts, events, material relations toward some ultimate goal."[14] The emphasis on *vision* linked to political action here anticipated Gramsci's later fascination with Machiavelli's "Jacobinism" in the *Notebooks*. The early Gramsci's fixation on human "will" and political action as the essence of historical change goes further in its celebration of subjectivity than any previous Marxist notion, even including Labriola's "praxis" philosophy. At times, perhaps writing under the infatuating spell of Giovanni Gentile's "action philosophy" and his friend Romain Rolland's notion of existential commitments Gramsci seemed almost contemptuously indifferent to the realm of material forces.[15] At these moments he appeared to be interested exclusively in the role of ideas, values, beliefs; the only real history was the type of flow and movement created by self-conscious individuals.[16] In other essays, however, he incorporated the materialist component of Marx in a way that indicated a search for the sort of philosophical synthesis to which he devoted so much of his attention in the *Notebooks*.[17] Probably the only valid generalization that can be made about Gramsci's work before 1919 is that his "Marxism", at best only crudely formed and based upon a limited familiarity with Marx's own writings, always coexisted in an uneasy tension with the strains of Italian philosophical idealism.[18]

Culture and Class Consciousness

Gramsci's early fascination with the theme of collective revolutionary will in the remaking of Italian society, thoroughly Crocean in its inspiration, helps to explain his persistent interest in culture or, more accurately, the relationship between politics and culture. A vision of cultural transformation was for Gramsci the natural extension of the Hegelian tradition. It was, moreover, the anticipation of later theoretical motifs—the notion of proletarian self-activity on his *Ordine Nuovo* writings, the concept of ideological hegemony (and counter-hegemonic politics) in the *Prison Notebooks*.

If Gramsci's Croceanism predisposed him to take culture more seriously than most of his party comrades were willing to do, it was his first political mentor Angelo Tasca who concretely pushed him in this direction. A leading PSI militant in Turin, and eventually a close collaborator with Gramsci during the *Ordine Nuovo* period, Tasca saw culture and education (an "active pedagogy") as the key to the formation of class consciousness, since the proletariat would have to develop its own cultural traditions and institutions to effectively challenge the bourgeoisie. When Gramsci became editor of *Il Grido del Popolo* in 1916 he immediately converted it into a journal of culture; through its pages he sought to impart a sense of immediacy to the theoretical ideal of "moral renewal" that was spawned by Italian idealism. He wrote regularly about theater, literature, poetry, language, and cultural history—about Dante, DeSanctis, Futurism, Pirandello, and Ibsen. During the formative 1916-1918 period, the combined influences of Henri Barbusse (and the *Clarte* group in France), Romain Rollard, and Charles Peguy compelled Gramsci to move beyond the study of intellectual and cultural elites and into the sphere of *popular* culture and consciousness—the everyday experiences of common people.[19]

Gramsci thus arrived at an understanding of "culture" much broader than those human activities conventionally associated with art and entertainment. It incorporated the entire realm of social consciousness—popular ideas, attitudes, habits, myths, folklore, etc.—that functioned as an ideological mediation in the class struggle, either confining or accelerating class politics The critique of capitalism was linked in Gramsci's mind to the idea of *civilta*, or quality of life; the struggle to overturn the bourgeois order was in great measure a *cultural* effort to reclaim this *civilta*, to transform civil society, consistent with the Hegelian dialectic of "overcoming" alienation. Traditional elite forms of culture, according to Gramsci, were the product of "mere intellect" and "pedantry", reinforcing in the great mass of people a sense of passivity. It was based upon an encyclopedic knowledge whereby man is viewed as a mere "container in which to pour and conserve empirical data of brute disconnected facts which he will have to subsequently pigeon-hole in his brain..." Gramsci added: "This form of culture is truly harmful, especially to the proletariat. It only serves to create misfits, people who believe themselves superior to the rest of humanity because they have accumulated in their memory a certain quantity of facts and dates which they cough up at every opportunity to almost raise a barrier between themselves and others. This form of culture serves to create that pale and broken-winded intellectualism (so well devastated by Romain Rolland) which has produced a whole crowd of boasters and day-dreamers more harmful to a healthy social life than tuberculosis of syphillis microbes are to the body's beauty and health."[20]

What, then, constituted the basis of a healthier and more creative type of culture? From Gramsci's viewpoint, the first objective was to state the problem more lucidly, to reconceptualize the very nature of cultural activity. Defined at the most general level, therefore, "Culture is the organization, the disciplining of one's inner self; it is the appropriation of one's own personality; it is the conquest of a superior consciousness whereby it becomes possible to understand one's own historical value, function in life, rights and duties."[21] This vision of culture, at once *popular* and *critical*, was for Gramsci hostile to the positivist world-view prevalent within academic culture. Hence: "It is through the unified criticism of capitalist civilization that the unified consciousness of the proletariat is formed and is forming. Here, criticism signifies culture, not spontaneous, naturalistic evolution."[22]

Gramsci saw this process of cultural regeneration as an indispensable element in the forging of revolutionary collective will. He observed that just as the French Revolution was preceded by the Enlightenment, so would the conditions of future socialist revolutions be shaped by "an intense critical effort of cultural penetration", one in which "the infusion of ideas through groups of men who were initially unresponsive" would instill class solidarity where before there was only social fragmentation and alienation. In eighteenth century France, "every new comedy of Voltaire, every new pamphlet was like a spark passing over a network of lines extended from nation to nation, from region to region." In this context "The bayonets of Napoleon's armies found the way already levelled by an invisible army of books and pamphlets and, an army which had been swarming out of Paris ... and had prepared men and institutions for the necessary renovation." The end result, Gramsci concluded, was "a magnificent revolution whereby ... an international, spiritual bourgeoisie was formed throughout Europe as a united consciousness aware in all of its sections of common sufferings and disgraces."[23] Written in 1916, these words exhibit a thematic language remarkably similar to what Gramsci would employ many years later in pressing the case for a "war of position" strategy in the *Prison Notebooks*.

Gramsci's theory of cultural transformation went to the very core of proletarian experience and pointed to the emergence of a class ideologically prepared and organizationally capable of carrying out the Marxian project of self-emancipation. Education, knowledge, culture—these would be the tools of the working class in its struggle to free itself from the omnipresent, stifling power of the traditional intellectuals. As Gramsci put it: "Education, culture, and the organized dissemination of knowledge constitute the independence of the masses from the intelligentsia. The most intelligent phase of the struggle against the despotism of professional intellectuals and the trust in divine law consists in the intensification of culture and the raising of consciousness."[24] Gramsci implied that it would be a grave mistake to put organization before consciousness insofar as the very form and direction of political organization ultimately depends upon the subjective dimension brought to it by the masses. Yet he was careful to stress the *dialectical* relationship between organization and consciousness so as to avoid the idealist tendency of abstracting ideological forces from their social totality. Thus, in his famous 1918 debate with Alfonso Leonetti, Gramsci maintained that Leonetti failed to "understand that until now organization has been a mode of being which determines a type of consciousness: that very type of consciousness which Leonetti supposes cannot develop until after we are free, i.e., until after we have conquered state power."[25]

Implicit in Gramsci's early reflections on culture, ideology, and class consciousness was a critique not only of the prevailing PSI doctrine but also of the "Leninism" that Gramsci himself embraced so euphorically after 1918. For, despite their vastly different strategic conceptions, both social democracy and Bolshevism accepted the Kautskian assumption of a social (and political) division of labor between intellectuals and masses. While Gramsci in his early work never really attempted to resolve this problem, he was at least sensitive to its political consequences; he felt that popular apathy and submissiveness might be reproduced *after* the socialist conquest of power, with new hierarchies emerging to suppress the spontaneous energies of the masses. Hence: "What takes place is not the result of what a few want, but of the fact that the great mass of men submit to the will of the few. They let things go... They allow men to rise to power which only mutiny will be allowed to overthrow. In fact, the fate which seems to dominate history is nothing but the illusory appearance of this indifference and of this absenteeism... The destiny of an epoch is manipulated according to narrow visions, immediate purposes, the ambitions and personal passions of small, active groups."[26]

To sweep away this indifference, to raise human beings out of their long-ingrained lethargy, to combat the whole system of ruling values upon which class domination rests—this was a guiding motif of Gramscian Marxism even before 1919, though one which was not theoretically elaborated until the *Prison Notebooks* (through the concepts of hegemony, war of position, and organic intellectuals). It is a preoccupation, moreover, closely associated with Gramsci's view of *democratization* as the necessary basis of revolutionary change. As distinct from Croce and Gentile, for whom the dialectic of cultural renovation was rooted in an enlightened intellectual elite, Gramsci saw proletarian self-activity as the locus of historical initiative. The Gramsci of 1918 was much closer to Georges Sorel and Rosa Luxemburg in his seemingly infinite faith in the capacity of the masses to generate their own sources of critical consciousness, their own culture, even their own intellectual leadership. Gramsci believed that without an emancipator *civilta*, forged through a revitalizing pedagogy tied to class struggle, real democratic institutions and practices could never be sustained; bureaucratic deformation would be unavoidable.[27] In sum: "Take away from the proletariat its class consciousness, and what have you? Puppets dancing on a string!"[28] But Gramsci's conceptualization of this process, however visionary, raises further questions: what precisely was the new cultural paradigm he anticipated and what forms could it be expected to assume? There was a certain frustrating vagueness to Gramsci's early writings on such points, almost as if the actual unfolding of revolutionary politics were so remote as to make superfluous any attempt at concretization. Or more likely there was still a great deal of confusion in his mind about such issues. In any case, Gramsci simply tended to fall back upon the Hegelian postulates he derived from Marx and Croce. For example, he wrote optimistically of the transition from bourgeois discipline ("mechanical and authoritarian") to socialist discipline ("autonomous and spontaneous"),[29] and from individualism to collectivism in which "bourgeois individualism necessarily creates in the proletariat this tendency to collectivism" and "individual-association is counterposed to the individual-capitalist."[30] Gramsci did further articulate his notion of social individuality, based upon the central Hegelian-Crocean problematic of alienation, as follows:

> For the proletariat, organization within its own class already necessarily replaces individualism, absorbing whatever there is in it that is eternal and rational: the sense of one's responsibility, the spirit of enterprise, the

respect for others, the conviction that freedom for all is the sole guarantee of individual freedoms, that the observation of contracts is an indispensable condition of civil existence...(Moreover), the wealth that each can produce above and beyond immediate needs belongs to the collectivity and constitutes the social patrimony: the exchangeability of the means of production is no longer necessary to stimulate capabilities and initiative, because labor has become a moral duty, activity is joy, and not a cruel struggle.[31]

Still, this formulation remained at a very general level, lacking the historical grounding and theoretical depth of even the early Marx, and barely hinting at the constituent elements of a transformative culture that for Gramsci had already become an indispensable element of socialist politics. At the same time, within the limits of his brief and topical essays, Gramsci did arrive at an historical analysis that he thought would specify the conditions of such a transformative process in Italy.

Lessons from Italian History

The most peculiar feature of modern Italian development, according to the young Gramsci, was the extreme political weakness of the bourgeoisie—in contrast, for example to the relative strength of its counterpart in England, the United States, and even France. Because the nineteenth century *Risorgimento* failed to establish a full national unification based upon the liberal principles it triumphed, capitalist expansion remained partial and fragmentary, confined to its regional base in the North (i.e., Piedmont, Liguria, and Lombardy). Taking his cue from Croce's important work on Italian history but moving beyond it, Gramsci argued that liberalism had never furnished any "coherent ideological direction" for the state or any legitimating "principle of order" for civil society as a whole. He mockingly suggested that "The liberals in Italy are a bad joke. They do not distinguish themselves in any way from other social currents. Politically they are a zero."[32]

The partial and unfinished character of the *Risorgimento* explains why the Italian bourgeoisie lacked the economic capacity for universal growth and adaptation, why its outlook was ideologically narrow and provincial, why it was forced to rely upon the most short-sided policies—petty economic nationalism, protectionism, corporatism, "right-wing reformism."Gramsci wrote that "Italy was not born with a bourgeois class already formed, having the same interests, and evenly spread throughout the country. It was in economic and political chaos...with no great political figure who ... could accelerate the birth of an organic economic class."[33] The emergent bourgeoisie, small and regionally confined, never evolved anything approximating a class consciousness and thus became parasitic on the state, devoid of any cohesive ideology that would give it a truly national (not to mention *international*) presence. Thus:

> The late entrance of Italy into capitalist activity has brought about this ideological confusion (which is reflected in the practical confusion of its actions and programs). The immature historical thinking on the part of economic nationalism wins out over the mature thinking of liberalism, which is not only a national but a truly international class doctrine which, therefore, tends to create an economic welding of the various national bourgeoisies and a growth of international capitalist wealth through liberalism.[34]

Gramsci identified three main dimensions to this problem. The first involved the "Southern Question": the historical failure of capitalism to expand into southern Italy, with the resultant division of the peninsula into an industrial North and a semi-feudal, traditional South. If Turin epitomized the urban culture of modern capitalism, the *Mezzogiorno* perpetuated a social life rooted in pre-industrial institutions and patterns of behavior. As a Sardinian, Gramsci was—like Croce and Gentile—in many respects a "Southerner" by virtue of his early upbringing; from the very outset he was sensitized to the colonized, impoverished situation of the peasantry. There is little doubt that Gramsci's early Sardinian nationalism had a profound impact on the development of his general theoretical and political outlook.[35] He responded with great enthusiasm to the pioneering work of Gaetano Salvemini on the *Questione Meridionale*. Though not a Marxist himself, Salvemini was the first theorist to systematically analyze the problem of uneven development in Italy, and his ideas became the inspiration for certain reform schemes designed to break down the *latifundias* (landed estates) and bring the peasantry into Italian political life. Salvemini's own political emphasis was directed toward peasant education and the extension of suffrage into the South.[36] Gramsci seized upon Salvemini's ideas and began to integrate them into his Hegelian-Marxist framework at a time when the PSI leadership was largely ignoring the role of the peasantry.

Whatever the political fragility of the bourgeoisie, Gramsci argued that from an economic standpoint the North had been able to establish a *colonial* domination over the South. He wrote in 1916 that "Unification brought the two parts of the peninsula in very close contact. The foolish centralization confused the needs and brought about the migration of all liquid funds from the South into the North to find greater and more immediate returns in industry, and the migration of men abroad to find the work that was lacking in their own country. Industrial protectionism raised the cost of living for the peasant in Calabria, without agrarian protectionism re-establishing the equilibrium since it was useless to those who hardly produced what was needed for their own consumption." For this reason, according to Gramsci, it was a fallacy to speak of the Southerners as lacking in energy and initiative. In Italy, as elsewhere, "capital always seeks the most secure and fruitful forms of employment." Thus, "where the factory already exists, it continues to develop through savings, but where any form of capitalism is uncertain and problematic, the savings sweated for and scraped with hard toil are distrustful and find investment where there is an immediate tangible return." The process of economic mobilization which accompanied World War I only accelerated this uneven development, for "while the Northern industrial enterprises find in the war a source of colossal profits, all the national productive potentiality engaged in the war industry clusters more and more in Piedmont, Lombardy, Emilia, and Liguria thus further weakening the little life that existed in the Southern regions."[37]

To speak of the unfinished bourgeois revolution was also to speak of the role of the Church and Catholicism, which was able to contain and disperse the economic and ideological advance of capitalism while maintaining its own hegemony. For Gramsci, the dominant presence of Catholicism, the weakness of the bourgeoisie, and uneven development between North and South were all intertwined, an outgrowth of the same historical pattern. The peculiar strength of Catholicism in Italy merely heightened the predicament of the liberals, since in the period before World War I ideological competition pitted a homogeneous tradition against a fragmented and unstable tradition lacking real popular strength. Inevitably, "degenerate and corrupt, without unity and national hierarchy, liberalism ended up subordinated to Catholicism, whose social energies are instead strongly organized and centralized." Gramsci added that "In the ecclesiastical hierarchy, Catholicism has a millenary frame, firm and ready for any kind of political struggle and conquest of social consciousness and power. The Italian state thus became the executor of the clerical program."[38]

But Catholicism did not, indeed could not, lay the foundations of a theocratic state; the secularizing forces unleashed by industrialization compelled the Church hierarchy to adapt in order to preserve its social and political power, with the result that "modernistic and democratic tendencies arise in the heart of Catholicism as an attempt to reconcile in the religious sphere the conflicts that emerge in modern society." In order to coopt the new ideologies "Catholics carry out a social action which is ever deeper and more widespread. They organize the proletarian masses, found cooperatives, trusts, banks and newspapers. They plunge into practical life and they necessarily intertwine their activity with that of the secular state, thus making the fortune of their particular interests dependent on its fortune." In this context, noted Gramsci, "the state absorbs the religious myth and seeks to make it into an instrument of government, well suited to drive back the assaults of the few absolutely secular forces organized by socialism."[39] Thus Catholicism abandoned its ideological universality with the aim of constituting itself as a particular sector of the bourgeoisie.

Gramsci believed that the political implications of Catholic hegemony for an emergent liberal bourgeoisie would be disastrous, insofar as "The constituting of the Italian Catholics into a political party is the greatest event in Italian history since the Risorgimento. The ranks of the bourgeoisie break up. The domination of the state will be bitterly contested and... the Catholic party could come out as a winner in competition with the liberal and secular conservative ranks of the bourgeoisie. The latter are corrupt, having no bonds of ideal discipline and no national unity : a noisy hornet's nest of petty cliques and gangs."[40]

Thirdly, the fact that the *Risorgimento* could never give rise to a unified national presence—i.e., could not transcend its narrow geographical and social base—closed off prospects for a strong liberal state. The failure of bourgeois democracy to achieve full expression in Italy would have profound implications for class conflict and political development well into the twentieth century. Writing at the end of 1918, Gramsci reflected that "The idea of the liberal or parliamentary state, typical of capitalist laisse-faire economy, has not spread in Italy with the same rhythm and intensity as in other nations... The essential goals of the secular state were neglected or approached empirically, and in its sixty years as a nation Italy did not have a political, economic, financial, domestic, or foreign life worthy of a modern state organism."[41] Unable to constitute itself as a dynamic and universalizing *economic* class, the liberal bourgeoisie was doomed politically; it was destined to become another victim of the national disunity and *campanilismo* (provincialism) which had chronically plagued the country. The root of the problem was that "the bourgeois class in Italy has not yet lived economically." In other words: "The spineless bourgeoisie has lacked concrete and straightforward programs because it was not a class of producers, but rather a bunch of politicians."[42]

A party system existed to be sure, but it was in constant disarray, "condemned to consuming itself in factional conflicts and always remaining the cheated and scorned victim of adventurers." Insofar as the parties evolved largely outside the sphere of mass politics, their ideologies, programs, and actions had meaning only within the elite institutional context of "demagogy" and petty squabbling among rival cliques. The celebrated Mazzinian dream of democratic participation lived on simply as myth; the struggle for change could manifest itself only through forms of sporadic revolt, initiated outside of the party system. As Gramsci noted: "There are no organic parties disciplined by a living program responsive to diffuse moral and economic interests. Opposition to the government manifests itself as revolt: it explodes suddenly, it is full of plots and secret understandings, threats and promises, and all of a sudden it quiets down... Because of its lack of scruples, its reluctance to welcome and respect party discipline, its love of empty originality and the tritest innovation, Italian bourgeois democracy is condemned to having no worthy political life."[43] As for the liberal bourgeoisie, it was ultimately forced to rely upon the venerated Italian practice of *trasformismo* in order to retain the precarious institutional power it won during the Risorgimento. *Trasformismo* involved the formation of elite alliances between contending political groups which agreed to subordinate their differences out of a common desire for stability; the dominant group normally extended concessions in exchange for support. When carried out effectively, as it was first under the leadership of Agostino Depretis (a left liberal) from 1876 to 1887 and later under the skillful manipulation of Giovanni Giolitti, this technique functioned to absorb opposition while creating a degree of national unity (or at least the *illusion* of unity). Given its narrow popular base, the bourgeoisie was constantly forced to seek allies—the Church, the southern landholders, the labor movement—to ensure its survival, but it predictably lost its historical identity in the process. This whole *modus operandi* was destined to collapse at the first signs of civil crisis, as indeed it did with the onset of the war.[44]

In Gramsci's analysis, *trasformismo* was a desperate liberal maneuver to achieve elite consensus as a means of staving off open class conflict. This was Giolitti's overriding mission for twenty years, during which time the appearance of democratic freedoms and mass participation coincided with the underlying reality of an "unchecked dictatorship." In "Class Intransigence and Italian History," which appeared in *Il Grido del Popolo* in early 1918 just as *trasformismo* was collapsing, Gramsci wrote: "The Giolittians would like to avoid the clash. They have no wish to battle over institutional programmes, which could make the nation's climate uncomfortably hot...they would like to resolve the problems confronting them within the parliamentary arena. In other words, they are carrying on within the same old tradition of minimizing important problems, excluding the nation from political affairs, avoiding any check by public opinion."[45] By a curious twist of irony, this very weakness of the bourgeoisie and the liberal state in Italy reduced the Socialists to the same level of political impotence:

> Just as the Socialist Party, the organization of the proletarian class, cannot enter into competition for conquest of the government without losing its intrinsic value and turning into a swarm of coachmen-flies, so too it cannot collaborate with any organized bourgeois parliamentary grouping without causing harm...The political decadence which class collaboration brings is due to the spasmodic expansion of the bourgeois party which is not satisfied with merely clinging to the state, but also makes use of the party which is antagonistic to the state. It thus becomes...a historical monster devoid of will or particular aims, concerned only with the possession of the state, to which it is encrusted like rust. State activity is reduced to mere legalities, to the formal settling of disputes, and never touches the substance; the state becomes a gypsy caravan held together by pegs and bolts—a mastodon on four tiny wheels.[46]

Gramsci's assessment turned out to be correct enough; within less than a year after this passage was written, the PSI would be in shambles, completely immobilized during the radical upsurge of the *Biennio Rosso*. Nor was the future of parliamentary democracy very promising.[47] For these and other reasons, Gramsci's early historical analysis contained massive implications for the future of Italian politics—and of course for Gramsci's own theoretical work. Yet if Gramsci's commentary during 1916-1918 reflected a cynical pessimism as far as revolutionary possibilities were concerned, his *long-term* outlook would eventually become just the opposite. In subsequent years he would construct much of his theory around these motifs—the fragility of bourgeois domination, the role of Catholicism, the Southern Question—thereby opening up new (and more optimistic) strategic avenues.[48]

Even by 1918 Gramsci had concluded that the ruling forces in Italy were uniquely vulnerable to ideological-political assault. The potential of capitalism to extend its sphere of growth and control generally depended upon the scope of its mass legitimacy. The failure of the Italian bourgeoisie to satisfy the unifying myths and objectives of the Risorgimento, the inability to constitute itself as a dynamic historical class, and the resulting weakness of bourgeois democratic institutions, would permit the proletarian-socialist movement to step into the void and assume for itself the task of national "renewal." This theme was absolutely central to Gramsci's Marxism, for he returned to it again during the council period, in the "Lyons Theses" (where he begins to outline a "national-popular" strategy for the PCI), and in the *Prison Notebooks*. In his early writings, however, Gramsci drew more limited but nonetheless far-reaching consequences: the fragility and provincialism of capitalism in Italy undercut the reformist solution that seemed fashionable in northern Europe, and called for a more distinctly frontal offensive.

Gramsci and the Bolshevik Revolution

By 1917, the wartime events had produced class polarization and political crisis throughout Europe, leading to a widespread sense of revolutionary optimism on the left. The gathering momentum of popular upsurges that Gramsci observed from his vantage point in Turin was hastened by the Bolshevik Revolution, which had explosive consequences in Italy as elsewhere on the continent. Gramsci and his Turinese comrades welcomed the Russian upheaval as nothing short of a major turning-point in history, the first blow in the shattering of European bourgeois civilization. This unrestrained exuberance permeated virtually all of Gramsci's essays throughout 1917-1918. Even before the actual conquest of power, at a time when the Bolsheviks were still mobilizing against Kerensky, Gramsci could write that "once again, the light comes from the east. It irradiates the old Western world which is left astonished and can only counterpose to it the commonplace and silly jokes of its newsmen."[49] In a later tribute to the "Russian Maximalist," he excitedly proclaimed: "New energies are provoked, new ideal forces are propagated. Thus men, all men, are finally the masters of their own destiny ... And the revolutionary fire spreads: it burns in new hearts and minds. It makes them into torches burning with new light, with flames that devour laziness and weariness."[50]

The October Revolution had a dual meaning for Gramsci: as a "theoretical event" it had the effect of overturning the rigid canons of scientific materialism which had blocked Marxism up to that point, while in *political* terms it was a truly *democratic* upheaval because it gave the oppressed masses for the first time the freedom to express their self-activity, to make history. The key for Gramsci was Lenin's steadfast insistence on the "actuality of revolution"— the notion that "He has been able to convert his thought into a force operating in history" and that "He and his Bolshevik comrades are persuaded that socialism can be realized at any moment."[51] In this monumental historical event Gramsci refocused the main concerns of his early work: Crocean-Hegelian philosophy, the role of mass consciousness, democratization.

In "Revolution Against *Capital*," one of the most familiar of Gramsci's early articles written at the height of the Bolshevik events, the Russian Revolution is characterized as an epochal puncturing of all the stale, lifeless, dogmatic tenets of what had come to be known as "historical materialism"—a reified Marxism embodied in the positivized interpretations of *Capital* that in Russia (as elsewhere) had become a text of the progressive bourgeoisie, which found in this volume a celebration of science, technology, capitalist innovation, and industrial growth. Whereas the "legal" Marxists and Mensheviks had accepted a strict definition of the stages of historical development (feudalism-capitalism-socialism), outlined in classical Marxism, Lenin and the Bolsheviks saw in the Russian case an "exceptionalism" that invalidated this schema. Hence the Mensheviks ended up as supporters of a Western-style bourgeois evolutionism, while the Leninists adopted an impatient voluntarism which sought to carry out socialist insurrection in a largely pre-industrial setting. Agreeing with Lenin, Gramsci described the Bolshevik Revolution as:

> ...the revolution against Karl Marx's *Capital*. In Russia Marx's *Capital* was the book of the bourgeoisie more than of the proletariat. It was the critical demonstration of the fatal necessity that in Russia a bourgeoisie had to be formed, that an era of capitalism had to begin, and that a western-type civilization had to be installed before the

proletariat might be even able to think about insurrection, class vindications, and revolution. Events have
overcome ideologies. Events have exploded the critical
schemes within which the history of Russia would have
had to develop according to the canons of historical
materialism. The Bolsheviks repudiate Karl Marx, they
affirm with the testimony of explicit action, with achieved conquests...[52]

Only by discarding the entire body of elaborate, self-confident
predictions based upon the "laws of *Capital*," overturning with it
the mystical powers of economic determinism, could the Bolsheviks have succeeded in conditions never analyzed by Marx or
Engels. From Gramsci's viewpoint, the revolutionary moment
dramatizes "living" over "abstract" theory, self-conscious action
over a fatalistic waiting for material conditions to "ripen." "Why,"
asked Gramsci, "should the Russian people wait until the history of
England repeats itself in Russia? Why must it wait for a bourgeoisie
to come into being in Russia and for class conflict to be generated in
order that a class consciousness be born and the catastrophe of the
capitalist world finally take place?"[53] Here of course Gramsci's
thinking paralleled Lenin's, with its emphasis on imperialism, war,
and uneven development as the basis of a revolutionary breakthrough occurring first in colonized, peripheral countries rather
than on the terrain of advanced capitalism (England, France, Germany) as Marx had projected. But while war played a crucial role in
awakening political passions in Russia, there was nothing "determined" about the revolutionary process itself, nothing that could
be neatly fitted into conventional historical models. Gramsci went
so far as to argue that "the Bolsheviks are not Marxist, that is all:
they have not compiled an external doctrine of dogmatic, indisputable statements on the basis of the Master's works. They live
the Marxist thought that never dies, which is the continuation of
Italian and German idealistic thought, which in Marx was con-
taminated with positivist and naturalistic encrustations. And this
thought always sees man—not brute economic facts—as the
supreme factor in history."[54]

Gramsci seized upon the Russian events to justify and further
specify his own concept of historical indeterminacy which he
inherited from Croce and Labriola. The pressing theoretical task
was not to arrive at a "scientific" analysis of capitalist development
that might permit prediction of the future; rather it was to move
toward an understanding of the particular historical circumstances under which a collective revolutionary will might be

formed. While necessary, analysis alone was theoretically and politically sterile, and efforts to positivize the study of history were debilitating. In Gramsci's words, "History is not a mathematical calculation: it does not have metric decimal system, a progressive numbering of equal quantities allowing for the four operations, equation and the extraction of roots."[55] After suggesting that the Bolshevik Revolution furnished "evidence that it is not economic structure which directly determines political action," he added that "every historical phenomenon is 'individual', development is governed by the rhythm of freedom; research must not focus on general necessity, but on particular necessity. The process of causation must be studied within Russian events and not from an abstract and general viewpoint." In one of his better-known passages, Gramsci continued: "The philistine does not see salvation outside pre-established schemes, he does not conceive of history other than as a natural organism that goes through fixed stages of predictable development. Nothing but an oak tree can come out of an acorn, to slowly grow and bear fruit after a certain number of years. But history is not a field of oaks, and men are not acorns."[56]

The great success of the Russian Revolution, then, derived from the capacity of political leaders to awaken popular consciousness and build effective organization, from their insistence that "socialism can be realized at any moment"[57]—not from the possession of "scientific" theory. Gramsci credited Lenin with being the first to understand that the combination of a weak bourgeoisie and strong proletarian class consciousness (despite a relatively small working class) made Russia a special case and permitted the unique growth of revolutionary forces. Lenin sensed that, even in a primarily agrarian setting, the Russian proletariat could become "the gigantic protagonist of history," though after 1905 he realized that a viable socialist movement would require peasant mobilization as well. As Gramsci summed it up, "through the Bolsheviks' propaganda the masses of workers and peasants began to realize what was happening and acquired an ever-growing political capacity and sensitivity." Borrowing some insights from Italian history, Gramsci fully endorsed Lenin's conclusion that "the bourgeoisie had neither the desire nor the ability to provide a democratic solution" in Russia and that, in the absence of Bolshevik intervention, the crisis most probably would have led to military dictatorship.[58] The second dimension of Gramsci's euphoric response to the October Revolution was more immediately political: the events set in motion new forms of mass participation and democratization—the unfolding of revolutionary self-activity on an unprecedented scale. After 1917, with the final overthrow of the provisional government, the old hierarchical structures gave way to new social wills, freedoms, and opportunities. Gramsci wrote that the "masses are continuously in upheaval and from this people-chaos they develop an ever-growing order in thought, a greater consciousness of their own power, of their own destinies."[59] If this passage seems rather far-fetched, it was nonetheless vintage Gramsci for the period. Actually, in contrast to what is generally assumed, Gramsci was a close observer of the Bolshevik Revolution and was comparatively well-informed about the post-revolutionary situation; the information coming out of Russia, however, was often one-sided and misleading, to the extent that Gramsci was thoroughly convinced in 1918 that the Bolsheviks were engineering a massive process of social transformation rooted in the soviets and factory committees, and that this represented a triumph of human freedom and democracy.

Gramsci's early commentary on the Russian events included very few references to the role of the vanguard party, although Lenin's leadership function is mentioned frequently; he viewed the revolution less as a "power phenomenon" than as "an event of mores," a "proletarian act" that "must necessarily result in socialist rule."[60] As distinct from a bourgeois revolution, which imposes the power and interests of a particular class on the whole of society, the proletarian revolution advances the *collective* interests of the general population. Thus in Russia the Bolshevik success "has destroyed authoritarianism and has replaced it with universal suffrage, extended to women as well. It has replaced authoritarianism with freedom, the Constitution with the free voice of universal consciousness." All of this was made possible because the revolution "has not just replaced power with power, but tradition with tradition; it has created a new moral atmosphere; it has brought about freedom of the spirit as well as bodily freedom."[61]

Gramsci expressed few doubts or reservations over the character of the revolution: it was a *popular* transformation based primarily in the local democratic organs (soviets, factory committees), with the party furnishing the essential coordination and strategic direction. It was a truly democratic revolution of workers and peasants. Immediately after the Bolshevik conquest of power, Gramsci wrote: "The Russian proletariat has offered us the first model of direct representation of producers: the soviets."[62] Six months later he was even more confident that "The proletariat has taken over the direction of political and economic life and realizes its order...The living nucleus of this hierarchy are the soviets and the popular parties. The soviets are the primordial organizations of integration and development, and the Bolsheviks became the party of government since they hold that state power must depend upon and be controlled by the soviets."[63]

In view of Gramsci's later positive attitude toward Jacobinism—and his association of it with *both* Lenin and Machiavelli—in the *Prison Notebooks*, it is intriguing to find such a hostile judgement of it in his early writings. To those contemporary observers who described the Bolshevik insurgency as a Jacobin phenomenon—a minority seizure of state power from above— Gramsci replied that the very proletarian or *mass* content of the political episode ruled out the need for a violent imposition of power, as in the case of the French Revolution. Thus: "The Russian revolution has ignored Jacobinism. The revolution has had to demolish autocracy, it has not had to conquer the majority with violence. Jacobinism is a purely bourgeois phenomenon: it characterizes the bourgeois revolution in France." This is why "socialist revolutionaries cannot be Jacobins."[64] Against the contention that the working class in Russia was still a small minority in 1917, and that the revolution despite its popular character would be forced by logic into a Jacobin stance, Gramsci countered:

> Jacobinism? Jacobinism is a wholly bourgeois phenomenon of minorities—even of potential ones. A minority which is certain of becoming an absolute majority...cannot be Jacobin and cannot have as its program perpetual dictatorship. It temporarily exercises dictatorial powers to allow the effective majority to get organized, to become conscious of its intrinsic necessities, and to establish its rule outside of any apriorism, according to the spontaneous laws of this necessity.[65]

In historical retrospect, it is easy to find in Gramsci's understanding of the Russian Revolution a vastly distorted image of an epochal process that was in fact Jacobin from the outset. The irony is that Gramsci's own theoretical sensibilities—recovery of the subjective dimension, popular self-activity, democratization— would later be harshly violated by the Bolshevik regime he so enthusiastically supported. No doubt his unrestrained sense of optimism about the Russian events, and his willingness to discount negative reports while glorifying what he genuinely perceived to be emancipatory changes, can be seen as a response to the severe criticisms of Lenin and the Bolsheviks which Gramsci read daily in the Italian bourgeois press. Still, one cannot fail to detect a certain innocence and naivete in Gramsci about Russia—an innocence and naivete that did not vanish even as the turn toward bureaucratic centralism became clearly visible. As late as 1921, he seemed oblivious to the bureaucratic tendencies at work within both the party-state and the economy, and in general he tended to ignore the many dilemmas and obstacles encountered by the Bolsheviks during this period.[66]

Vision and Continuity

The composite picture that emerges of the young Gramsci during 1915-1918—of a Gramsci writing on the eve of the dramatic *Biennio Rosso*—is one perhaps best depicted by Gwyn Williams as a theorist whose vision was "distinctly mythic, grandiose, and semi-utopian."[67] The identification of "vision" with Gramsci is most appropriate, for in these years and up until the council debacle of autumn 1920, he often conveyed a mood of almost messianic optimism—much like the Marx and Engels of the *Communist Manifesto*. It was a "vision" generated out of a hybrid, poorly-integrated theoretical synthesis of Marx, Croce, Labriola, Rolland, and Lenin, and which, inevitably, produced the kind of ambiguities and inconsistencies found in Gramsci's initial writings (reflected, for example, in his distorted perception of the Russian Revolution). This dimension of the early Gramsci explains the absence of any comprehensive strategic outlook until the events of the *Biennio Rosso* imposed it on him. One searches in vain for any treatment of the state, political power, of role of the party (not to mention unions and councils) in this period. Yet it would be a serious mistake to dismiss the relevance of this formative work for Gramsci's later theoretical evolution, much less to posit a fundamental break between the young "idealist" Gramsci and the "mature" Marxist (or Leninist) thinker of the *Prison Notebooks*, given the broad thematic overlap and continuity which—as should become evident in the following chapters—was a definitive feature of Gramsci's Marxism.

Footnotes

1. For several historical reasons, the Hegelian tradition struck especially deep roots in Italian national culture, even predating the influence of Croce in the work of Bertrando Spaventa and others. See Paul Piccone, "From Spaventa to Gramsci," *Telos*, no. 31, spring 1977. Piccone observes that, in contrast to Germany, England, and the U.S., in Italy national unification developed in opposition to Catholic cultural and political hegemony so that, by the mid-nineteenth century, Hegelianism became a kind of "lay religion." (p.41)

2. Quoted from one of Gramsci's prison letters to his sister-in-law, Tatiana, in Fiori, *Antonio Gramsci: Life of a Revolutionary*, p. 104.

3. Gramsci's most important essays of the 1915-1918 period were published in *Il Grido del Popolo* (which he edited for a brief period beginning in August 1917), *Avanti!* (Turin edition), and *L'Ordine Nuovo*. These have been assembled in various Gramsci anthologies published in Italy: the aforementioned *Scritti Politici* and *Scritti giovanili*, as well as in G. Ferrata and N. Gallo, eds., *2000 pagine di Gramsci* (Turin: Einaudi, 1972). English translations of some of this material have been collected in the Hoare and Cavalcanti-Piccone volumes already cited.

4. "The Study of Philosophy," in *Selections from the Prison Notebooks*, p. 336.

5. Quoted in Fiori, *Antonio Gramsci*, p. 106.

6. On this dimension of Croce's thought, see *Etica e politica* (Bari: Laterza, 1945) and *What is Living and What is Dead in the Philosophy of Hegel* (London: MacMillan, 1915). For useful secondary accounts see Emilio Agazzi, *Il Giovane Croce e il Marxismo* (Turin: Einaudi, 1962); H. Wildon Carr, *The Philosophy of Benedetto Croce* (London: MacMillan, 1927); and Giacinto Lentini, *Croce e Gramsci* (Rome: Mori, 1967).

7. See Alastair Davidson, *Antonio Gramsci*, p. 105.

8. Labriola's main ideas are presented in V. Gerrantana and A. Guerre, eds., *Saggi sul materialismo storico* (Rome: Editori Riuniti, 1964). In English, see *Essays on the Materialist Conception of History* (Chicago: Charles Kerr, 1908) and *Socialism and Philosophy* (St. Louis: Telos Press. 1980). Paul Piccone, in his introduction to the

latter volume, writes that Labriola had anticipated the trajectory of Western Marxism in the work of Lukacs, Korsch, and Gramsci already in the 1890s (pp. 48-49). While this may be true, it should be mentioned that Labriola was simultaneously attracted to some of the more scientific components of orthodox Marxism. Labriola died in 1904, just as the classic Marxist debates were getting under way.

9. "Il Nostro Marx," May 4, 1918, in *Scritti politici*, pp. 120-21. See also "Our Marx," in Cavalcanti and Piccone, *History, Philosophy, and Culture in the Young Gramsci*, p. 9.

10. "Mysteries of Poetry and Culture." October 19, 1918, in *History, Philosophy, and Culture*, p. 18.

11. "La critica critica," January 12, 1918, in *Scritti politici*, pp. 95-96. See also *History, Philosophy, and Culture*, pp. 38-39. This essay was written in response to an article by Claudio Treves in the PSI journal *Critica Sociale*, in which Treves observes the "horrifying lack of culture in the new generation of Italian socialists."

12. "The Russian Utopia," July 25, 1918, in *History, Philosophy, and Culture* pp. 152-153.

13. *Ibid.*, p. 153.

14. "Tre principi, tre ordini," February 11, 1917, in *Scritti politici*, pp. 42-43.

15. Gramsci was attracted to Gentile's ideas for only a brief period, during 1917-1918, but they clearly had an impact on his overall philosophical development. At this time, Gramsci referred to Gentile's conception of the historical "act" as a major contribution to Italian idealist thought. Later, in the *Prison Notebooks*, Gramsci wrote that Gentile represented one of the major idealist currents which opened the way to a new Marxian synthesis. See "Problems of Marxism", *SPN*, p. 389. Gentile flirted with the young Marx for a while in the 1890s, but then followed his extreme idealist inclinations toward a conservative politics, ending up in the orbit of fascism. Along with Labriola and non-Marxist theorists like Rodolfo Mondolfo, Gentile owed his greatest intellectual debt to Croce. The themes they articulated in common—the critique of positivism and industrialism, commitment to a cultural and moral renewal of Italian society, the emphasis on collective subjectivity— were all ones that Gramsci himself critically appropriated. But Gentile's idealism departed from this Crocean matrix in its attachment of ideological and "spiritual" goals to the authoritarian state. As Mussolini's first Minister of Education in 1923, Gentile was responsible for conceptualizing and enacting the fascist educational reform. On Gentile's philosophy, see his *La Riforma della dialettica hegeliana* (Florence, 1954). For secondary treat-

ments, see A. Signorini, *Il Giovane Gentile e Marx* (Milan: Feltrinelli 1966) and Giacomo Marramao, *Marxismo e revisionismo in Italia* (Bari: Laterza, 1971). For the influence of Gentile on Gramsci, see Davidson, *Antonio Gramsci*, pp. 97-98 and 107, and Buci-Glucksmann, *Gramsci and the State*, pp. 295-305.

16. "Astrattismo e intransigenza," May 11, 1918, in *Scritti politici*, pp. 124-27. See also "Tre principi, tre ordini," *op. cit.* p. 43.

17. For example, "Il nostro Marx," *op. cit.*, pp. 120-23, and "The Russian Utopia," in *History, Philosophy, and Culture*, pp. 149-155.

18. As an activist and journalist in the PSI, Gramsci had of course read a good deal of Marx and Engels, though he had apparently not read *Capital* before 1919. To what extent Gramsci actually considered himself a "Marxist" between 1915 and 1918 is uncertain, and in any case his work contained relatively few references to Marx or Marxists. The most likely interpretation is that Gramsci approached Marx much as he approached Croce: he adhered to the broad contours and "spirit" of the theory while remaining critical of various specifics. For an asessment of Gramsci's relationship to both influences, see Guido Tagliabue, "Gramsci tra Croce e Marx," *Il Ponte*, May 1948, pp. 429-438.

19. Of interest in view of footnote 18 is that each of these French writers stood clearly outside of the Marxist tradition. (The same could be said of another French influence on Gramsci, the syndicalist Georges Sorel, although Sorel's relationship to Marxism was quite different from that of Barbusse, Rolland, or Peguy). What each shared was an interest in working toward democratic educational and cultural reforms. Barbusse's periodical *Clarte* constituted a sort of model for Gramsci's *L'Ordine Nuovo*. Peguy's impact on Gramsci's thinking at this time was especially strong: it was he who insisted most vocally that it was not the great intellectuals but the common people who make history. For Gramsci, Peguy was "the man who wore himself out in a daily endeavor to educate himself, and sacrificed his own artistic personality, to give the youth of France a new consciousness, to send it on its way by the living example of his own toil to attain a world-view which was both more profound and would achieve more." Ferrata e Gallo, eds., *2000 pagine di Gramsci*, vol. I., p. 205, cited in Davidson, *Antonio Gramsci*, p. 100.

20. "Socialism and Culture," January 29, 1916, in *History, Philosophy, and Culture*, pp. 20-21.

21. *Ibid.*, p. 21.

22. *Ibid.*, p. 22.

23. *Ibid.*, pp. 21-22.

24. "Freedom First," August 31, 1918, in *History, Philosophy, and Culture*, p. 51. Gramsci added that the obstacles in Italy were particularly formidable, since unlike most European countries it "never underwent the liberal experience. Italy has known few liberties and illiteracy today is even more widespread than statistics indicate." (*Ibid*).

25. *Ibid.*, p. 50.

26. "Indifferents," from *La citta Futura*, February 11, 1917, in *History, Philosophy, and Culture*, pp. 64-65.

27. There is a certain parallelism here between Gramsci's concerns and those of Robert Michels, whose critique of the German Social Democratic Party was by this time well known. Gramsci himself never developed a theory of bureaucracy, but he was aware of Michels' work, seemed to be influenced by it, and later devoted space in the *Prison Notebooks* to an assessment of *Political Parties*. Gramsci was appreciative of Michels' contributions to an analysis of bureaucracy, but rejected the notion of an "iron law of oligarchy" as simply another expression of the "positivist sociology of elites." After his imprisonment, Gramsci repeatedly asked for copies of Michels' books—including *Il proletariato e la borghesia nel movimento socialista italiano* (Turin: Bocca, 1908)—which he received. See Davidson, *Antonio Gramsci*, pp. 244, 246.

28. "Class Intransigence and Italian History," May 18, 1918, in Hoare, ed., *Antonio Gramsci: Selections from Political Writings, 1910-1920*, p.47

29. "Discipline," February 11, 1917, in *History, Philosophy, and Culture*, p. 49.

30. "Individualism and Collectivism," March 9, 1918, *op. cit.*, pp. 61-62.

31. *Ibid.*, p. 61.

32. "The Italian Liberals," September 12, 1918, in *History, Philosophy, and Culture*, p. 108.

33. "Clarifying Ideas about Bourgeois Reformism," December 1918, *op. cit.*, pp. 104-105.

34. "Clarifying Ideas about Bourgeois Reformism," December 11, 1917, *op. cit.*, p. 95.

35. On this point, see Davidson, *Antonio Gramsci*, ch. 2. Quite possibly Davidson attaches too much significance to Gramsci's early Sardinian identity, given the importance of the formative Turin years, yet Davidson does provide a needed corrective to a common inclination on the part of Gramsci scholars to ignore or downplay the Sardinian period.

36. Salvemini began to call attention to the "Southern Ques-

tion" as the decisive element of Italian politics in the 1890s, mainly in the journal *La Voce*, which Gramsci read quite regularly. Salvemini's writings on this topic are collected in the volume *Scritti sulle questione meridionale 1896-1955* (Turin: Einaudi, 1955). Gramsci was familiar with Salvemini's writings even before he left Sardinia, and in 1911 as a student at the University of Turin he listed Salvemini as one of his favorite authors. See Davidson, *Antonio Gramsci*, pp. 42, 55. Salvemini too was a member of the PSI, but even before Gramsci's entry into the party he abandoned his efforts to convince the leadership that it should take up issues related to the *Mezzogiorno*.

37. "The South and the War," April 1, 1916, in *History, Philosophy, and Culture*, pp. 102-03. In contrasting the urban capitalist setting of Turin with the underdeveloped South, Gramsci was keenly aware of what this meant for the socialist movement in Italy: "Turin is a modern city. Capitalist activity pulsates in it with the crashing noise of cyclopic factories that amass in a few thousand square feet thousands and thousands of proletarians. Turin has more than a half million inhabitants. Humanity there divides into two classes with such a sharpness as nowhere else in Italy. We do not have democrats as petty reformists. We have a bold, aggressive capitalist bourgeoisie, we have powerful organizations, and we have a socialist movement which is complex, varied, rich in impulses, and intellectual needs." "Culture and Class Struggle," May 25, 1918, *op. cit.*, p. 110.

38. "The Italian Catholics," December 22, 1918, in *History, Philosophy and Culture*, pp. 112-113.

39. *Ibid.*, p. 113.

40. *Ibid.*, p. 115. The Catholic political formation that Gramsci had in mind here was the *Popolari* (Popular Party), which was organized in the immediate postwar years and achieved success of the sort Gramsci anticipated. By 1921, the *Popolari* had forged the country's second largest party, winning 1,750,000 votes and 100 seats in the chamber of deputies; they also presided over mutual aid societies, trade unions, and agricultural cooperatives totaling 1,200,000 members. See Serge Hughes, *The Fall and Rise of Modern Italy* (New York: Macmillan, 1967), pp. 116-17. Catholicism before World War I was a loosely-organized political force with probably even less cohesion than Liberalism, and with a confused and ambivalent attitude toward the post-Risorgimento state.

41. "The Italian Catholics," *op. cit.*, pp. 111-12.

42, "Clarifying Ideas about Bourgeois Reformism," December 11, 1917, *op. cit.* p. 94.

43. "Italian Democracy," September 7, 1918, *op. cit.*, pp. 115-16. In this same article Gramsci complained that "newspapers replace parties. This is the reason for the lack of continuity in Italian political life, the confusion, the petulant arrogance of certain demonstrations and the servility which necessarily concludes them." *Ibid.*, p. 116.

44. On the rise and collapse of *trasformismo* during the Giolitti reign, see William A. Salomone, *Italy in the Giolittian Era* (Philadelphia: University of Pennsylvania Press, 1960) and Rita Cambria, *I Liberali Italiani e il Socialismo* (Milan: Marzorati, 1979).

45. "Class Intransigence and Italian History," May 18, 1918, in *Political Writings-I*, pp. 42-43.

46, *Ibid.*, p. 45. This assessment of the PSI represents a dramatic reversal from what Gramsci had been writing a few years earlier. Thus, in late 1914 he depicted the PSI as a "maturing, potential state antagonistic to the bourgeois state", as "the only party that lives and knows its various postions." "Active and Operative Neutrality," October 31, 1914, in *History, Philosophy, and Culture*, p. 117.

47. For an extensive treatment of the relationship between Liberals and Socialists, see Cambria, *op. cit.*

48. On Gramsci's general analysis of Italian history, see Giuseppe Galasso, "Gramsci e il problema della storia italiana", in *Gramsci e la cultura contemporanea* (Rome: Editori Riuniti, 1969), vol. II, pp. 305-354.

49. "Notes on the Russian Revolution," April 29, 1917, in *History, Philosophy, and Culture*, p. 128.

50. "The Russian Maximalist," July 28, 1917, *op. cit.*, p. 133.

51. *Ibid.*

52. "The Revolution Against *Capital*", November 24, 1917, in *History, Philosophy, and Culture*, p. 123.

53. *Ibid.*, p. 125.

54. *Ibid.*, p. 123.

55. "The Russian Utopia," July 25, 1918, *op. cit.*, p. 150.

56. *Ibid.*, pp. 151-53.

57. "The Russian Maximalist," *op. cit.*, p. 133.

58. "Lenin's Work," September 14, 1918, in *History, Philosophy, and Culture*, pp. 135-37. For an excellent account of Gramsci's evaluation of Lenin at this time, see Alastair Davidson, "Gramsci and Lenin, 1917-1922," *Socialist Register* (London: Merlin Press, 1974), pp. 125-150.

59. "The Revolution Against *Capital,"op. cit.*, p. 124.

60. "Notes on the Russian Revolution," *op. cit.*, p. 126. Gramsci

was responding here to claims on the part of bourgeois journalists that the Bolshevik Revolution was simply a modern version of the French Revolution with its Jacobinism, reign of terror, etc.

61. *Ibid.*, pp. 127-28.

62. "The Constitutional Assembly and the Soviets," January 26, 1918, in *History, Philosophy, and Culture*, p. 146.

63. "The Russian Utopia," *op. cit.*. p. 154. Gramsci added: "The Soviets and the Bolshevik party are not closed organisms: they are continually integrated. Here is the domination of freedom, the guarantee of freedom." (*Ibid.*)

64. "Notes on the Russian Revolution," *op. cit.*, p. 127.

65. "The Constitutional Assembly and the Soviets," *op. cit.*, p. 146. In his early essays Gramsci sometimes referred to Jacobinism as a form of "messianism"—an abstract but inevitably authoritarian doctrine. The shift in Gramsci's assessment that occurred in the *Prison Notebooks* can be explained only in part, if at all, by his fundamental rethinking of the Russian situation; of much greater significance, as we shall see, was the more vanguardist (Leninist?) conception of the party he adopted beginning in 1921.

66. Among leading European Marxists Gramsci was hardly alone in his spirited defense of the Bolshevik party-state, as the examples of Korsch, Lukacs, and Bordiga show. Of course with Gramsci's involvement in the PCI and the Comintern, the pressures to follow the Bolshevik line were intense. Nonetheless, it might be recalled that there was already a vigorous "left communist" opposition within the Russian party by 1919; moreover, fairly extensive critiques of Lenin's theory and strategy of revolution were developed by Luxemburg, Kautsky, and the Council Communists, among others, even *before* 1920. On the left communists, see Robert B. Daniels, *The Conscience of the Revolution* (New York: Simon and Schuster, 1960), chs. 3,5, and 6; on Luxemburg, see "Organizational Questions on Russian Social Democracy", in Dick Howard, ed., *Rosa Luxemburg: Selected Political Writings* (New York: Monthly Review Press, 1971), pp. 283-306; on Kautsky, see *The Dictatorship of the Proletariat* (Ann Arbor: University of Michigan Press, 1964); on the Council theorists, see Anton Pannekoek, "World Revolution and Communist Tactics," in Serge Bricianer, ed., *Pannekoek and Workers' Councils* (St. Louis: Telos Press, 1978), pp. 175-210.

67. Gwyn Williams, *Proletarian Order* (London: Pluto Press, 1975), p. 91.

3 The Factory Councils: Insurrection and Defeat

Gramsci's whole theoretical and political outlook underwent dramatic changes in response to the explosive upheavals that shook Italy in 1918-1920. In many ways, however, these changes extended and concretized the Hegelian-Crocean predisposition of his early period. Gramsci was the main intellectual architect of an Italian council communism that coincided with the emergence of the *Ordine Nuovo* movement in Turin, and which paralleled similar revolutionary formations in Russia, Hungary, and Germany. Now, for the first time, Gramsci's thought assumed more directly political and *strategic* dimensions. It was a period in which he abandoned the PSI as a vehicle for socialist transformation; incorporated the "critical" themes of consciousness, alienation, and collective self-activity into the *structural* context of the council movement; formulated a theory of workers' control and proletarian democracy; and began to confront more squarely issues posed within the Marxist tradition. It was, finally, a time when he was forced by tragic necessity to draw lessons from the defeat of the council insurrections, the dispersion of a once-potent Italian left, and the subsequent rise of fascism.

War, Crisis, and Class Polarization

The *Biennio Rosso* of post-World War II Italy—a "Red Two Years" of popular upsurge that began with radical dreams and collapsed in exhausted despair—stands as a great European political landmark. An expression of the massive wave of working-class struggles that swept across the continent in the aftermath of

69

the war and the Bolshevik Revolution, a movement constituting the first political threat to capitalism in Italy, it contained all the elements of a rapidly-unfolding, suspenseful, at times amusing, and ultimately tragic, historical drama.

There was the unremitting cycle of political and economic warfare, from lockouts and mass strikes to demonstrations, public assemblies, and street clashes which culminated in the Turin General Strike of April 1920 and the "Occupation of the Factories" in September of the same year. There was the spectre of a fragile capitalist order on the verge of collapse, retreating in the face of a proletarian assault that seemed to be inventing new forms of struggle by the day, as if a new civilization were about to be actualized at any moment. There were the angry and sometimes violent encounters within the radical opposition itself over every conceivable strategic question: spontaneism vs. vanguardism, factory councils vs. party and unions, popular self-management vs. structural reforms, abstentionism vs. electoralism—as well as the urgent debates concerning the timeliness of armed insurrection, and relations with the Comintern and the Bolsheviks. There was the final, climactic moment of political crisis when the alternative "socialism or barbarism" inescapably presented itself but could not be turned to the advantage of the left—a moment characterized by Amadeo Bordiga as "the revolution that failed." And there were, of course, the actors in the drama: the skillfully manipulative liberal Premier, Giolitti; the legendary Socialist leader G. M. Serrati; the industrialist Giacomo Olivetti; the anarchist Errico Malatesta; the Turin communists Angelo Tasca and Palmiro Togliatti; the ultra-Leninist Bordiga; the omnipresent Comintern leadership; the behind-the-scenes theoretical figure of Georges Sorel; and finally, Gramsci, who plunged head-first into the battle only to emerge beaten, isolated, and depressed at a time when political reaction made its first ominous stirrings—the same Gramsci who later complained that "history teaches, but it has no pupils."

The *Biennio Rosso* had its roots in the prewar years, when the delicate ideological consensus that Giolitti was able to engineer through *trasformismo*—and with it the containment of the labor movement—began to disintegrate. Rapid economic growth after 1900, with the emergence of the great "industrial triangle" of Milan, Turin, and Genoa, brought Northern Italy firmly into the orbit of European industrial society. Within scarcely more that a decade, the region became a leading producer of autos, rubber, cement, textiles, chemicals and appliances. The workers who came to the new factories were paid low wages even in comparison with what their counterparts elsewhere received, working conditions were often tortuous, management was harshly paternalistic, and the trade unions were themselves authoritarian. Industrial workers joined the PSI and the trade-union movement in large numbers, though many were attracted to syndicalism and anarchism (especially in Piedmont).

Like other parties affiliated with the Second International, the PSI proclaimed a revolutionary theory and strategy that masked an ardently reformist practice. Since its politics were shaped less by the "maximalist" leadership of Serrati than by the main inspiration of parliamentary socialism in Italy, Filippo Turati, the PSI centered its struggle around liberal reforms in the political sphere (e.g., universal suffrage, which was finally granted in 1911) and limited reforms in the economic sphere. This strategy resulted in large membership and electoral gains that by 1919 gave the party 156 seats in the Chamber of Deputies. The PSI's trade-union partner, the General Confederation of Labor (CGL), functioned mainly as a bargaining instrument with capitalist management; its premise (theoretically articulated by Claudio Treves) was to strengthen working-class economic power with the goal of precipitating a general crisis that would hasten the "natural death" of capitalism. While nominally revolutionary in commitment, the concrete organizational identity of both the PSI and CGL was forged, first, out of a frenzied hostility to all forms of "spontaneism" (anarchism, syndicalism) and, secondly, out of its institutionalized position as mediator between government, capital, and labor that was part of Giolitti's *trasformismo* scheme.

Although conflict between the proletarian masses and an increasingly deradicalized and cautious PSI-CGL directorate had spilled into the open even before 1914, such a reformist scenario might have worked had it not been for the outbreak of the war and the Russian Revolution. The military debacle left Italy in a state of numbness: out of more than six million men conscripted for the war effort, 600,000 were killed and roughly 700,000 suffered permanent disability. Defeat and disruption led to a severe economic decline, characterized by food shortages, unemployment, inflation and a sharply falling lira—all linked to a drastic fall in industrial production and exacerbated by widespread, painful social dislocation. Production fell by 15 percent in mining, 40 percent in engineering, and 20 percent in chemicals. Moreover, as Paolo Spriano writes, "the whole productive apparatus was blocked; masses of immobile capital were frozen in investments which the ending of the war made unprofitable. Naturally, strikes too ran parallel to the shrinkage in production: in 1920, there were 1,881, with 1,267,953 strikers and 16,398,227 lost working days, the highest figure ever."[1]

Popular militancy spread rapidly; already by 1917-1918 a series of strikes, street demonstrations, and land occupations had begun to erode the PSI-CGL reformist hegemony while the breakdown of labor discipline meant that, in the words of Gwyn Williams, "A mass of workers well to the left of the PSI had suddenly emerged on the streets."[2] Syndicalism appealed to many workers, reflected in a membership growth of the Italian Syndicalist Union (USI) from 100,000 to 300,000 during the war and to 900,000 by 1920. Dramatic news of the October Revolution fed this unrest and gave new encouragement to popular struggles in Turin and elsewhere, where remarkable industrial development after the turn of the century (spurred by auto manufacturing) gave rise to a skilled, concentrated, and relatively homogenous working class that prompted comparisons with Petrograd on the eve of the Bolshevik Revolution. Out of Turin's general population of little more than half a million by 1917, 150,000 were factory workers—the vast majority of them bound together by an intimate communications network and by a common militancy. It was in Turin too that the entrenched reformists within the PSI and CGL came under the most virulent and sustained challenge by a proletarian movement that was determined to create its own popular forms, notably the *consigli di fabbrica*, or factory councils, which became the core of Turin council communism during the *Biennio Rosso*. Not surprisingly, Turin appeared as the seedbed of new theoretical and strategic perspectives that would subject the Marxism of PSI to devastating attacks from which it would never recover.

Ordine Nuovo Confronts the Socialist Party

The popular revolt that swept through Italy during 1918-1920 irreversibly transfigured the old political terrain: the Socialist Party (to a greater extent than even capitalism) was crumbling from its own internal crisis, a new but doomed revolutionary left emerged out of the ashes, and the bourgeoisie—frightened and desperate after barely surviving the proletarian onslaught—began searching for more authoritarian methods to ensure its domination. Despite a theoretical commitment to the "dictatorship of the proletariat" and its adherence to Comintern principles after 1919, the PSI leadership struggled valiantly to institutionally mediate any form of mass insurrection in order to preserve the reformist hegemony so patiently constructed by Turati. The long-awaited moment of crisis summoned no heroic political response from the PSI and CGL hierarchies (even the maximalist Serrati argued only for "party unity"), eliciting merely a powerful "fear of revolution" that could be explained more by their deep entrenchment in bourgeois institutions than by any presumed collapse of moral will or courage. Against this poured out the spontaneous energies of large radicalized sectors of the working class and peasants, crystallizing into a movement directed as much against the established Marxist organizations as against the capitalist order itself.

These mass struggles gave powerful impetus to three major leftist tendencies—anarchism, syndicalism, and above all a council communism born out of the Turin working-class movement.[3] By mid-1919, tens of thousands of workers, both skilled and unskilled, entered the rapidly-expanding factory councils, which grew out of the elitist and impotent CGL-affiliated grievance committees (commissioni interne) at Fiat and other industrial enterprises Proletarian demands, which went beyond wage claims and working conditions to address issues of *control*, could no longer be absorbed within the conventional union framework. In September 1919, more than 2000 workers at Fiat Brevetti elected 32 commissars (delegates) as the fist initiative toward a broader system of councils. The first assembly of councils in Turin met a month later, representing about 30,000 workers. All of this coincided with a massive rank-and-file upsurge against the trade-union leadership that for years had been viewed as authoritarian and generally unreceptive to workers input from below. This embryonic council movement gave expression to new modes of class consciousness and, ultimately, pressed for a revolutionary strategy that directly challenged the dominant PSI-CGL reformist model, not only in Piedmont but elsewhere. Though neither strictly anarchist nor syndicalist, the council movement assimilated their anti-union bureaucracy, anti-reformist tendencies and emphasized many of the same Sorelian goals: direct democracy at the point of production, working-class solidarity, collective self-management of the factories.[4]

In May 1919 the Turinese council revolutionaries founded the journal *L'Ordine Nuovo*, which through the efforts of Gramsci, Togliatti, Tasca, Umberto Terracini and others, sought to establish a theoretical-strategic grounding for what was an explosive but still highly-amorphous popular insurgency. Anticipating, in Gramsci's works, the beginning of a "new era of humanity." the journal set out to analyze and facilitate the transition to a new order; the factory councils were envisioned as the first step toward more mature forms of socialist democracy (soviets) as the "embryo" of a new proletarian state. At the same time, the content of *L'Ordine Nuovo* was very eclectic and was also, to a surprising extent, influenced by working-class movements outside of Italy (the shop-steward movement in England, the IWW in the United States, syndicalism in France, and of course the soviets in Russia). Gramsci and Tasca were easily the dominant intellectual forces, but the contributors from abroad were many and diverse, including Henri Barbusse, Bertrand Russell, John Reed, Max Eastman, and Romain Rolland as well as Sorel and Lenin. Yet this periodical, closely linked as it was to the factory councils, appealed primarily to a working-class audience because it was able to capture the spirit of the movement and translate it into popular language. Gramsci observed that "the workers loved *L'Ordine Nuovo*... because in it they sense their own inner striving: how can we be free? How can we become ourselves?"[5]

One reason the factory councils occupied center stage in 1919-1920, aside from the powerful impact of the Bolshevik Revolution, was the overwhelming sense of impending political upheaval that characterized the Italian left. There was a general mood of eschatological optimism regarding new possibilities that would arise out of the chaos; to virtually everyone it seemed that capitalism had finally lost the historical initiative, that bourgeois society was crumbling on all fronts, and that out of the catastrophe would come renewal and the seeds of a new revolutionary order manifested in the organic diffusion of councils. In this context the ideas promulgated by the *Ordinovisti* in Turin were widely accepted, not simply by the upper eschelons of labor seeking job autonomy, but by broad sectors of workers in auto, textile, chemical, tire, and metal production, by janitors as well as technicians, unskilled as well as skilled strata.

Already by 1919 it had become clear to Gramsci and the *Ordinovisti* that neither the Socialist Party nor the trade unions could be salvaged as instruments of revolutionary struggle. The impatience of the Turin group within the PSI had been visible for some time; talk of party "renewal" gave way to talk of an alternative political strategy rooted in local organs of self-activity. It was natural for the emergent *Ordine Nuovo* movement, situated as it was in the "Petrograd of Italy", to look for inspiration to the Bolshevik experience in Russia, where factory committees and soviets evolved rapidly into structures of "dual power" and became probably the most important locus of mass insurrection. At this point the role of the party was not yet clear to most European leftists and in any case few had anticipated the future bureaucratic degeneration of the Soviet party-state. For Gramsci, the factory councils in Italy were the nucleus of future soviets—the basis of a socialist state that would lend democratic content to the "dictatorship of the proletariat." The virtue of this approach was that it would eventually lead to "new forms of state power," to democratized social and authority relations, rather than to simply another "government by functionaries."[16]

What Gramsci derived from the Russian Revolution, regardless of its ultimate factual validity, was a sense of the insurrectionary moment—a scenario of crisis and overthrow of the old institutions—that would unleash unprecedented democratic impulses. After all, the Bolsheviks *did* destroy bourgeois state power and seemed to overturn the entire traditional social structure in the process; and of course the upheaval, commonly viewed as a "revolution of the soviets," demonstrated the function of collective will in history. All of this simply confirmed Gramsci's overall outlook, which stressed the Sorelian themes of class warfare, forcible destruction of the bourgeois state, and workers' control of production.[7] In this period Gramsci assumed that given the international crisis of capitalism, the institutional and social differences between Russia and Italy did not weigh heavily enough to force any rethinking of political strategy. The later distinction between "Eastern" and "Western" fronts did not really figure during the council phase.

Gramsci's *Ordine Nuovo* writings were thus infused with a spirit of impatience, optimism, and confrontation. While never an abstentionist, he believed that a truly revolutionary movement would have to sustain its autonomy and identify *outside* of the main political institutions in capitalist society—e.g., parliament, the party system, state bureaucracy, trade unions and local government. While these forms could be utilized for limited, tactical purposes, only the local organs of proletarian democracy could serve as the *strategic* basis of socialist transformation. On this point Gramsci was in perfect theoretical agreement with Lenin.[8]

By late 1919, and early 1920 Gramsci had worked out his critique of the PSI and the CGL, which merged into his broader analysis of the capitalist state and his increasingly mature theory of council communism. Gramsci's basic point of departure was that both the party system and the trade-union structure were formed on the terrain of bourgeois democracy—that they were essentially products of capitalist development—and thus were necessarily bound to the logic of that system. Because there could be no revolutionary mobilization or systemic rupture within bourgeois political institutions, the very concept of a parliamentary road to socialism upheld by the Second International was nothing but an illusion. Such a strategy, if successful on its own terms, would only function to integrate the proletariat into the existing state institutions. For Gramsci, the revolutionary movement would have to "be prepared...(and) armed for the conquest of social power." In a context where the broad masses of Italian people were "shapeless" and "atomized," the leadership above all "does not want them given to believe that it is possible to overcome the present crisis through parliamentary and reformist action." Hence the movement had "planted itself in the parliamentary circus" not "through any democratic illusion or reformist tenderness, but strictly in order to create the conditions for the triumph of the proletariat; in order to ensure the success of the revolutionary effort directed towards installing a proletarian dictatorship embodied in the system of councils, *outside and against Parliament.*"[9]

These passages were not written during isolated moments of council euphoria but actually typified Gramsci's thinking during the *Biennio Rosso*—and later. He typically argued that the revolutionary process would have to be "natural"—i.e., organic in the sense that its main locus would not be in the state but in civil society, with the transition requiring a fundamental break with the bourgeois public sphere and all of its constitutional and pluralistic trappings. Socialist transformation could

> ...only be identified with a spontaneous movement of the working masses brought about by the clash of contradictions inherent in the social system characterized by private property. Caught in the pincers of capitalist conflicts, and threatened by condemnation without appeal to the loss of civil and intellectual rights, the masses break with the forms of bourgeois democracy and leave behind them the legality of the bourgeois constitution.[10]

This scenario (and the theory behind it) was connected to one of Gramsci's early overriding premises; that the bourgeois class in Italy was too weak to carry out a vigorous capitalist development on its own, and was much too fragile to legitimate its political domination. By the end of World War I, moreover, the bourgeoisie had even further exhausted its historical role. Just as the market economy was collapsing, so too were liberal institutions and norms.

The bourgeoisie itself, from Gramsci's viewpoint, posed no real obstacle to socialist revolution on the peninsula; indeed, only the collaborationist parties and unions stood in the way. There existed no political space for a reformist solution to the crisis, no rationale for pursuing an electoral strategy. In Gramsci's words: "As a political force, capitalism has been reduced to corporate associations of factory owners. It no longer possesses a political party whose ideology also embraces the petty-bourgeois strata in the cities and countryside, and so ensures the continued survival of a broadly-based legal state... Since the bourgeoisie is exhausted and worn out as a ruling class, capitalism is exhausted as a mode of production and exchange... the working class is ineluctably summoned by history to take upon itself the responsibilities of a ruling class... Only the proletariat, through its creation of a new organ of public authority, the soviet system, can give dynamic expression to the fluid and incandescent mass of workers and restore order to the general upheaval of the productive forces."[11]

With the spread of the factory councils in Turin throughout 1919 and 1920, Gramsci's patience with the obstinate Socialist Party leadership was wearing thin. His call for a "renewal" of the PSI in May 1920 therefore must be understood as the demand for a complete overhaul, of total reconstitution, of the party rather than for specific organizational and policy revisions. The problem was that the PSI, after years of electoralism, had become an institutionalized fixture of the capitalist state and had consequently lost "its own precise and distinct character." A working-class party in name only, it had evolved into a "petty-bourgeois parliamentary party" lacking cohesiveness, discipline, and a doctrine and tactics of its own. The result was that "neither the Party leadership nor *Avanti!* counterposed a genuinely revolutionary conception to the incessant propaganda which the reformist and opportunists were disseminating in parliament and in the trade-union bodies."[12] Gramsci viewed the PSI as a party much like other bourgeois parties, with more or less the same commitments, interests, and priorities. Possessing little beyond a loose conglomeration of interests and constituencies, it "watches the course of events like a spectator; it never has an opinion of its own to express, based on the revolutionary theses of Marxism and the Communist International; it never launches slogans that can be adopted by the masses, to lay down a general line and unify or concentrate revolutionary action."[13]

The PSI did, however, win impressive political victories on the electoral terrain; in 1919 it gained 32 percent of the vote and elected

156 deputies to parliament, making it the second strongest party in the country. But with each new success the party fell more and more under the influence of parliamentarians and interest groups with a vision that did not go much beyond exchange relations based upon votes and patronage. In order to broaden its electoral base the PSI leadership inevitably abandoned whatever ideological and strategic coherence it had in the first place so that the party became, according to Gramsci, little more than a "conglomeration of forces" lacking real direction—"no different from the English Labor Party."[14] The Socialist Party was

> ...revolutionary in terms of the general statements contained in its programme... It moves and cannot help but move slowly and belatedly. It runs the permanent risk of becoming an easy prey for adventurers, careerists, and ambiguous men without political capacity or seriousness. Because of its heterogeneous character and the numerous sources of friction in its machinery...it has never been in a position to take upon itself the burden and responsibility for initiating and carrying out the revolutionary actions that the ceaseless pressures of events demand of it. Here we have the explanation for the historical paradox that, in Italy, it is the masses who drive and 'educate' the Party of the working class and not the Party that guides and educates the masses.[15]

The political impotence of the PSI in the face of the postwar crisis in Italy could therefore be attributed to the logic of a parliamentarist strategy that, in looking almost exclusively to the bourgeois state, undercut prospects for revolutionary change directed through autonomous centers of proletarian struggle.

If the Socialist Party had become thoroughly immersed in the capitalist state system, the trade unions (notably the CGL) compromised their socialist identity in a different fashion: confined by a narrow economism, they were never able transcend the worker-employer relationship enough to politicize the everyday struggles of workers. This mechanical separation of politics and economics, an endemic feature of bourgeois society that orthodox Marxism itself replicated, gave rise to a partial (and thus reformist) involvement of both parties and unions in their respective spheres. Whereas the PSI failed to establish any real presence at the point of production, the CGL was unable to broaden or politicize the immediate material demands of workers.

While Gramsci's attitude toward the trade union movement was in certain respects equivocal—for example, he defended it as a necessary instrument for building proletarian unity and securing economic benefits under capitalism—his writings of the *Biennio Rosso* period reflected a growing skepticism towards the unions as potentially *revolutionary* forms. In most European countries, Gramsci observed, the unions came into being as radical mechanisms of working-class struggles but eventually ended up as bargaining components within the capitalist managerial structure. The Italian CGL was no exception to this general developmental tendency, despite its "Marxist" and "socialist" pretensions. Thus: "...one must conclude that trade unionism is not a means to revolution, is not a moment in the proletarian revolution, is not the revolution in the process of being accomplished and realized."[16] Moreover, far from instilling a class consciousness in workers that would at least prepare them for socialist transformation, the unions achieved just the opposite:

> The unions' normal course of development is marked by a continuous decline in the revolutionary spirit of the masses. The union increases their material strength, but weakens or completely destroys their appetite for conquest; their *elan vital* wilts, and heroic intransigence is succeeded by the practice of opportunism—'bread and butter' demands. An increase in quantity results in a decrease in quality, and a facile accommodation to capitalist forms; it results in the workers acquiring a stingy, narrow petty- and middle-bourgeois mentality.[17]

Gramsci pointed to three dimensions of this problem. In the first place, the unions represented labor as a commodity to be bought, sold, and negotiated within the corporate structure, advancing the economic demands only of particular sectors. They dealt with workers primarily as wage-earners and consumers rather than as *producers* who themselves had created the material foundations of capitalism and who were therefore capable of playing a central role in transforming it. By late 1919 Gramsci had concluded that "Trade unionism stands revealed as nothing other than a form of capitalist society, not a potential successor to that society. It organizes workers not as producers, but as wage-earners, i.e., as creatures of the capitalist, private property regime, selling the commodity labor. Trade unionism combines workers on the basis of the tools they use or the material they transform; in other words, trade unionism combines workers on the basis of the form that the capitalist regime, the regime of economic individualism impresses on them."[18] It follows that, insofar as the unions simply reproduced the workers' status as commodities within capitalist production, they thereby negated the formation of collective subjectivity—that is, the workers' sense of themselves as historical actors. From Gramsci's viewpoint the proletariat would never see itself as a *producing* class—it would never overcome its atomization and alienation—until it understood itself as part of the totality, "as an inseparable part of the whole labor system" capable of experiencing the "unity of the industrial process."[19] Gramsci saw in craft unionism, which had a strong presence in Italy, the living negation of this dialectic.

Secondly, Gramsci viewed the CGL as an expression of capitalist legality to the degree that it sought to establish a contractual relationship between wage labor and industrial management within the shared norms of the corporate economy. In this context the union structure operated to *mediate* between labor and capital rather than challenge the legitimacy of that relationship; the CGL could therefore never become the basis of a "future society of producers". It would be childish, Gramsci suggested, to "maintain that the trade union in itself possesses the capability to overthrow capitalism. *Objectively*, the trade union is nothing other than a commercial company, of a purely capitalistic type, which aims to secure, in the interests of the proletariat, the maximum price for the commodity labor, and to establish a monopoly over this commodity in the national and international fields. The trade union is distinguished from capitalist mercantilism only *subjectively* insofar as, being formed necessarily of workers, it tends to create among the workers an awareness that it is impossible to achieve industrial autonomy of the producers within the bounds of trade-unionism."[20] The historical limitations of the trade union movements in the relatively advanced countries were thus essentially structural: union leaders could not possibly commit themselves to overturning bourgeois rationality or subverting wage-labor as a key element of capitalist exploitation, without simultaneously abandoning the very basis of their stewardship.

The third deradicalizing impulse of the union movement was a logical extension of the first two: insofar as it achieved power by representing labor as a commodity within the system of industrial legality, it naturally gravitated toward the bureaucratic form. As the unions grew in membership and organizational strength, they took on the characteristics of other corporate structures—they became hierarchical, specialized, rigidly disciplined, and (over time) remote from the everyday struggles of the majority of workers. Because of their attachment to the norms of capitalist rationality, they could effectively press for tangible economic reforms but could never, in Gramsci's view, advance the more radical demand for workers' control of production; indeed, true democratic participation at the workplace would inevitably threaten the vested interests of union leaders.

In one of his most important *Ordine Nuovo* articles, "Unions and Councils," Gramsci wrote that the trade unions' efforts to control the labor market as a commodity sooner or later gave rise to a central office staffed by various functionaries, "organizational technicians," and specialists. In this way each union "acquires the ability to negotiate agreements and take on responsibilities." At the same time, however, "this office becomes divorced from the masses it has regimented, and removes itself from the eddies and currents of fickle whims and foolish ambitions that are to be expected in the excitable broad masses."[21] Gramsci went on to argue that, whereas the emergent factory councils were the "negation" of industrial legality and looked to "spark off the class war at any moment," the trade union "represents legality" and "by virtue of its bureaucratic form, tends to prevent class war from every breaking out."[22] Not only workers' self-management, then, but any type of mobilization at the point of production was anathema to the union bureaucracy. Thus:

> In Italian conditions, the trade-union official sees industrial legality as a permanent state of affairs. Too often he defends it from the same perspective as the proprietor. He sees only chaos and willfulness in everything that happens amongst the working masses. He does not universalize the worker's act of rebellion against capitalist discipline as rebellion; he perceives only the physical act, which might in itself be trivial... In these conditions, the trade-union discipline can be nothing other than a service rendered to capital.[23]

Reflecting on the massive growth of the CGL, Gramsci reluctantly concluded that the union leaders and the workers they "represented" stood in fundamentally antagonistic relationship to each other; the union structure became outmoded, thereby *blocking* the revolutionary process. Far from instilling class consciousness, the unions actually reproduced bourgeois ideology in its manifold expressions—passivity, indifference, deference to authority, competitive individualism. Above all, the workers developed a sense of impotence in the face of union control and manipulation. Hence "They feel that even in their own house, in the house they built with tenacious and patient efforts, cementing it with blood and tears—even in this house, the machine crushes man and bureaucracy crushes any creative spirit." The workers could only be angered by this situation but they nonetheless felt powerless to change it, since "the words and intentions of individual men are too puny to stand up to the iron laws inherent in the bureaucratic structure of the trade-union apparatus."[24]

Writing at a time of proletarian upheavals in Italy and elsewhere, Gramsci seems to have relegated the union movement to historical obsolescence, for he offered little hope for an internal reconstitution of the unions that might transform them into anti-capitalist forms. They had negated the essence of proletarian self-activity that for Gramsci was the cornerstone of Marx's theory. Like the Socialist Party, therefore, the unions would have to be rejected as a potential agency of socialist transformation; the craft unions, the Chambers of Labor, the industrial federations, and the CGL were all labor organizations "specific to the period of history dominated by capital" and thus "an integral part of capitalist society."[25] There can be no avoiding the conclusion that

> The trade union has an essentially competitive, not communist, character. It cannot be the instrument for the radical renovation of society. It can provide the proletariat with skilled bureaucrats, and with technical experts on general industrial matters, but it cannot form the basis of proletarian power. It offers no scope for the selection of proletarian individuals who are capable and worthy of running society. It cannot throw up the hierarchies which will embody the *elan vital* and the rhythm of progress of communist society.[26]

Gramsci however did not completely abandon these labor organizations for they were still viable as limited, tactical, *defensive* tools of struggle. But in the spring of 1919, with the founding of *Ordine Nuovo*, he looked to situate the revolutionary process elsewhere—in the factory councils as autonomous centers of proletarian activity that he hoped would evolve into politically mature "soviets". At first he thought it would be possible to *merge* these three forms, but then in the euphoria of the *Biennio Rosso* he began to stress the primacy of the councils, insisting that the "proletarian dictatorship can only be embodied in a type of organization that is specific to the activity of producers, not wage-earners, the slaves of capital."[27]

Gramsci's Theory of Proletarian Democracy

The appearance of *L'Ordine Nuovo* and the rise of the factory councils in Turin furnished Gramsci with the ideal opportunity to extend concretely his Crocean and Sorelian inclinations of the time—to specify, in other words, the institutional embodiment of those initial, loosely-articulated theoretical stirrings. In this phase of Gramsci's thought, the factory councils appeared as the expression of proletarian self-emancipation, collective solidarity, and cultural renewal; in contrast to the hierarchical party and trade-union structures, they were rooted in everyday life and thereby could prefigure the future communist society. The councils imparted *form* to Gramsci's Hegelian focus on ideological-cultural struggle; they mediated between the universal project of socialist transformation and localized popular revolt in the sense that, as Gwyn Williams suggests, "it is in these new configurations that the mass acquires consciousness of its historical responsibilities and of its definite mission. It is the *councils* then which are the crucial *areas of translation.*"[28]

The council movement derived much of its spirit and sense of direction from the newspaper *L'Ordine Nuovo*, which averaged 5,000 subscribers—most of them workers in the Turin area—during 1919-1921. Gramsci and his intellectual comrades did not publish the periodical as theorists detached from the lives of the workers but as political activists committed to educating working people, to providing new theoretical insights into an already explosive and radicalizing situation. Gramsci wrote: "I, Togliatti, and Terracini were invited to hold debates in educational institutes and factory assemblies; the shop committees invited us to small group discussions...The development of the shop committees became the central problem, indeed the *idea* behind the *Ordine Nuovo*: the fundamental problem of a working-class revolution, the problem of 'liberty' for workers. *Ordine Nuovo* became for us and our supporters the 'newspaper' of the factory councils."[29]

Gramsci foresaw a transition to socialism in his *Ordine Nuovo* essays that stood qualitatively apart from both the Social Democratic and Leninist-Bordighist models. (It must be remembered that Gramsci's "Leninism" of this period was a *council*-based theory, closer to *State and Revolution* than to the vanguardist Lenin of the Bolshevik Party.) He followed Sorel and the Italian syndicalist tradition insofar as he located the revolutionary dialectic at the point of production, mainly within the factory.[30] He saw in the actuality of emergent Turin councils the genesis of an independent movement that might solidify a previously "shapeless" mass consciousness and unleash class warfare against the bourgeoisie. Such a movement would have a distinct political identity, and power base, outside of the capitalist state, the party system, and the unions; hence the councils allowed for an "escape from the dominion of union corporatism and party sectarianism."[31]

On one level the councils served to transform alienated wage-laborers into self-conscious producers, or social individuals, while on another they embodied in primitive form the features of a democratic socialist state in which the political division of labor would finally be abolished. Gramsci, as we have seen, held that a revolutionary, non-bureaucratic politics could not be realized within the sphere of bourgeois democracy. Surveying the councils and the soviets (which he mistakenly thought were the basis of revolutionary power in Russia), he insisted that

> The socialist state already exists potentially in the institutions of social life characteristic of the exploited working class. To link these institutions, coordinating and ordering them into a highly centralized hierarchy of competences and powers, while respecting the necessary autonomy and articulation of each, is to create a genuine workers' democracy here and now—a workers' democracy in effective and active opposition to the bourgeois state, and prepared to replace it here and now in all its essential functions of administering and controlling the national heritage.[32]

True, the silhouette of the *party* always loomed in the background—though its larger political role and its relationship to the councils was never satisfactorily discussed in the *Ordine Nuovo* writings—but Gramsci's break with the major left currents of his time (including syndicalism) in the course of his grappling with the problems of council communism cannot be doubted.

Gramsci's critique of bureaucratic organizations and of the bourgeois state was closely linked to his theory of proletarian democracy: underlying both was a concept of revolution that was grounded in the historic effort of oppressed classes to reconquer civil society against the authoritarian state. Socialist transformation would therefore have to be an *organic* process evolving beneath the facade of liberal democratic institutions, rooted in the relations of production and in the dialectic of everyday life. One of the fallacies of social democracy—and of classical Jacobinism as well—was its preoccupation with the existing state apparatus as a set of structures to be taken over, administered, and transformed from above, thus undercutting any genuine thrust toward democratization of civil society. For Gramsci, this model of political activity erred in accepting "the historical reality produced by capitalist initiative;" it reflected "the same mistaken mentality as the liberal economists [who] believe in the perpetuity and fundamental perfection of the democratic state."[33] Movements which set out to "conquer" the old state institutions can only wind up hopelessly ensnared in the logic of capitalist development—a logic that works against autonomous mass power in hundreds of ways. Instead of constructing new political forms, they reproduced the old ones which remain embedded in the bourgeois social division of labor.

If the Socialist Party looked to the *conquest* of state power, for Gramsci the alternative was a *process* of revolutionary development culminating in a new "network of proletarian institutions." This Gramscian schema appeared especially viable at moments of capitalist crisis in Europe, where bourgeois domination was weakening and seemed more vulnerable to assault from below. Speaking for the Turinese council movement, Gramsci wrote: "We...remain convinced, in the light of the revolutionary experiences of Russia, Hungary and Germany, that the socialist state cannot be embodied in the institutions of the capitalist state. We remain convinced that with respect to these institutions, if not with respect to those of the proletariat, the socialist state must be a fundamentally new creation." It followed that the struggle for a communal order "cannot be accomplished by parliamentary democracy. So the formula 'conquest of the state' should be understood in the following sense: replacement of the democratic-parliamentary state by a new type of state, one that is generated by the associative experience of the proletarian class."[34]

In his article "The Factory Council," Gramsci wrote with excitement that the birth of workers' councils throughout Europe was "a major historical event—the beginning of a new era in the history of the human race. For now the revolutionary process has burst into the light of day, and entered the phase where it can be controlled and documented."[35] It was in the sphere of production, in the factory, that the nucleus of a socialist economy *and* state would originate. The council would constitute the medium through which economics, politics, and culture intersected and became reconstituted; Gramscian theory had thus begun to transcend the mechanical separation of these spheres typical of orthodox Marxism, pointing toward a much richer understanding of mass consciousness. During the *Ordine Nuovo* period Gramsci never wavered from the belief that "the actual unfolding of the revolutionary process takes place subterraneously, in the murky depths of the factory and of the minds of the countless multitudes that capitalism subjects to its laws." It is here that "relations are those of oppressor to oppressed, exploiter to exploited, where freedom for the worker does not exist, and democracy does not exist. The revolutionary process takes place where the worker is nothing but intends to become all..."[36]

As in Russia, the factory councils and soviets took form in the midst of crisis, when the old system of authority was decomposing and the moderate leftist organizations were losing credibility. Gramsci saw in the Italian councils potentially effective instruments of class struggle and democratization: they would simultaneously wage "mortal combat" against capitalism and bring the workers "priceless gains in terms of autonomy and initiative." Hence the working class begins to develop an entirely new class consciousness—and understanding of its historical mission:

> Insofar as it constructs this representative apparatus, the working class in effect completes the expropriation of the *primum mobile*, of the most important instruments of production of all—the working class itself. It thereby rediscovers itself, acquiring consciousness of its organic unity and counterposing itself as a whole to capitalism...It presents the factory in a new light, from the workers' point of view, as a form in which the working class constitutes itself into a specific organic body, as the cell of a new state—the workers' state—and as the basis of a new representative system—the system of councils.[37]

This Gramscian ideal of council democracy assumed that new state forms would have to be the expression of everyday proletarian life. Whereas the bureaucratized parties and unions were increasingly remote from the masses, the factory councils by virtue of their immersion in the workplace could instill a psychological sense of revolutionary subjectivity. the councils would enable the workers to take *control* of production themselves by overthrowing management and allowing them to go beyond limited reform efforts that inevitably left bourgeois relations of production intact. In this way the council movement could build upon and *broaden* the spontaneous impulses of class struggle; the old hierarchical discipline would give way to more collective, organic forms of interaction. As Gramsci put it: "once the councils exist, they give the workers direct responsibility for production, provide them with an incentive to improve their work, instill a *conscious* and *voluntary* discipline, and create a producer's mentality—the mentality of a creator of history."[38]

To carry out this tack—to make significant inroads into bourgeois claims to legitimacy—the councils would assume critical *pedagogical* functions: the workers would have to be educated to the point where they had the capacity to operate a new economy and a new state. New values, habits, and above all skills would have to be cultivated. Gramsci insisted that "If the working class, which has a vital interest in the establishment of communism, is to be given the preparation it needs to attain its historical goals, it must be organized as the dominant class. The proletariat needs to acquire the sort of mentality that the bourgeois class possesses at present— in the sense that it needs to acquire the art of governing, the art of bringing an initiative... to a successful conclusion, though certainly not in the sense that it needs to acquire the art of exploitation."[39] From this viewpoint, there could be no workers' state, surely no democratic socialist system, in the absence of ideological-cultural preparation on the part of the great majority of people. A revolution which destroyed capitalist power but which failed to produce a new proletarian governing class would likely fall "into the hands of adventurers and political intriguers" and end up as a "counterfeit of the bourgeois state." Hence the working class must do everything possible "to train itself and educate itself in the management of society," to build a pedagogical network "through its own channels and its own systems—meetings, congresses, discussions, mutual education."[40] Observing the rapid proliferation of councils in Turin, Gramsci concluded that they were the ideal setting for the realization of such tasks.

In sum, the factory councils appeared as original and innovative forms of class struggle that, even in their embryonic phase of development, could be the repository of a growing proletarian sense of dignity, confidence, and comradely socialist spirit in *every sector* of the work force, affecting through their presence other institutions (including the trade unions). Because of their small size and the active participation of *all* workers regardless of union affiliation, job classification, or skill level,[41] the councils also stimulate tendencies toward collective self-management for, in Gramsci's words, "the whole mass participates in the life of the council and feels itself to be something through this activity."[42] Local organs (potentially) unite structure and consciousness in such a way that a previously fragmented and divided class is dialectically transformed into a powerful "single organism."

The influence of the *Ordinovista* theorists (notably Gramsci) on the concrete development of the Turin councils was immense; the gap between Gramsci's theory of proletarian democracy and the official proclamations of the council movement was narrowed in the context of the *Biennio Rosso*. Although the "Programme of the Workshop Delegates" which appeared in November 1919 was officially signed by the "*Gruppo di Studio*", Gramsci was no doubt its main author. The "Programme" affirmed that the councils would operate according to "the principle of the democratic mandate" and that, "the elected (delegates) must be nothing other that the executors of the will of the masses." The factory delegates would be the "sole" and "authentic" representatives "by virtue of their being elected by all workers at their workplace on the basis of universal suffrage." The system of representation would evolve vertically from the work-crew through the workshop, factory, union of the factories in a given industry, enterprises in a city, province, region, the nation, and the world. In all cases the council would be organized at the point of production, with the delegates accountable to "the whole of the proletariat in the factory" and subject to instant recall.[43] The "Programme" further instructed each council to set up a school on the factory premises.[44] Triumphantly, this document stated that "The assembly of all the Turin plant delegates asserts with pride and assurance that their election and the establishment of the council system represents the first concrete indication of the communist revolution in Italy."[45]

As the "Programme" suggested, and as Gramsci in his more utopian moments affirmed, the Turin councils were to be the initial step in a much larger process: the factory organs would build toward urban soviets, which in turn would constitute the nucleus of a democratic proletarian state. Fearful of isolation and counterattack, the *Ordinovisti* urged the expansion of councils beyond their narrow Piedmont base. The "Programme" established as a major priority the goal of ensuring that "the system of workers' councils...should spread irresistibly throughout Italy, and that within the shortest possible time a national congress of worker and peasant delegates from all over Italy should be called."[46] While this project failed miserably, to attribute the problem to a geographical or cultural provincialism on the part of the *Ordinovisti* would be much too simplistic.

From a broader political viewpoint, Gramsci's version of revolutionary councilism departed fundamentally from earlier party (and union) centered strategies in three crucial respects. In the first place, the councils emerged as local checks on bureau-cratization within the larger mass organizations and on Jacobin forms of elitism within the state. Their small scale would presumably enable them to effectively counter authoritarian tendencies. Yet the *Ordine Nuovo* essays were also a source of much confusion and ambiguity regarding the possible future relationship between councils, unions, and party—a significant issue in view of Gramsci's later development. During the period 1918-1921 Gramsci seemed to vaccilate between the assumption (hope?) that a vigorous council movement would ultimately democratize the party and union structures, thus converting them into agencies of class struggle, and the expectation that an expanded council network itself would totally supersede the large-scale forms insofar as they had become institutionalized parts of the capitalist system. A second and closely related advantage of the councils was their presumed capacity to sustain proletarian autonomy and movement identity apart from the dominant institutions. Perhaps they could counter the fatal effects of deradicalization that a number of theorists —Michels, Lenin, Luxemburg, Sorel, Gramsci himself— had detected in the parties of the Second International.[47] This theme permeated Gramsci's work throughout his life: it would reappear writ large in the *Prison Notebooks*, where he explored the problems of "ideological hegemony," "war of position," and counter-hegemonic movement in another historical context.

Finally, the councils would prefigure in their collective patterns of life-activity the unfolding of a future socialist economy and state. Such an organic process of transition was possible because, as we have seen, the new order "already exists potentially in institutions of social life characteristic of the working class." The capitalist infrastructure could be subverted and broken down from within as the ever-proliferating councils stimulated the growth of emancipatory social and authority relations.[48] At the same time, the developmental process whereby the factory organs evolve into full-fledged soviets—i.e., into more distinctively *political* bodies— always remained unclear in Gramsci. Nowhere did he indicate, moreover, the extent to which the principles of proletarian democracy might be generalized beyond the sphere of production and into the community, incorporating other aspects of social existence. Still, Gramscian theory was unique in its attempt to furnish a connecting link between councils and the state; this dynamic was missing not only from Sorelian syndicalism but also from the more "mature" versions of council communism associated with Korsch and Pannekoek. The *Ordine Nuovo* contributions therefore stand, for their time, as the most innovative theoretical effort to specify the constituent elements of a democratic state and a non-bureaucratic transition to socialism.

A Different View: Bordiga and Tasca

The exuberant optimism of Gramsci and the other *Ordinovisti* concerning the revolutionary potential of the factory councils was not widely shared outside of Turin. Indeed the appearance of the councils, and their theoretical justification in the pages of *L'Ordine Nuovo*, triggered an intense debate on the Italian left during 1919-1921; the response in general was hostile, ranging from a skeptical cynicism to bitter opposition, with the attitudes of the PSI and CGL leaderships characterized by the latter. Much of this hostility could be attributed to bureaucratic inertia and to the fear of "spontaneism" on the part of the established left organizations. Some no doubt grew out of a longstanding resentment toward Turinese chauvinism in other parts of Italy. Still, Gramsci's ideas were subjected to rather harsh criticism within his own circles—from both the "left" (Amadeo Bordiga) and the "right" (Angelo Tasca).

Bordiga was quick to seize upon the obvious weaknesses of the council movement (notably, its isolation) to drive home his attack and distinquished his own politics from Gramsci's. The councils were depicted in Bordiga's Naples-based journal, *Il Soviet*, as politically impotent, economistic, gradualist structures designed at best to modify the trade unions. For Bordiga, local factory organs represented a diversion from the principal task of forging a revolutionary party capable of seizing state power: in this ultra-Leninist schema reformism and councilism turned out to be opposite sides of the same coin. He called for a unified vanguard organization that could decisively insert itself into the class struggle. It was the Bordiga faction that took the initiative in breaking with the PSI and forming a new Communist party in early 1921—a momentous step that Gramsci likewise came around to supporting. It was this same *Il Soviet* group which carried out a relentless assault on reformists and "opportunists" of all stripes, which insisted upon a classical definition of the proletariat, and which called for total and principled abstention from all bourgeois institutions.

At no point did the Bordighists actually *oppose* the establishment of factory councils, so long as the workers were behind it; their attitude was more complicated. So long as the capitalists controlled state power, the councils were necessarily confined to trade-union style activities (resistance, reforms). As Bordiga put it, "Control *within the factory* has a revolutionary and expropriative significance only after central power has passed into the hands of the proletariat." Hence the transition to socialism would involve first and foremost the conquest of political power by a vanguard party, the "communist class party," with all other organizational forms secondary. From this viewpoint, the council advocates were misled by the old syndicalist illusion that "the proletariat can achieve emancipation by making advances in economic relations while capitalism still holds political power through the state."[49] After observing that the Turin councils did indeed often take over the management of the workshops, Bordiga cautioned:

> We would not like the working masses to get hold of the idea that all they need do to take over the factories and get rid of the capitalists is set up councils. This would indeed be a dangerous illusion. The factory will be conquered by the working class—and not only by the workforce employed in it, which would be too weak and non-communist—only after the working class as a whole has seized political power. Unless it has done so, the Royal Guards, military police, etc.—in other words, the mechanism of force and oppression that the bourgeoisie has at its disposal, its political power apparatus—will see to it that all illusions are dispelled.[50]

Bordiga pointed out that the recent history of many European countries had shown how factory-based organs can be absorbed into large-scale structures; they can readily coexist with the bourgeois-democratic political system. In some cases (e.g., Germany and Austria) the councils emerged as corporatist adjuncts to the capitalist managerial structure. Movements in these countries failed to articulate viable *political* structures (party, soviets) that could generate and protect autonomous bases of proletarian power, that could break totally with the bourgeois public sphere. For Bordiga, the source of confusion for the *Ordine Nuovo* comrades was their inability to distinguish between the councils and soviets in the Russian context: whereas the former served to exercise control over *production*, the latter embodied a new system of political representation once the proletariat had gained power, "taking the place of parliament and the bourgeois administrative assemblies."[51] Since the councils express the interests of particular sectors of the working class rather than broad segments of the community, they could not—as Gramsci had assumed—constitute the nucleus of a new proletarian state. For this reason council theory and Marxism had little in common:

> To identify in the role of liberation organs of the proletariat, the stages of the political process with their economic counterparts is to lapse into the petty-bourgeois caricature of Marxism called economism (which in turn can be classified into reformism and syndicalism). Overemphasis on the factory council is just a resurrection of this hoary old error, which unites the petty-bourgeois Proudhon with all those revisionists who believe they have transcended Marx.[52]

Tasca's critique of Gramsci, which he launched in the middle of 1920, contained a number of surface parallels to Bordiga's despite its entirely different political motivation. While Tasca was an early ally of Gramsci and a member of the *Ordine Nuovo* group, he grew increasingly skeptical of the council form, especially after the spring 1920 defeats in Turin; he feared the movement's painful isolation, and even more its collision course with the party and unions. He came to share Bordiga's earlier definition of the factory organs as "syndicalist" and viewed them as auxiliary to the mass working-class organizations. He was also committed to the development of Russian-style soviets. Tasca saw the formation of Italian councils as a positive advance, but he thought that Gramsci had vastly exaggerated their role, even within the sphere of production, where in Tasca's opinion both the trade unions and the state would be the main catalysts of the transition. Whereas Gramsci at times indicated that the councils would *transcend* the union structure, Tasca looked to a *merger* of the two, with the councils exercising a democratic counterweight to the labor bureaucracy. Tasca's critical approach to *Ordine Nuovo* was part of his generally more conservative, institutionally-focused politics which later emphasized parliamentarism, the mass party, and internal modification of the bourgeois state; no doubt he would have settled for a revitalized PSI, had such an alternative presented itself.

In his contribution to the "polemics" over the *Ordine Nuovo* program in June and July, 1920, Tasca heaped scorn on Gramsci's thesis that the councils were the foundation of a "workers' state." He argued that because the factory council was confined to the workplace it could never challenge the totality of capitalist domination: "In terms of state structure, the soviet stands in relation to the factory council in the same way as economic determinism stands to class consciousness."[53] Hence the soviets and not the councils were the political forms appropriate to the transitional process, and the economy would have to be organized through this newly-reconstituted state. Elements of the old institutional apparatus, the party, and the union movement would all be incorporated into the socialist governing machinery. After denouncing Gramsci's "abstract and anti-historical" view of the factory councils, Tasca went on:

> Gramsci has even lagged behind the syndicalists, who mistakenly, in our view, identified the process of development of the unions with that of the revolution, as Gramsci now identifies the emergence of the factory councils with the creation of the 'workers' state'...In other words, Gramsci has repeated the error of the syndicalists and made it worse. For in the first place, industrial unions are more suited to the direct management of production than factory councils, in accordance with the demands of production such as we inherit it from the bourgeoisie and such as we shall have to develop.[54]

Comparing the historical status of the union and councils in Italy, Tasca concluded that the latter should be assigned a clearly "secondary role in the management of production."[55] Gramsci had envisaged for the unions, along with the party, an essentially "protective" role vis-a-vis the councils—that is, the larger organizations would simply help clear the way for the fullest possible expansion of what he considered to be the only authentic proletarian democratic forms. Tasca simply reversed this schema, arguing that the spread of local workplace organs would strengthen the unions and party and enable them to consolidate the new socialist government. In the long run, it was the unions which possessed real structural durability, which must "carry out a socialization programme" since "it is possible to conceive of the unions managing production without the factory councils, but not the other way round."[56] Tasca conceded that the councils were vital expressions of political upheaval at times of crisis, but he expected the unions to reappear as the hegemonic force once stability returned (as occurred in Russia), so that "in the present period it is up to the unions to carry the class struggle from the field of resistance to that of conquest."[57]

The council debates reflected some deep theoretical and strategic differences that would resurface from time to time throughout the 1920s. On the one hand, Gramsci was at odds with the very temperament and spirit of Bordiga's insular vanguardism; on the other, he thought that Tasca's vision of a reformed, democratized trade-union movement was hopelessly utopian.

Gramsci's conflict with Bordiga was not really over the question of "Leninism" (especially given the amorphous meaning of the label in 1919-1920) but rather over what Gramsci saw as Bordiga's mechanical, ultra-centralist interpretation of Lenin.[58] If Gramsci was too naively optimistic in his expectation that the councils would lead to a new proletarian state, Bordiga on the other side placed excessive faith in a small, disciplined nucleus of professional revolutionaries whose actions would be guided by correct theory. In Bordiga's contempt for "spontaneity" Gramsci saw an insensitivity to the complex process of consciousness transformation that produced a manipulative, elitist approach to revolutionary politics—what in the *Prison Notebooks* he would later describe as "Cadornism" or "Voluntarism". As for Tasca, Gramsci replied that for him "the problem of the factory council was simply a problem in the arithmetic sense of the work: the problem of how to organize at once the *whole* of the class of Italian workers and peasants."[59] Gramsci complained that Tasca was a very inattentive reader of *L'Ordine Nuovo* who "grasped nothing of its theoretical development"; the only thing which preoccupied Tasca was his desire "to open a new era in the trade-union movement." Tasca failed to see the qualitatively new character of the councils, which were subject to their own logic and momentum—not that of the unions or party.[60]

What seems abundantly evident from the council debates, regardless of the merits of the contending points of view, is that Gramsci's theory of proletarian democracy was quite ambiguous or even mute on some critical issues. For example, the key dynamic relationships in the transition were never clearly specified: councils and unions, councils and party, councils and soviets, councils and state. It appears that Gramsci made little effort to resolve these questions in his *Ordine Nuovo* writings, probably because of the fast pace of events and the messianic hopes which they generated. Indeed, it might be argued that Gramsci's chief shortcoming during this period was his excessive *optimism*. In any case, while there can be no doubt that Gramsci theorized the councils as *foundations* of a workers' state, a great deal of ambiguity remains in this formulation. Were the factory councils expected to evolve into broader regional or national federations of councils, for example along the lines of Pannekoek's schema? Were they to develop into, or alongside of, community-based soviets? What structure (or structures) would constitute the coordinating mechanism for production and political decision-making? While Gramsci obviously had in mind a revolutionary process entailing more that the councils, his failure to specify this process opened him and the *Ordinovisti* to damaging criticisms.

The combined Bordiga-Tasca attack was most telling in the area of Gramsci's productivism—a certain one-sidedness that he inherited from Sorel. In the aftermath of the council collapse, Gramsci himself quickly came to recognize this bias—what some critics called the "moral supremacy of the producer"—and managed to transcend it in his later work. Other disagreements, however, did reflect basic strategic splits which would have long-term implications for the Italian and European left.[61] Whatever their political differences, Bordiga and Tasca shared much the same outlook: a reliance upon large-scale organizational forms, professional leaders, and institutional hierarchies. To this Gramsci opposed his prefigurative and molecular conception which, despite the catastrophe of the Turin council movement, he would carry forward into his later political thinking. He always retained an understanding of class struggle that stressed the transformation of civil society ("war of position") as the necessary prelude to the conquest of power ("war of movement"). Put another way, in comparison with both Bordiga and Tasca, Gramsci was more interested in working out the constituent elements of a democratic transition to socialism, for which the councils were seen as a vehicle in 1918-1920.[62]

Turin: Failure of a Movement

As the political situation unfolded, the events of 1920 rapidly outpaced these strategic discussions: the Italian left itself was completely overwhelmed. The class strife that built toward the climactic phase of the *Biennio Rosso* began to intensify in early 1920. The increased scope and militancy of the council movement set the stage for a powerful counter-offensive by industrialists in Piedmont and Liguria, which involved massive lockouts and troop occupations in many factories. What followed was a general strike in Piedmont, "defensive" in its inception, that mobilized more than 500,000 workers for most of the month of April; the spontaneous upheavals which accompanied the strike marked probably the most dramatic episode in postwar European working-class history. Such an assessment was shared by neither the PSI nor CGL leaderships, however, for they maintained an attitude of fearful antagonism toward the strike wave that was sweeping though Northern Italy; the Milan edition of *Avanti!*, for example, refused to publish the Turin strike bulletins. The fear of revolution that swept through the bourgeoisie and the party system also gripped the Socialists.[63] In the end, the appeal for an Italian general strike went unheeded— the PSI dismissing it as adventurism and the Bordighists offering only "principled doctrinal criticism" to the effect that the *state* and not the factory must be viewed as the primary arena of contestation. Catastrophic defeat was unavoidable. So too were the bitter recriminations that followed, producing an irreversible mood of antagonism between the Turin radicals and PSI-CGL hierarchies.

The collapse of the Piedmont general strike generated an atmosphere of retreat and confusion on the Italian left, followed by a mood of reformism that took control of even the council movement. With the factory councils in disarray, many of the *Ordinovisti* began to look in different directions—Tasca toward a reconstituted trade-union formation, Togliatti and his new "electionist communist" group toward parliamentary politics. Gramsci, however, stubbornly stood his ground. For him, the defeat was only a surface phenomenon, a temporary setback at the level of institutional politics; the general strike, though it achieved few tangible gains, did raise working-class consciousness and inspired new modes of struggle. Gramsci thus remained firmly optimistic: beneath the facade of order and stability could be detected a rapidly-decomposing bourgeois society in which the old class and power relations would continue to be sharply challenged. Despite the chaos of the councils, he persisted in a strategic commitment to a total break with the bourgeois structures, arguing that contractual organizations such as parties and trade unions would inevitably impede the revolutionary process, which he still insisted must unfold within civil society, or more accurately within the sphere of production. Hence: "The revolution is proletarian and communist only to the extent that it is a liberation of the proletarian and communist forces of production that were developing within the very heart of the society dominated by the capitalist class."[64]

Events would soon validate Gramsci's analysis, for just five months after the Turin general strike came the heroic sequel—the occupation of the factories—that seemed to put Italy even closer to the edge of revolution. An upsurge that engulfed most of northern Italy during the entire month of September, 1920, and involved the occupation of more than 200 factories by 500,000 workers, it revitalized the dormant council movement and inspired a renewal of syndicalism. As in April, the revolt began modestly as a defensive move to preempt a lockout by industrialists over a bargaining statement—an action designed, as Tasca put it, to be a "simple substitute for the strike weapon." But the turmoil that grew out of attempts to take over and manage the factories, under chaotic and burdensome conditions, quickly politicized the workers and broadened the agitation far beyond its April confines. From Milan, Genoa, and Turin the occupations spread to Rome, Salerno, Reggio-Emilia, Padua, and elsewhere, moving through the major industrial sectors: autos, machine tools, textiles, rubber, footwear, chemicals, etc.

While the council structures as such did not spread beyond their Piedmont origins (the few that did being quickly absorbed by the unions), the occupations everywhere were infused with a sense of proletarian solidarity and a drive towards workers' control. Along with the red and black flags hoisted atop factories went the banners reading "We want no wealth but freedom." Production output in the occupied sectors was lower than normal, mainly because of the confusion and material shortages, but by all accounts the takeovers proceeded in orderly and peaceful fashion, typified by a kind of "communist" regimen: "No one could enter or leave without permission. Workers were searched at the exits and thieves severely punished. Alcohol was strictly forbidden. The corps of red guards kept watch inside the plants to check for possible trouble-makers."[65] Within two weeks the occupations were in full swing and a revolutionary euphoria spread through the air. The assembly of the workers' leagues proclaimed that "The struggle of the metal workers (who were the first to act) opens a new era in the class struggle which will close only with the establishment of workers' control over all production."[66] The industrialists too thought revolution was imminent. Giovanni Agnelli, apparently convinced that capitalism was too badly maimed to resurrect itself, was on the verge of surrendering Fiat-Centro to the occupying workers, asking "How can you build anything with the help of 25,000 enemies?"[67]

Yet within less than a month after they began, the occupations had run their course, leaving in their wake an exhausted and embittered proletariat that could no longer summon the energy to combat the bourgeoisie, not to mention the Socialist Party and trade-union apparatus as well. Once again, the insurgency could not sustain any revolutionary alternative to the PSI-CGL hegemony. But this failure was not merely the result of Socialist treachery and even less of actual or threatened state repression, though of course these were factors; it was to a greater extent the outcome of a skillful cooptation process that involved the collaboration of government, the progressive industrialists (e.g., Agnelli and Olivetti), and the trade unions. This was Premier Giolitti's most brilliant stratagem of all—the final, gallant moment in the pre-war scheme of *trasformismo*, the last desperate attempt to save Italian capitalism by means of an elite-engineered "reformist solution." In this maneuver Turati and other PSI leaders were quite willing accomplices; they helped provide the ruling class with a way out of the crisis. At the peak of the upsurge, Giolitti was able to usurp the initiative from the radical militants who floundered without a sense of history and without the capacity to translate their struggles onto the political terrain.

What did emerge from the *Biennio Rosso* was the nebulous, CGL-initiated principle of "union control" which on paper meant equal trade-union involvement in enterprise management and state economic planning. While many Socialists and leftists (including Tasca) endorsed this arrangement because it would presumably give workers *some* authority, Gramsci denounced it as fraudulent insofar as it would only serve to institutionalize class conflict without altering any (exploitative) aspect of production.[68] In reality all of this meant very little, especially with the growing reactionary counter-offensive that would soon make a mockery of such agreements. So while the triumvirate of institutional forces managed to coax the workers out of the plants behind the promise of broad new concessions (a task made easier by the demoralization that had set in by late September), the anticipated "new era" of institutionalized class relations—the prospect of a reconsolidated capitalism designed to augment productivity and labor discipline within a bourgeois democratic framework—would die early under the fascist avalanche. Yet from the outset Giolitti's plan was marked for what it was—a skillful capitalist maneuvre to coopt labor, but one destined to fail. Even PSI leader Serrati reacted angrily: "It is evident that the control won over the factories, once it starts to work, can only be either mystification of corruption. If it becomes effective, it will inevitably transform workers into interested aides to bourgeois management."[69]

It turned out that Gramsci's analysis of the Italian bourgeoisie was essentially correct; it was unquestionably a weak, defensive social force that could not rule on its own. Capitalism needed the crutch of *trasformismo*. But this fragility, which Gramsci thought would ultimately favor the left, now signaled just the opposite—it cleared the way for Europe's first fascist dictatorship. Giolitti's "order" collapsed, giving way to Mussolini's "order". After the hopes and illusions of the *Biennio Rosso* were finally crushed, Gramsci in the midst of his own depression prophetically grasped this new twist to his argument: "...the political power of capitalism is tending to be identified increasingly with the upper ranks of the military, the Royal Guard and the swarm of adventurers who have cropped up since the Armistice, aspiring each and every one to become the Kornilov or Bonaparte of Italy. Thus the political power of capitalism can only be expressed today in a military coup d'etat and the attempt to impose an iron nationalist dictatorship which will drive the brutalized Italian masses to revive the economy by sacking neighboring countries sword in hand."[70] With capitalism in a state of collapse, the real postwar alternatives seemed to be socialist revolution or fascist reaction; in any case, the Giolitti-inspired vision of an "enlightened" or progressive bourgeois solution became the most tragic illusion of all.[71]

It seemed hardly possible that in the space of only a few years such an unprecedented anti-capitalist explosion could so easily give way to fascism, that an organized proletarian movement capable of immobilizing the entire country could submit so quickly and so completely to annihilating defeat by the Mussolini regime, to the extent that the left would remain a dormant political force in Italy for at least two decades. This defeat raises some fundamental questions about the historical situation that produced *Ordine Nuovo* and shaped its possibilities and limits. Could the *Biennio Rosso* in fact have led to a general revolutionary rupture in Italy, as is commonly assumed? If so, were the obstacles that led to failure *internal* to the left opposition itself (i.e., strategic and tactical) or external to it, the result of a successful campaign by the bourgeoisie to coopt and domesticate the insurgency? If not, then what was the character of the political situation that *did* erupt in postwar Italy, and what realistic left advances were possible given the balance of forces, available strategic options, and the level of mass ideological preparation?

The initial point to be made is that, whereas the council movement won great victories in Turin, it lacked the power necessary to sustain them; organs of workers' control that at one moment galvanized the entire Piedmont proletariat rapidly vanished the next moment. The masses that had so resolutely broken with the established institutions were just as completely reintegrated into them, and the historical initiative soon passed to the Italian right. This sequence of developments was due not only to the paralysis of the PSI, but to internal weaknesses of the emergent factory councils themselves. The weaknesses were many, the most crucial being the fatal political isolation bred of Piedmont "exceptionalism:" during this period the region was the base of Italian industrial development, typified by a system of factory production and urban working-class culture duplicated nowhere else on the peninsula. Not surprisingly, the *Ordine Nuovo* tendency spawned by these conditions was itself unique, nourishing a regionalism which ruled out attempts to expand council politics beyond Turin and a few other northern cities. The characterization of Turin as the "Italian Petrograd" only reinforced its identification as the center of the most "advanced" proletarian movement in Italy—a sense of superiority that was theoretically justified by an exclusivist and moralistic productivism. (Ironically, Gramsci's extreme Sorelian celebration of the factory contradicted his own preoccupation with the peasantry and the "Southern Question" in both his earlier and later writings.) Of all the significant leftist formations operating in Italy at this time—the Socialists, the CGL, anarchists, Bordighists—only the factory council movement lacked a truly national presence.[72]

Within the city itself, a phenomenon known as "factory egoism" appeared, limiting the possibilities of coordinated struggle and planning even among the relatively unified Turinese workers. Cut off from the rest of Italy and politically alienated from the PSI and CGL, the councils were inevitably engulfed by their own isolation as much as by the force and cunning of the bourgeoisie. The absence of an organizational center—of leadership and political direction—was particularly visible during the occupation of the factories when the workers were trying to simultaneously manage production and sustain a revolutionary movement. Thus any critique of the *Ordinovisti* for their failure to pose the question of armed insurrection and seizure of state power must take this predicament into account.[73]

A further point is that the actual, living, functioning councils which appeared in 1918-1920 rarely approximated the ideal type of Gramsci's theoretical formulations; in fact, he always referred to the real factory organs as the "nucleus" or "embryo" of the fully-developed council. Of the hundreds of councils in Turin, most grew out of the old internal commissions and they moved only haltingly and unevenly toward democratic involvement of all workers. Normally the small labor teams in a plant would elect a representative, or commissar, who would vote to select an executive committee of 3 to 9 members. The principle of delegation (rather than direct democracy) prevailed, but it was compatible with the ongoing participation of most workers in meetings, educational sessions, and direct forms of action. In any event, the systematic over-representation or domination of technical workers as in the German case was not evident in Turin.[74] Of course the councils ran into numerous political and economic obstacles, some of which have been mentioned. The intransigent opposition of the PSI and CGL seriously undercut recruitment efforts and presented the *Ordinovisti* with yet another combat front. Where the councils did take over large enterprises (e.g., Fiat), immediate organizational and technical problems arose: how to satisfy the demand for managerial expertise, obtain supplies and market finished goods in a hostile economic atmosphere, coordinate the diverse activities of plants and whole enterprises, impose labor discipline (e.g., against absenteeism) without violating the new democratic norms, and so forth. Finally, there was the difficulty of carrying out tasks under constant police surveillance and the threat of military intervention. From the standpoint of efficiency, by most accounts the factory councils met these challenges with mixed results before the final collapse.[75]

Yet the obstacles went much deeper. While most commentators have described the political conditions of the *Biennio Rosso* as a "revolutionary situation," such a view may well be too facile: there is plenty of evidence to suggest that the Italian masses were in fact *not* prepared to carry out any revolutionary transformation. This should not be confused with the question of armed *insurrection*, though here too the degree of preparedness was not equal to the task. Commenting on the occupation, Tasca wrote that "armed insurrection was impossible because nothing was ready." Another Turinese militant at Fiat-Centro estimated that a sortie from the factories to engage in armed combat in the streets would be finished in ten minutes, given the primitive weaponry and limited ammunition available to the workers. The larger problem was more vastly political in nature: the movement, however militant and broadly supported, could not transcend its own divisive and even self-destructive parochialism. In the absence of any coordinating "center," without any real communication links, the insurgency could only wind up trapped in a formless spontaneism. The sharp fragmentation of popular forces from factory to factory, city to city, and region to region—in part a continuation of the Italian legacy of *campanilismo*—arrested the movement short of the political-institutional sphere, which it ultimately ceded to the liberal-reformist alliance.

From this classic predicament it might be concluded that the key missing ingredient needed to convert chaos into purpose, defeat into revolution, was a globalizing force in the presence of vanguard revolutionary party. Thus Williams observed that "Every factory looked to its own defenses, like *a militia*. There was no coordination. There was no communist party."[76] Such a protagonist, at least in theory, would have furnished the general direction, planning, and leadership necessary to pull the popular forces out of their pre-political morass. Unified and disciplined, it would have been in a position to seize upon the moment of crisis that the left had for so long been awaiting. In other words, Bordiga, despite his annoying sectarianism, was essentially on the right track.

This conventional Leninist response, however, is only superficially valid, for the problem of spontaneism must be confronted at yet a deeper level: the collapse of the *Biennio Rosso* is ultimately explained by the ideological character of the industrial workers. To whatever extent the crisis might have permitted a revolutionary seizure of power, in retrospect it is clear that no cohesive *popular* force was prepared to initiate and carry out a process of social transformation. The proletarian masses of the North, despite their heroic spirit and innovative struggles, generally failed to move beyond their cultural and regional boundaries; their internal divisions could not readily have been overcome by a Jacobin organizational unity. Moreover, since these struggles were almost totally cut off from other regions of Italy, any attempt to establish a socialist government with its main base of support in the "industrial triangle" would only have reproduced the old geopolitical fragmentation that was the legacy of the *Risorgimento*. The legitimacy of such a state would obviously be extremely fragile.

From the standpoint of the ideological development of the Italian workers, then, this period cannot be accurately viewed as a "revolutionary situation" that required for its complete historical actualization only a vanguard party capable of unifying the amorphous masses. This very amorphousness, manifested in the "factory egoism", localism, and feeble integration of even the most advanced Piedmont struggles, was itself a sign that socialist consciousness was lacking—that civil society had yet to undergo significant changes in this direction—and suggested that a Jacobin solution would have meant an even more mechanical imposition of centralized political power than was the case in Russia. Conversely, this very uneven and atomized class consciousness also explains why the northern workers, so militant one moment, could so easily yield to the reformist ploys of the PSI and CGL leaders the next.[77]

Even Gramsci, whose optimism led him to stress the "actuality of revolution" and to exaggerate the transformative potential of the Turin workers, reluctantly arrived at these same conclusions in the very midst of the factory occupations when he observed that "the enemy to combat and overcome will no longer be outside the proletariat, will no longer be an external physical power that is limited and can be controlled. The enemy will lie within the proletariat itself, in its ignorance, its laziness, its ponderous slowness in understanding, when the dialectic of class struggle has been internalized within every individual consciousness. The new man, in his every act, has to fight the 'bourgeois' lying in ambush."[78] Here again, from Gramsci's viewpoint, the Bordighist approach in its Jacobin preoccupation with organizational identity, leadership, and political power sidestepped the entire problem of mass consciousness. Gramsci's already keen sensitivity to this issue—to the way in which bourgeois attitudes, values, and social relations penetrate the everyday life of workers—anticipated his subsequent conceptual emphasis on ideological hegemony in the *Prison Notebooks*.

The Fate of Council Communism

As a deeply-involved revolutionary activist, Gramsci would have found it difficult to retreat into the comfortable sphere of ideology and culture as a means of avoiding troublesome organizational questions that arose in the aftermath of the council defeat. On the contrary, he began to more seriously wrestle with the issue of the *party* in late 1920, arguing along with Bordiga and others that a new kind of party formation (inspired partly by the Bolshevik experience) would be needed to replace the discredited PSI. With fascism taking the offensive and the left in a state of paralysis, Bordiga's power-oriented vanguardism gained in appeal while the *Ordinovista* council-based strategy appeared more and more futile. The Bordighists were thus in a position to impose their Jacobin vision on the nascent Communist Party, which consequently bore all the features of a disciplined, sectarian organization during the formative 1921-22 period.

Gramsci himself was an extremely depressed and somewhat marginal figure at this time, fortunate indeed not to be excluded from any leadership role in the new party, and he had little choice but to go along with the dominant mood. It is tempting to interpret these developments as the inevitable triumph of party over councils, centralism over spontaneism, to which Gramsci was bound to yield through the inexorable flow of events and logic. But this would be profoundly misleading, in theoretical if not also in political terms. Gramsci's imminent rise to a position of intellectual and political leadership in the PCI—not to mention the entire corpus of his writings—would reveal that his strong antagonisms toward Bordiga and the Bordighist model never disappeared, but were merely suppressed or muted for a brief time (presumably in the interests of party unity). While the conception of a revolutionary party increasingly occupied Gramsci's thought after 1920, his vision of a "mass" or "national-popular" party was always distinct from Bordiga's centralist schema, as a replay of the Gramsci-Bordiga debates in 1923-24 would illustrate. If Gramsci did in fact enter a Jacobin phase beginning in 1926, his philosophy and political strategy were nonetheless firmly stamped with the imprint of his early Hegelianism and councilism which collided with Bordiga's mechanical Marxism at virtually every level.

Gramsci's loss of optimism concerning revolutionary prospects in Italy after 1920 inevitably produced a marked shift in his theoretical orientation toward the factory councils. The destruction of the Turin movement raised many questions about the efficacy of a "dual power" approach which glorified the spontaneous self-activity of the proletarian masses. While Gramsci continued to push for workers' and peasants' councils as a means of checking party bureaucracy, he openly voiced his criticism (and self-criticism) of *Ordine Nuovo* politics, suggesting above all that the struggles were too confined to the factories. The defeat, he felt, was partly a *strategic* failure: in looking almost exclusively to control of the productive apparatus, the movement essentially abdicated the political terrain—it did not contest for state power, where the bourgeoisie concentrated its instruments of violence, its administrative machinery, even much of its economic strength. Even in the midst of the September occupations, Gramsci observed:

> ...the pure and simple occupation of the factories by the working class, though it *indicates* the extent of proletarian power, does not in itself produce any new, definitive position. Power remains in the hands of capital; armed force remains the property of the bourgeois state; public administration, the distribution of basic necessities, the agencies disposing of credit, the still intact commercial apparatus all remain under the control of the bourgeois

class. The proletariat has no coercive means to break the sabotage of the technicians and white-collar workers, it cannot secure its own supplies of raw materials, it cannot sell the objects it produces. The occupation of the factories in and of itself...cannot be seen as an experience of communist society.[79]

At a time when many plants throughout Piedmont were occupied by workers, political and military power remained firmly in the hands of the bourgeoisie; lacking its own cohesive party and a people's militia, the council movement was more easily encircled and crushed than otherwise would have been the case. As Gramsci put it, "how could the workers at the same time be in the factory and on the streets to defend their conquests, if there is not a state organization to train a loyal and well-positioned armed force, ready in all circumstances and for all eventualities?"[80] As things turned out, the unprecedented political energy that had sustained workers through their heroic actions over many months became rapidly dissipated. The ideological limitations previously mentioned (spontaneism, localism, factory egoism) were thus dialectically intertwined with organizational problems that, even if they were not soluble in the context of the *Biennio Rosso*, yielded some important lessons for the future.

Gramsci's celebrated "turn" toward the party at this juncture was a much less radical departure from his earlier outlook than is commonly assumed. He had for several years carried out his own work within the PSI framework, and even his harsh attacks on the party leadership in 1918-1920 were directed mainly toward internal "renewal" rather than complete abandonment: with the final collapse of the PSI as a viable oppositional force in 1920, however, Gramsci naturally gravitated toward a Comintern-inspired alternative. Moreover, even in the most "syndicalist" moments of his *Ordine Nuovo* involvement, Gramsci never repudiated the concept of a party that would perform certain indispensable political functions: leadership, overall strategic direction, organizational coordination. Still, it is fair to say that during the period of council euphoria the party formation *did* recede into the background, both theoretically and practically. And the bias of Gramsci's writings was toward the primacy of *economics*, toward a view of revolutionary process in which the proletarian struggle for control over production would precede the contestation for state power—not vice-versa, as Bordiga had understood it.[81]

If Gramsci's early references to the role of the party nowhere approach the systematic quality of the *Prison Notebooks*, certain generalizations can nonetheless be derived from the totality of his writings before his imprisonment. Above all, it seems evident that Gramsci fairly consistently adhered to a dialectical conception of the relationship between politics and economics, party and councils, structure and consciousness, suggesting the outlines of a more complex strategic model limited to neither the vanguardist nor spontaneist extremes. In a typical passage, Gramsci wrote that "the various sequences of historical events are not separate and independent; they are moments of a single dialectical process of development in the course of which relations of cause and effect intervene, reverse and interact." He added that "the revolution as the conquest of social power on the part of the proletariat can only be conceived as a dialectical process, in which political power makes possible industrial power and vice-versa."[82] This is not to say that Gramsci always managed to avoid stressing one extreme or the other; but just as he did not ignore the party in his *Ordine Nuovo* writings, neither did he totally jettison his commitment to working-class self-activity, the councils, and the organic transformation of civil society in later phases of work (*including* the prison years).[83]

The concept of a revolutionary party that emerges from Gramsci's dialectical theory, therefore, differs significantly from the centralist model of Lenin of Bordiga. It is tied to an understanding of conflict and change grounded in "natural" processes, where new political formations would have to correspond to emancipatory development within civil society, within the "sphere of production and exchange." Echoing Marx, Gramsci insisted that the party cannot be a Jacobin force standing above these processes, seeking to mold it through external impositon, but must become an "agent" of social transformation insofar as it helps to define and coordinate those historical forces already in motion. The party emerges as a constitutive element of proletarian consciousness, not as a prime mover itself that substitutes for the collective revolutionary will of the masses:

> We must strive to promote the organic creation of a communist party that is not a collection of little dogmatist or Machiavellis, but a party of revolutionary communist action; a party with a precise consciousness of the historical mission of the proletariat and the ability to guide the proletariat...in other words, a party of the

masses who, through their own efforts, are striving to
liberate themselves autonomously from political and
industrial servitude through the organization of the
social economy, and not a party which makes use of the
masses for its own heroic attempts to imitate the French
Jacobins.[84]

Gramsci's theory of a mass party rooted in everyday social life
and local democratic structures, though barely sketched in his
pre-prison writings, reflects a pervasive unity in the overall
development of his political ideas. As will become apparent in the
following chapters, the organic and prefigurative dimension of the
Ordine Nuovo contributions—inseparable from a strategic conception of factory councils and soviets—ultimately converges with
the major themes of the *Prison Notebooks*: philosophy of praxis,
hegemony, mass consciousness, organic intellectuals, and "war of
position."

From this perspective, it would be mistaken to conclude that
the councils simply vanished from Gramsci's later theoretical
commitments—or that he lost sight of their unique historical
impact on European working-class politics. The revolution may
have failed, but the council experiences continued to live on in the
collective consciousness of the workers. Six years after the Turin
defeat, Gramsci would write that

...the occupation of the factories has not been forgotten by
the masses, and this is true not just of the working-class
masses but also of the peasant masses. It was the general
test of the Italian revolutionary class, which as a class
showed that it was mature; that it was capable of
initiative; that it possessed an incalculable wealth of
creative and organizational energies. If the movement
failed, the responsibility cannot be laid at the door of the
working class as such, but at that of the Socialist Party
which failed in its duty; which was incapable and inept;
which was at the tail of the working class not at its
head.[85]

The Turin council movement did in fact give birth to precisely the
kind of legacy Gramsci mentioned; the *Biennio Rosso* became the
watershed of a cohesive and militant working-class culture in
northern Italy, helping to keep alive a socialist presence throughout the Mussolini years. With the collapse of fascism, this tradition
reappeared during 1943-47 in the form of the Committees for
National Liberation (CLNs)—mass-based Resistance organizations

in the factories and communities. It achieved new expression in the late 1960s and early 1970s, when the new radicalism and extra-parliamentary left revived the themes of soviets, workers' control, and democratization through the *comitati di base* (committees of the base) and other grassroots structures.

Hence if council communism was a failure in its own time, this fact surely does not exhaust consideration of its later relevance and impact. Perhaps the most fatal deficiency of traditional council theory, including the Gramscian version, was its exclusive productivism; in this respect the various critiques of *Ordine Nuovo* are valid enough.[86] Yet the general *content* of the issues raised by the factory council struggles—popular self-management, social revolt, prefigurative politics—cannot be reduced to their specific historical *form*. Not only has council communism re-emerged in new and different settings, moving beyond the old productivist boundaries more suitable to early competitive capitalism, it has permeated the entire Western Marxist legacy since the 1920s and thereby contributed to sustaining a critical, non-statist radicalism through the decades of fascism, Stalinism, and the postwar deradicalization of the Communist parties.[87] Gramsci's *Prison Notebooks* bear all the marks of this influence.

Whatever the immediate fate of the factory councils in Turin, the short-lived *Ordine Nuovo* experiment did pose a set of questions virtually unique within Marxism: what are the forms, practices, and attitudes appropriate to the creation of democratic socialist authority relations? What are the constituent elements of a proletarian, non-bureaucratic state? How can revolutionary sensibilities be translated into everyday life? Implicit in the raising of such questions, however unsatisfactory they might have been answered, was the effort to formulate a new kind of politics which, in Gramsci's own work, would not achieve culmination for at least another decade—and then, ironically, under the eye of the fascist censors. Gramsci was to become one of the few Marxists to conceptualize the transition to socialism in non-economistic terms, as a process that would transform social and authority relations as well as the mode of production. The factory councils were simply an initial, partial, and distorted expression of this vision.

FOOTNOTES

1. Paolo Spriano, *The Occupation of the Factories: Italy 1920* (London: Pluto Press, 1975), p. 43. This volume, translated by Gwyn Williams, appeared originally in Italy under the title *L'Occupazione delle fabbriche* (Turin: Einaudi, 1964). Spriano, who is best known for his five-volume history of the Italian Communist Party, has written extensively on the early Turin working-class movement. His two previous volumes were: *Socialismo e classe operaia a Torino dal 1892 al 1913* (Turin: Einaudi, 1958) and *Torino operaia nelle grande guerra* (Turin: Einaudi, 1960).

2. *Proletarian Order*, p. 64.

3. This period also witnessed the appearance of an ultra-centralist vanguardism inspired by Bordiga and his followers. Although the split between Bordiga's group and the council communism identified with Gramsci would leave an enduring imprint on the Italian political landscape, as would the classic Bordiga-Gramsci debates, they shared a common hostility to reformism and parliamentarism that would later make them fleeting allies when, in the midst of the post-council political debris, they joined forces to create the PCI as an alternative to the discredited PSI.

4. It would probably be more accurate to argue that the distinction between these traditions—anarchism, syndicalism, and councilism—was effectively blurred during the *Biennio Rosso* events. More that that, there was a good deal of active cooperation among diverse groups as the struggles unfolded. As Guerin notes, much of the underlying theory of the councils was actually anarchist (or anarcho-syndicalist), with two of the leading Turin militants of this current (Pietro Ferrero and Maurizio Garino) providing contributions. The manifestoes of the council movement were commonly signed by representatives of the different tendencies. See Daniel Guerin, *Anarchism* (New York: Monthly Review, 1970), p. 110.

5. Quoted in Williams, *Proletarian Order*, p. 95, from *L'Ordine Nuovo*, August 14, 1920.

6. Gramsci was very explicit about the debt that the Italian council movement owed to the Russians. Thus: "The idea of the councils system, based upon the power of the working masses around their place of work, around production units, arose as a result of the concrete historical experiences of the Russian proletariat; it is the fruit of the theoretical labors of Russian communist comrades...". "Sindacato e Consigli," November 8, 1919, in *Scritti politici*, p. 263. See also "Syndicalism and the Councils," in *Political Writings-I*, pp. 112-13.

7. Gramsci was familiar with Sorel's work even before the *Biennio Rosso*, having read *Saggi di critica del Marxismo* (translated into Italian in 1903) and other subsequent writings. Sorel was generally well-received by the Italian left—he intersected with Croce, Gentile, Salvemini and even Tasca —and his influence on the young Gramsci, and later the *Ordinovisti*, was substantial. Sorel had stressed in his work a number of themes consonant with Gramsci's interests before 1921, and in some cases well after: the critique of orthodox Marxism, a celebration of heroic proletarian struggles at the point of production, a passionate sense of activism and voluntarism, the importance of ideology and culture in revolutionary politics. Like Mussolini, Gentile, and futurists like Marinetti, Sorel moved rightward in the wake of proletarian defeats.

8. If the overlap between *Ordinovista* theory and syndicalism was considerable, Gramsci himself always self-consciously distanced his viewpoint from that of the syndicalists. He felt that syndicalism lacked a commitment to engage in ongoing political education and real political activity. Thus he wrote that "the error of syndicalism consists...in presenting itself as the initiator of a 'spontaneist,' libertarian tradition" when it was "in fact one of the many disguises of the Jacobin and abstract spirit." He added that "the apoliticism of the apoliticals was merely a degeneration of politics" since "the syndicalists worked outside of reality, and hence their politics were fundamentally mistaken." See "The Conquest of the State," July 12, 1919, in *Political Writings-I*, pp. 74-75. These words could just as easily have been written by Lenin. What both Gramsci and Lenin shared here that set them apart from syndicalism was not only a commitment to overthrow bourgeois state power, but equally a concern for *structural* definition (councils, soviets, party) of the revolutionary process.

9. "Revolutionaries and the Elections," November 15, 1919, in *Political Writings-I*, pp. 128-9 (italics mine).

10. "Il Partito e la rivoluzione," December 27, 1919, in *Scritti politici*, p. 292. Also "The Party and Revolution," in *Political Writings-I*, pp. 142-43.

11. "The Communist Party," September 4, 1920, in *Political Writings-I*, p. 336. Gramsci further added, prophetically, that "the political power of capitalism can only be expressed today in a military *coup d'etat* and the attempt to impose an iron nationalist dictatorship which will drive the brutalized Italian masses to revive the economy by sacking neighboring countries sword in hand." (*Ibid*)

12. "Per un rinnovamento del Partito socialista," May 8, 1920, in *Scritti politici*, pp. 317, 319. See also "Towards a Renewal of the Socialist Party," in *Political Writings-I*, pp. 192, 194.

13. *Ibid*. pp. 316-17 and p. 191.

14. "Il Paritito comunista", October 9, 1920, in *Scritti politici*, p. 365. See also "The Communist Party," *op. cit.* p. 337.

15. *Ibid*.

16. "Syndicalismo e Consigli," November 8, 1919, in *Scritti politici*, p. 260. See also "Syndicalism and the Councils," *Political Writings-I*, p. 109.

17. *Ibid*.

18. *Ibid*.

19. *Ibid*. It should be noted here that for Gramsci the proletarian struggle to attain the mentality of producer was the same thing as the acquisition of class consciousness. This meant that the worker would have to develop not only a broad sense of class identity (entering into "collaboration between manual workers, skilled workers, administrative employees, engineers, and the technical directors") but also of the nation and the world. *Ibid*., pp. 261-62 and 110-111. Gramsci later built upon this theme in the *Prison Notebooks*.

20. "Le Masse e i capi," October 30, 1921, in *Scritti politici*, p. 501. See also "Masses and Leaders," in *Political Writings-II*, p. 76. This essay was written more than a year after the collapse of the Turin council movement, indicating that the defeat of *Ordine Nuovo* did not alter Gramsci's general analysis of the trade unions.

21. "Sindacati e consigli," June 12, 1920, in *Scritti politici*, p. 337. See also "Unions and Councils," in *Political Writings-I*, p. 265. Once again, the influence of Michels was quite evident.

22. *Ibid*., p. 338 and 266. This conflicting nature of councils and unions led Gramsci to conclude in 1920 that the councils should never be subjected to a hierarchical dependency upon the trade-union structure.

23. *Ibid.*, p. 341 and p. 268.

24. "Sindacato e consigli," October 11, 1919, in *Scritti politici*, p. 246. See also "Unions and Councils," in *Political Writings-I*, p. 98. Here once again Gramsci was in agreement with Lenin's critique of trade unionism formulated in *What Is To Be Done?* Lenin wrote that "the history of all countries shows that the working class, exclusively by its own efforts, is able to develop only trade-union consciousness, i.e., the conviction that it is necessary to combine in unions, fight the employers, and strive to compel the government to pass necessary labor legislation." Lenin further contended that the only choice for workers was between bourgeois and socialist ideology, that in fact "the *spontaneous* development of the working-class movement leads to its subordination to bourgeois ideology...for the spontaneous working-class movement is trade-unionism...and trade-unionism means the ideological enslavement of the workers by the bourgeoisie." See Robert C. Tucker, ed., *The Lenin Anthology* (New York: W.W. Norton, 1975), pp. 24, 29. All of this of course consonant with Gramsci's later theory of ideological hegemony spelled out in the *Prison Notebooks*.

25. *Ibid.*, p. 247 and 99.

26. *Ibid.*, p. 247 and pp. 99-100.

27. *Ibid.*, p. 248 and p. 100. Gramsci's use of the term "dictatorship" here must be understood in its generic Marxian sense—that is, as a transitional political form between capitalism and full communism in the sense employed not only by Marx, Engels, and Lenin but also by Kautsky, Luxemburg, and others.

28. Williams, *Proletarian Order*, p. 165. (Italics in original).

29. From *L'Ordine Nuovo*, August 14, 1920, quoted in Lynne Lawner, ed., *The Prison Letters of Antonio Gramsci*, pp. 138-39.

30. For an extensive discussion of the influence of Sorelian syndicalism on the Italian left during the *Biennio Rosso* period, see Enzo Santarelli, *La revisione del marxismo in Italia* (Milano: Feltrinelli, 1977), pp. 80-116.

31. Quoted in Williams, *Proletarian Order*, p. 161.

32. "Democrazia operia," , June 21, 1919, in *Scritti politici*, p. 206. See also "Workers' Democracy," in *Political Writings-I*, p. 65.

33. "La conquista dello stato," July 12, 1919, in *Scritti politici*, pp. 223-24. See also "The Conquest of the State," in *political Writings-I*, p. 76.

34. *Ibid.*, p. 222 and p. 76. Here Gramsci specified that "the proletarian state is embodied in a system of workers', peasants', and soldiers' councils." (*Ibid.*)

35. "Il Consiglio di fabbrica," June 5, 1920, in *Scritti politici*, pp.

333-34. See also "The Factory Council," in *Political Writings-I*, p. 262.

36. *Ibid.*, p. 333 and p. 261.

37. *Ibid.*, p. 335 and p. 263. Gramsci adds that, for this process to be completed, it would have to take on an *international* dimension—i.e., "The workers' state, since it arises in accordance with a given pattern of production, has within it the seeds of its own development, of its own dissolution as a state and of its organic incorporation into a world system." (*Ibid.*)

38. "Sindacato e consigli," *op. cit.*, p. 341. Also "Unions and Council," *op. cit.*, p. 101. Gramsci's reference to "discipline" here and elsewhere in his *Ordine Nuovo* writings clearly should not be confused with any endorsement of Taylorism. He is quite obviously committed to a *different*, non-capitalist, potentially socialist kind of discipline. The definite productivist bias of Gramsci and the *Ordinovisti* during this period has been a source of confusion on this point. Gramsci's "productivism" had more in common with Sorelian syndicalism and other variants of council communism (e.g., Pannekoek) that with Taylorist schemes of capitalist rationalization. For an argument linking the theory of the factory councils and Taylorism, see Martin A. Clark, *Antonio Gramsci and the Revolution that Failed* (New Haven: Yale University Press, 1977), p. 70.

39. "Governing Party and Governing Class," March 6, 1920, in *Political Writings-I*, p. 169. Gramsci hastened to add that "even if it wanted to, the proletariat could never cultivate an exploiter's mentality." (*Ibid.*)

40. *Ibid.*, p. 171.

41. This point is critical for two reasons: first, the trade unions represented only those workers (often not even a majority) who were paid members and, second, the Turin council movement resisted the tendency of other council formations (e.g., in Germany) to build around only the most "advanced"—the most skilled, educated and organized—workers, whose interests were mainly to secure job or professional autonomy in the face of capitalist rationalization. This is not to argue, however, that in *practice* the Turin councils were completely free of this second limitation, with all of its negative political consequence. For an analysis of this phenomenon in the German case, see Sergio Bologna, "Class Composition and the Theory of the Party at the Origin of the Workers-Council Movement," *Telos*, Fall 1972, pp. 3-27.

42. "Sindacati e consigli," *op. cit.*, p. 340. See also "Unions and Councils," *op.cit.*, p. 267. Gramsci stressed that "The Council's

strength consists in the fact that it is in close contact—indeed identified—with the consciousness of the working masses, who are seeking their autonomous emancipation..." (*Ibid.*)

43. "The Programme of the Workshop Delegates," November 8, 1919, in *Political Writings-I*, pp. 115-19.

44. *Ibid.*, p. 122.

45. *Ibid.*, p. 118.

46. *Ibid.*

47. Strangely, while Gramsci's critique of orthodox Marxism has been widely discussed, little attention has been devoted to the analysis of deradicalization implicit throughout his writings, especially in the *Ordine Nuovo* period. Yet Gramsci was a keen observer of the various conservatizing tendencies at work on the European left. Already in late 1919 he prophetically pointed to the integrative tendencies at work in the German council movement, as follows: "German social-democracy effected the paradox of violently forcing the process of the German proletarian revolution into the form of its own organization, believing that it was thereby dominating history. It created *its own* councils, by fiat, and made sure its own men would have a majority on them. It shackled and domesticated the revolution." See "Il Partito e la rivoluzione" December 27, 1919, in *Scritti politici*, p. 292. See also "The Party and the Revolution," in *Political Writings-I*, p. 143.

48. Gramsci's frequent references to "efficiency," "productivity", and "discipline" must be understood within this larger *prefigurative* dimension of his theory. It is thus misleading to suggest that Gramsci was merely interested in the councils as mechanisms for restructuring capitalist management. For this argument, see Enzo Rutigliano, "The Ideology of Labor and Capitalist Rationality in Gramsci," *Telos*, no. 31, Spring 1977, pp. 93-96.

49. Amadeo Bordiga, "Towards the Establishment of Workers' Councils in Italy," (From *Il Soviet*, January 1, 1920), in *Political Writings-I*, pp. 214-15. (italics in original)

50. Bordiga, "Seize Power or Seize the Factory?", February 22, 1920, *op. cit.*, p. 236.

51. "Towards the Establishment of Workers' Councils in Italy", *op. cit.*, p. 216. Bordiga thus looked to the soviet as the true instrument of proletarian "representation," Thus: "The political soviet represents the collective interests of the working class, insofar as this class does not share power with the bourgeoisie, but has succeeded in overthrowing it and excluding it from power. Hence the full significance and strength of the soviet lies not in this

of that structure, but in the fact that it is the organ of a class which is taking the management of society into its own hands." "Is This the Time to Form 'Soviets'?" *op. cit.*, pp. 204-5.

52. "Towards the Establishment of Workers' Councils in Italy," *op. cit.*, pp. 226-27.

53. Angelo Tasca, "Polemics over the *L'Ordine Nuovo* Programme," June 12 and 19, 1920 (from *L'Ordine Nuovo*), in *Political Writings-I*, pp. 273-77.

54. *Ibid.*, p. 281. The Italian usage of the terms "syndicalism" is commonly interchangeable with "trade union movement," and that is Tasca's meaning here.

55. *Ibid.*, July 3, 1920, p. 287.

56. *Ibid.*, p. 285.

57. *Ibid.*, p. 288.

58. Another side of Bordiga's vanguardism was his sectarianism and abstentionism, which even Lenin criticized on the basis (correct, as it turned out) of his reading of a few numbers of *Il Soviet*. See *Left Wing Communism* (New York: International Publishers, 1940), p. 48.

59. "On the *L'Ordine Nuovo* Programme," August 28, 1920, in *Political Writings-I*, p. 294.

60. *Ibid.*, p. 298.

61. The council debates, which were overt and heated during the *Biennio Rosso* but temporarily muted at the founding of the PCI, resurfaced in 1922 and lurked behind every important party debate until fascist repression made such divisions meaningless. It should be noted that, while the party figured more prominently in Gramsci's thought after 1921, he had in mind a *different conception* of the party and of the revolutionary process than did Bordiga. For further discussion of these debates, see: Paolo Spriano, *Gramsci e L'Ordine Nuovo* (Rome: Editori Riuniti, 1965); Franco De Felice, *Serrati, Bordiga, Gramsci* (Bari: De Donato, 1971); Ernesto Ragionieri, "Gramsci e il dibattito teoretico nel movimento operaio internazionale," in *Gramsci e la cultura contemporanea*, vol. I. pp. 101-147; Alastair Davidson, "Gramsci and Lenin," *op. cit.*: and Gwyn Williams, *Proletarian Order*, ch. 9.

62. It has been argued (for example by Gwyn Williams) that the "cult of Gramsci" in Italian Communist historiography has seriously distorted the historical stature of both Gramsci and Bordiga in favor of the former. This is true enough, since Bordiga's catalytic leadership and initiative were indispensable to the formation of the PCI at a moment of debilitating crisis within the Italian left (a crisis, incidentally, which left Gramsci too demoralized to function

politically). Still, it is necessary to distinguish between "political role" and "theoretical legacy," and it is in the latter sphere that Gramsci's influence has been preponderant. Examples of attempts to "rehabilitate" Bordiga include Williams, *Proletarian Order*, epilogue and Andreina de Clementi, *Amadeo Bordiga* (Turin: Einaudi, 1970).

63. For a description of those events, see Spriano, *The Occupation of the Factories*, chs. 1-5 and Gwyn Williams, *Proletarian Order*, ch. 8.

64. "The Two Revolutions," July 3, 1920, in *Political Writings-I*, p. 305. In stressing the need for a complete break with bourgeois institutions, Gramsci ironically appeared closer to Bordiga than to his *Ordinovista* comrades Tasca and Togliatti.

65. Spriano, *The Occupation of the Factories*, p. 65.

66. Quoted in *Ibid.*, p. 66.

67. Quoted in *ibid.*, p. 123.

68. See Williams, *Proletarian Order*, pp. 248-276 and Martin Clark, *Antonio Gramsci and The Revolution that Failed*, ch. 9.

69. Quoted in *The Occupation of the Factories*, p. 109.

70. "The Communist Party," September 9, 1920, in *Political Writings-I*, p. 336.

71. This counters Franklin Adler's argument that Gramsci and the *Ordinovisti* vastly underestimated the strength of Italian capitalism—especially the progressive sector headed by Olivetti and Fiat—to carry out its own program of rationalization in the postwar period. Adler's claim overlooks the important fact that Gramsci's analysis—if not his misplaced optimism—was vindicated by historical events: the absence of a broad social-geographical base and ideological consensus underlying bourgeois democracy in Italy made the liberal wing of the bourgeoisie uniquely vulnerable to both the left and the right. See Franklin Adler, "Factory Councils, Gramsci, and the Industrialists," *Telos* no. 31, spring 1977, especially pp. 70-88.

72. Cammett argues that the inability of *Ordine Nuovo* to build a national presence stemmed more from disunity and fragmentation within the council movement itself than from Piedmont or Turin exceptionalism. It would seem, however, that *both* were factors and that they were mutually reinforcing. See John Cammett, *Antonio Gramsci and the Origins of Italian Communism*, p. 108.

73. This qualification applies to Bordiga's critique of *Ordine Nuovo* for its localism and productivism. In early 1920, in the midst of the council upheavals, Bordiga argued: "It would be better if

these endless and useless adventures that are daily exhausting the working masses were all channeled, merged, and organized into one great, comprehensive upsurge aimed directly at the heart of the enemy bourgeoisie." See "Seize Power or Seize the Factory?", *op. cit.*, p. 236. The point here is that, given their geo-political isolation, the Turinese revolutionaries alone could not possibly have mounted such an attack.

74. See Spriano, *The Occupation of the Factories*, ch. 6.

75. *Ibid.*, p. 85.

76. *Proletarian Order*, p. 253.

77. Speaking from afar, at the Third Comintern congress, Clara Zetkin expressed this matter well: "It was not simply a matter of putting the PSI on trial...I see something else, namely, that the masses who were then in ferment in Italy had made no greater progress than their leaders. Otherwise, comrades, if the masses had really been animated by a revolutionary will, if they had been conscious, they would...have booed offstage their trembling union and political leaders and taken up the fight themselves." Quoted in *The Occupation of the Factories, p. 167.*

78. "The Communist Party," *op. cit.*, pp. 331-32.

79. "The Occupation," September 5, 1920, in *Political Writings-I* p. 327.

80. *Ibid.*, p. 328.

81. See, for example, "Controllo operaio," December 27, 1919, in *Scritti politici*, pp. 411-12.

82. "Two Revolutions", July 3, 1920, in *Political Writings-I*, p. 308. It should be noted that this essay was written *during* the *Biennio Rosso*, not afterwards.

83. While it is true that various Hegelian themes reappeared in the *Prison Notebooks*, the factory councils essentially disappeared from view—for several possible reasons. First, Gramsci probably felt that he had explored this problem adequately and now wanted to devote his limited energy to other issues, such as the party. Secondly, during these years he was increasingly preoccupied with fascism and the instrumental means whereby the Italian left might avert destruction. Finally, insofar as the legacy of defeat still surrounded *Ordine Nuovo* it is probably safe to conjecture that Gramsci wanted to at least temporarily distance himself from the particular forms (councils) associated with that defeat.

84. "Two Revolutions," *op. cit.*, p. 309. Probably Gramsci's best early essay on the role of the mass party was "The Communist Party," *op. cit.*, pp. 330-39.

85. "Once Again on the Organic Capacities of the Working Class", October 1, 1926, in *Political Writings-II*, p. 417.

86. For a critique of Gramsci's productivism in 1918-20, see Clark, *Antonio Gramsci and the Revolution that Failed*, pp. 210-11. Clark suggests that massive unemployment further undermined the productivist schema. (p. 210) See also Richard Gombin, *The Radical Tradition* (London: Methuen and Co., 1978), pp. 91-92.

87. For further development of this point, see Jacoby, *Dialectic of Defeat*, ch. 4.

4 Marxism, Philosophy, and Politics

Gramsci's imprisonment by the Italian fascist regime came almost exactly six years after the collapse of the Turin factory council movement. During the interim, the left opposition had been forced into a defensive position, dispersed, and finally devastated by the fascist advance; Gramsci's arrest in November 1926, coming at a time when Mussolini had consolidated his dictatorship, appeared to symbolize this catastrophic moment. With the Communist Party thrown into disarray—its leading members were either jailed, exiled, or driven underground—the logic of the situation dictated retrenchment and, for theorists like Gramsci, a fundamental rethinking of Marxist categories in the aftermath of failure and defeat. Throughout Europe the two main revolutionary alternatives to the Second International (the Comintern parties and council communism) had themselves run aground, leaving an increasingly bureaucratized Soviet party-state as the global hegemonic agent of "Marxism." While Gramsci's harsh confinement produced the inevitable depression associated with extended personal and political isolation, it also furnished time for reflection. The end result of roughly eight years of such "reflection"—the *Prison Notebooks*—was a monumental attempt to reconceptualize a Marxism that could no longer stand on its old foundations. The hundreds of pages devoted to this project constitute one of the most original contributions to Marxist philosophy in the twentieth century.[1]

While Gramsci's prison writings would have no major impact for at least two decades after his death, owing to difficulties in getting the materials published and then translated, they belong by virtue of their origins, motivation, and spirit to the post-World War I neo-Hegelian revival within Marxism. They reflected all of the influences associated with the first appearances of Western Marxism: German or Italian idealist philosophy, Sorelian syndicalism, "left" or council communism. In Italy the *Notebooks* would be seen as an extension of an indigenous radicalism running from Croce and Labriola through Gentile, Mondolfo, Salvemini, and postwar Marxism; elsewhere they would parallel the theoretical departures of Luxemburg, Korsch, Lukacs, Reich, and the early Frankfurt School, despite the nearly total absence of direct contact or influence in one direction or the other. What all of these traditions and theorists shared was a profound sense of disillusionment with orthodox Marxism and with social-democratic reformism—a disillusionment that sooner or later fueled the search for a new dialectical synthesis. For most, including Gramsci, this search led to the rediscovery of a philosophical discourse that had been unceremoniously jettisoned by Engels, Plekhanov, Kautsky, and other leading purveyors of scientific materialism.[2] Philosophy, notably *Hegelian* philosophy, was now in the process of being rehabilitated. Yet, instead of inspiring a retreat from politics, the rediscovery of philosophy—the return to basic questions of history, knowledge, purpose—actually opened up new ways of looking at politics.[3] If a nascent Western Marxism represented a flight from *economics,* and from the crisis theory associated with deterministic formulas, it emphatically did not signal an escape from politics. Probably in no theorist of the time was the nexus philosophy-politics more salient than in Gramsci.

Borrowing a phrase employed by Labriola, Gramsci commonly referred to Marxism in the *Notebooks* as the "Philosophy of Praxis;" while this may have been a linguistic device to fool the fascist censors, it further revealed the deeply philosophical understanding Gramsci had of his work. Philosophy too was a terrain of class struggle, the necessary source of intellectual and cultural renewal that Marxism would require to gain ascendancy, the very basis of socialist efforts to theoretically critique and transcend bourgeois society. Just as important, it was a source of *internal* criticism and reconstitution within Marxism itself—the methodological underpinnings of a revitalized theory grounded in a new historical awareness: the failure of revolutionary movements in Europe, the rise of fascism and Stalinism, the apparent eclipse of the industrial proletariat as revolutionary subject, the emergence of new ideological mediations. Above all, *Marxist* philosophy was for Gramsci a powerfully transformative enterprise intertwined not only with politics but with historically-constituted social life. It was (at least potentially) the first truly collective or "popular" philosophical synthesis, qualitatively distinct from all past intellectual systems: "At the level of theory the philosophy of praxis cannot be confounded with or reduced to any other philosophy. Its originality lies not only in its transcending of previous philosophies but also and above all in that it opens up a completely new road, renewing from head to toe the whole way of conceiving philosophy itself."[4]

The "Leitmotif" of Gramsci's Thought

It is probably safe to say that the young Gramsci was only tangentially concerned with philosophical issues, despite the intensity of his commitment to certain Hegelian themes and to refining the Crocean idealism he had inherited. Even this limited interest was not primarily centered in the Marxian paradigm; it was more or less restricted, as we have seen, to the boundaries of Italian neo-Hegelianism. During the subsequent 1919-1926 period, moreover, Gramsci was naturally consumed with more immediate political involvements, so that he did not return to extended philosophical discourse until well after his arrest, in the late 1920s and early 1930s. This renewed effort in the prison writings differed significantly from the initial explorations in two vital respects: it was far more *systematic,* and it was more clearly directed toward restoring the theoretical unity of *Marxism*—i.e., toward reconstituting the "philosophy of praxis" on new foundations. Whatever its ultimate flaws, Gramsci's intellectual project in the *Prison Notebooks* was an attempt to carry out a kind of "philosophical revolution."[5]

Ironically, what made such a "revolution" in thought even conceivable was the sense of ambiguity that Gramsci had come to express toward Marxism itself. Of course in *political* terms he was a *Marxist* by 1920-21, and perhaps earlier, but this did not keep him from having serious *theoretical* reservations which he was forced to repress throughout the PCI years but which, given the space for contemplation in prison, he finally articulated with great lucidity. His sentiment that Marxism was profoundly incomplete and one-sided—a theoretical system badly in need of overhaul—was at the same time counter-balanced by his recognition of it as the most powerful philosophy of the historical period since "the philosophy of praxis presupposes all this cultural past: Renaissance and Reformation, German philosophy and the French Revolution, Calvinism and English classical economics, secular liberalism and this historicism which is at the root of the whole modern conception of life."[6] The problem was that the actually existing Marxism associated with both the Second and Third Internationals was marred by a crude scientism and an equally primitive economic determinism. In the *Notebooks* Gramsci set out to correct this fatal deficiency through a reincorporation of the dialectic, much along the lines of Lukacs and Korsch in another context.

This return to a dialectical philosophy—to a transcendence of the antinomies idealism-materialism that Marx was the first to *pose*—constituted the pervasive "Leitmotif" of Gramsci's work. In outlining the methodology needed for evaluating the contributions of a theorist, Gramsci emphasized that the "Search for the Leitmotif, for the rhythm of the thought as it develops, should be more important than that for single casual affirmations and isolated aphorisms."[7] When applied to Gramsci's own theory, we arrive at a dialectical unity wherein a series of dualisms have been conceptually integrated within the framework of transformative collective action (i.e., praxis): philosophy and politics, theory and history, subject and object, consciousness and social being.

Insofar as previous philosophies (Greek idealism, Catholicism, French materialism) had asserted the primacy of one dimension over the other, they simply reproduced what Gramsci called an "empty metaphysics" that could never furnish the basis of revolutionary action. On the idealist side there was Croce, whom Gramsci criticized for adhering to a "pure conceptual dialectic" devoid of concrete historical substance; on the materialist side there was Bukharin, whose sterile "laws of causality" and search for a system of predictable empirical regularities led him to an antihistorical "flat evolutionism". With this critique as a point of departure, Gramsci looked to the dialectic as a corrective to both speculative idealism and mechanical determinism, since neither could capture *history* in its rich flow and complexity. He observed that when Marx took over the dialectic from Hegel, he did not *substitute* a materialist for an idealist dialectic as was commonly supposed but actually integrated the social or "material" dimension into the Hegelian system—a fundamentally different process.

In this fashion Marx had reunited philosophy and politics.

But the historical legacy of European Marxism before World War I unfortunately diverged from its origins, the result in great measure of Engels' unique influence on German Social Democracy after Marx's death. "Philosophy" was abandoned in favor of "science," leading to a rather strict distinction between "utopian" and "scientific" socialism and to a simplistic reconceptualization of the dialectic itself contained in the Engelsian formula of a materialist or "natural" dialectic. For better or worse, scientific materialism gained widespread acceptance beginning in the 1880s, in part because Marxists desperately sought a firm methodological grounding as a counter to religious or metaphysical ideologies which had so thoroughly shaped popular consciousness. What often emerged out of these early philosophical struggles was a Marxist epistemology that reduced the sphere of human ideas and consciousness to mere reflections of objective historical forces or "economic determinants". The return to a mechanical "base-superstructure" model within orthodox Marxism would have pernicious theoretical and political consequences. In Gramsci's words, "The claim, presented as an essential postulate of historical materialism, that every fluctuation of politics and ideology can be presented and expounded as an immediate expression of the structure, must be contested in theory as primitive infantilism, and combated in practice with the authentic testimony of Marx, the author of concrete political and historical works."[8]

Following the spirit of Labriola, Gramsci insisted that the all-consuming philosophical debates around idealism versus materialism and voluntarism versus determinism were sterile and misleading; from the standpoint of constructing a praxis-oriented theory, this conventional dualism would have to be overcome. Labriola perhaps more than any other theorist was able to grasp the instinctive *originality* of Marxist philosophy in its dialectical transcendence of *all* traditional intellectual systems. He did not choose to compensate for the idealism of "pure intellectuals" with an equally one-dimensional and "banal materialism." Thus: "Labriola distinguishes himself from both currents by his affirmation (not always, admittedly, unequivocal) that the philosophy of praxis is an independent and original philosophy which contains in itself the elements of further development, so as to become, from an interpretation of history, a general philosophy. This is the direction in which one must work, developing Antonio Labriola's position..."[9] The implications of this insight for Gramsci's future work would be enormous.

Yet Labriola's philosophical outlook was, as Gramsci hints in the above passage, ambiguous and at times even contradictory; the "philosophy of praxis" was itself infused with a persistent scientific bias. The more compelling frame of reference for Gramsci's interpretation of Marx was based upon memory and what little of Marx's writings was available to him.[10] Without question Gramsci's route to a revitalized Marxism was through a return to Marx himself, to a Marx who did not overturn Hegel but who appropriated and enriched Hegelian philosophy. In other works, Gramsci implicitly looked to the *critical* side of Marx in which science and philosophy, material conditions and consciousness were dialectically merged to produce a new totality. It is this spirit of Marx which pervaded the *Prison Notebooks*. Reflecting on the birth of Marxist philosophy, Gramsci wrote:

> Hegel, half-way between the French Revolution and the Restoration, gave dialectical form to the two moments of the life of thought, materialism and spiritualism, but his synthesis was 'a man walking on his head.' Hegel's successors destroyed this unity and there was a return to materialist systems on the one side and spiritualist on the other. The philosophy of praxis, through its founder, relived all this experience of Hegelianism, Feuerbachianism and French materialism, in order to reconstruct the synthesis of dialectical unity, 'the man walking on his feet.'[11]

Gramsci noted that precisely the kind of rupture which afflicted Hegelianism would occur later within Marxism, thus robbing the theory of that very subversive character which made it unique.

In constructing this "synthesis of dialectical unity," Marx was able to locate the essence of historical change in concrete social and economic forces which achieve political expression through the mediation of consciousness. He dispensed with simple, mechanical cause-and-effect relations. Committed to the notion of proletarian self-emancipation—to the Hegelian vision of a "universal class"— Marx could not possibly have viewed history (the transition to socialism) as a natural process unfolding apart from purposive human activity. Consciousness could never be understood as the direct reflection of objective conditions; it was, instead, the crucial mediation between human activity and nature, between politics and the sphere of production. To the extent that Marx regarded production as his central theoretical category, human actors were perceived as an integral part of that world, as creatures of it, rather than as standing apart from it. This epistemology, which still owed much to the German idealist tradition, clearly typified Marx's early work; exactly how much it shaped his later writings is a matter of debate, but undeniable traces can be found in the *Grundrisse* and *Capital.*[12]

At the same time, whatever Marx's seminal contributions to Western philosophy, it would be misleading to suggest that orthodox Marxism had no antecedents in Marx's own theory, or that it shared none of the epistemological assumptions that entered into his later writings. Elements of *continuity* in nineteenth century Marxism can be readily identified. I have devoted attention to the "scientific" component of Marx's thought (and not merely of Engels') in chapter one. It was this dimension which increasingly prevailed over and submerged the "critical" tendency in Marx's post-1848 work, revealing a quasi-positivist theorist who sought to discover the "laws" of capitalist development, who believed it was possible to specify the objective determinants of revolution, who at times downplayed the role of political will and mass consciousness in favor of historical "necessity."[13] Marx's obsession with the sphere of production and work was, moreover, tied to an understanding of "science" that was patterned after the natural sciences. From this viewpoint, *Capital* was a volume that itself remained tied to the logic of capitalist development, for its positivist emphasis upon laws of economic motion ultimately precluded any real dialectical approach.[14] Marx's most important work, therefore, contained a huge gap between the analysis of existing social reality and the conceptual framework required for its transcendence, i.e., for class struggle leading to revolutionary transformation. This flaw necessarily damaged the theoretical coherence of classical Marxism.[15]

Gramsci's "return to Marx" in the *Prison Notebooks* was accordingly as much a projection of his own philosophical sensibilities onto Marx as it was the fresh rediscovery of a dialectical philosophy within the general corpus of Marx's writings. It would be more accurate to say that there were *parallels* between Gramsci's "philosophy of praxis" and the critical side of Marx, which Gramsci could have construed as the totality of classical Marxism given his limited sources. Yet the young Gramsci was hardly unmindful of Marx's scientific bent and its political implications:

his analysis of the Bolshevik conquest of power as a "Revolution against *Capital*," it will be remembered, portrayed the Russian events as overturning the mechanistic, ahistorical premises of Marx's great opus. Interestingly enough, Gramsci chose to ignore or gloss over this positivist component of Marx in the *Notebooks*, perhaps because he was now more anxious to consolidate his Marxist lineage. Thus his devastating attacks on crude materialism and scientism were reserved for the orthodox Marxists and later scientific materialists like Bukharin. The point here is that, whatever its antecedents, the "philosophy of praxis" which Gramsci formulated while in prison was more original than probably even he realized.

The Crisis of Italian Idealism

Having been socialized into the intellectual world through Crocean philosophy, Gramsci became increasingly uncomfortable with it after 1920—especially as Croce himself drifted away from socialism and some of his disciples (including Gentile) began to embrace fascism as the new expression of collective political will. The *Prison Notebooks* signaled Gramsci's final break with his Italian idealist heritage, though its guiding themes would remain deeply embedded in his work. After recognizing Croce's powerful contributions to Italian philosophy and to his own development, Gramsci would now explicitly distance himself from Croce's "pure" intellectualism and his "contemplative" attitude toward theory and politics. The prison writings can be understood as an attempt by Gramsci to wrestle with the ghost of Croce, to work through the idealist tradition with the aim of going beyond it by integrating it into a larger philosophical synthesis. Gramsci's relationship to Croce thus paralleled Marx's to Hegel: in each case a dialectic of consciousness was initially adopted and then reconstituted on social foundations, allowing for a historicized conception of revolutionary politics, or praxis. If Marx seized hold of the "left" tendency in German philosophy, exposed its contradictions, and pushed beyond its limits, Gramsci likewise came to view his task as the radicalization of an Italian idealism that had fallen into deep crisis after World War I.

Gramsci saw in both Hegel and Croce the necessary point of departure for the philosophy of praxis, since it was they (each in their own cultural context) who most fully elaborated the basic categories—dialectic, totality, consciousness, collective will—of this new synthesis. They had discovered the essence of a totally new *conception* of philosophy, even if they had failed to historicize it adequately. Thus Gramsci observed that "In the history of philosophical thought Hegel represents a chapter on his own, since in his system, in one way or another, even in the form of a 'philosophical romance,' one manages to understand what reality is." From this angle, Marxism constitutes a "reform and a development of Hegelianism," transforming it into the most conscious expression of historical contradictions."[16] For Gramsci, then, there could be no doubt that "Hegelianism is (relatively speaking) the most important of philosophical motivations of our author [Marx], particularly because it attempted to go beyond the traditional conceptions of idealism and materialism in a new synthesis...which represents a world-historical moment of philosophical inquiry."[17]

Yet the new, praxis-defined philosophy would require for its realization the ultimate dissolution of the Hegelian system, the eclipse of a German idealism that had encountered its historical limits. In Gramsci's words: "From the disintegration of Hegelianism derives the beginning of a new cultural process, different in character from its predecessors, a process in which practical movement and theoretical thought are united (or are trying to unite through a struggle that is both theoretical and practical)."[18]

From the viewpoint of the young Marx, Hegel's thought had become abstract in the sense that it was detached from real historical forces; the projection of history as unfolding collective self-consciousness tore philosophy from its worldly object, thereby destroying its *transformative* possibilities. Marx's corrective led not to a rejection of consciousness but to its grounding in the interplay between material (class) forces, consciousness, and political struggle. It was not only through productive activity but also within the realm of politics (praxis) that Marx believed human beings would achieve the fullest self-expression, insofar as the transition to a communist society would involve more than the maturation of economic conditions: it would ultimately require a class-based *political* revolution. Thus by reducing an understanding of the social world to the level of mental processes, to "mere phantoms," Hegel had negated the possibility of analyzing and acting upon concrete developments and events. His contemplative approach robbed history of its political dimension even as it affirmed the power of human consciousness and will. For Marx, therefore, the function of philosophy was to provide a logical framework in which the social division of labor could be comprehended in the very process of its being transformed—in which the knowledge of history was simultaneously an awareness of how to overcome alienation—as part of a dialectical totality.

Gramsci's critique and transcendence of Croce more or less followed this pattern. Like Hegel, Croce had conceptualized historical development as the unfolding of self-consciousness, as creative human will overpowering the material world. Croce's analysis of nineteenth century Italy, for example, focused almost exclusively upon what he called the "ethico-political" sphere—that is, upon transformations at the level of politics, ideology and culture.[19] It was through his prolific work that Hegel was finally "translated" into the Italian context. Croce's thought was vital to Gramsci's intellectual formation in several important areas: against traditional philosophy he affirmed the role of the dialectic; against Catholicism he embraced a secular humanism; and against the fetishism of science he formulated a powerful critique of positivism. Above all, Croce's vital contribution to the study of Italian history—his brilliant insights into the ideological or consensual underpinnings of politics—would be incorporated into Gramsci's theory of "hegemony" in the *Prison Notebooks*. Finally, Gramsci admired Croce for his great literary success, for his tremendous impact upon the national culture, for the style of his prose which he compared to that of Manzoni. In one of his prison letters Gramsci wrote: "...one must remember that Croce's thought does not always appear as a massive, indigestible system. His greatest quality had always been the ability to disseminate his ideas about the world in a series of brief, unpedantic writings, which the public readily absorbs as 'good sense' and 'common sense'."[20] It seems that on the whole Gramsci found in Croce an ever-present source of critical inspiration—a counterpoint to the mechanical Marxism that permeated the European left.

Imposing as Croce's intellectual presence might have been, Gramsci found it much too one-dimensional. The key problem was that Croce's theory of history scarcely took into account the role of material conditions, social structure, or class forces; the dialectic worked mainly through changes within the "superstructure" (notably political, cultural, and intellectual leadership), and indeed this seemed applicable to the post-Risorgimento period that occupied most of Croce's attention. Despite a brief flirtation with Marxism, Croce had in fact dismissed the materialist conception of history as a "theological" approach that worshipped economics as a kind of "hidden god".

Gramsci's reaction against this philosophical idealism—contained in his *Il materialismo storico e la filosofia di Benedetto Croce* and scattered elsewhere throughout the *Notebooks* and his letters—indicated a pronounced contempt for Croce's simplistic understanding of Marxist theory. Thus Gramsci pointed out how absurd it was that "Croce dares to maintain that historical materialism marks a return to a kind of medieval theology and to pre-Kantian and pre-Cartesian philosophy. This is really astonishing and makes one wonder whether he is not perhaps, in spite of his Olympian serenity, dozing off a little too often, more than Homer did." [21] More specifically, Gramsci characterized Croce's work as "speculative history" in that it completely overlooked both the moment of class struggle and the coercive dimension of state power—elementary premises of Marxism but apparently foreign to Crocean philosophy. Croce's "pure conceptual dialectic" embraced a certain utopianism:[22] by detaching consciousness from material conditions, ideology from class forces, and subject from object it in effect treated the ethico-political sphere "as if it had just appeared from the blue." It was ironically Croce himself who had adopted a religious frame of mind:

> Croce is so involved in his own method and speculative language that these are the only standards he can use. When he writes that in the philosophy of praxis the structure is like a hidden god, this would hold good if the philosophy of praxis were speculative philosophy and not absolute historicism—an historicism that is completely free from all transcendental and theological vestiges.[23]

Gramsci defined Crocean philosophy as "speculative" not only because it placed great emphasis on the ethico-political realm but because it lost sight of the dialectical relationship between this and other aspects of the social totality. In other words, Croce was mired in an extreme subjectivist idealism. The advantage of Marxism was that it could in principle assimilate the ethico-political dimension, whereas the speculative approach could never escape its flat one-sidedness; as a "form of anti-historicist abstraction" that dissolved history into an inert series of concepts and categories,[24] Croceanism represented a new kind of spiritualism and, finally, a hostility toward politics. At one point in the *Notebooks* Gramsci suggested the possibility of an "anti-Croce" critique much along the lines of Engels' *Anti-Duhring*.[25] It turned out that the very quality which bestowed upon Croce his great influence was simultaneously linked to the intractable contradictions of his idealist philosophy: as a leading intellectual hero-figure Croce could not escape the elitist, anti-popular implications of his own stature.

As Gramsci mockingly noted: "It is evident from his writings that Croce is justly proud of his position as leader of world culture and acknowledges the responsibility that entails. His work is clearly directed toward an international elite."[26]

The obsolescence of Crocean philosophy was, in Gramscian terms, most visibly illuminated by its marked inability to comprehend the ebb and flow of organized politics, by its near silence concerning the development of concrete political formations. In this sense Croce's emphasis on the ethico-political was too confined to the momentary, diffuse expressions of "will" and "passion". Italian idealism consequently failed to generate a social or political theory relevant to the explosive historical changes after 1914: World War I, the breakdown of *trasformismo*, the upheavals of the *Biennio Rosso*, and the rise of fascism. There could be no compelling analysis of organized violence and conflict in such a theory. For Gramsci, "Croce's conception of politics/passion excludes parties, since it is not possible to think of an organized and permanent passion. Permanent passion is a condition of orgasm and spasm, which means operational incapacity. It excludes parties, and excludes every plan of action worked out in advance. However, parties exist and plans of action are worked out, put into practice, and are often successful to a remarkable extent."[27] Here Croce's view of politics reproduced many of the contradictions associated with Sorel's notion of "myth." For Croce, however, this flaw stemmed from the most fundamental of all his philosophical errors—the failure to incorporate a material or economic component into his historical methodology. Thus: "Politics becomes permanent action and gives birth to permanent organizations precisely insofar as it identifies itself with economics." Gramsci argued that while politics is in certain vital respects distinct from economics, the two realms are also integrally linked on the terrain of class struggle and therefore cannot be understood independently of each other.[28] In developing as a reaction against the economism of orthodox Marxism, therefore, Croce's particular form of historicism went too far in denying the role of productive forces.

In the end, Croce's moralistic and detached liberalism turned to conservatism while the idealist tradition which he galvanized— at one point a catalyst behind the evolution of a distinct Italian Marxism—disintegrated as an intellectual and cultural force in its own right. It became confined to a small aristocratic elite of intellectuals, many of them Southern in origin, who were harshly antagonistic to both Catholicism and Marxism. Meanwhile, Gramsci, having absorbed into his own philosophy of praxis what was most progressive and critical in Croceanism, set out on a completely different path. But still another set of philosophical roadblocks remained.

Bukharin and the Materialist Impasse

If German and Italian idealism first paved the way for Marxism but then deteriorated as an autonomous philosophical expression, Marxism itself—in a valiant effort to appropriate a "materialist" dialectic—retreated into its own narrow, insular shell. Instead of fulfilling the Hegelian and early Marxian promise of a new (revolutionary) philosophical synthesis, orthodox Marxism embellished a scientific materialism that simply repeated the flaws of traditional metaphysical philosophy. Hence the critique that was levelled against Hegelianism and Croceanism could equally well have been applied to the dominant tendency within Marxism itself. In gradually slipping back into a crude determinism, orthodox theory in effect lost its critical edge and its transformative content—indeed its very *identity* as an emancipatory philosophy distinct from all preceding systems of thought. In Europe, as we have seen, this positivized Marxism corresponded to a phase of relative political stability between the early 1880s and World War I. While it had origins in the writings of the later Marx, it realized its fullest expression in the work of Engels, Kautsky, and Plekhanov—as well as the Lenin of *Materialism and Empiriocriticism*—and would ultimately constitute the main foundations of Soviet Marxism ("dialectical materialism") after the Bolshevik consolidation of power.[29]

To a greater extent than his precursor Labriola, Gramsci had taken the lead within Italian Marxism against this form of materialism. It is enough to recall his early (1918) essay "Revolution against *Capital*" in which he celebrated the Russian events as a triumph of political voluntarism over the stale objectivist formulas derived from orthodox theory. From the outset Gramsci had rejected the neo-Kantian distinction between fact and value, subject and object, philosophy and history; the key to understanding historical process was not the uncovering of formal rules and regularities but rather the grasping of a collective self-consciousness in the absence of which events lose all meaning. Yet it was not until his prison writings that Gramsci would have the opportunity to systematically elaborate his philosophical critique of materialism, which he did with an effectiveness rarely equalled.

In the *Prison Notebooks* he denied more firmly than ever that a revolutionary theory could be built upon materialist premises, opposing to it an active, political conception of knowledge necessary for praxis.

The main thrust of Gramsci's critique in the *Notebooks* was directed against the leading Soviet (and Comintern) theorist Nikolai Bukharin, who in his introductory "texts" presented Marxism as a science that could explain historical change through a formal system of causal laws.[30] Bukharin undertook one of the initial post-revolutionary efforts to codify Marxist philosophy into a logical framework possessing many of the attributes of the natural sciences. His "Manual", as Gramsci referred to it, sought to root the dialectic in objective social processes that were viewed as unfolding independently of human perception and intentionality; it affirmed the external reality of the "thing in itself," laying claim to a scientific rigor and precision that would allow prediction of events. Within this schema human action was viewed as the product of historically-determined patterns, the expression of social forces that permit only the most limited influence of subjective factors: ideology, consciousness, political will.

From Gramsci's point of view, this kind of epistemology merely became a substitute for the concrete historical analysis of contending class and political forces; it assumed, on the basis of formal a priori statements, what needed to be explored in *specific* contexts where economics, politics, and culture merge into complex relationships. By ignoring the subjective dimension of this totality, Bukharin forgot that "Reality does not exist on its own, in and for itself, but only in an historical relationship with the men who modify it, etc." Gramsci likened Bukharin's materialist fetishism of the objective world to a mystical faith in an "unknown God" which has supernatural powers to manipulate forces controlling human behavior. Under such conditions history, social conflict, and dialectical change are all dissolved into a false universality. Insofar as "objectivity" possesses any real meaning, it would have to be expressed through the world-historical struggle for a classless society, the realization of which would for the first time unify subject and object:

> Objective always means 'humanly objective' which can be held to correspond exactly to 'historically subjective,' in other words, objective would mean 'universal subjective.' Man knows objectively insofar as knowledge is real for the whole human race *historically* unified in a

single unitary cultural system. But this process of historical unification takes place through the disappearance of the internal contradictions which tear apart human society...There exists therefore a struggle for objectivity (to free oneself from partial and fallacious ideologies) and this struggle is the same as the struggle for cultural unification of the human race.[31]

To the extent that Gramsci's theory of knowledge incorporated the active, conscious, political dimension of human existence, an understanding of social activity would have to take into account the whole sphere of "immediate particulars" (everyday feelings, sentiments, needs, passions) that tends to resist and break through abstract categories of analysis. The major problem with statistical laws, even assuming such laws could be established, is that they negate the spontaneous element of historical flux. For Gramsci, the search for highly regularized patterns of behavior was viable "in the science and art of politics only so long as the great masses of the population remain (or are at least reputed to remain) essentially passive, in relation to the questions which interest historians and politicians."[32] Bukharin's entire project, therefore, rested upon essentially static premises.

In fact, Gramsci rejected the very *possibility* of constructing a scientific Marxism based upon the formal, statistical properties of disciplines like physics, chemistry, and astronomy. If Marxism were to be understood as the "science" of capitalist development, what "laws" had this science actually produced in nearly a century? Gramsci was rather amused by Bukharin's scientific pretensions, which he equated with the most hollow type of theoretical formalism: "The so-called laws of sociology which are assumed as laws of causation have no causal value: they are almost always tautologies and paralogisms. Usually they are no more than a duplicate of the observed fact itself. The only novelty is the collective name given to a series of 'petty facts'."[33] Contained in Gramsci's philosophy of praxis was a critical alternative to this type of methodology. The theorist would be better advised to identify certain broad "tendencies" at work in a particular society with the aim of facilitating the most effective political intervention. Viewed from this angle, theory and history, theory and strategy would have to be dialectically interwoven. Hence even "objective" conditions would only become historically intelligible through the unfolding of human beings, given shape, and applied to specific political outcomes.

Gramsci argued that Bukharin's scientism worked to sever this dialectical relationship: above all it divorced theory from history by raising the formal techniques and methods of analysis to an independent status, as ends in themselves detached from their substantive focus. If bourgeois society were to be not only analyzed but also overturned, then the task of theory must be to unravel the complex diversity and specificity of historical processes. Bukharin's quest for general principles underlying an imputed universal order would therefore necessarily lose in political relevance what it might have gained in logical clarity. In standing "above" the tension and conflict of mundane social processes, the theorist necessarily loses sight of those very historical contradictions which shape knowledge and vision. Gramsci noted that Marx never distinguished between the theoretical and historical-practical components of his own work. He might have cited Marx's contention in *Theses on Feuerbach* that "The question whether objective truth can be attributed to human thinking is not a theoretical but a practical question. In practice man must prove the truth, that is, the reality and power, the this-sidedness of his thinking. The dispute over the reality or non-reality of thinking isolated from practice is a purely scholastic question."[34]

There was a remarkable similarity here between Gramsci's critique of Bukharin's "Manual" and Korsch's attack on orthodox Marxism in the early 1920s. Korsch had insisted that Marxist theory was itself embedded in history and therefore reflected all of the distorted, partial, contradictory aspects of capitalist development; the theoretical project could not be abstracted from its specific referents in time and place. The implication was that theoretical concepts (forces of production, class, alienation, revolution) have no timeless meanings and therefore must be reconstituted in accordance with changing historical conditions. As Korsch put it: "To accord theory and autonomous existence outside of the objective movement of history would obviously be neither materialist, nor dialectical in the Hegelian sense; it would simply be an idealist metaphysic." He adds: "For example, many bourgeois interpreters of Marx and some later Marxists thought they were able to distinguish between the historical and the theoretical-economic material in Marx's major work *Capital*; but all they proved by this is that they understood nothing of the real method of Marx's critique of political economy."[35]

The historicist emphasis in Gramsci's Marxism also denied a separation of the universal and concrete elements of theory: this was one Hegelian premise he never abandoned. Paralleling Korsch's thought, Gramsci wrote: "It is not enough to know the *ensemble* of relations as they exist at any given time as a given system. They must be known genetically, in the movement of their formation. For each individual is the synthesis not only of existing relations, but of the history of these relations."[36] Efforts to construct logically tight formal models mystify or occlude historical processes rather than illuminate them by ignoring the uniqueness of class and political configurations—and the way they are mediated by ideological and cultural influences—even *within* the parameters of capitalist development. Such efforts also overlooked the fact that intellectual activity (including its Marxist expression) is itself part of a complex history shaped by particular traditions and limitations. The very notion of a "pure" theory set off from the world surrounding it is nothing but a fiction, since "the philosophy of praxis is an expression of historical contradictions, and indeed their most complete, because most conscious, expression: this means that it too is tied to 'necessity' and not yet to a 'freedom' which does not exist and, historically, cannot yet exist."[37] For Gramsci, then, "scientific" attempts to purge Marxism of its historicist dimension—of its intimate relationship to concrete social forces—could only render the theory uselessly abstract:

> It has been forgotten that in the case of a very common expression (historical materialism) one should put the accent on the first term—'historical'—and not on the second, which is of metaphysical origin. The philosophy of practice is absolute 'historicism,' the absolute secularization and earthiness of thought, and absolute humanism of history. It is along this line that one must trace the thread of a new conception of the world.[38]

Insofar as Bukharin's abstract formalism served to detach theory from its historical object, the role of the theorist was likewise transformed. Gramsci claimed that the theorist whose function is shaped by a scientific ethos, or by the search for sociological laws and mathematical formulas, sooner or later adopts an instrumental attitude and loses an understanding of the rhythm and flow of mass politics. As the reverse side of speculative idealism, scientific materialism instills in its adherents a disintegrated, contemplative, elitist orientation antithetical to the sphere of political action. Thus:

> Indeed in politics the assumption of the law of statistics

as an essential law operating of necessity is not only a scientific error, but becomes a practical error of action. What is more it favors mental laziness and superficiality in political programmes. It should be observed that political action tends precisely to arouse the masses from passivity...So how can it be considered a law of sociology?[39]

Gramsci went on to suggest that the sociological assumptions required for such a positivized Marxism would be increasingly undermined by countervailing tendencies within advanced capitalism, since "With the extension of mass parties and their organic coalescence with the intimate (economic-productive) life of the masses themselves, the process whereby popular feeling is standardized ceases to be mechanical and causal (that is produced by the condition of environmental factors and the like) and becomes conscious and critical."[40]

Bukharin's objectivist philosophy thus failed to escape the metaphysical pitfalls of pre-Marxian systems. It naively took for granted the existence of a natural world independent of conscious human purpose—a world ostensibly created prior to human perception which develops according to its own internal logic, where "reality" is an immutable, overpowering force that people internalize as part of everyday "common sense." Once the subjective realm is disposed of in this way, faith in the predictability of historical events can be embraced with a kind of religious passion. The commitment to socialist transformation, insofar as it was retained, amounted to accurately foreseeing the moments or phases of transition through an understanding of the structural development of capitalism. Gramsci viewed the Marxist impulse toward scientific prediction—linked as it generally was to a crude and messianic "crisis" scenario—as a fatalistic delusion that destroyed political initiative, which it did in the Italian Socialist Party before 1920. In Italy it was Antonio Graziadei who took up the banner of scientific Marxism, which many theorists (within the PCI as well as the PSI) believed was appropriate to the new technological era. Gramsci thought that this was simply an ill-designed effort to legitimate Marxism, a sad pretense at resolving concrete political tasks by means of "scientific analysis". Thus:

The situating of the problem as a search for laws and for constant, regular and uniform lines is connected to a need, conceived in a somewhat puerile and ingenious way, to resolve in preemptory fashion the practical problem of the predictability of historical events...In reality one can foresee only the struggle, but not the concrete moments of the struggle, which can but be the results of opposing forces in continuous movement, which are never reduced to fixed qualities since within them quantity is continuously becoming quality. In reality one can 'foresee' to the extent that one acts, to the extent that one applies a voluntary effort and therefore contributes concretely to creating the result 'foreseen,' Prediction reveals itself thus not as a scientific act of knowledge, but as the abstract expression of the effort made, the practical way of creating a collective will.[41]

The "future", then, can be nothing more than the application of human will to the historical material that is available; it is a complex interplay of subjective and objective forces. A methodological emphasis on prediction blocks imaginative foresight by restricting political activity to a preconceived "effective reality" for, as Gramsci wrote, "Only the man who wills something strongly can identify the elements which are necessary to the realization of his will." Prediction "precisely acquires that importance in the living brain of the individual who makes the prediction and who by the strength of his will makes it come true."[42] Gramsci therefore had in mind something both more modest and more ambitious than the positivist theories of prediction rooted in statistical probability; by "prediction" he meant "seeing the present and the past clearly as movement," not in any objective or final sense but as part of a collective political struggle to achieve certain (revolutionary) historical objectives.[43] Without this element of political consciousness, forecasting the future is nothing but an empty exercise by those whom Gramsci called "Byzantine theorists"—Marxists who valued theory for its own sake, as a "pastime"—with no action referents.

In its uncritical appropriation of science, technology, and "material forces", the positivist Marxism epitomized by Bukharin's *Historical Materialism* had in effect capitulated to the dominant forms of bourgeois thought and culture. From a Gramscian perspective it was natural to find "dialectical materialism" equated with "common sense".[44] This was a step backward even from the late Marx and Engels, and explains why Gramsci saw in scientism "transcendental" residues which Marxism would have to *combat*. At no point did Gramsci define his own philosophy as "materialist" and, like Marx, never did he use the term "dialectical materialism" to characterize his methodology. The originality of Gramsci's philosophy therefore lies not in its materialism but rather in its struggle for a dialectical synthesis of theory and history, philosophy and politics.

Toward A Philosophy of Praxis

Gramsci's near-obsession with philosophical issues in the *Prison Notebooks* grew out of a commitment that would be central to Western Marxism: to restore unity and dynamism to a Marxist theory that had by the 1920s become deadened and conservative. This task required rediscovery of the *critical* side of Marxism with its emphasis on an indeterminate history, class consciousness, and above all for Gramsci, politics. If classical Marxism was in fact the product of "the highest development of culture" for its time— classical German philosophy, English classical economics, and French political radicalism—then it can be said that Gramsci's thought expressed those very tendencies as they were filtered and passed on via Marx, Croce, Sorel, Labriola, and Lenin. The hybrid result was an unsystematic but new dialectical philosophy:

> The true fundamental...significance of the dialectic can only be grasped if the philosophy of praxis is conceived as an integral and original philosophy which opens up a new phase of history and a new phase in the development of world thought. It does this to the extent that it goes beyond both traditional idealism and traditional material-ism, philosophies which are expressions of past societies, while retaining their vital elements. If the philosophy of praxis is not considered except in subordination to another philosophy, then it is not possible to grasp the new dialectic, through which the transcending of old philosophies is effected and expressed.[45]

Human knowledge was for Gramsci simultaneously a product of objective structural forces and a creative *transforming* agent capable of reshaping those forces. Gramsci noted for instance that the "objective" conditions necessary for the overthrow of capital-ism had prevailed in Europe for many decades; it was precisely the "subjective" conditions (revolutionary class consciousness, politi-cal cohesion) that were lacking, and that were hence most problematic. Historical obstacles and boundaries were therefore to a great extent themselves subjective and would constitute an enslaving force until opposed by the conscious self-activity of ordinary people. Gramsci assumed that human beings were innately driven to resist this enslavement a part of the struggle to recover their social individuality: "To transform the external world, the general system of relations, is to potentiate oneself and to develop oneself...For this reason one can say that man is essentially 'political' since it is through the activity of transforming and consciously directing other men that man realized his 'humanity' and 'human nature'."[46]

At the same time, Gramsci distinguished his own voluntarism, anchored in an historical understanding of class forces and strategic possibilities, from non-Marxist approaches like the fascist notion of "volunteers" or Gentile's exaltation of the "act" which viewed the willful activity of a few leaders as a powerful causal force that could transcend external restraints. For Gramsci, this reactionary Jacobinism was the logical extension of an uncontrolled, "monist" idealism which lost sight of the necessary dialectical interaction between purposive human activity and historicized social processes. In other words: "Philosophy of the act (praxis, development), but not of the 'pure' act, but rather of the real 'impure' act, in the most profane and worldly sense of the word."[47]

A key theme of Gramsci's philosophy of praxis was the inseparability of consciousness (thoughts, feelings, will) and historical reality (the specific "*ensemble* of relations")—another way of expressing the intimate relationship between philosophy and politics. Throughout the *Prison Notebooks* one finds repeated, in different ways, the notion that material forces acquire meaning only through human definition and engagement, through a wide range of ideological and cultural mediations. From this angle, Marxism could only be understood as the critical theory of politically committed actors, since "the existence of objective conditions, of possibilities of freedom is not yet enough: it is necessary to 'know' them, and to know how to use them. And to want to use them. Man, in this sense, is concrete will, that is, the effective application of the abstract will or vital impulse to the concrete means which realize such a will."[48] To the extent that human activity is "determined" by social structures, therefore, it is also the (potential) subject or creator of new initiatives that challenge those same structures. Or, as Gramsci put it, "Structure ceases to be an external force which crushes man, assimilates him to itself and makes him passive, and is transformed into a means of freedom, an instrument to create a new ethico-political form and source of new initiatives."[49]

In Hegelian terms, Gramsci envisaged the transition from the realm of necessity to the realm of freedom as a conscious, self-actualizing process whereby oppressed (or "subaltern") strata reach awareness of their alienated existence within the social division of labor and then burst through the old boundaries of thought and action. Scientific Marxism provided few insights into this process, for it was locked into static, ahistorical categories: if human beings were strictly the product of material forces, how could they ever hope to change the world? Gramsci often poked fun at the materialist inclination to fetishize structures (the state, mode of production) as if they could somehow be created and held together without the support of living, breathing persons:

> Thus one could imagine a recruit explaining to the recruiting officers the theory of the state as superior to individuals and demanding that they should leave in liberty his physical and material person and just enroll that mysterious something that contributes to building that national something known as the state.[50]

It is clear from this passage that Gramsci's Marxism could not be forced into the conventional base-superstructure model without distorting the theory beyond recognition. While he did employ these concepts occasionally, in terms of their reciprocity, he generally preferred the Hegelian distinction state-civil society and at times introduced his own notion of an *"ensemble* of relations," or social totality. In any event, however ambiguous Gramsci's methodology was in this area, there can be no doubt that his approach was rather novel among Marxists: he accepted the primacy of neither the "base" nor the "superstructure." On the one hand, Gramsci devoted relatively little attention to the concerns of production in the *Notebooks*, and he clearly did not view he economy as "determinant" in any sense; on the other hand, while he did theoretically focus on the role of ideology and consciousness these phenomena were never relegated to the "superstructure"—or assigned a derivative status—but were dynamically incorporated into a social totality that included both civil society and the state.[51]

Understood in this fashion, Gramsci's philosophy of praxis appears as more than just another synonym for "Marxism;" it signaled in fact the possibility of a *reconstituted* Marxism based in a merging of philosophy and politics scarcely visible in the pre-

Gramscian Marxist tradition. This nexus philosophy-politics was not a submerged or merely implicit aspect of Gramsci's prison writings, but was a guiding thematic that shaped all his major concepts. In the *Notebooks* philosophy became an emancipatory force—the basis of a theoretical "organizing principle" for an emergent moral-political (socialist) order, the source of a new community, world-view, and language for "subaltern" groups opposing capitalist domination. Philosophy contained a new revolutionary logic—the basis of a socialist "moral-intellectual" unity. In other words, "the philosophy of praxis had two tasks to perform: to combat modern ideologies in their most refined form, in order to be able to constitute its own group of independent intellectuals; and to educate the popular masses, whose culture was medieval."[52] As a necessary dimension of class struggle, philosophy for Gramsci was a *collective* intellectual enterprise that would bring into being a subversive "integrated culture". In sum:

> We have established that philosophy is a conception of the world and that philosophical activity is not to be conceived solely as the 'individual' elaboration of systematically coherent concepts, but also and above all as a cultural battle to transform the popular 'mentality' and to diffuse the philosophical innovations which will demonstrate themselves to be 'historically true' to the extent that they become concretely—i.e., historically and socially—universal.[53]

Given this premise, the philosophy of praxis was not to be confused with the detached and speculative modes of discourse typical of conventional systems of thought, including orthodox Marxism. Gramsci viewed philosophy as the conceptual medium whereby ideas are translated into cohesive social and political forces. He concluded that "for a mass of people to be led to think coherently and in the same coherent fashion about the present world, is a 'philosophical' event far more important and 'original' than the discovery by some philosophical 'genius' of a truth which remains the property of a small group of intellectuals."[54]

Thinking "coherently" in this context meant for Gramsci the presence of a discourse whereby the masses develop the capacity to free themselves from the encapsulating forms of traditional hegemony—in this case religion (spiritualism) and common sense (vulgar materialism). Without a solid grounding in *critical* philosophy, wherein subject and object, thought and action are dialectically united, no such transcendence could ever be realized.

Gramsci stated that "Philosophy is criticism and the superseding of religion and 'common sense.' In this sense it coincides with 'good' as opposed to 'common' sense. Religion and common sense cannot constitute an intellectual order, because they cannot be reduced to unity and coherence even within an individual consciousness, let alone collective consciousness."[55] The one-dimensional and therefore conservative nature of both religion and common sense corresponds to Gramsci's extensive critique of idealism and materialism explored in earlier sections of this chapter; its implication for the problems of ideological hegemony and mass consciousness will be taken up later.

Yet religion in the Italian setting posed a very special range of issues, given the powerful historical impact of Catholicism on the cultural and intellectual life of the nation, and therefore also on its philosophical traditions. Gramsci contrasted the theological elitism of the Church with the inherently "popular" thrust of Marxism. Catholicism had always been willing to allow the masses to drift along in their ignorance and passivity, while the philosophy of praxis by its very nature seeks to build an organic unity between intellectuals/leaders and the popular strata, refusing "to leave the 'simple' in their primitive philosophy of common sense, but rather to lead them to a higher conception of life." Insofar as religious ideology instilled an attitude of political fatalism into those subjected to it, the gulf between intellectuals and masses was merely reinforced and legitimated; the aim of Marxism, on the other hand, is to overcome this dualism by constructing "an intellectual-moral bloc which can make politically possible the intellectual progress of the mass and not only of small intellectual groups."[56] In Gramscian terms, therefore, the philosophical legacy of both idealism and Catholicism ultimately led to the same political consequences. Both traditions anxiously retreated from a commitment to political education and cultural renewal tied to the transformation of civil society, since philosophy and intellectual life in general was considered the preserve of a privileged elite.

At this juncture Gramsci's notion of a "democractized" or "popular" philosophy represented a decisive shift even within Marxism, to the degree that previous Marxist theorists had accepted the social division of labor implicit in the traditional conception of intellectual activity. Gramsci's philosophy of praxis opened up a radical redefinition of the theoretical enterprise itself. The first dramatic step was to collapse the historical distinction between philosophy and everyday life: "Everything is political, even philosophy or philosophies and the only 'philosophy' is history in action, that is, life itself."[57] From this assumption followed something equally novel —the contention that all human beings are in the final analysis "philosophers." In a celebrated passage Gramsci insisted that:

> Each man, finally, outside his professional activity, carries on some form of intellectual activity, that is, he is a 'philosopher,' an artist, a man of taste, he participates in a particular conception of the world, has a conscious line of moral conduct, and therefore contributes to sustain a conception of the world of to modify it, that is, to bring into being new modes of thought.[58]

Gramsci conceded that as professionals or "specialized workers" certain established philosophers were expected to be more intellectually advanced than the great mass of the population—they can think with more "logical rigor," are familiar with the history of thought, etc.—but he stressed that the difference is one of "quantity" rather than "quality." Even this difference, moreover, was small in comparison with that between specialists and non-specialists in other areas, indicating to Gramsci that the prospects for a truly democratized philosophical discourse were not as remote as even Marxists had assumed.[59] Of course the realization of such an intellectual egalitarianism would finally depend upon *praxis*, upon the general level of progress toward socialist transformation.

The philosophical outlook which emerged from the *Prison Notebooks* constitutes, in however unsystematic form, the basis of an alternative to the scientific materialism that has been the hegemonic Marxist paradigm since the 1930s. In this sense Gramsci's philosophy of praxis belongs distinctly to the Western Marxist tradition. Neo-Hegelian in inspiration, it has contributed to sustaining the possibility of a critical-dialectical theory against the simple appeals of Soviet-style Marxism, which long ago degenerated into a "scientific" ideology that serves mainly to legitimate a bureaucratic-centralist system of rule.

Gramsci's entire theoretical project—above all his effort to articulate a popular-democratic vision of revolutionary transformation—was prefigured in his philosophy. At its core was the principle of dialectical totality,[60] with its non-determinist framework of viewing history and politics; rather than adhering to a set of a priori assumptions about history, Gramsci chose to look at a *multiplicity* of factors within the "*ensemble* of relations." In refusing to yield to the methodological premises of orthodox Marxism, the philosophy of praxis laid the foundations for a concrete historical analysis without lapsing into either empiricism or economism; introduced the possibility of exploring social divisions and forms of domination outside the sphere of production (even if Gramsci did not extend his own analysis very far in this direction); and paid serious theoretical attention to ideological-cultural phenomena as such. Gramsci's methodological framework obviously lacked the simple precision and logical coherence of scientific materialism. Yet for Gramsci such "precision" and "coherence" was false, since the very historicity of knowledge guaranteed that there could be no rigid formulas for determining the collapse of capitalism, the transition to socialism, or even the constituent elements of theory itself. It would be illusory, indeed fraudulent, to claim more than a comprehension of broad developmental outlines and tendencies requiring politics for their actualization. Because philosophy was a dynamic *social* enterprise inseparable from history, moreover, it was always in the process of "becoming"—in other works, it could never give rise to a fixed system of thought so long as the "*ensemble* of relations" was changing, so long as intellectuals themselves were engulfed by conflict and uncertainty. As Gramsci noted:

> The philosophy of praxis is consciousness full of contradictions, in which the philosopher himself, understood both individually and as an entire social group, not merely grasps the contradictions, but posits himself as an element of the contradiction and elevates this element to a principle of knowledge and therefore of action.[61]

The Marxism which is the culmination of Gramsci's fragmentary but innovative work hardly constitutes anything resembling a finished *system*: it is a creative Marxism in which categories of history, dialectic, totality, and praxis are interconnected. Gramsci's creative Marxism, however, should not be confused with the "voluntarist" and "subjectivist" interpretations that stress its supposedly "liberal" or "idealist" qualities.[62] Such interpretations distort the philosophy of praxis found in the *Prison Notebooks* and completely miss the significance of Gramsci's rich theoretical contributions within the Marxist tradition. For what Gramscian philosophy historically represents, in fact, is precisely the supersession of old divisions—between philosophy and politics, thought and action, intellectuals and masses—characteristic of the Western intellectual tradition, Marxism included, in favor of an emergent revolutionary synthesis.

Footnotes

1. Gramsci's philosophical work (which included a large portion of the *Prison Notebooks*) has rarely received the attention it merits, especially in English-language commentaries. This is regrettable, given the extent to which the body of Gramsci's theory cannot be fully understood without reference to the philosophical underpinnings. This lacunae is probably explained by the fact that Gramsci was one of the few Western Marxists to concentrate on *politics*, thus diverting the textual focus in that direction. Then, too, the philosophical terrain had for so long been monopolized by Lukacs. For two extensive treatments of Gramsci's philosophy, see Nicola Badaloni, *Il Marxismo di Gramsci* (Turin: Einaudi, 1975), and Vicenzo Merolle, *Gramsci e la filosofia della prassi* (Rome: Bulzoni, 1974). No comparable full-length studies in English presently exist, the closest to it being Paul Piccone, "Gramsci's Hegelian Marxism," *Political Theory*, February 1974, pp. 32-45.

2. Some theorists (e.g., Pannekoek, Luxemburg, and Lenin) hoped to reconcile conventional scientific materialism with a transformative politics, but this proved futile.

3. This interpretation differs radically from that of Perry Anderson, who presents Western Marxism as a tradition of "political isolation and despair" born of earlier defeats. He argues that "Western Marxism...inverted the trajectory of Marx's own development itself. Where the founder of historical materialism moved progressively from philosophy to politics and then economics...the successors of the tradition that emerged after 1920 increasingly turned back from economics and politics to philosophy—abandoning direct engagement with what had been the great concerns of the mature Marx, nearly as completely as he had abandoned direct pursuit of the discursive issues of his youth." *Considerations on Western Marxism*, pp. 42, 52. By linking economics and politics here Anderson gives a completely false picture of Western Marxist concerns, which did largely ignore the former but not the latter. For a reply to Anderson, see Jacoby, *Dialectic of Defeat*, esp. pp. 6-7.

4. "Problems of Marxism," *Selections from the Prison Notebooks* (hereafter SPN), p. 464.

5. This is the term employed by Leonardo Paggi. See his "Gramsci's General Theory of Marxism," in Chantal Mouffe, ed.,

Gramsci and Marxist Theory, pp. 115, 118.

6. "Problems of Marxism," *SPN*, p. 395. Gramsci added that "the philosophy of praxis is the crowning point of this entire movement of intellectual and moral reformation, made dialectical in the contrast between popular culture and high culture." (p. 395)

7. "Problems of Marxism," *op. cit.*, pp. 383-84.

8. "Problems of Marxism," *op. cit.*, p. 407.

9. "Problems of]Marxism," *op. cit.*, p. 390. Among the early critics of orthodox Marxism (e.g., Bernstein, Sorel, Croce, and Pannekoek) Labriola was the only theorist to retain this dialectical philosophy.

10. Aside from numerous references to *Theses on Feuerbach* and the preface to *A Contribution to the Critique of Political Economy*, citations of Marx's writings in the *Prison Notebooks* were rather sparse. Gramsci's citations of ideas and passages from *The Holy Family*, *The German Ideology*, and *Capital* were reconstructions from memory, and were therefore sometimes understandably lacking in precision.

11. "Problems of Marxism," *op. cit.*, p. 396.

12. Whereas theorists writing in the tradition of Louis Althusser and French structuralism posit an epistemological "break" separating the early from the later Marx, others like Shlomo Avineri present Marx's thought as the continuous development along Hegelian lines. While Avineri tends to overlook the positivist encrustations of Marx's later work, his interpretation more accurately captures the overall "leitmotif" of classical Marxian theory. For examples of these two contrasting interpretations, see Louis Althusser and Etienne Balibar, *Reading Capital* (London: New Left Books, 1970), and Shlomo Avineri, *The Social and Political Thought of Karl Marx* (Cambridge: Cambridge University Press, 1971).

13. For an excellent treatment of this problem, see Gouldner, *The Two Marxisms*, ch. 3. Gouldner argues that the main thrust of Marx was deterministic, that already in Marx there was a certain hostility toward philosophy as an "idealist" enterprise.

14. Albrecht Wellmer refers to the "latent positivism" of Marx's philosophy of history, contending that for the Marx of *Capital* the material conditions of historical change—of the "transition to a classless society"—were at the same time sufficient conditions. See *Critical Theory of Society* (New York: Seabury Press, 1974), pp. 67-120.

15. In his discussion of this issue, Andrew Feenberg suggests that *Capital* establishes no causal connection between capitalism

and socialism. See his *Lukacs, Marx and the Sources of Critical Theory* (Totowa, N.J.: Rowman and Littlefield, 1981), p. 57.

16. "Problems of Marxism," *op. cit.*, pp. 404-05.

17. "Problems of Marxism," *op. cit.*, p. 465.

18. "Problems of Marxism", *op. cit.*, p. 417. Gramsci added here, in a passage that foreshadows his own philosophical orientation, that "What matters is that a new way of conceiving the world and man is born and that this conception is no longer reserved to the great intellectuals, to professional philosophers, but tends rather to become a popular, mass phenomenon..."(Ibid.)

19. Gramsci often referred in his prison writings to Croce's *Storia d'Italia dal 1871 al 1915*. The English translation is *A History of Italy, 1871-1915* (Oxford: Clarendon Press, 1929).

20. "Letter to Tatiana," April 25, 1932, in Lawner, *op. cit.*, p. 233. Commenting further on Croce's style, Gramsci added that it "corresponds to his moral life and has an almost Goethean serenity and composure." (*Ibid*)

21. "Letter to Tatiana," December 1, 1930, in Lawner, *op. cit.* p. 189. Gramsci expressed this same sentiment in *Il Materialismo storico e le filosofia di Benedetto Croce* (Turin: Einaudi, 1966), pp. 217-18.

22. *Il Materialismo storico*, pp. 216 and 240-41. See also, "The Study of Philosophy," *SPN*, p. 356.

23. "Letter to Tatiana," May 9, 1932, in Lawner, *op. cit.*, pp. 236-37. Gramsci went on to refer to Croce as the "high priest of contemporary historicist religion." ' (*Ibid*, p. 238).

24. *Il Materialism storico*, pp. 190-91, 240. In describing the Crocean dialectic as confined to the sphere of conceptual abstraction, Gramsci often employed the phrase "*dialettica dei distinti*". See also "Problems of Marxism", *SPN*, p. 437.

25. *Il Materialismo storico*, p. 200. Gramsci indicated that any "anti-Croce" treatise should likewise be an "anti-Gentile". See also "The Study of Philosophy", *SPN*, p. 371.

26. "Letter to Tatiana", April 18, 1932, in Lawner, *op. cit.*, p. 230. Elsewhere Gramsci wrote that "Croce in reality is a kind of lay Pope"—except that as an intellectual of the Risorgimento he could not hope to influence the Italian masses in the manner of the Catholic hierarchy. *Il Materialism storico*, p. 250.

27. "The Modern Prince," *SPN*, pp. 138-39. For a further critique of Croce's Sorelian equation of politics with "passion," see *Il Materialismo storico*, pp. 242-45.

28. *Il Materialismo storico*, pp. 237-38. See also "The Modern Prince," pp. 139-40. At other points Gramsci compared the meta-

physics of Croce's "idealist sociologism" with conventional "positivist sociologism." See *Il Materialismo storico*, p. 217.

29. A critical Marxist tendency flourished in Russia, even within the Bolshevik Party, during the period of most intense revolutionary activity (1916-1920), but it quickly gave way to scientific Marxism after the end of the Civil War. Lenin's own writings during this period—the *Philosophical Notebooks, State and Revolution*—represented a departure from both his earlier and later materialist bent. Bureaucratization reinforces this positivist evolution and by 1921 repressed the left communism that was most closely linked to critical Marxism. See Robert Daniels, *The Conscience of the Revolution*, chs. 5,6.

30. The Bukharin volume which Gramsci set out to demolish in the *Notebooks* is *The Theory of Historical Materialism, A Manual of Popular Sociology* (Moscow, 1921). The English translation is *Historical Materialism, A System of Sociology* (London: Allen and Unwin, 1926). Despite the superficial and often dogmatic level of theoretical discussion contained in this work, Bukharin was an enormously influential theorist in the Third International during the 1920s. While Bukharin's scientism may appear exaggerated, its basic premises were accepted by Comintern leaders and theorists even if Lenin himself felt uneasy about them—the Bolshevik leader characterizing Bukharin as a "brilliant theorist" but "ignorant of the dialectic". Bukharin's work was subjected to extensive criticism by both Lukacs and the Soviet Marxist Abram Deborin in the early 1920s; although Gramsci's assessment would not come for nearly another decade, it was by far the most devastating. Gramsci's critique spans pp. 419-472 of his "Problems of Marxism" in the *Notebooks*. For an excellent general treatment of Bukharin's thought, see Stephen F. Cohen, *Bukharin and the Bolshevik Revolution* (New York: Vintage Books, 1975).

31. "Problems of Marxism," *SPN*, p. 445.

32. "Problems of Marxism," *SPN*, pp. 428-29.

33. "Problems of Marxism," *SPN*, p. 430.

34. "Theses on Feurbach," in *Karl Marx and Frederick Engels: Selected works* (New York: International Publishers, 1968), p. 28.

35. Karl Korsch, *Marxism and Philosophy* (New York: Monthly Review Press, 1970), pp. 58-59. While these essays were written in 1923, there is no evidence that Korsch's work had any direct influence on Gramsci, who did not cite Korsch in the *Prison Notebooks*.

36. "The Study of Philosophy," *SPN*, p. 353.

37. "Problems of Marxism," *SPN*, p. 405.

38. "Problems of Marxism," *SPN*, p. 465. Elsewhere Gramsci referred to the concept "subjective universal", to an "objectivity that is part of man and being." Thus: "We know reality only in relation to man, and since man is historical becoming, knowledge and reality are also a becoming and so is objectivity, etc," (*Ibid.*, p. 446).

39. "Problems of Marxism," *SPN*, p. 429.

40. *Ibid*,

41. "Problems of Marxism," *SPN*, pp. 437-38.

42. "The Modern Prince," *SPN*, p. 171.

43. *Ibid.*

44. Gramsci remarked here that "'Politically' the materialist conception is close to the people, to 'common sense'. It is closely linked to many beliefs and prejudices, to almost all popular superstitions (witchcraft, spirits, etc.). This can be seen in popular Catholicism, and, even more, Byzantine orthodoxy. Popular religion is crassly materialistic..." "Problems of Marxism", *SPN*, p. 396.

45. "Problems of Marxism," *SPN*, p. 435.

46. "The Study of Philosophy," *SPN*, p. 360.

47. "The Study of Philosophy," *SPN*, p. 372.

48. "The Study of Philosophy," *SPN*, p. 360. In another section of the *Notebooks* Gramsci expressed this same point in a more epistemological fashion: "If it is true that man cannot be conceived of except as historically-determined man—i.e., man who has developed, and who lives in certain conditions, in a particular social complex or totality of social relations—is it then possible to take sociology as meaning simply the study of these conditions and the laws which regulate their development? Since the will and initiative of men themselves cannot be left out of account, this notion must be false. The problem of what 'science' itself is has to be posed. Is not science itself 'political activity' and 'political thought,' inasmuch as it transforms men and makes them different from what they were before?" "State and Civil Society," *SPN*, p. 244.

49. "The Study of Philosophy," *SPN*, p. 367.

50. "Problems of Marxism," *SPN*, p. 470.

51. Interpretations which present Gramsci as a "theorist of the superstructure" thus miss this important departure in Gramsci's thought, which is fully intelligible only in the context of his dialectical philosophy. For such an interpretation, see Norberto Bobbio, "Gramsci and the Conception of Civil Society", in Mouffe, ed., *Gramsci and Marxist Theory*, pp. 19-47. Bobbio sees in Gramsci a reversal of Marx's dialectic of the infrastructure since Gramsci's

concept of civil society is understood as excluding the realm of material relations. Thus Bobbio contends that, in deriving his view of civil society from Hegel, Gramsci includes within it "not the whole of material relationships, but the whole of ideological-cultural relations; not the whole of commercial and industrial life but the whole of spiritual and intellectual life." (p. 31) Not only is this formulation totally incompatible with Gramsci's philosophy of praxis—as reflected above all in his critique of Crocean idealism—but it saddles Gramsci with an outlook from which, theoretically speaking, economics is banished.

52. "Problems of Marxism," *SPN*, p. 392.

53. "The Study of Philosophy," *SPN*, p. 348.

54. "The Study of Philosophy," *SPN*, p. 325.

55. "The Study of Philosophy," *SPN*, pp. 325-26. Here Gramsci's conception of a critical Marxism, though nowhere explicitly defined as such in the *Prison Notebooks*, would seem to converge at points with the Critical Theory tradition that was first articulated at about the same time by theorists of the Frankfurt School (Max Horkheimer, Theodor Adorno, Herbert Marcuse, et. al.). But there were some crucial differences, notably in the more clearly-defined linkage between philosophy and politics that one finds in Gramsci.

56. "The Study of Philosophy," *SPN*, pp. 332-33.

57. "The Study of Philosophy," *SPN*, p. 357.

58. "The Intellectuals," *SPN*, p. 9. The only previous Marxist theorist who seemed to be moving in this direction was, once again, Korsch. See *Marxism and Philosophy*, pp. 75-81.

59. Alberto Martinelli was the first commentator to draw attention to the centrality of the dialectic for Gramsci's theory of revolution. See "In Defense of the Dialectic: Antonio Gramsci's Theory of Revolution," *Berkeley Journal of Sociology*, vol. XIII, 1968, pp. 1-27.

60. "Problems of Marxism," *SPN*, pp. 404-05.

61. It should be recalled that in his own time, and especially during the early years, Gramsci was attacked for his "Bergsonian" idealism by orthodox theorists within the PSI. More recent interpretations have stressed the *positive* implications of Gramsci's presumed idealism, often seeking to demonstrate its compatibility with liberalism and pluralist democracy. Some examples include: Norberto Bobbio, "Gramsci and the Conception of Civil Society," *op. cit.*; Paul Piccone, "Gramsci's Hegelian Marxism," *Political Theory*, February 1974; Giorgio Galli, "Gramsci e le teorie delle 'elites'", in *Gramsci e la cultura contemporanea*, pp. 201-216; Carl Marzani, The *Open Marxism of Antonio Gramsci* (New York:

Cameron Associates, 1957), introduction; Eugene Genovese, "On Antonio Gramsci", *Studies on the Left*, March-April 1967; and H. Stuart Hughes, *Consciousness and Society* (New York: Vintage Books, 1958), epilogue to ch. 5. An excellent critique of the tendency to see Gramsci's Marxism in strictly idealist terms is the introduction by Carlo Salinari and Mario Spinella to the Italian anthology of Gramsci's writings. See *Antonio Gramsci: Antologia degli Scritti,* (Rome: Editori Riuniti, 1963).

5 The Theory of Ideological Hegemony

Classical Marxism derived much of its ideological strength from a convincing theoretical projection of imminent capitalist crisis leading to systematic breakdown and, ultimately, to some form of socialist transformation. Given the presumed automatic character of this historical process, the theory inspired a great deal of messianic faith in a commitment to the revolutionary potential of the urban proletariat. As the Erfurt Programme of German Social Democracy made clear in 1891, the capitalist mode of production could not be expected to survive its own explosive contradictions—an optimism buttressed by an underlying mood of scientific certainty. By the turn of the century, however, this scenario was beginning to lose its credibility, especially in the more advanced countries (England, Germany, France, Sweden, Holland) where capitalism had in fact consolidated its economic and political power, and where the working class was clearly not being transformed into a cohesive revolutionary force. Instead of the anticipated class polarization, leading to widespread socialist consciousness and insurrectionary politics, the overwhelming trend was toward stabilization, a fragmented class consciousness, and political reformism. This trend, although dramatically interrupted during the European upheavals of 1917-1923, actually became more pronounced with capitalist development so that, by the mid-1920s, the traditional crisis schema had lost its credibility.

Marxist efforts to confront this predicament generated a wide range of fresh theoretical (and strategic) responses; out of frustrated hopes and political despair came intellectual creativity. The task was to understand not only why capitalism seemed to have infinite

153

adaptability, but also why even where cataclysmic crises did occur—as in Germany, Italy, and Hungary—it turned out to be not the left but the *right* which managed to seize the initiative.

The first and probably most compelling reassessment came from Bernstein, who located the problem within the very trajectory of capitalist transformation: new levels of technology and material affluence, growth of the new middle classes, rise of trade unionism and improved living standards, and new political opportunities presented by universal suffrage—all this suggested an entirely different working-class politics than classical Marxism had envisioned. Since capitalism in 1900 was a completely different system from what Marx had analyzed in *Capital*, Bernstein concluded that the dialectic of class struggle no longer made sense. There was little reason to believe that, in the context of flourishing and adaptive bourgeois societies, the majority of workers would be driven necessarily toward insurrectionary activity. Henceforth reformist consciousness would be the *norm*, and not the aberration, for workers in the advanced countries. For Michels, on the other hand, the attenuation of class conflict was a function of conservative internal party and trade-union organization. The bureaucratization of the SPD, for example, created a privileged elite stratum whose outlook increasingly diverged from the presumed radical militancy of rank-and-file members, resulting in "embourgeoisement" and ideological stagnation. Sorel too advanced the thesis of a narrowly bureaucratic and cautious leadership diverting the energies of a proletariat originally committed to the overthrow of capitalism. But where Michels focused upon organizational degeneration, Sorel emphasized *ideological* cooptation: by steering the working-class movement away from the point of production, where its historical mission was to wrest economic control from bourgeois management, and entire stratum of trade-union officials, parliamentarians, and "Marxist" intellectuals sapped class militancy by importing various liberal, pacifist, and reformist ideologies into socialist politics. From the viewpoint of Luxemburg, the problem was simply one of proletarian "immaturity," which meant that subjective factors lagged behind objective conditions (owing in part to the ideological influence of national competition). However, while in many countries political and cultural advances among workers did not keep pace with economic development, Luxemburg clearly viewed this as something *contingent*—a temporary gap that would be closed in time. Finally, Lenin's explanation centered around the emergence of an "aristocracy of labor", which he derived from his theory of imperialism. Thus the growing internationalization of capital permitted the European bourgeoisie to domesticate leading sectors of labor by virtue of a vastly-strengthened economic position made possible by new market outlets, sources of cheap labor, and raw materials. Imperialism laid the groundwork for new (and possibly more durable) modes of class collaboration.

With the exception of Bernstein, who in any event abandoned Marxism altogether, all of these theorists shared the assumption (derived from Marx) that the proletariat in the developed capitalist societies was an *inherently* revolutionary force—that, a few roadblocks here or there notwithstanding, it would ultimately be driven to overthrow the general interests of capital. Any absence of socialist class consciousness was due to contingent or "external" factors that would sooner or later be neutralized. Lenin, of course, added the qualifier that revolutionary class consciousness would have to be introduced and activated by a vanguard elite; still, he accepted the conventional Marxist premise that the workers, once presented with a viable socialist alternative, would respond rationally and positively.

Only with the appearance of neo-Hegelian Marxism in the 1920s and 1930s was the issue of proletarian consciousness—or, more accurately, the relationship between bourgeois ideology and proletarian consciousness—taken up as something theoretically *problematic*. No conventional assumptions were taken for granted. Thus the contributions of Lukacs, Korsch, Reich, and the early Frankfurt School all, in one way or another, sought to demonstrate that the stabilization of capitalism could not be understood without looking closely at the unfolding of working-class social existence itself. What factors shaped proletarian subjectivity and consciousness? Why had a reformist, pragmatic outlook become so universal among workers in the advanced countries? Neo-Hegelianism assumed that answers to such questions would require a much deeper, historical probing than previous Marxists had been willing to contemplate. Of course the failure of European working-class movements to carry out revolutionary struggles was indeed attributable in some measure to those factors mentioned above— changing class structure, organizational conservatism, leadership cooptation, imperialism — but the effective *impact* of these causes could not be fully analyzed without reference to the *internal* dynamics of class formation and development.

Whatever the nature of Gramsci's earlier political affiliation with the Comintern, his theoretical work in the *Prison Notebooks* belongs unequivocally to the neo-Hegelian tradition: indeed, his interest in the variable and complex expressions of class consciousness can be detected in virtually every page of those writings.

Gramsci's famous notion of ideological hegemony—a term refer-ring to the forms of bourgeois ideological and cultural domination—is the conceptual matrix that supplied coherence and meaning to the innumerable far-ranging discussions of ideology and con-sciousness in the *Notebooks*. Without question it represents a major contribution to the legacy of Western Marxism. For Gramsci, the concept of hegemony contained not only a powerful critique of mechanistic crisis theories—for him there was no method for predicting the death of capitalism—but also an implicit under-standing of the system's ability to reproduce itself despite its persistent economic contradictions. An intensified theoretical focus on the problem of hegemony (and *counter*-hegemony) there-fore indicated that the transition to socialism could not be ade-quately comprehended simply by looking at irreconcilable antagon-isms in the mode of production.

Gramsci's unique presentation of ideological themes through his concept of hegemony effectively set off his philosophy of praxis from scientific materialism, which had monopolized the definition of ideology within Marxism before the 1920s. In stressing the role of objective conditions, scientific Marxism accepted as axiomatic the notion that politics, ideology, and culture were reflections of the material "base"—i.e., that they were elements of the "super-structure." Subjectivity was regarded as mere "appearance," with little independent or continuous existence of its own; ideology was thus understood as the distorted expression of social reality, as a form of rationalization or "false consciousness."[1] Armed with this one-dimensional perspective, it was no wonder that orthodox Marxism offered few insights into why revolutionary prospects in the West had collapsed. Gramsci was uncompromisingly hostile to reductionist theories, even in his early writings. Influenced by Croce's thematic of the "ethico-political" in Italian history, he never doubted that ideas play an *active* role in class struggle—a theoretical outlook that, as I suggested in chapter four, forced him to reconceptualize the base-superstructure motif inherited from classical Marxism. In Gramsci's case, preoccupation with the ideological-cultural sphere grew out of historical events and political experiences that preceded his imprisonment: the collapse of social democracy, defeat of the factory council movement, and the triumph of fascism. Yet, while for this reason the *Notebooks* reflected a certain sense of political retreat if not pessimism, the concept of hegemony turned this around, adding a positive twist insofar as it broadened understanding of capitalist domination and the means for combating it.

The Consensual Basis of Domination

There is no evidence to suggest that Gramsci ever denied the primacy of economic factors in shaping historical development over the long run. On the contrary, he argued that the mode of production was crucial during periods of stability or slow evolutionary change, when the established institutions persisted more or less intact. But this framework, though perhaps useful for studying patterns of continuity, could not explain the critical *transformative* phases of history characterized by open conflict, upheaval and revolution, when one system was giving way to another. In Gramsci's view, only a critical-dialectical theory that went beyond economic determinism could take into account the rich interplay of diverse conflicting social forces at these "conjunctural" moments of revolutionary change. In the place of the base-superstructure model Gramsci substituted the more dynamic and historicized notions "*ensemble* of relations" and "historical bloc", which allowed for the systematic investigation of concrete situations and events. Rather than putting forth a set of universal propositions linked to a single "root cause" and derived in dogmatic fashion, theory would specify and analyze the relation of forces as it actually unfolded.

Contained in this methodological departure was Gramsci's radical critique of economism: "real history" is too complex and multifaceted to be reduced to a primal force. In "The Modern Prince" Gramsci observed that "It may be ruled out that immediate economic crises of themselves produce fundamental historical events; they can simply create a terrain more favorable to the dissemination of certain modes of thought, and certain ways of posing and resolving questions involving the entire subsequent development of national life."[2] Reflecting on the causes of the French Revolution, he added:

> ...the rupture of the equilibrium of forces did not occur as the result of direct mechanical causes—i.e. the impoverishment of the social group which had an interest in breaking the equilibrium, and which in fact did break it. It occurred in the context of conflicts on a higher plane than the immediate world of the economy; conflicts related to class 'prestige' and to an inflammation of sentiments of independence, autonomy, and power. The specific question of new historical realities is a partial aspect of the question of the relations of force, at the various levels.[3]

Beyond a general historicist rejection of economism, Gramsci stressed that Marxism itself originated out of a philosophical system—nineteenth century idealism—and took form through the imperatives of historical research, political struggle, and cultural self-definition, largely within the "subjective" realm that later Marxists were so anxious to theoretically obliterate. Moreover, at several points in the *Notebooks* Gramsci approvingly referred to Marx's dictum that human beings develop consciousness and become political actors in the ideological sphere, in support of the claim that consciousness decisively affects the content and outcome of class conflict. Thus: "To the extent that ideologies are historically necessary they have a validity which is 'psychological'; they 'organize' human masses and create the terrain on which men move, acquire consciousness of their position, struggle, etc."[4] For Gramsci, ideas, beliefs, cultural preferences, and even myths and superstitions possessed a certain "material" reality of their own since in their power to inspire people towards action they interact with economic conditions, which otherwise would be nothing more than empty abstractions. In other words, the contradictions of capitalist society do not "explode" but are actualized and even manipulated by human will-power. A Marxism which degenerates into economism, however seductive it might be in its simplicity, eventually "loses a great part of its capacity for cultural expansion", especially among intellectuals.[5] Thus in Gramsci's thought ideology was never viewed as merely a distorted or mystified image of something more basic; while hardly distinct from the social totality, it did embody a special logic and political relevance that had escaped the grasp of scientific Marxists.[6]

The concept of hegemony integrated these insights into a theoretically coherent framework and allowed Gramsci to sidestep the tiresome debates around "base" versus "superstructure". Previous Marxist thinking located the source of ruling-class power primarily in the mode of production and secondarily in state power; forms of domination and control outside these spheres were typically ignored. While this might have been adequate for understanding class relations in pre-capitalist societies, it could not do justice to the greater complexity of bourgeois systems where class domination was more refracted through ideological and cultural mediations. Hence greater attention would have to be devoted to the "consensual" basis of power, particularly greater in the advanced European countries. As noted in chapter three, the collapse of the Turin factory council movement in 1920 had already produced this sensitivity in Gramsci, who concluded that the enemy to combat was not only the bourgeoisie but was also something that existed within the proletariat itself, in its fragmented and economistic consciousness. This awareness surfaced again in his contribution to the "Lyons' Theses" in 1926—especially in his analysis of the Southern Question—but he did not address the problem theoretically until the *Notebooks*. On those occasions when Gramsci used the term "hegemony" during his PCI period, he did so in a more restricted Leninist framework: it applied either to the general political ascendancy of a socialist formation or to the leading position of the working class in an alliance of forces, but never to the character of class domination in capitalist societies. Indeed, Gramsci no doubt borrowed this term from the Russian and Comintern settings, where it was referred to casually by such theorists as Lenin, Plekhanov, and Bukharin. The concept of ideological hegemony in the *Notebooks*, however, differed fundamentally from its Russian usage.[7]

Gramsci approached the problem of hegemony from two separate angles. On one plane, he set out to differentiate opposing modes of political control, contrasting the functions of "domination" (direct physical coercion) with those of "hegemony" or "direction" (ideological manipulation, consent), which actually cut across the distinction between state and civil society.[8] Bourgeois society is characterized by a "dual nature" exemplified by Machiavelli's Centaur, half-animal and half-human—"the levels of force and consent, authority and hegemony, violence and civilization...."[9] In dwelling upon the former, Marxists had virtually ignored the latter, with disastrous consequences for political strategy. Hence one of Gramsci's main tasks was to restore the consensual side of politics. Inspired by Croce's idea of the "ethico-political," he fell back on a tradition not too far removed from the theory of an epochal "spirit" found in Montesquieu and Hegel, but Gramsci tore away its abstract, mystical trappings by reformulating it as an element of class relations and political domination. The point was that no social order could sustain itself over the long run primarily on a foundation of organized state power, that on the contrary the inclination of a ruling class to rely upon repression and violence was a sign of *weakness* rather than strength. What contributed to real political durability was the scope of popular support or ideological consent.[10]

The second aspect of hegemony centered around Gramsci's analysis of insurgent movements as they strive to create their own consensual legitimacy or counter-hegemonic presence in both civil society and the state. For the proletariat to wrest power from the bourgeoisie it would ultimately have to become "hegemonic" precisely in the sense of moving beyond the restrictive "economic-corporate" phase of special group, sectional, or even class interests to the political or "universal" phase in which a new moral-intellectual organizing principle for society as a whole could be advanced. Hegemony is attained when

> ...one's own corporate interests, in their present and future development, transcend the corporate limits of the purely economic class, and can and must become the interests of other subordinate groups too. This is the most purely political phase, and marks the decisive passage from the structure to the sphere of complex super-structures...bringing about not only a unison of economic and political aims, but also intellectual and moral unity, posing all the questions around which struggle rages not on a corporate but on a 'universal' plane, and thus creating the hegemony of a fundamental social group [class] over a series of subordinate groups.[11]

As this passage suggests, a strong motivation behind the theory of hegemony was the rejection of economism in both its method-ological and political dimensions. Yet this did not mean that the ideological-cultural sphere was autonomous or that the economy as such played no role in the exercise of hegemony—two common misinterpretations of Gramsci's Marxism. His thinking was more dialectical, more attuned to the complexity of the bourgeois system of domination: if "hegemony is ethical-political, it must also be economic, must necessarily be based on the decisive function exercised by the leading group in the decisive nucleus of economic activity."[12]

Gramsci's definition of ideological hegemony was therefore rather broad. It encompassed the whole range of values, attitudes, beliefs, cultural norms, legal precepts, etc. that to one degree or another permeated civil society, that solidified the class structure and the multiple forms of domination that pass through it. The arenas of ideological-cultural transmission are infinite: the state, legal system, workplace, schools, churches, bureaucracies, cultural activities, the media, the family. Hegemony quite clearly embraces far more than single, well-defined ideologies (e.g. liberalism) that can be said to reflect (and mystify) the interests of dominant classes. In capitalist societies it might include not only the competitive individualism diffused by liberalism but also the social atomization and depoliticization produced by bureaucracy, the fatalism instilled by religion, the state-worship fanned by national-ism, and the sexism which grows out of the family. Even within systems of the same type, patterns of hegemonic development vary dramatically, owing in part to the impact of traditional residues or "survivals" such as the persistence of feudal agrarian classes in southern Italy long after industrialization had begun. Whatever the patterns, Gramsci observed that ruling elites always sought to justify their power, wealth, and status *ideologically,* with the aim of securing general popular acceptance of their dominant position as something "natural", part of an eternal social order, and thus unchallengeable.

It follows that the impact of the hegemonic apparatus depends upon the extent to which the mechanisms transmitting values, life-styles, and cultural orientations succeed in transforming popular consciousness; for this to occur the ruling ideas must become deeply-embedded in the fabric of social relations and national traditions. Gramsci pointed out that insofar as these ruling ideas are internalized by the majority of people and become a defining motif of everyday life, they appear as "common sense"— i.e., as the "traditional popular conception of the world."[13] At this level hegemony performs functions that the military and police machinery could never carry out: it mystifies power relations, public issues, and historical events; it encourages fatalism and passivity toward political action; it justifies various types of system-serving deprivation and sacrifice. Hence the structure of ideological domination works in many ways to induce the oppressed strata to accept or "consent to" their own daily exploitation and misery.

But this binding relationship between dominant and subordinate classes could not be realized without the presence of an intellectual stratum tied to relatively coherent world-views rooted in philosophy, science, sociological theory, law, and so forth. In Gramsci's words, " 'common sense' is the folklore of philosophy."[14] Hegemony thus operates in a dualistic manner: as a "general conception of life" for the mass of people, and as a "scholastic programme" or set of moral-intellectual principles which is reproduced by a sector of the educated stratum.[15]

If the values of the dominant ideological paradigm were in Gramsci's view reproduced mainly throughout civil society, it was nonetheless the state which generally assumed the most important hegemonic functions. This emphasis corresponded to a definite shift in theoretical focus toward the state within the *Notebooks* as a whole. In contrast to Lenin, however, for whom the state was primarily a coercive bureaucratic apparatus superimposed upon civil society,[16] Gramsci saw the state as a mobilizer of both force and consent, violence and ideology—especially in the advanced capitalist countries where the problem of mass loyalty had taken on a new dimension. Gramsci thus rejected the simple Leninist equation of governing structures with class dictatorship. Reflecting upon Italian political history, he arrived at a more dialectical relationship between state and civil society in which the institutions of political power appear as the complex sphere of social and ideological forces. Hegemony constituted the linkage between social relations and the state in a way that never entered Lenin's theory.[17] From this viewpoint, the state is significant for two reasons: it is an arena of ideological and political contestation, and it is the medium through which the dominant class seeks to mobilize or "universalize" popular consent. (The first proposition belongs to the topic of revolution and political strategy, and will be explored further in chapter 7.)

An underlying theme of the *Notebooks* (particularly "The Modern Prince") involved the "pedagogical" role of the state. As Machiavelli observed centuries before, state power has the unique capacity to "nationalize" the interests of specific political groups because it alone can counter the pressures of social and regional fragmentation. It functions as the repository of a moral-intellectual unity which transcends class divisions through appeals to religion, constitutional-legal norms, cultural and linguistic traditions. Yet while states historically carried out such hegemonic activities, with varying levels of success, only with the rise of capitalism did the state apparatus expand its ideological presence throughout civil society. As Gramsci wrote:

> The previous ruling classes were essentially conservative in the sense that they did not tend to construct an organic passage from the other classes into their own, i.e., to enlarge their class sphere 'technically' and 'ideologically': their conception was that of a closed caste. The bourgeois class poses itself as an organism in continuous movement, capable of absorbing the entire society, assimilating it to its own cultural and economic level. The entire function of the state has been transformed; the state has become an 'educator', etc.[18]

Thus Gramsci's concept of hegemony introduced an expansive view of the state while previous Marxist theory had largely instrumentalist view of the state and politics.[19] At the same time, Gramsci's analysis of hegemony as mediation between state and civil society represented (for his time) a novel way of understanding ideological phenomena—one that circumvented the limitations of both abstract idealism and economism.

In posing the issue of ideological domination thusly, Gramsci was not arguing that ruling-class adaptability was infinite; on the contrary, he regarded the actual exercise of hegemony as *problematic,* the scope and content of which would have to be investigated historically. Hegemony is part of a dynamic, always-shifting complex of relations, not the legitimating core of a static and all-encompassing totalitarian rule where political opposition is completely absorbed. Here Gramsci directed a good deal of his attention to the degree of equilibrium which exists between state and civil society. The correlation between political institutions and their consensual support could vary from stable to precarious—a balance that, owing to historical, economic, and cultural factors, determines the ideological "resources" that ruling classes can mobilize in periods of crisis. An additional variable in this picture is the ability of elites to manipulate popular consciousness through education, mass media, the legal system, and culture, especially in the industrialized countries where technology and bureaucracy permit further rationalization of control functions. As far as European history was concerned, however, Gramsci found that *disequilibrium* rather than broad ideological consensus was the general rule.

As an example of fragile hegemony Gramsci cited nineteenth century Germany where, much like the Italian Renaissance, intellectual and cultural life was restricted to a small nucleus of elites who had little contact with the general population. The dominant strata of intellectuals, politicians, and artists exercised little ideological influence within civil society as a whole, and so their hegemonic role—their power to shape popular consciousness—was extremely limited; hence in the absence of an imposing *Weltanschauung* or "organizing principle" popular social forces were able to exercise more autonomy. Not only the feudal aristocracy but the emergent bourgeoisie failed to establish the conditions necessary for a national community; as in Italy, regionalism and social cleavage prevailed over unifying tendencies to the degree that broad consensus could not be formed. The state evolved as a hollow shell, more or less detached from civil society. Without real "organic or disciplinary bonds" connecting the interests and outlooks of antagonistic classes, ideological domination became "merely a phenomenon of abstract cultural influence," virtually ensuring the subsequent imposition of authoritarian rule as a means of achieving national unity through statist forms of popular mobilization.[20] This dialectic of late German historical development, which paralleled the Italian case in many ways, continued well into the twentieth century, though Gramsci himself devoted little attention to the Bismarckian period, Weimar, and the rise of Nazism. It contrasted dramatically with an earlier phase of German politics—the Reformation—in which the agent of change was the great mass of people rather than an insular elite stratum.

Gramsci noted a similar comparison between the Renaissance and the French Revolution. While the Renaissance had nourished a thriving cultural, social and political life, it was almost totally removed from the daily existence of the majority of Italian people; it had been mainly limited to a "restricted intellectual aristocracy" or, in Croce's words, the "courtly circles." The ideological-cultural forces set in motion by the Renaissance, though powerful, were largely self-contained and failed to produce a lasting equilibrium between state and civil society. The French Revolution, on the other hand, burst upon the scene as a profoundly *mass* phenomenon—a "national-popular" movement that generated a cohesive political community.[21] To be sure, this Jacobin imposition from above had its violent and coercive moment, but once the convergence of elites and popular strata, town and countryside, was achieved the essence of a unified French nation-state had been secured. Such a process never really occurred in modern Germany or Italy.

The theory of consensual power outlined in the *Notebooks* provided a far broader and more strategically viable understanding of revolutionary change in the advanced countries than any of the Marxist "breakdown" schemas could furnish. Gramsci contended that the transition to socialism would have to be accompanied by a general crisis of hegemony involving above all the collapse of old authority patterns. This historical process could take one of two forms: either a gradual deterioration of ruling class legitimacy or sudden, dramatic shifts in popular consciousness leading to widespread rejection of traditional ideologies. In either case the first stages of crisis would typically involve mass expressions of apathy, cynicism and confusion as well as outbursts of primitive revolt. Next would probably follow more overt and politicized forms of class struggle characterized by the spread of anti-authoritarian norms in many spheres of public life, the unfolding of new social relations, the development of anti-system subcultures, the adoption of new language codes, and so forth. On the elite level, this erosion of consensus would be met with increasing state dependence upon force and repression. Whatever the exact scenario, Gramsci believed that the crisis of hegemony would involve a fairly lengthy transitional period during which political responses tend to be unpredictable and often contradictory. Indeed, the contestation of social forces is inevitably shaped by the contradictions of class society. Thus:

> If the ruling class had lost its consensus, i.e., is no longer 'leading' but only 'dominant', exercising coercive force alone, this means precisely that the great masses have become detached from their traditional ideologies and no longer believe what they used to believe previously, etc. The crisis consists precisely in the fact that the old is dying and the new cannot be born: in this interregnum a great variety of morbid symptoms appears.[22]

Thus, in the stripping away of these protective hegemonic facades, the directly exploitative and repressive nature of the system of class domination becomes less and less opaque. In this fashion, according to Gramsci, the "crisis of the modern state" occurs when the ruling strata are robbed of their "spiritual prestige and power" and are reduced to their "economic-corporate" existence, which reveals more clearly than ever the real cause of oppression.[23] A crisis of such proportions may occur when "the ruling class had failed in some major political undertaking for which it has requested, or forcibly extracted, the consent of the broad masses (war, for example), or because the huge masses...have passed suddenly from a state of political passivity to a certain activity, and put forward demands which taken together...add up to revolution."[24] Yet Gramsci noted that such a sequence of events, which he also referred to as a "crisis of authority", could be resolved either to the advantage of reaction ("Caesarism") or revolution, depending upon the levels of preparation within the left itself as well as any number of "imponderable factors" (which recalls Machiavelli's notion of *fortuna*).[25]

Consistent with the philosophy of praxis formulated in the *Notebooks*, Gramsci insisted that there was nothing mechanical about the crisis of bourgeois society: because the crisis was not the product of economic causes alone, or of a breakdown in the productive apparatus of capitalism, socialist revolution could not be analyzed in terms of a cataclysmic series of events. He realized that the erosion of ideological hegemony was only a necessary but never a sufficient precondition for fundamental change; demystification of the old class and power relations would not automatically give rise to new forms of critical consciousness. At best, the cultural expansion of working-class struggles would be precarious and uneven. What matters here, as we shall elaborate in chapter 7, is the degree of ideological preparation, organizational cohesion, and social unity ("homogeneity") of a revolutionary movement that seeks to contest state power. With the subversion of traditional systems of domination a new "integrated culture", grounded in changing social and authority relations, [26] would be necessary to give that process democratic content. The struggle for hegemony, moreover, is an ongoing phenomenon, continuing well beyond the actual transfer of state power:

> ...from the moment in which a subaltern group becomes really autonomous and hegemonic, thus bringing into being a new form of state, we experience the concrete birth of a need to construct a new intellectual and moral order, that is, a new type of society, and hence the need to develop more universal concepts and more refined and decisive ideological weapons.[27]

It follows that the struggle for ideological hegemony on the part of subordinate groups has two phases: to penetrate the false and irrational world of social appearances tied to the dominant order, and to create a new universe of belief systems, cultural values, and social relations constitutive of an emergent democratic socialism.

Gramsci and Lukacs

Of course Gramsci was not the first Marxist to rediscover the theme of subjectivity or to develop a theory of ideological domination. Already in the early 1920s, Georg Lukacs, in his classic *History and Class Consciousness*, had elaborated his concept of reification as a means of explaining the continuing hold of bourgeois ideology and culture over the working class in central Europe. Lukacs' formulation and Gramsci's notion of hegemony suggest certain intriguing parallels, not only in their theoretical motivations but in their political implications. The similarities are indeed rather striking— far more than is generally realized, at least judging from the dearth of comparisons found in both the Lukacs and Gramsci literature.[28] Yet there are some critical differences, with far-reaching consequences for Marxist politics and strategy in the advanced capitalist societies.

Like Gramsci, Lukacs concluded on the basis of his own political involvement that class struggle would have to be mounted on two terrains: one against the structural impediments of capitalist economic and political power, the other involving an internal consciousness transformation of the working class itself, through the unfolding of its self-activity. It will be recalled that Gramsci, in the midst of the Italian factory council defeats of 1920, sadly observed that the workers themselves—however militant and sacrificing—had not been ideologically prepared to carry out a socialist revolution, that the bourgeoisie in fact was still "waiting in ambush" within the minds of thousands of individual proletarians. This realization prefigured Gramsci's later theory of hegemony. Reflecting on the precarious situation in central Europe, Lukacs argued that "authentic" class consciousness, even within the rapidly proliferating workers' councils, was still only a distant prospect given the inclination of the proletariat to confine itself to bourgeois categories of thought and action. The effort to realize socialism, according to Lukacs, "is not just a battle waged against an external enemy, the bourgeoisie. It is equally the struggle of the proletariat *against itself*: against the devastating and degrading effects of the capitalist system upon its class consciousness. The proletariat will only have won the real victory when it has overcome these effects within itself."[29]

Both Gramsci and Lukacs shared broad and *critical* philosophical interests—rare within Marxism—linked to a patient struggle to unravel the subjective requirements of social transformation. From this angle they both emphasized the dialectical movement of social totality. Central to Gramsci's philosophy of praxis was the incorporation of progressive elements within the German and Italian idealist tradition as a counter to the crude determinism of orthodox Marxism; he always associated economism with *bourgeois* theory and consciousness. Lukacs expressed the same idea when he wrote: "...the class consciousness of the bourgeoisie is geared to economic consciousness. And indeed the highest degree of unconsciousness, the crassest form of 'false consciousness' always manifests itself when the conscious mastery of economic phenomena appears to be at its greatest. From the point of view of the relation of consciousness to society this contradiction is expressed as the *irreconcilable antagonism between ideology and economic base*."[30] One of the more pernicious effects of economism was its rigid separation of political and economic phenomena, which , as the history of the Second International had shown,destroyed the possibility of a unified strategic perspective. The Leninist critique of economistic Marxism, though inspired by somewhat different preoccupations, strongly influenced Gramsci's theoretical discourse in the *Notebooks*. Its earlier impact on Lukacs was no less profound.

Thus:

> The most striking division in proletarian class consciousness and the one most fraught with consequences is the separation of the economic struggle from the political one. Marx repeatedly exposed the fallacy of this split and demonstrated that it is in the nature of every economic struggle to develop into a political one (and vice-versa). Nevertheless, it has not proved possible to eradicate this heresy from the theory of the proletariat. The cause of this aberration is to be found in the dialectical separation of immediate objectives and ultimate goal and, hence, in the dialectical division within the proletarian revolution itself.[31]

The concept of reification gave theoretical expression to Lukacs' departure from scientific materialism in *History and Class Consciousness*. Borrowing from Marx's theory of the fetishism of commodities in *Capital* and Max Weber's notion of rationalization, Lukacs was able to present the most systematic account of how the forms of capitalist ideological domination evolved and became universalized throughout bourgeois society, engulfing proletarian existence at the same time. Reification could therefore be understood as the mystifying ideology unique to the "laws" of the market, exchange relations, and instrumental values—that is, the world of commodity production as a whole. Capitalist industrialization, and with it the appearance of bureaucracy and technology, gave life to the first truly comprehensive process of transformation in which all human institutions, values, and social relations were subordinated to a single principle: the market. As new forms of consciousness accompanied this transformation, the commodity itself took on the appearance of a law-like force working independently of human will. With capitalist production overturning all tradition and colonizing previously autonomous realms of social existence, human relationships became commodified—in other words, they became assimilated into the realm of objects or "things".

Lukacs observed that this "rationalization of the world" at times appears to be uniform or total, penetrating to the very core of the human psyche and soul. Insofar as capitalism succeeded in creating a unified economic system, its inherent drive was toward a "unified structure of consciousness that embraced the whole of society." Accordingly:

> The transformation of the commodity relation into a thing of ghostly 'objectivity' cannot therefore content itself with the reduction of all objects for the gratification of human needs to commodities. It stamps its imprint upon the whole consciousness of man; his qualities and abilities are no longer an organic part of his personality, they are things which he can 'own' or 'dispose of' like the various objects of the external world. And there is no natural form in which human relations can be cast, no way in which man can bring his physical and psychic 'qualities' into play without their being subjected increasingly to this reifying process.[32]

With each new phase of capitalist development, therefore, reification extends further beyond the sphere of market relations as such, so that bourgeois ideological domination reproduces itself through a variety of mediations: a positivist philosophical tradition, instrumentalized politics, fragmented social relations, and alienated labor. In this context there appears to be no escape for the proletariat insofar as its consciousness becomes nothing more than a mirror reflection of *bourgeois* consciousness, insofar as "the proletariat shares with the bourgeoisie the reification of every aspect of its life."[33] Indeed, for Lukacs reification was the very prerequisite for capitalist economic growth to the extent that flourishing market relations depend upon "free" workers who can openly sell their labor-power as a commodity without undue restrictions. "As the commodity becomes universally dominant", Lukacs argued, "the fate of the worker becomes the fate of society as a whole; indeed, this fate must become universal as otherwise industrialization could not develop in this direction."[34] For this reason the factory too becomes a microcosm of capitalist society in its entirety, an arena in which workers are subjected to bureaucratic discipline and bourgeois socialization, where they are left with only their precarious labor-power. The result is that "this self-objectification, this transformation of a human function into a commodity reveals in all its starkness the dehumanized and dehumanizing function of the commodity relation."[35]

In Lukacs' framework, then, reification performs a doubly mystifying function: it alienates human beings from each other and from nature, and it distorts thinking about a social and historical reality that has assumed an illusory "natural" character. The proletariat is denied its sense of collective awareness, the knowledge it needs to oppose capitalist domination, and therefore the very capacity to transform the world within which it remains imprisoned. By concealing this mundane reality of class conflict from workers, the process of rational objectification serves to destroy or at least impede the formation of critical consciousness.

Yet Lukacs, as a Marxist committed to revolutionary change, was never prepared to concede that the working class would be forever reduced to a passive spectator of an historical process that had totally escaped its control. In pulverizing and atomizing consciousness, the commodity at the same time must inevitably generate *resistance*; Lukacs thus retained the dialectic as the key to political struggle and social transformation. But for Lukacs, in contrast to orthodox Marxism, the breakdown of capitalism would not result from economic crisis strictly speaking because such a crisis was no guarantee that revolutionary class consciousness would somehow miraculously appear where before it had been absent. Only *cultural* breakdown, characterized by a far-reaching process of de-reification, would allow the working class to press beyond the boundaries of capitalism in the fullest sense. Here again Lukacs' orientation anticipated that of Gramsci, for whom a similar generalized crisis of ideological hegemony was a prerequisite for the transition to socialism. In Lukacs' view, the transition could only occur once the reification mechanisms of bourgeois society (including above all the commodity structure) exhausted their utility as purveyors of meaning and purpose, thereby opening up space for the diffusion of new (proletarian, but also universal) forms of rationality. The theoretical vision expressed in *History and Class Consciousness*, despite its "Leninist" conclusions, points emphatically toward a politics of cultural transformation.[36]

At the same time, Lukacsian theory contained serious flaws similar to those found in classical Marxism. If for Lukacs reified consciousness was the inevitable expression of an expanding market structure that destroyed proletarian subjectivity in its totalistic sweep, then it is fair to ask—within the framework of such a theory—how the working class could be expected to recover its lost subjectivity and constitute itself as an historical agent of change. How is reification to be overcome? What are the dynamic social forces necessary for a revolutionary politics? Lukacs unfortunately provided no convincing answers to such questions. In theorizing the possibilities of dialectical change, Lukacs' reliance upon a vision of cultural transformation was inadequate to the degree that the phenomenon of reification, in reducing workers to the status of mere objects, precisely closed off such an alternative.[37]

Lukacs' understanding of bourgeois ideological control was simply too all-encompassing and one-dimensional. Given this outlook he found himself retreating by default toward an orthodox Marxist productivism: for reification to be undermined, the entire commodity structure (i.e., the capitalist mode of production) itself would have to collapse. Ultimately, the only recourse was one or another variant of objectivist crisis theory.

As a theory of ideological domination, therefore, Lukacs' contribution was simultaneously too restrictive and too global when compared with Gramsci's concept of hegemony. It was too *restrictive* in linking reification exclusively to the sphere of production, too *global* insofar as it expected every aspect of social life to become fully immersed in the commodity form. Ideological hegemony, as we have seen, incorporates a variable and dynamic element grounded in no single structure or process. Gramsci applied the notion to vastly different settings—preindustrial and industrial—as well as to the realm of complex mediations in class and political struggle: nationalism, religion, liberalism, intellectual and cultural traditions. Rarely were the hegemonic ideologies explored by Gramsci in the *Notebooks* strictly reducible to the systems of production. Moreover, the functions of hegemony were also understood to vary greatly in their binding power from society to society; there was no presumed universalizing pattern to capitalist expansion (as Gramsci's analysis of Italian development revealed), no "iron cage" of reified consciousness.[38] The degree of equilibrium between state and civil society was always uncertain, a problem to be investigated.

It might be argued that Gramsci had overlooked the mystifying consequences of a reification process associated with advancing levels of capitalist rationalization in Europe. There is some truth to this, since Gramsci in fact devoted most of his historical analysis to *transitional* or residual ideological forces (e.g., religion) which of course made sense in the case of Italy. Nonetheless, once he turned his attention to the more developed countries—as in his essay "Americanism and Fordism"—he revealed an almost Lukacsian sensitivity to the problem of rationalization, which he saw as an increasingly powerful form of hegemony.

Italy: A Fragile Hegemony

Gramsci's fascinating treatment of Italian history in the *Notebooks*, while tentative and sketchy, can be seen as an extension of his earlier preoccupations in which he stressed the continuing dynamic connection between an incomplete bourgeois revolution and the "Southern Question."[39] Borrowing from both Machiavelli and Croce, while injecting the class dimension that they lacked, Gramsci now incorporated his previous historical insights into his theory of ideological hegemony. In the *Notebooks* he concluded that Italy, like Germany, represented the quintessential case of a sharp and perpetual disequilibrium between state and civil society, between ruling ideas and popular culture. For centuries, in other words, the peninsula had been under the spell of a chronically feudal hegemony, which reproduced itself through the period of national unification.

From at least the time of Machiavelli, when the first stirrings of nationalism appeared, Italy had been characterized by deep sociopolitical fragmentation involving divisions among the various city-states, between religious and anti-clerical traditions, between North and South, and later between industrial capitalism and feudal agrarianism. Italian civil society lacked the cohesion of England, the United States, and even France, where a sense of national "spirit" had accompanied and to some extent even preceded capitalist transformation. Gramsci believed that a full explanation of this predicament would have to go back to the Roman Empire—to the origins of Catholicism, the medieval Communes, and the "problem of the intellectuals". Catholicism turned out to be a major source of difficulty since Italy was the seat of the Vatican, whose powerful hegemonic role far overshadowed that of various social classes, reducing them to a narrow corporatist presence with little expansive potential. As Gramsci put it, Church domination "brought about an internal situation which may be called 'economic-corporate' —politically, the worst of all forms of feudal society, the least progressive and the most stagnant. An effective *Jacobin* force was always missing, and could not be constituted; and it was precisely such a Jacobin force which in other nations awakened and organized the national-popular collective will, and founded the modern states."[40]

The *Risorgimento* of the 1860s and 1870s, despite its vision of Italian unification, simply compounded the old social and regional divisions; it came no closer to establishing the kind of ideological bond between elites and popular strata embodied in Machiavelli's dream of a national community. The new industrial groups, based mainly in Piedmont, set out to "conquer" Italy and managed to "dominate" its political life, but they were never able to "lead" or mobilize consent with the result that northern liberalism became a "dictatorship without hegemony," the pathetic expression of an unfulfilled bourgeois-democratic revolution.[41] Because of their awkward isolation, these groups were inevitably drawn toward political coercion as the primary means of protecting their economic interests and securing their role as "arbiter of the Nation." This meant that the centralized state (and with it the monarchy) would have to be the agency of power and legitimation, replicating in effect the earlier authoritarian and ideologically destabilizing function of the Church. In other words, hegemony was lacking insofar as the State replaces the local social groups in leading a struggle for renewal.[42] At the same time, one of the main structural embodiments of northern liberalism during the *Risorgimento*— Mazzini's *Partito d'Azione,* or Action Party—was a frail, divided political force without "even a concrete programme of government." Steeped in the traditional rhetoric of Italian literature, leaders of the Action Party "confused the cultural unity which existed in the peninsula...with the political and territorial unity of the great popular masses, who were foreign to that tradition and who, even supposing they knew of its existence, couldn't care less about it."[43]

The legacy of the *Risorgimento* was thus a fragile bourgeios hegemony, in contrast to the vigorous Jacobin expansion of the French Revolution; the "Italian bourgeoisie was incapable of uniting the people around itself, and this was the cause of its defeats and the interruptions of its development."[44] Unable to penetrate beyond its own restricted social base, the northern industrial class was compelled to rely not only upon the state but upon alliances with pre-capitalist forces (notably the southern landholders). To a much greater extent than elsewhere, Gramsci noted, the development of capitalism in Italy was impeded and distorted by its necessary compromise with feudal survivals — the monarchy, Church, landholding aristocracy, southern traditionalism. In one of his last pre-prison writings, he noted that "as a result of its specific development, the specific national conditions of capitalist development, Italian society has conserved many relics of the past: a whole series of institutions and political relations which weigh on the situation and cloud its fundamental lines."[45] The consequences, which persisted well into the twentieth century, were severe economic imbalance marked by periodic social crises, a huge gulf between urban and rural sectors, parasitism and an inefficient managerial structure. Politically, of course, the embryonic institutions of bourgeois democracy were feeble and lacked consensual support insofar as the state itself had little organic presence in civil society. And the virtual absence of a national "collective will," either from above or from below, further reflected what one writer termed a cultural "crisis of progress" despite the great optimism of the nineteenth century Italian liberalism.[46]

Throughout the post-*Risorgimento* years, as Salvemini and Gramsci both observed, the South remained semi-feudal, industrially backward, and colonially dependent upon the North. Gramsci pointed out that continued northern domination blocked any significant accumulation of capital—and with it the rise of a "broad capitalist bourgeoisie"—in the *Mezzogiorno*.[47] More specifically, the "hegemony of the North" amounted to a "territorial version of the town-country relationship" in which "the North concretely was an 'octopus' which enriched itself at the expense of the South," that is "in direct proportion to the impoverishment of the economy and the agriculture of the South."[48] Thus southern Italy was "reduced to the status of a semi-colonial market, a source of savings and taxes," and kept disciplined by repression and patronage (public jobs awarded to intellectuals). The very weak character of southern urban development, moreover, led to a bizarre situation "which sometimes took the form of a literal subjugation of the city to the countryside."[49]

From the perspective of ideological hegemony, Gramsci was fascinated by the role of southern intellectuals, who had risen from the ranks of the aristocracy and, once attached to the state, became effective legitimating agents of traditionalism within the orbit of northern liberal domination. This phenomenon further reinforced the already sizeable gap between intellectuals and masses and, above all cut short the formation of a peasant-based culture of resistance. Thus: "Over and above the agrarian bloc, there functions in the South an intellectual bloc which in practice has so far served to prevent the cracks in the agrarian bloc becoming too dangerous and causing a landslide.... It is a remarkable fact that in the South, side by side with huge property, there have existed and continue to exist great accumulations of culture and intelligence in single individuals, or small groups of great intellectuals, while there does not exist any organization of middle culture."[50] Gramsci had in mind the conservative function not only of low-level intellectuals such as priests and civil servants but also of "great" individual thinkers like Croce and Giustino Fortunato. For example, Gramsci wrote that Croce's preoccupation with the ethico-political sphere helped to reproduce the myth of Italian cultural unity, thereby covering up the vast historical *differences* between North and South while downplaying the "moment of struggle."[51] In general, this incorporation of the most active southern elements transformed the intellectuals, who otherwise might have supplied leadership to mass peasant opposition, into accomplices of northern colonial policy. The unfortunate outcome was that popular discontent in the *Mezzogiorno*, lacking strategic direction, found "expression only in an anarchic turbulence" which was simply treated as a "matter for the police" and the courts.[52]

The strength of Catholicism in all areas of Italy, like the persistance of feudal social relations in the South, constituted for Gramsci yet another part of the historical logic which led to a weak bourgeois hegemony. Having resisted the incursions of industrialization, secular liberalism, and anti-clericalism, the Church emerged still ideologically powerful even if philosophically discredited; an obstacle to capitalist expansion, it remained a bastion of cultural legitimacy in its own right, by far the most important rallying point of conservative mobilization in the country. Reflecting on the 1870-1890 period, Gramsci wrote:

> The greatest weakness of the state in this period consisted in the fact that outside it, the Vatican grouped around itself a reactionary and anti-state bloc made up of landowners and the great mass of backward peasants, controlled and led by the rich landlords and priests. The Vatican's programme had two elements: it sought to struggle against the unitary, 'liberal' bourgeois state; and at the same time, it aimed to form the peasants into a reserve army against the advance of the socialist proletariat, stimulated by the development of industry.[53]

While Gramsci appeared to retreat somewhat from this harshly critical stance in the *Notebooks*, his fragmentary comments on religion nonetheless revealed certain insights into the profoundly conservative impact of Catholicism in modern Italian development. All observers agreed that religious ideology had penetrated deeply into popular and even working-class consciousness. Yet Marxists of Gramsci's generation typically assumed that Catholicism would rather quickly give way to the secularizing influence of material forces (i.e., capitalist transformation) or would later simply wither away as a by-product of the transition to socialism. Gramsci, however, approached the problem somewhat differently: religion had to be understood as a specific component in the larger matrix of domination—as a hegemonic tradition possessing a logic irreducible to economic conditions—and therefore as a distinct terrain of political struggle. He rejected facile assumptions about the "automatic" disappearance of religious values with higher levels of industrialization; in this respect such values were obviously much more than historical "relics" or survivals. The Church had to be understood as a concrete political formation in its own right. As Gramsci noted, religion must be approached "not in the confessional sense but in the secular sense of a unity of faith between a conception of the world and a corresponding norm of conduct. But why call this unity of faith 'religion' and not 'ideology,' or even frankly 'politics'?"[54]

But the Church in Italy was not merely part of the institutional status quo, a privileged fortress of economic wealth and social power centered around the Vatican and the Pope. Nor was Catholicism a strictly metaphysical or theological set of beliefs. Religious hegemony performed a worldly function to the degree that it contained popular rebellion—for example, by instilling in the masses the idea of a "natural" or "God-given" character of existing structures and social relations (private property, the family),[55] the importance of transcendental concerns over everyday, "earthly" collective action, the "moral" virtues of poverty and meekness, and the sacrosanct nature of all forms of established authority. Gramsci further argued, as we have seen, that the Church hierarchy made every effort to constitute itself as a special ecclesiastical order with an intellectual discourse beyond the reach, of the masses; such an order could only reinforce the passivity, fatalism, and parochialism already deeply embedded in Italian popular consciousness, especially in the South and the Islands. In this fashion Catholicism reproduced the "common sense" of pre-capitalist patterns of social and political life.[56]

Yet if Catholic hegemony served to restrict popular insurgency—notably among the peasantry—it likewise impeded capitalist development by producing the sort of disequilibrium between state and civil society referred to earlier. In failing to mobilize a broad national consensus around its class interests, the Italian bourgeoisie found itself burdened by a perpetual instability which ruled out the formation of strong liberal leadership. Politics often took the form of rivalry or intrigue among corporatist elite factions having little mass presence. Under these circumstances the bourgeoisie was naturally inclined toward *trasformismo*—an intricate but generally effective process of elite coalition-building described in chapter two. Gramsci carried his analysis of this phenomenon even further in the *Notebooks*, maintaining that "the entire state life of Italy from 1848 onwards has been characterized by *transformism*."[57] Gramsci identified two distinct phases in this bourgeois gambit to accomplish through methods of state engineering the kind of ruling legitimacy it lacked within civil society. The first, from 1860 to roughly 1900, was a "molecular" *trasformismo* in which individual representatives of democratic opposition forces were assimilated into a "conservative-moderate" governing bloc. At the time of the Risorgimento and after, the moderates were able to incorporate one-by-one the leaders of the militantly progressive (but hardly unified) Action Party by awarding them high government posts and other favors, with the result that "the popular masses were decapitated, not absorbed into the ambit of the new state."[58] The second phase, from 1900 onwards, involved the systematic cooptation of leftist parties and groups, including the Socialists, within the liberal orbit through the shrewd machinations of Premier Giolitti. Over time the ideological distinctions between "left" and "right" became more and more blurred, with the logic of elite consensus operating to override the demands and priorities of emerging mass constituencies.

In the *Notebooks* Gramsci referred to this political dynamic as "passive revolution"—a shifting equilibrium of forces which integrates opposition into the state apparatus while postponing real structural change and denying full entry of the masses into the political system. The ruling elites, in the absence of either ideological consensus or organizational cohesion, were able in this fashion to manage class conflict. At times Gramsci called this process "revolution/restoration"—a dialectic of radical upsurge and reconsolidation combined in the same phase of activity—which he at times equated with the strategic concept "war of position."[59] During the early *Risorgimento* period, for example, Cavour became visible as a proponent of a gradualist "passive revolution," hoping for limited and realistic gains within the existing power framework, whereas Mazzini was a "visionary apostle" rather than a "realistic politician" insofar as he pressed for radical transformation through direct popular initiative. Cavour easily prevailed, setting the contours of Italian development for the next century; for Gramsci, a Mazzinian victory would have given rise to an Italian state more consonant with "modern" development.[60] From the viewpoint of Gramsci's assessment of the actual historical forces at work, however, it would have been difficult to imagine an alternative outcome.

If the failure of bourgeois integration made for a tenuous

stability during the Risorgimento years, mass movements remained incapable of pressing this situation to their advantage. Incursions were made, but these movements lacked the unity made possible by organization and leadership to challenge the "traditional organic forces" (emergent bourgeoisie, landholders) which possessed "parties of long standing" and "rationally formed leaders."[61] This logic prevailed in one form or another until World War I. Not only the liberal elites, but those representing the left opposition as well, became in some measure detached from broad bases of popular support during this period. While a "passive revolution" was the only recourse available to a weak bourgeoisie desperate to avoid mass upheavals, such an arrangement was always fragile: indeed, the strains of industrialization and then the war would ultimately explode its very foundation. Yet, in the end, it was this precarious nature of bourgeois hegemony in Italy which, as Gramsci had predicted, gave rise to a new and more authoritarian recycling of the "passive revolution"—a dictatorial version of the old alliance between industrial and agrarian elites—culminating in fascism.[62]

"Americanism" and Technological Rationality

At the other extreme, far removed form Italy, Gramsci looked to the United States as an example of a society in which the ruling bourgeoisie had established the most complete ideological hegemony. Like many other European Marxists, he believed that the unique success of American capitalism could be explained by the absence of a feudal stage of development and, as it turned out, he was able to connect this insight nicely to his theory of hegemony. Gramsci observed that the first Anglo-Saxon pioneers who settled America brought with them a new "moral energy," a "new level of civilization" untrammeled by preindustrial residues that made possible the virtually limitless expansion of a unified capitalist mode of production, political system, and culture. The optimistic vision of progress through economic growth that the early colonialists implanted on fresh terrain assumed a certain rhythm and momentum of its own—a kind of self-propelling ideology. If in Europe class conflict tended to fit the traditional Marxist pattern, with the rising middle classes caught between the aristocracy and the proletariat, in the U.S. the great strength of bourgeois ideology undercut both conservative and socialist polarities, thus denying class conflict the explosive political impact it would have else-where.

With no feudal restraints, obstacles to capitalist development in the U.S. were more readily overcome than in the more tradition-bound European countries. As Gramsci put it, "The non-existence of vicious parasitic sedimentations left behind by past phases of history has allowed industry, and commerce in particular, to advance on a sound basis."[63] He wrote that the early American settlers were the

> ...protagonists of the political and religious struggles in England, defeated but not humiliated or laid low in their country of origin. They import into America...apart from moral energy and energy of the will, a certain level of civilization, a certain stage of European historical evolu-tion, which, when transplanted by such men into the virgin soil of America, continues to develop the forces implicit in its nature but with an incomparably more rapid rhythm than in Old Europe, where there exists a whole series of checks (moral, intellectual, political, economic) incorporated in specific sections of the popula-tion, relics of past regimes which refuse to die out, which generate opposition to speedy progress and give to every initiative the equilibrium of mediocrity, diluting it in time and space.[64]

The key element of American politics was that the whole life of the country had always revolved around capitalist productive activity, from which emerged a new type of human being, a new work process, a new dynamic material culture with no feudal survivals (monarchy, nobility, peasantry) and, as a corollary to all this, a weak socialist tradition in comparison with other capitalist societ-ies. Gramsci added that the very type of social existence found in liberal capitalism paved the way toward the later success of bureaucratic-corporate forms of rationality; indeed, the ideological phenomenon that Gramsci labelled "Americanism" seemed to apply to *both* liberalism and technological rationality—or at least their convergence appeared "natural" in a setting where bourgeois hegemony met so little resistance.

The American state, in contrast with the Italian and German states, therefore was able to sink deep roots in civil society; popular support for bourgeois institutions was widespread, even among workers. Class struggle, which took on even more militant expressions in the U.S. than in Europe, was never politicized to the point where mass-based socialist movements could effectively challenge the capitalist order. Reform and protest struggles were confined to either the corporate-economic sphere of the two-party system, with but a few short-lived exceptions such as the Industrial Workers of the World (IWW), while Marxism was successfully marginalized as an alien world-view adhered to only by misguided utopians and eccentrics. "The absence of the European historical phase," Gramsci noted, referring to feudalism, "has left the American popular masses in a backward state."[65] This permitted the bourgeoisie to manage the system's crisis-tendencies more adequately than elsewhere, rendering impotent any fundamental challenge to capitalist structures and values.[66]

American religious traditions too exercised a strong hegemonic influence, but of a sort quite different from Catholicism in Italy. Whereas the Roman Church had embraced an "other-worldly" form of conservatism in pre-capitalist Europe, the Protestantism forged by the Reformation—and later translated into the American experience by the Puritans—was closely linked to the rise of the bourgeoisie, with its dedication to the temporal values of hard work, thrift and frugality, sacrifice, self-discipline, and so forth. Much along the lines of Weber's thesis in *The Protestant Ethic and The Spirit of Capitalism*, Gramsci argued that such values were both the measure of religious salvation and the core consciousness of an emerging capitalist society. Hence a strong emphasis on earthly achievements and good deeds, in accordance with the Puritan concept of predestination, could be easily adapted to a material world obsessed with efficiency, private property, and profits. Gramsci found that the Protestant ethic was more universally assimilated by the popular masses in the U.S. than in any European country, owing in part to the absence of an established Church. Moreover, as he suggested in "Americanism and Fordism," the puritanical regulation of moral-personal life in the U.S. laid the groundwork for the later appearance of an historically new type of person—the "trained gorillas" so totally submerged in the rationalized work process that pleasure, sensuality, and critical thinking were almost totally stifled.[67]

This analysis, however, implies a concept of "Americanism" much broader than the simple historical convergence of liberalism and puritanism for in the twentieth century an entirely new phenomenon entered the picture: "Fordism". By the 1920s American enterprises, with Henry Ford leading the way, became the "prototype of the new industrialism" made possible by innovative forms of machine technology and bureaucratic control over the human labor force. The ideology which was the natural expression of this process—technological rationality—was now assimilated into the complex network of bourgeois hegemony. Gramsci saw in the process of rationalization the leading edge of a new epoch: the ruling classes were no longer only obsessed with efficiency but were now mobilizing to stave off economic crisis and reconsolidate the system on firmer ideological ground. This logic applied simultaneously to the rise of a bureaucratic-corporate economy in the U.S. and the ascendance of a fascist dictatorship in Italy. In each case, "Fordism" represented "the passage from the old economic individualism to the planned economy."[68]

Marxism before Gramsci had contributed precious little to a theoretical understanding of bureaucracy. Because of a strong productivist bias, Marxists had either ignored the problem altogether or merely viewed it as a direct structural expression of bourgeois class interests. Of course Marx himself wrote well before the appearance of large-scale organizations (either public or private) and thus could offer at best only a distant glimpse into a future shaped by bureaucratic and technological change, as he did in the *Grundrisse*. Of course Marxism originally evolved as a theory of classical competitive capitalism—a system in which the state, political parties, and bureaucracy were not fully articulated and thus could easily be viewed as derivative of or secondary to the material "base." Later orthodox Marxists carried this framework well into the twentieth century, long after bureaucracy had begun to evolve as an independent force requiring a more sophisticated conceptual approach.

It is therefore no coincidence that the two theorists who first confronted bureaucracy as a new and distinct form of domination in bourgeois society—Max Weber and Robert Michels—were not Marxists. Nor is it suprising that their view of social organization as a complex of relations irreducible to class structure was fiercely criticized by Marxists at the time. Writing from a liberal viewpoint, Weber approached bureaucracy as the fount of a new rationality tied to the irreversible logic of industrialization in any context. From this viewpoint bureaucratization gave rise to centralized modes of planning, a specialized division of labor, and, perhaps most vital, a new legitimating principle that was expected to prevail over all forms of traditionalism. Here Weber referred to a far-reaching "rational-legal" ideology with its celebration of instrumental norms, routinized methods of work and decision-making, professionalization, a codified system of law, and social hierarchy. The impact of bureaucratization, both structurally and ideologically, was to rationalize the mechanisms of political control and at the same time transform the general population into loyal, fragmented, and depoliticized subjects. Michels, as we have seen, applied this Weberian schema to an analysis of prewar German Social Democracy and concluded from it that large-scale organization posed insurmountable obstacles to socialist politics. Bureaucracy, as far as Weber and and Michels were concerned, was the defining motif of the industrialized societies after the turn of the century.

Gramsci was clearly influenced by this line of thinking, but only insofar as it could be made compatible with a critical Marxist framework that took into account the role of class forces. As the lynchpin of a "Fordist" organized and planned capitalist economy, bureaucracy and technology were not simply fixed elements of a universal industrialization process; they were also part of a broader system of *domination*, and the technological rationality which they embodied would become a hegemonic force of major proportions. In the *Notebooks* Gramsci paid a good deal of attention to the destructive effects that new industrial and administrative techniques—notably "scientific management," or Taylorism—had upon working-class consciousness and politics.[69] It could be said that his concept of "Fordism" was, like Lukacs' theory of reification, an implicit attempt to merge the concerns of Marx and Weber. In any case, Gramsci was probably the first Marxist to anticipate the massive consequences of rationalization for capitalist development as a whole: the transition to an administratively integrated state-corporate economy, the appearance of new forms of social control, the degradation of work and working-class consciousness. His opportunity to reflect upon the Italian fascist experience of the 1920s and 1930s no doubt contributed to this theoretical foresight.

Gramsci anticipated in Taylorism a hegemonic force in advanced capitalism equivalent in some ways to the function of religious ideology during feudalism and early capitalism. The new instrumental and secular "theology" of technological rationality which emanated from a convergence of science, technology, and large-scale organization would, within the structure of bourgeois class relations, impose even more rigid barriers to critical thought and action. The rationalization of production and work, already well advanced in the U.S., required a "collective man" or "mass worker" who would passively perform routine tasks and who would unthinkingly conform with a suffocating labor discipline imposed by the technocratic regimen in the interests of "efficiency". The physical and mental subordination of a new generation of workers to capital, through the apparatus of machine specialization and the new forms of ideological control, would be nearly total. As Gramsci added, however, this kind of labor discipline would also have to be accompanied by material concessions from capitalist management: "In America rationalization had determined the need to elaborate a new type of man suited to a new type of work and productive process. This elaboration is still only in its initial phase and therefore (appropriately) idyllic. It is still at the stage of psycho-physical adaptation to the new industrial structure, aimed for through high wages."[70] Given the absence in the U.S. of pre-capitalist "sedimentations." working-class resistance to rationalization was likely to be minimal in comparison with Europe.

In Italy, on the other hand, tradition-based opposition to capitalist restructuring suggested that this process would move in an authoritarian direction—i.e., it would have to unfold *against* the liberal state. Thus Gramsci saw in the rise of fascism a novel form of state capitalism; the outgrowth of a herculean effort by bourgeois elites to rationalize the economy in the face of mounting contradictions and obstacles. Centralized state planning became the main pillar of a reorganized productive system which, following Mussolini's corporatist model, would presumably institutionalize class conflict and consolidate the fragile position of the bourgeoisie without threatening the Church and other traditional interests. Thus: "In reality the corporative trend had operated to shore up crumbling positions of the middle classes and not to eliminate them, and is becoming, because of the vested interests that arise from the old foundation, more and more a machinery to preserve the existing order..."[71] Fascism in fact marked a dramatic triumph of capital over the proletariat, which itself had struggled to bring into being "newer and more modern industrial requirements" but found these efforts coopted by management.[72]

Whether channelled through "Fordism" or corporatism, through the liberal state or fascist dictatorship, Gramsci viewed rationalization as everywhere destructive of all intellectual, creative, and even human content within the labor process. It reduced workers' lives to virtual nothingness. Taylorism, for example, had the cynical purpose of

> ...developing in the worker to the highest degree automatic and mechanical attitudes, breaking up the old

psycho-physical nexus of qualified professional work, which demands a certain active participation of intelligence, fantasy, and initiative on the part of the worker, and reducing productive operations exclusively to the mechanical, physical aspect. But these things, in reality, are not original or novel: they represent simply the most recent phase of a long process which began with industrialism itself.[73]

By reducing workers to obedient automatons, rationalization would (insofar as it succeeded) break down their very capacity to respond creatively to new situations and thereby destroy their impulse to resist exploitation. Gramsci described Henry Ford as an innovative corporate general who was the first to perceive the immense productivity *and* control benefits to be derived from regulation the complete moral-psychological being of workers. The ultimate goal was to create a routinized psychic structure compatible with the imperatives of capitalist labor discipline. In other words, the "industrialists are concerned to maintain the continuity of the physical and muscular-nervous efficiency of the worker. It is in their interests to have a stable, skilled labor force, a permanently well-adjusted complex, because the human complex (the collective worker) of an enterprise is also a machine which cannot, without considerable loss, be taken to pieces too often and renewed with single new parts."[74]

It follows that the very logic of Fordism moved toward an unprecedented regulation of both work and "private" life; indeed, in Gramscian terms, rationalization was bound to obliterate the distinction between public and personal realms to a degree that even Puritanism could not have imagined. Of course in the American setting, as we have seen, Puritan religious ideology had historically cleared the way for this development insofar as it molded collective personalities to accept an externally imposed system of repression. The result was a unique interconnection of social forces: capitalism, bureaucracy, the family, religion. While the *Notebooks* contained no real theory of the family or sexuality, they did present a line of argumentation that, within Marxism, had been pursued only in the work of Wilhelm Reich.

Gramsci understood the history of industrialism as the struggle of human beings to dominate and tame not only nature but *themselves* as well—that is, to subordinate their wildest, most passionate, most uncontrollable impulses, or what he called "animality." He wrote: "It has been an uninterrupted, often painful and bloody process of subjugating natural (i.e., animal and primitive) instincts to new, more complex and rigid norms and habits of order, exactitude and precision which are the necessary consequence of industrial development."[75] Gramsci suggested that capitalism requires the stabilization of sexual relations within the monogamous family for the purpose of guaranteeing an obedient and hardworking labor force; the increasingly organic relationship between production and family was solidified first by Puritanism and later by Fordist rationalization. Thus as capitalism expands and comes to rely more and more upon technology and bureaucracy, "these new methods demand a rigorous discipline of the sex instincts...and with it a strengthening of the 'family' in the wide sense and the regulation and stability of sexual relations."[76] Rationalization simply carries a step further the repressive sexuality and authoritarian personality that was already a functional expression of early capitalism, the family, and religion. In more graphic terms: "It seems clear that the new industrialism wants monogamy: it wants the man as worker not to squander his nervous energies in the disorderly and stimulating pursuit of occasional sexual satisfaction. The employee who goes to work after a night of 'excess' is no good for his work."[77]

Gramsci saw in this coerced fusion of public and personal morality a dangerous trend toward a totally-administered society in which Fordism would probably become a type of "state ideology."[78] This was in fact the trajectory of European fascism in Gramsci's own lifetime. The American model, on the other hand, was not likely to fulfill such Orwellian projections: *state* regulation of personal and social life never approached fascist levels, while Puritanism and sexual repression subsequently *declined* with capitalist rationalization. Gramsci, like Reich, vastly exaggerated the capitalist requirements for stable monogamous sexual relations. From the standpoint of ideological hegemony, however, Gramsci's historical understanding of "Americanism" was well ahead of its time. More significantly, his view of technological rationality as a significant hegemonic force in the advanced capitalist societies represented a new theoretical departure within Western Marxism. The sketchy notes assembled in "Americanism and Fordism" might therefore be viewed as a preliminary statement to the later work on rationalization by theorists identified with the Frankfurt School, notably Herbert Marcuse.[79]

If Gramsci was correct in assuming that capitalist rationalization would give rise to a repressed and depoliticized mass consciousness, then the conventional Marxist expectation of growing class polarization with higher levels of industrialization would presumably have to be discarded. With proletarian subjectivity seemingly absorbed into the bureaucratic-corporate structure with the appearance of the assembly-line mass worker, capital accumulation could now occur in a relatively smooth, crisis-free fashion. In this respect Gramsci's commentary in "Americanism and Fordism" can be read as a theoretical concession to the traumatic *political* defeats suffered by the European working class in the early 1920s. Gramsci may well have been resigned to a lengthy phase of capitalist stabilization made possible by modern technocratic engineering. Surely he bemoaned the disappearance of the type of skilled and rebellious worker who formed the nucleus of the Turin factory council movement. For what the rise of the routinized "collective worker" signaled more than anything was the irretrievable loss of class autonomy vis-a-vis capital, and hence the eclipse of authentic struggles for proletarian self-management which could materially pose the question of socialism.

Gramsci's analysis of rationalization, though fragmentary and tentative, in effect shared more in common with Marx's theory of the fetishism of commodities and Lukacs' concept of reification than his general, more dialectical, notion of ideological hegemony would suggest. Pushed to its extreme, this emphasis inevitably suppresses that side of Marxism which looked to revolutionary self-activity as the main historical dynamic and which, moreover, best converges with Gramsci's philosophy of praxis and his previous optimism captured by the notion "actuality of the revolution." To the extent that rationalization can be said to enable the capitalist productive system to regenerate itself indefinitely, the agencies of resistance tend to vanish; the dialectic of class struggle is superseded by the triumph of absolute bourgeois hegemony. For if the workers are indeed reduced to "trained gorillas"—i.e., are transformed into passive, atomized, and degraded objects—by the new technocratic regimen, then the very psychological basis of proletarian subjectivity is eroded. Of course this was not the precise conceptual framework that Gramsci was interested in building. He wanted to grasp the central features of an entirely new phase of industrial development in the West—an organized and planned (state) capitalism that was beginning to engulf all spheres of autonomous social activity. For this purpose the old Marxist base-superstructure dichotomy was even more outmoded than before. Thus despite lapsing into a certain one-dimensionality here, Gramsci did perceptively identify the main structural and ideological barriers to socialist transformation posed by a rationalized political economy.[80] At the same time, this system would become the source of new and explosive contradictions of its own; it would constitute the terrain of a refocused dialectic of change which Gramsci barely glimpsed but could hardly have theoretically formulated during the period of his imprisonment.

Gramsci's more general theory of ideological hegemony nonetheless seemed to *imply* the possible emergence of countervailing tendencies to rationalized domination; beneath this near-totalitarian surface, workers (the unskilled as well as the skilled) would presumably be driven to resist. Indeed, Gramsci intimated as much when he wrote of the separation between purpose and actuality that could be expected to prevail in even the most draconian of Fordist ventures. Since routinization of the labor process can never fully obliterate critical consciousness, even the American industrialists "have understood that 'trained gorilla' is just a phrase, that 'unfortunately' the worker remains a man and even that during his work he thinks more, or at least has greater opportunities for thinking, once he has overcome the crisis of adaptation without being eliminated: and not only does the worker think, but the fact that he gets no immediate satisfaction from his work and realizes that they are trying to reduce him to a trained gorilla, *can lead him into a train of thought that is far from conformist"*.[81]

When viewed as part of Gramsci's overall theory, then, this concept of rationalization actually pointed to a new phase of class struggle and, equally significant, to a new arena in which it would be waged, although such implications were nowhere clearly spelled out in the *Notebooks*. The new arena was that of ideological-cultural struggle, which for Gramsci assumed new meaning in the developed countries where hegemony had become more decisive than force as an instrument of bourgeois rule, where the relationship between state and civil society was far more intimate than in earlier capitalist of semi-developed systems like Russia. In a famous passage Gramsci noted that

> In Russia the state was everything, civil society was primordial and gelatinous; in the West, there was a proper relation between state and civil society, and when the state trembled a sturdy structure of civil society was at once revealed. The state was only an outer ditch, behind which there stood a powerful system of fortresses and earthworks: more or less numerous from one state to the next, it goes without saying—but this precisely necessitated an accurate reconnaisance of each individual country.[82]

This idea is filled with implications for political strategy, which will be explored in chapter seven. The point here is that, from Gramsci's admittedly very sketchy treatment, the appearance of an increasingly complex *"ensemble* of relations" in advanced capitalism (the emergence of political parties and parliaments, the rise of a technical stratum within the labor force, the expanded role of education and mass media, the penetration of civil society by the state) gave the struggle for ideological hegemony an immediacy and even centrality that it did not have previously.

Hegemony and Class Struggle

Gramsci's theory of hegemony inspired a serious Marxist rethinking of issues connected to the state and political power, and, indirectly, to political *strategy* for the developed countries. In strategic terms, his theory revolved around the distinction between "organic" and "conjunctural" phases of revolutionary change, which is roughly equivalent to his well-known dichotomy between "war of position" and "war of movement" that will be discussed more fully later. Such a point of departure, though very rudimentary, permitted Gramsci to focus upon the efforts of subaltern groups to achieve ideological-cultural supremacy—to assume a position of "leadership" (*direzione*) within civil society—as the prerequisite for taking state power.

If the Leninist fixation on the "conjunctural" dimension—the struggle for political and military control over the state machinery—made sense in the case of Tsarist Russia, where "the state was everything and civil society nothing," in the West a new strategy was needed to take account of the deeper ideological "entrenchment" of the bourgeoisie. Reflecting on the failure of conventional crisis theory in the general European context, Gramsci wrote that for most of the advanced capitalist societies (with Italy only marginally included) "civil society has become a very complex structure and one which is resistant to the catastrophic 'incursions' of the immediate economic element (crisis, depressions, etc.)." Under these circumstances of strengthened hegemony, "a crisis cannot give the attacking forces the ability to organize with lightning speed in time and space" and "still less can it endow them with fighting spirit."[83] Referring to Trotsky's comparison of the "Eastern" and "Western" fronts,[84] Gramsci noted that the former (i.e., Russia) had fallen suddenly while the latter necessarily obliged a more protracted and multi-dimensional phase of combat prior to the conquest of power. It followed that both the orthodox Marxist *and* Leninist schema of a "catastrophic" rupture in the mode of production allowing for the rapid intervention of an armed revolutionary force must be jettisoned in favor of this counter-hegemonic model.[85]

Gramsci sometimes referred to the Protestant Reformation and the French Revolution as historical examples of successful counter-hegemonic politics. In each case the overthrow of the traditional order did not come as a dramatic event or episode but rather through a long and gradual phase of ideological-cultural ferment set in motion by subversive currents (Protestantism, the Enlightenment) linked to emergent social forces. The transfer of institutional power was but a single moment in a continuous modification of class relations that occurs largely "underneath the surface" of formal structures, norms, and laws. Socialist transformation in the West was expected to follow this general pattern: working-class ascendancy within civil society would be a necessary prelude to frontal assaults on the bourgeois state. Of course a Bonapartist-type seizure of power might conceivably intercept such a process, but lacking broad consensual support it would be neither democratic nor egalitarian.

But the struggle for hegemony was never simply a conflict of ideas and values in the Crocean sense, as is often mistakenly assumed. For Gramsci the class struggle passed through *both* the "conjunctural" and "organic" phases in a way that defies conventional formulas; the oppressed classes do not advance harmoniously but usually surge ahead and suffer defeats, come together and break up, all the while moving towards a variety of historical blocs and political formations. But there can be no question that Gramsci placed an overriding emphasis on the need for some kind of prior transformation of civil society:

> ...the supremacy of a social group manifests itself in two ways, as 'domination' and as 'intellectual and moral leadership.' A social group dominates antagonistic groups, which it tends to 'liquidate,' or to subjugate perhaps even by armed force; it leads kindred and allied groups. A social group can, and indeed must, already exercise 'leadership' before winning governmental power (this indeed is one of the principal conditions for the winning of such power).[86]

Gramsci's theory of hegemony possessed a sweeping power and

originality, but was ultimately flawed by a certain diffuseness; like many innovative concepts, it broke new theoretical ground but in the process left a whole array of critical questions unanswered. Above all, Gramsci's analysis of rationalization implied such a blurring of the distinction between civil society and state that these categories—so vital to his notion of hegemony—may have lost their conceptual utility. With no clear boundaries, the phases or "moments" of class struggle which Gramsci outlined in the *Notebooks* tend to lose their specificity. Gramsci's failure to explore the hegemonic and counter-hegemonic mechanisms within advanced capitalism, including the role of bourgeois democratic institutions,[87] was no doubt symptomatic of this problem. In the context of organized state capitalism, which Gramsci of course could not fully anticipate, theoretical and political efforts to isolate civil society are illusory. Perhaps it was the weight of just this realization that drove him to appropriate Lenin's "primacy of politics" in certain sections of the *Notebooks*.

Whatever its peculiar defects and limitations, the version of Marxism that emerged from Gramsci's discussion of hegemony looked fundamentally different from the orthodox and Leninist versions which preceded it. Though its influence would not be felt until years later, Gramscian Marxism contributed immensely to the development of a critical-dialectical theory insofar as it refocused attention on the ideological conditions necessary for a *democratic* socialist transformation in the West. The concept of hegemony was vital to such a renewal because it encouraged the thematic reintegration of ideology, culture, and consciousness into a Marxian framework without joining the common flight from *politics*. In doing so, it restored emphasis upon political education as a "moral-intellectual" force that would subvert the legitimating principles of bourgeois society and further lay the foundations of a secular and emancipatory "integrated culture". It would be a revolutionary pedagogy firmly grounded in the praxis of everyday political struggles. For Gramsci, this meant a vast theoretical reconstruction of Marxism along a whole range of decidedly "subjective" problems: the formation of mass consciousness, role of the intellectuals, nature of the party, and genesis of political strategy.

Footnotes

1. For a general discussion of this traditional Marxist approach to ideology, see Martin Seliger, *The Marxist Conception of Ideology* (Cambridge: Cambridge University Press, 1977), chapters 2-4. See also Richard Lichtman, "Marx's Theory of Ideology," *Socialist Revolution"* no. 23, April 1975, pp. 45-76, for a treatment that illustrates some of the dilemmas and limitations of the classical orientation.

2. "The Modern Prince," *SPN*, p. 184.

3. *Ibid*.

4. "The Study of Philosophy," *SPN*, p. 377.

5. "The Modern Prince," *SPN*, p. 164.

6. As Chantal Mouffe argues, Gramsci was really the first Marxist to elaborate a critique of economism on the basis of this understanding of ideology. Here again the influence of Croce and Sorel is rather easy to detect. See "Hegemony and Ideology in Gramsci," in Mouffe, ed., *Gramsci and Marxist Theory*, esp. pp. 169-70.

7. Some commentators have exaggerated the importance of the Russian origins of the concept of hegemony in order to show a closer linkage between Leninist and Gramscian theory than was in the fact the case. See Christine Buci-Glucksmann, *Gramsci and the State*, pp. 174-75, and Perry Anderson, "The Antinomies of Antonio Gramsci," *New Left Review* no. 100, November 1976-January 1977, pp. 15-19.

8. Gramsci did not adhere to this distinction consistently throughout the *Notebooks*. At times he suggested that hegemony corresponds rather strictly to civil society, For example: "What we can do...is to fix two major superstructural 'levels': the one that can be called 'civil society', that is the ensemble of organisms commonly called 'private', and that of 'political society' or 'the State'. These two levels correspond on the one hand to the function of 'hegemony' which the dominant group exercises throughout society and on the other hand to that of 'direct domination' or command exercised through the state and 'juridical' government." See "The Intellectuals." *SPN*, p. 12. In general, however, Gramsci clearly incorporated the state into his understanding of hegemony. Thus he referred to the "integral meaning" of the state as "dictatorship and hegemony." See "State and Civil society," *SPN*, p. 239. At another

point he wrote that, "the general notion of the state includes elements which need to be referred back to the notion of civil society (in the sense that one might say that state = political society + civil society, in other words hegemony protected by the armor of coercion)." "State and Civil society," *SPN*, p. 263. The thrust of Gramsci's contribution to the Marxist theory of the state is weakened here not only by such ambiguity but also by his failure to clearly specify the boundaries between political and civil society. For example, modern political parties and interest groups would not appear to belong exclusively to either the state or civil society.

9. "The Modern Prince," *SPN*, pp. 169-70.

10. Parallels between the themes of "hegemony" in Gramsci, "reification" in Lukacs, and "legitimacy" in Max Weber are quite striking. (Lukacs will be considered in the following section.) As for Weber, his analysis of ideology in the industrial societies centered mainly around the process of bureaucratization; legitimacy referred essentially to the "rational-legal" ethos, to instrumentalized forms of rationality typical of an administered (yet constitutional) system. Gramsci's concept of hegemony, on the other hand, corresponded (though not perfectly) to the *class* basis of domination; although it did not rule out the theme of bureaucratic rationality, it was viewed as one of many *forms* of ideological control which mediated class conflict. For whatever reasons, Gramsci chose not to confront the implications of Weberian theory in the *Notebooks*.

11. "The Modern Prince," *SPN*, pp. 181-82.

12. "The Modern Prince," *SPN*, p. 161.

13. "The Modern Prince," *SPN*, p. 199. Elsewhere Gramsci wrote that "Every philosophical current leaves behind a sedimentation of 'common sense': this is the document of its effectiveness. Common sense is not something rigid and immobile, but is continually transforming itself, enriching itself with scientific ideas and with philosophical opinions which have entered ordinary life." "The Study of Philosophy," *SPN*, p. 326.

14. *Ibid*.

15. "Notes on Italian History," *SPN*, pp. 103-04. The role of the intellectuals in Gramscian theory will be explored further in chapter 6.

16. Lenin went to great lengths to make his position on the state clear. For example: "...if the state is the product of the irreconcilability of class antagonisms, if it is a power standing *above* society and '*alienating* itself *more and more* from it,' it is clear that the liberation of the oppressed class is impossible not only without a violent revolution, *but also without the destruction* of the

apparatus of state power which was created by the ruling class and which is the embodiment of this 'alienation.' " "State and Revolution," in Robert C. Tucker, ed., *The Lenin Anthology* (New York: W.W. Norton, 1975), p. 315.

17. This point was never spelled out by Gramsci in any one place; it simply had to be inferred from his overall theoretical position. For an excellent discussion of this issue, see Nicola Auciello, *Socialismo ed egemonia in Gramsci e Togliatti,* pp. 67, 123-26.

18. "State and Civil Society," *SPN*, p. 260.

19. On this point Mouffe suggests that Gramsci's notion of hegemony opened up a new conception of politics and power. See "Ideology and Hegemony in Gramsci," *op. cit.*, pp. 199-201.

20. "The Modern Prince," *SPN*, p. 188.

21. Gramsci's analysis of this problem—including references not only to the French Revolution but to the Renaissance and the Reformation—is contained in "Problems of Marxism," *SPN*, pp. 393-99. Although valid from the perspective of hegemony, Gramsci's treatment unfortunately made no effort to determine the impact of economic conditions upon the degree of equilibrium. This theoretical weakness recurred from time to time in Gramsci's discussion of hegemony.

22. "State and Civil Society," *SPN*, p. 276.

23. "State and Civil Society," *SPN*, p. 270.

24. "State and Civil Society," *SPN*, p. 210.

25. *Ibid.* Here Gramsci observed that the crisis of authority, which gives oppositional forces new opportunities, is equally filled with dangers and pitfalls since the subaltern classes are generally less capable of responding to rapidly-changing situations with political and organizational skill than are the ruling classes, so that new levels of repression are a likely outcome. Hence: "The traditional ruling class, which has numerous trained cadres, changes men and progammes and, with greater speed than is achieved by the subordinate classes, reabsorbs the control that was slipping from its grasp. Perhaps it may make sacrifices, and expose itself to an uncertain future by demagogic promises; but it retains power, reinforces it for the time being, and uses it to crush its adversary and disperse his leading cadres, who cannot be very numerous or highly trained" (pp. 210-11).

26. The importance of connecting an emergent hegemony with the unfolding of new social relations grounded in everyday life cannot be stressed too much. Failure to comprehend Gramsci's broad and dialectical view of ideology (or culture) had been a source

of great confusion among critics who understand hegemony in its narrow idealist sense, as a detached system of values and beliefs. For an excellent discussion of this point, see Nicola Badaloni, "Liberta' individuale e uomo colletivo in A. Gramsci," in Franco Ferri, ed., *Politica e storia in Gramsci* (Rome: Editori Riuniti, 1977), pp. 9-21.

27. "Problems of Marxism," *SPN*, p. 388. This passage is typical of many in the *Notebooks*, which should dispel the common misconception that Gramsci viewed the struggle for hegemony as something more or less separate from the struggle for state power. Here, as elsewhere, Gramsci did not isolate the ideological from the structural components of revolutionary transformation.

28. One noteworthy exception to this rule is Feenberg's *Lukacs, Marx, and the Sources of Critical Theory*, pp. 152-54, although there is little explicit discussion here of parallels between reification and hegemony.

29. Georg Lukacs, *History and Class Consciousness* (Cambridge, Mass: MIT Press, 1971), p. 80. (Italics in the original.)

30. *Ibid.*, p. 64. (Italics in the original.)

31. *Ibid.*, pp. 70-71.

32. *Ibid.*, pp. 100-101.

33. *Ibid.*, p. 149.

34. *Ibid.*, pp. 90-91.

35. *Ibid.*, p. 92.

36. This point is emphasized by Feenberg, who writes: "What Lukacs calls for is thus a politics of cultural change that would challenge capitalist society at its 'spiritual' roots, that is to say, in its most basic definition of reality, in its paradigm of rationality, in its founding practices." See *Lukacs, Marx and the Sources of Critical Theory*, p. 196.

37. For a similar critique, see Andrew Arato and Paul Breines, *The Young Lukacs and the Origins of Western Marxism* (London: Pluto Press, 1979), pp. 138-40.

38. There is no commentary on Lukacs' theory of reification in the *Notebooks*, and it is unclear how familiar Gramsci was with Lukacs' work. The single reference to Lukacs was a misplaced criticism of his "undialectical" treatment of the relationship between human activity and nature. See "Problems of Marxism," *SPN*, p. 448. It seems evident here that Gramsci wanted to distinguish his own "philosophy of praxis" from Lukacs' presumably more "idealist" philosophy.

39. Aside from his early (1915-1918) writings, Gramsci further

explored these themes in his later PCI period. See, for example, the "Lyons' Theses", especially pp. 343-46, and "Some Aspects of the Southern Question," in *Political Writings-II,* pp. 441-462.

40. "The Modern Prince," *SPN*, p. 131. (Italics in original.) Gramsci added that peculiar to Italian development was the legacy of a "rural bourgeoisie" characterized by "parasitic" tendencies.

41. "Notes on Italian History," *SPN*, p. 106.

42. "Notes on Italian History," *SPN*, pp. 105-06.

43. "Notes on Italian History," *SPN*, pp. 62-63. Here Gramsci was referring to a certain holdover from the insular and elitist Renaissance tradition which he contrasted with an emphasis in French political literature on "the necessity of binding the town (Paris) to the countryside." (*Ibid.*, p. 63.)

44. "Notes on Italian History," *SPN*, pp. 53-54.

45. "We and the Republican Concentration," October 13, 1926, *Political Writings-II*, pp. 422-23.

46. Remo Bodei, "Gramsci: volonta, egemonia, razionaliza-zione," in Ferri, *Politica e storia in Gramsci*, pp. 86-87.

47. "Some Aspects of the Southern Question," in *Political Writings-II*, p. 458.

48. "Notes on Italian History," *SPN*, pp. 70-71.

49. "Notes on Italian History," *SPN* pp. 94, 99.

50. "Some Aspects of the Southern Question," in *Political Writings-II*, p. 459.

51. "Notes on Italian History," *SPN*, p. 118. On Croce's general role in Italian politics, Gramsci suggested that "it is precisely in civil society that intellectuals operate especially (Benedetto Croce, for example, is a kind of lay pope and an extremely efficient instrument of hegemony—even if at times he may find himself in disagreement with one government or another)." *Ibid,.* p. 56.

52. "Notes on Italian History," *SPN*, p. 94.

53. The "Lyons' Theses," January 1926, in *Political Writings-II*, p. 346.

54. "The Study of Philosophy," *SPN*, p. 326.

55. Gramsci described "popular religion" as "crassly material-istic" and suggested that Catholicism in particular "always recognized a political personality only in property, implying in other words that man is not worthy for his own sake but only insofar as he is completed by material goods." "The Study of Philosophy," *SPN,* p.361.

56. On Gramsci's equation of religion and "common sense," see "The Study of Philosophy," *SPN,* pp. 323, 326.

57. "Notes on Italian History," *SPN*, p. 58.

58. "Notes on Italian History," *SPN*, pp. 97-98.

59. "Notes on Italian History," *SPN*, pp. 108-09.

60. *Ibid.*

61, "Notes on Italian History," *SPN*, p. 112.

62. An excellent analysis of this trajectory is contained in John A. Davis, *Gramsci and Italy's Passive Revolution* (London: Croom Helm, 1979), pp. 20-23. For an overview of the entire post-Risorgimento period, see Paul Ginsborg, "Gramsci in the Era of Bourgeois Revolution in Italy," in the same volume, pp. 31-65. See also Giuseppe Galasso, "Gramsci e il problema della storia italiana," in Rossi, ed., *Gramsci e la cultura contemporanea*, pp. 305-354.

63. "Americanism and Fordism," *SPN*, p. 285.

64. "The Intellectuals," *SPN*, p. 20.

65. "Americanism and Fordism," *SPN*, pp. 286-87.

66. Gramsci's analysis of American "exceptionalism" here bore a close resemblance to the later interpretation of Louis Hartz in his *Liberal Tradition in America* (New York: Harcourt, Brace and World, 1955). Of course Gramsci's understanding of U.S. history, based as it was upon inadequate source material, lacked the depth and systematic quality of Hartz' account. It also revealed a poor grasp of the importance of slavery and black history, an understandable omission but one that necessarily qualifies some of the generalization. Yet when one examines the problem from a comparative perspective, Gramsci's insights into the unique character of bourgeois hegemony in the U.S. remain impressive for their richness and originality.

67. "Americanism and Fordism," *SPN*, pp. 300-305.

68. "Americanism and Fordism," *SPN), p. 279*.

69. Gramsci's assessment of Taylorism and rationalization in general differed radically from Lenin's. Out of his enthusiasm for the adoption of Western technological and scientific methods in Russia, Lenin embraced the new forms of rational social engineering made possible by Taylorism. See Rainer Traub, "The Fate of 'Scientific Management' in the (Early) Soviet Union," *Telos,* no. 37, pp. 82-92.

70. "Americanism and Fordism," *SPN*, p. 286.

71. "Americanism and Fordism", *SPN*, p. 294. Gramsci added that corporatism was an ideology obsessed with modernization while at the same time seeking to avert a "monstrous catastrophe." It therefore hoped to "proceed by very slow and almost imperceptible stages to modify the social structure without violent attacks." *(Ibid.)* For a discussion of Gramsci's approach to corporatism, see Franco De Felice, "Rivoluzione passiva, fascismo, e americanismo in Gramsci," in Ferri, ed., *Politica e storia in*

Gramsci, esp. pp. 202-213.

72. "Americanism and Fordism," *SPN*, p. 292.

73. "Americanism and Fordism," *SPN*, p. 302.

74. "Americanism and Fordism," *SPN*, p. 303.

75. "Americanism and Fordism," *SPN*, p. 298.

76. "Americanism and Fordism," *SPN*, p. 300.

77. "Americanism and Fordism," *SPN*, p. 304-05. This passage could also be read as a critique of Soviet rationalization efforts in the 1930s, when Stalin initiated a campaign to strengthen the family and return to traditional social and sexual relations as a means of bolstering labor discipline. Gramsci's negative assessment of Trotsky's earlier design to militarize Soviet production in some measure anticipated this logic. (*Ibid.*, p. 301.)

78. "Americanism and Fordism," *SPN*, p. 304.

79. Marcuse's *One-Dimensional Man* (Boston: Beacon Press, 1964), which probably best fits into this theoretical tradition, presents in more systematic form concepts which Gramsci had just begun to explore in 1931. Sections of *Studies in Critical Philosophy* (Boston: Beacon Press, 1972), written in 1932 and 1936, reflected the early Weberian influence on Marcuse and already anticipated his later preoccupation with the theme of rationalization. Max Horkheimer too had begun to examine the impact of technological rationality on a variety of phenomena—science, the family, social theory—in the 1930s. See *Critical Theory: Selected Essays* (New York: Seabury Press, 1972).

80. This linkage between Gramsci's theory of hegemony and his analysis of capitalist rationalization is generally overlooked in the literature. For one such example, see Enzo Rutigliano, "The Ideology of Labor and Capitalist Rationality in Gramsci," *Telos* no. 31, spring 1977, pp. 91-99.

81. "Americanism and Fordism," *SPN*, pp. 309-10. (Italics mine.)

82. "State and Civil Society," *SPN*, p. 238. Or, as Gramsci wrote in a more strategic vein: "The massive structures of the modern democracies, both as state organizations and as complexes of organizations in civil society, constitute for the art of politics as it were the 'trenches' and the permanent fortifications of the front in the war of position; they render merely 'partial' the element of movement which before used to be 'the whole' of war, etc." (*Ibid.*, p. 243.).

83. "State and Civil Society," *SPN*, p. 235.

84. Gramsci's reference (*Ibid.*, p. 236) was to a statement made by Trotsky in his report to the Fourth World congress of the

Comintern in 1922, at which Gramsci was present. However, following this commentary Gramsci hastened to express his disagreement with "Bronstein's famous theory about the *permanent* character of the movement," implying that a convergence of the two "fronts" within the same worldwide revolutionary process was highly improbable. (pp. 236-37)

85. The strategic consequences Gramsci drew from his theory of hegemony (and counter-hegemony) here should further dispel any ambiguity concerning his supposedly "Leninist" application of the concept. Thus, for example, while Salvadori is correct in arguing that Gramsci's approach to hegemony has little in common with the contemporary PCI version, his contention that "Gramsci's theory of hegemony is the highest and most complex expression of Leninism" must by questioned. See Massimo Salvadori, "Gramsci and the PCI: two conceptions of hegemony," in Mouffe, *Gramsci and Marxist Theory*, p. 252. For a different perspective emphasizing a non-Leninist angle, see Giuseppe Vacca, "La 'quistione politica degli intelletuali' e la teoria marxista dello stato nello pensiero di Gramsci," in Ferri, *Politica e storia in Gramsci*, pp. 463-70.

86. "Notes on Italian History," *SPN*, p. 57.

87. Strangely enough, Gramsci's preoccupation with the role of parties, unions, and parliament in his pre-prison writings did not carry over into the *Notebooks*; indeed his earlier critiques gave way to almost complete silence on this topic—explicable no doubt in part by the situation in Italy, where fascist dictatorship rather than bourgeois democracy became the key issue of the 1930s. At any rate, in the absence of any clear reassessment it is fair to assume that Gramsci's hostile attitude to bourgeois democracy presented in chapter three did not undergo any basic change. Surely nowhere did Gramsci link his theory of hegemony—or more specifically his distinction between "Eastern" and "Western" fronts—to a parliamentary-based strategy for the advanced countries, as Eurocommunist theorists have mistakenly concluded. At the same time, Anderson is correct to note the vagueness in some of Gramsci's theoretical formulations here. See "The Antinomies of Antonio Gramsci," *op. cit.*, pp. 27-29.

6 Class Consciousness and the Formation of Intellectuals

The great ambiguity of classical Marxism on the role of popular consciousness in revolutionary change had already become evident by the turn of the century. Confined largely to the paradigm of capitalist development, early Marxism often reproduced the very logic of that paradigm (reflected in an attachment to neo-Ricardian economics), thus sidestepping the difficult problem of how an *alternative* to capitalism might be realized. The theory expressed a certain methodological antagonism toward what were regarded as "utopian" concerns: the *forms* of class conflict, the development of proletarian organization, culture, and community, the transformation of consciousness, and the social psychology of political rebellion. This was to be expected, given the theoretically disabling effects of scientism and economism within a tradition that remained tied to the primacy of production. In any case, the phenomenon of revolutionary consciousness was scarcely even discussed before the explosive prewar debates around political strategy finally forced the issue.

Much of this silence had its origins in Marx's own writings, in which the sphere of ideology and consciousness was viewed as a direct manifestation of class dynamics; "socialism" was understood as a complex of forces, barely visible from a distance, that would take root naturally within the very dialectic of capitalist evolution. Scattered references to the role of the political vanguard in the *Manifesto* and elsewhere notwithstanding, the dominant motif of nineteenth century Marxism was the contradiction between wage-labor and capital, which would lead inexorably to proletarian transcendence of the mature capitalist system. Marx apparently thought that the very weight of the bourgeois social division of labor would by itself drive workers toward socialist consciousness, with everyday struggles at the point of production—within the factory—constituting a "school" for revolution. Accordingly, bourgeois ideology was nothing more than a simple cover for ruling-class interests, a thinly-disguised intellectual deception that would quickly unravel in the midst of class conflict. The vision of a self-interested and rapidly-expanding proletariat ready to assault the bourgeois fortress inspired a mechanical and dichotomistic approach to mass consciousness which was bound to ignore the variable historical modes of class formation.[1]

This theoretical outlook gave rise to an even more positivized Marxism of the late Engels and the Second International, for which the problem of consciousness was merely a troublesome kind of "bourgeois idealism" that stood in the way of a coherent materialist analysis of historical development. As a result, Marxist politics entered into a strategic impasse: movements and parties wound up imprisoned in their own social immediacy, restricted on the whole to the momentary ebb and flow of practical activity, incapable of mobilizing workers around any broad social vision. While the more successful social-democratic parties, like the SPD in Germany, were able for a time to generate significant popular support, they failed to instill much political dynamism; the masses were not psychologically involved in the life of the party. In other words, mobilization was broad but superficial. To the degree that feelings, emotions, and values were all considered to be "irrational", secondary, or idealist, then expressions of class consciousness could be interpreted as rational-cognitive responses to fairly predictable situations, as the outgrowth of a certain utilitarian psychology. Not surprisingly, class conflict was reduced to a species of interest-group politics.

But such a framework could not grasp the historical complexity of class formations in the transition to socialism. If workers were to be understood as making their own history, or at least as participating decisively in the revolutionary process, then class forces would have to be analyzed as part of the larger totality of life experiences, social relations, cultural activity, and so forth; resistance to capitalism would accordingly take many diverse forms, not all of them "rational." The working class, much like the bourgeoisie before it, was an assemblage of social-forces-in-evolution rather than merely a discrete bundle of material interests, a class whose consciousness was embedded in a whole network of associations and institutions as well as traditions peculiar to it—the accumulated culture of decades and generations.[2] The factories and working-class neighborhoods may not have been "schools" of revolution, but they could nonetheless be seen as the infrastructure of an emergent class solidarity. Orthodox Marxism, in its haste to assert "scientific" over "utopian" dimensions of theory, either lost sight of this subjective element of class formation or took it for granted. In either case, one finds in the leading theorists of classical social democracy little appreciation for the type of workplace and community-based ideological supports needed to break the dependency of workers on the established institutions and sustain long periods of struggle.[3] Conversely, those factors which tend to fragment or depoliticize working-class existence, and which thus intrude upon fixed class-based ideological formulas—e.g., the family, religion, nationalism, race—were likewise all but ignored or dutifully reduced to their proper material foundations.[4]

In the absence of a conceptual model sensitive to the mediations between economic conditions and political action—i.e., to the historical forms of class consciousness—there could be no criteria for evaluating the successes *or* failures of socialist movements. And this was not a strictly theoretical matter. Thus, when structural breakdown did occur in Europe after World War I, leading to massive anti-capitalist upheavals, the social-democratic parties failed to take advantage of these new opportunities in part because they conceded the ideological-cultural terrain to the bourgeoisie. The conditions for successful insurgency might have been "ripe," but "subjective" responses did not meet the "objective" historical imperatives. The problem was that large sectors of the proletariat (not to mention the peasantry and petty bourgeoisie) had never really internalized socialist politics; dispersed and in retreat, many actually went in the direction of fascism. The European working class, far from having emerged as a "class for itself," came increasingly under the spell of bourgeois hegemony during the 1920s and 1930s as capitalist reconsolidation assumed more harshly authoritarian forms.

The depth of this problem went largely unrecognized within prewar Marxism. Some initial and bold but not very systematic efforts to break through the barriers of orthodoxy were made by Labriola, Gustav Landauer, Luxemburg and, on the fringes of Marxism, by Sorel and the Council Communists but it was only after the war—indeed after the stunning political defeats of the early 1920s—that Marxist theorists began to seriously address the issue of consciousness. By the late 1920s a critical tradition grounded in new ways of linking theory and consciousness was established in the work of Korsch, Lukacs, Reich, the early Frankfurt School, and (just tentatively at this point) Gramsci.

The key insight of this theoretical renovation, as Luxemburg stressed, was that the revolutionary process could not develop upon a foundation of psychological inertia or passivity and that the "solution" to a lagging mass consciousness was not to be found in a vanguard elite. Where before the proletariat as imputed universal subject of history existed in the form of theoretical abstraction and little more, now it would have to be constructed in its flesh-and-blood totality.[5] As Reich later observed, the fatal weakness of the European left was its failure to articulate a "mass psychology" that would permit it to "speak the language of the broad masses" with imagination and emotional appeal. Marxism was too schematic and abstract, too preoccupied with material forces: "While we presented the masses with superb historical analyses and economic treatises on the contradictions of imperialism, Hitler stirred the deepest roots of their emotional being. As Marx would have put it, we left the praxis of the subjective factor to the idealists; we acted like mechanistic economistic materialists."[6] Reich's point was that, despite the broad spirit of rebellion in Germany during the 1920s and 1930s, "socialism" never became a concrete vision for large numbers of people, never became internalized, while fascism or "national socialism" was very deeply compelling insofar as it captured the emotional and even "romantic" sentiments of everyday life.

Reich chastized Marxists for having lost touch with the needs, desires, fears, and anxieties of the masses out of a singular interest in the objective contradictions of capitalism. Theory in effect had projected an artificial and incorrect understanding of historical process onto the consciousness of oppressed strata, thereby falling into the trap of an inverted subjectivism or what Lukacs called "abstract utopianism."[7] Having lost sight of the mundane, sensuous character of popular ideology, Marxism lapsed into the fallacy of a "ready-made class consciousness" deduced from the objective position of the working class within capitalism as a whole. For Reich, however, class struggle was inconceivable apart from efforts to transform personality structure—to combat bourgeois culture in every area of social life. Thus:

> We make and change the world only through the mind of man, through his will for work, his longing for happiness,

in grief, through his psychological existence. The 'Marxists' who degenerated into 'economists' forgot this a long
time ago. A global economic and political policy, if it
means to create and secure international socialism, must
find a point of contact with trivial, banal, primitive,
simple everyday life, with the desires of the broadest
masses....Only in this way can the objective sociological
process become one with the subjective consciousness of
men and women, abolishing the contradiction between
the two.[8]

Few Marxist theorists or leaders, unforunately, chose to pursue
this line of reasoning very far. Reich's prescription merely illuminated the tragic fate of the German left, which, like its Italian
counterpart, eventually fell prey to the forces of reaction. And
Gramsci arrived at many of the same conclusions, but without
Reich's explicit social-psychological foundations or his theoretical
concern with Freud.[9] Such conclusions, interestingly, had their
origins in the young Gramsci—in the writings of the *Ordine Nuovo*
period and even before—anticipating by more than a decade his
seminal contributions on the problem of consciousness in the
Prison Notebooks. Already during these early years Gramsci had
rebelled against the political instrumentalism and economism of
his own Italian Socialist Party and correctly predicted, well before
the rise of fascism, that the PSI would become paralyzed by its
ideological narrowness and lack of "cultural expansiveness."

"Common Sense", Spontaneity, and Beyond

Gramsci began with the assumption that social movements
can never be anything more than the collective consciousness
which defines them and expresses their potential at any historical
moment. As the foundation of political "will," such consciousness
does not simply shift with the cyclical tendencies of capitalist
development; it is not the immediate result of crisis and breakdown
but instead contains its own logic which no economistic formula
can adequately comprehend. From this viewpoint, consciousness
transformation was an integral part, a dialectical component, of the
general remaking of civil society that would depend upon profound
changes in the "ensemble of relations." The masses would have to
be transformed from "passive" spectators into "active" subjects.[10]
The following passage reveals Gramsci's thinking during his
formative years:

Man is above all else mind, consciousness—that is, he is a product of history, not nature. There is no other way of explaining why socialism has not come into existence already, although there have always been exploiters and exploited, creators of wealth and selfish consumers of wealth. Man has only been able to acquire a sense of his worth bit by bit, in one sector of society after another ...And such awareness was not generated out of brute physiological needs, but out of intelligent reasoning, first of all by a few and later by entire social classes who perceived the causes of certain social facts and understood that there might be ways of converting the structure of repression into one of rebellion and reconstruction. This means that every revolution had been preceded by an intense labor of social criticism, of cultural penetration and diffusion.[11]

The PSI leadership, however, possessed none of these insights—a fact that in Gramsci's opinion helped to explain why the Socialists were incapable of acting decisively during the postwar crisis. PSI strategy under the reformist Turati was shaped by an institutionally-centered parliamentarism on the one hand and a fatalistic vision of capitalist collapse on the other. It viewed consciousness as an outgrowth of material necessity, as part of the natural evolution of the proletariat in which "socialism" appears once the capitalist mode of production has exhausted its potential. This was standard Second International orthodoxy, the legacy of Engels and Kautsky, whereby reformism and scientism came to occupy two sides of the same coin. The PSI leadership instinctively looked to the bourgeois state machinery as the main source of political initiative, which pushed the party toward a collaborationism that, in the wake of the *Biennio Rosso*, helped to restore capitalist order in Italy. For Gramsci, this historic impasse could not be explained apart from the PSI's naturalistic approach to mass consciousness.[12]

As an example of the PSI's myopic theory Gramsci cited the party's blanket rejection of a strong prewar cultural tendency known as Futurism. Although a good deal of Futurist art and literature expressed hostility to the traditional order—to capitalism, the academic establishment, high culture, Catholicism—PSI Marxists found it lacking in "socialist" content and thus chose to ignore its progressive challenge. But Gramsci saw in it something altogether different: an ideological-cultural or aesthetic subversion of conventional values that, while not explicitly "Marxist", was nevertheless "preparing new ground in the class struggle"; in this sense at least Marinetti and his Futurist disciples could be considered "revolutionaries".[13] If socialism were to fully affirm its claim to political ascendancy, it would have to create a cultural life superior to that of the bourgeoisie and, in doing so, would have to build upon the embryonic but imperfect currents of cultural protest and revolt.[14] Gramsci believed that Futurism, in the period before it drifted toward reactionary populism, embodied this potential.

Gramsci's answer to the PSI's sterile Marxism, as we have seen, was the council communism of the *Ordine Nuovo* movement. It sought to rekindle class consciousness at the point of production, largely outside of the institutional network of the parties, parliament, and trade unions; the councils were to recover that proletarian subjectivity which capitalism had deformed and the PSI had ignored. Victimized by PSI sabotage, state repression, and its own spontaneism, *Ordine Nuovo* collapsed soon after it appeared, giving way in 1921 to the Communist Party as the main left alternative to the Socialists. But the PCI, a small organization controlled by the "abstentionist" Bordiga faction, progressed little beyond the PSI in its capacity to face the issue of consciousness. The Bordighists wanted to build an ultra-centralized vanguard organization as a means of safeguarding revolutionary identity. Thus, at a time when Mussolini was moving to consolidate fascist power, the PCI leadership was primarily concerned with sustaining ideological and organizational autonomy. Gramsci's reaction was a "united front"—a broad *popular* force—that could combat fascism while also preserving its socialist commitments. Bordiga's line prevailed until his arrest in 1924, and it was not until the Lyons Congress in early 1926 that Gramsci's position was adopted by the central committee; by this time, however, the party was about to be forced underground.

Returning to the problem of consciousness in prison, Gramsci was moved to do some of his most original and important work. His earlier frustrations with the PSI, the council movement, and the PCI surely must have been a powerful motivating force. At the same time, his concern for the politics of everyday life, his fascination with the role of popular attitudes and beliefs, and his activist temperament must have made incarceration all the more difficult to endure. This was no doubt one of the reasons why he read a good many popular novels and journals in prison, for through them he was able to understand better a certain range of aspiration, need, and emotion prevalent among the Italian masses. But after years of incarceration Gramsci found that no reading could be very enlightening so long as he was cut off from friends, family, and comrades—from the very pulse of ordinary activity. Already in November 1928 he expressed the following sentiments to his sister-in-law Tatiana:

> I do a great deal of reading. But I enjoy it much less than I used to. Books and magazines contain generalized notions and only sketch the course of events in the world as best they can; they never let you have an immediate, direct, animate sense of the lives of Tom, Dick and Harry. If you're not able to understand real individuals, you can't understand what is universal and general.[15]

Ironically, Gramsci's theoretical work remained alive despite the absence of this immediate dialectic between the "animate" and the "universal", but of course he could draw abundantly from his pre-prison experiences.

A critical theme of the *Notebooks* was that class struggle matures on a "higher plane than the economy;" a decisive rupture with the bourgeois "ensemble of relations" would never occur without a profound consciousness transformation at the popular level. Granted that capitalism was beset with ongoing structural crises, these were not enough to explain the rise and decline of concrete movements. As Gramsci noted: "It may be ruled out that immediate economic crises of themselves produce fundamental historical events; they can simply create a terrain more favorable to the dissemination of certain modes of thought, and certain ways of posing and resolving questions involving the entire subsequent development of national life."[16] Yet consciousness was not a matter for abstract paradigms of thought, detached from material conditions, but was rather a *concrete political force*—a complex syndrome of ideas, beliefs, and even myths integral to the life-world of a "collective organism" (social stratum or class) and the *sine qua non* of praxis. Consciousness was above all the medium through which the oppressed strata become self-determining revolutionary subjects. Whatever the degree of working-class militancy, "no mass action is possible if the masses in question are not convinced of the ends they wish to attain or the methods to be applied."[17]

One of the fatal errors of traditional Marxism, Gramsci observed, was the tendency to fetishize concepts like "class," "state," "party," and "mode of production," assigning them to a trans-historical universality which obscured their social concreteness and thereby concealed the individual human actors who infused these concepts with purpose. Here he contrasted the psychological sensibility of a critical perspective with the "external attitude" typical of a mechanistic approach. The latter in effect transferred political initiative from self-conscious human beings to structural entities possessing a kind of collective personality, inducing a sort of immobility:

> The individual expects the organism to act, even if he does not do anything himself, and does not reflect that precisely because his attitude is very widespread, the organism is necessarily inoperative. Furthermore, it should be recognized that, since a deterministic and mechanical conception is very widespread...each individual, seeing that despite his non-intervention something still does happen, tends to think that there indeed exists, over and above individuals, a phantasmagorical being, the abstraction of the collective organism, a kind of autonomous divinity, which does not think with any concrete brain but still thinks, etc.[18]

This Sorelian-flavored passage reveals Gramsci's insights into the bureaucratic dangers of hierarchical forms operating "above" everyday popular existence, detached from local struggles which may not be "revolutionary" but which have democratizing potential. In mass mobilization the initial problem is not spontaneism but Jacobinism, since where organization becomes a self-contained instrument, with clear-cut boundaries between politics and social life, the self-conscious, collectivizing dimension of change is lost. Commenting on the disastrous failure of postwar PSI strategy, Gramsci wrote that for party leaders "what was 'spontaneous' was inferior, not worth considering, not even worth analyzing. In reality, the 'spontaneous' was the most crushing proof of the party's ineptitude, because it demonstrated the gulf between fine-sounding programmes and wretched deeds."[19] He called the PSI theorists to task for failing to appreciate the *developmental* potential of "primitive" rebellion—e.g., populism, urban insurrection, utopianism, cultural revolt—which had long been a feature of the Italian landscape.[20] Because the initial stirrings of protest were inevitably "impure," infused with elements of bourgeois hegemony, it would be foolish to think that insurgency would follow ideologically coherent lines from the outset; political opposition is always contradictory and uneven. The vital challenge for Gramsci was how socialists could help advance pre-political struggles beyond spontaneity, how they could integrate expressions of alienation, despair, and anger into a viable revolutionary movement.

This brought Marxism face-to-face with the psychological realm of "common sense." As a philosophy of praxis, Marxism could not revert to the luxury of competing with the old "systemic philosophies" at the level of elite discourse but would have to insert itself into the mundane and even "trivial" concerns of the masses. From this angle the historical role of theory was to politicize the incoherent and fragmentary ideas bound up with common sense, which assumes a multitude of expressions, rather than to uncover a distilled revolutionary truth that looks like a "baroque form of Platonic idealism." In Gramsci's words: "Indeed, because by its nature it tends toward being a mass philosophy, the philosophy of praxis can only be conceived in a polemical form and in the form of perpetual struggle. Nonetheless the starting point must always be that common sense which is the spontaneous philosophy of the multitude and which has to be made ideologically coherent."[21]

In Gramscian terms, therefore, the dilemma was how to move beyond social immediacy without at the same time destroying spontaneous impulses. Whereas the anarchists and syndicalists glorified common sense as innately rebellious, Gramsci defined it as a disaggregated collection of sentiments, ideals, hopes, and myths in which "one can find there anything one likes,"[22] whether conservative or reformist, reactionary or revolutionary. Such diversity and mixture of ideologies was inescapable given the power of bourgeois hegemony:

> There exists in the totality of the working masses many distinct wills: there is a communist will, a maximalist will, a reformist will, a liberal democratic will. There is even a fascist will, in a certain sense and within certain limits. So long as there exists a bourgeois regime, with a monopoly of the press in the hands of capitalism and thus the possibility of the government and political parties to impose political issues according to their interests, presented as the general interest, so long as the freedom of association and meetings of the working class are suppressed and restricted, so long as the most impudent lies against communism are diffused at will, it is inevitable that the working class will remain fragmented, that is with many different wills.[23]

This notion of a contradictory and rather formless yet dynamic mass consciousness is one that Gramsci adhered to throughout the *Notebooks*. The prospects for socialist consciousness would depend upon a critique and transcendence of "natural" or pragmatic belief-systems insofar as "common sense is an ambiguous, contradictory, and multiform concept, and that to refer to common sense as a confirmation of truth is nonsense."[24] As noted in chapter three, Gramsci argued that Catholicism was the type of popular ideology which reinforced the most fragmentary and superstitious world-views, whereas the task of Marxism was to raise mass consciousness above this mundane level—to create "good sense" in place of "common sense" (*senso buono* as opposed to *senso commune*). Bourgeois hegemony is so pervasive that all unmediated psychological impulses will be more or less conditioned by ruling ideologies; common sense, therefore, could never be more than a limited and *distorted* negation of the capitalist system. Spontaneous forms of class struggle could never bear positive elements of a new order.[25]

Here Gramsci insisted that the transition from common sense to good sense, from spontaneity to critical consciousness, must emerge neither directly out of the social reality of productive relations nor out of the moment of cataclysmic "explosion." This outlook conflicted not only with orthodox Marxism but also with Leninism to the extent that it too relied heavily upon a crisis scenario. Still, Lenin would have agreed with Gramsci's contention that revolutionary consciousness could not be expected to *originally* develop through the self-activity of the oppressed strata. In other words: "Ideas and opinions are not simultaneously 'born' in each individual brain: they have had a center of formation, of irradiation, of dissemination, of persuasion—a group of men, or a single individual even, which has developed them and presented them in the current form of political reality."[26]

It follows that the ideological expressions of insurgent social forces are rarely fixed and stable but are recurrently changing through the influence of political events, social disruptions, and new philosophical or scientific discoveries. Change can take a revolutionary direction only through the introduction of a counter-hegemonic "external element," since otherwise popular revolt would be absorbed into the prevailing system of hegemony or, worse, mobilized in the direction of reactionary populism. Regarding this latter possibility Gramsci had in mind the success of fascist appeals among workers and peasants in Italy, from which he concluded that "neglecting, or worse still despising, so-called spontaneous movements, i.e., failing to give them a conscious leadership or to raise them to a higher plane by inserting them into politics may often have serious consequences."[27]

The emergence of a collective political will is always gradual and uneven, part of a counter-hegemonic *movement* in which intellectuals are destined to play a leading role. The pre-political stage is typified by a simple but often militant anti-authoritarianism such as "dislike of officialdom—the only form in which the state is perceived." Gramsci suggested that this "generic hatred is still 'semi-feudal' rather than 'modern' in character, and cannot be taken as evidence of class consciousness—merely as the glimmer of such consciousness, in other words, merely as the basic negative, polemical attitude."[28] From a *political* standpoint, anti-authoritarianism could give rise to various expressions of adventurism or "utopianism;" it could evolve toward a mature critical consciousness (Marxism); or it could drift back into a sense of fatalistic despair and passivity in the wake of repression or defeat. The mood of the rural masses in the Italian South, which Gramsci had studied very closely, typically swung back and forth between the two poles of spontaneous revolt and fatalism.

Gramsci's developmental view of consciousness transcended the old dichotomies: science vs. ideology, vanguard vs. mass, "true" vs. "false" consciousness. The ebb and flow of political struggle, the persistence of bourgeois hegemony, and the uneven nature of class formation all function to blur such facile theoretical distinctions. Such an historicist approach to the actual evolution of social formations ruled out highly-structured conceptions of popular ideology.[29] For Gramsci, moreover, since virtually all aspects of daily life impinge upon consciousness in one way or another— serving to either uphold or subvert the system of hegemony—the entire relationship between politics and consciousness was broadened and redefined.[30]

Pushed to its extreme, the historicist understanding of popular consciousness was bound to lead to the theoretical predicament of relativism—the assumption that there cannot be any "revolutionary" consciousness separate from the actual historical class definition of itself. Seeking to avoid this trap, Gramsci was anxious to specify the process whereby spontaneity would finally be abandoned in favor of a critical subjectivity tied to ultimate socialist *goals*. One such formulation in the *Notebooks* involved a transition from the "corporate-economic" to the "political" stage, where the question of the "*state*," or the "*ensemble* of relations," is raised to the point where the interests of one stratum or group "can and must become the interests of other subordinate groups too." Insofar as the "corporate" ideology was defined by a narrow sense of economic self-interest (for example in much of the trade-union movement), it could never pass beyond bourgeois reformism, for the expression of working-class demands within competing sectors of the economy (crafts, occupations, enterprises) runs counter to class solidarity and development of a systemic perspective. Only when "previously germinated ideologies become 'party'," allowing for a "unison of economic and political aims," can hegemony be contested on a "universal" plane.[31] Gramsci might well have had the failure of the Turin council movement in mind here.

Elsewhere in the *Notebooks* Gramsci equated the triumph of critical consciousness over spontaneity with a shift from the Crocean sphere of absolute ideals to the political terrain. Insurgent social groups can achieve a degree of "independence" from the ruling class only when moral-intellectual resistance is crystallized into a global (political) force. Thus:

> Critical understanding of self takes place...through a struggle of political 'hegemonies' and of opposing directions, first in the ethical field and then in that of politics proper, in order to arrive at the working out at a higher level of one's own conception of reality. Consciousness of being part of a particular hegemonic force (that is to say, *political* consciousness) is the first stage towards a further progressive self-consciousness in which theory and practice will finally be one...This is why it must be stressed that the political development of the concept of hegemony represents a great philosophical advance as well as a politico-practical one. For it necessarily supposes an intellectual unity and an ethic of conformity with a conception of reality that has gone beyond common sense and has become...a critical conception.[32]

Following Lenin, Gramsci assumed that consciousness transformation would depend upon the leading role of the intellectuals, but he departed from Lenin to the extent that he insisted that popular social forces themselves must ultimately constitute the real agency of change. In this sense, as I shall argue in the following sections, Gramsci's theory of the intellectuals and his general approach to consciousness were hardly "Leninist". His outlook was counter-hegemonic insofar as he looked to the formation of a national-popular "integrated culture" that would be transmitted through everyday social processes rather that an organized elite structure which, regardless of its "democratic" intentions, would only reproduce hierarchical power relations.[33] Rejecting the Kautskian thesis of an autonomous and scientifically motivated intellectual stratum, Gramsci wrote that "the principle must always rule that ideas are not born of other ideas, philosophies of other philosophies; they are a continually renewed expression of real historical development."[34] Here again the dialectical content of Gramscian theory stands out in his attempt to overcome the familiar dualism of intellectual vs. popular element, organization-leadership vs. spontaneity, and theory vs. ideology. Reviewing the *positive* achievements of the Turin factory council experience, Gramsci summed up his approach to consciousness as follows:

> It [the leadership] applied itself to real men, formed in specific historical relations, with specific feelings, out-looks, fragmentary conceptions of the world, etc..... This element of 'spontaneity' was not neglected and even less despised, It was educated, directed, purged of extraneous contaminations; the aim was to bring it into line with modern theory [i.e., Marxism]—but in a living and historically effective manner. The leaders themselves spoke of the 'spontaneity' of the movement, and rightly so. This assertion was a stimulus, a tonic, an element of unification in depth.... It gave the masses a 'theoretical' consciousness of being creators of historical and institutional values, of being founders of a state. The unity between 'spontaneity' and 'conscious leadership' or 'discipline' is precisely the real political action of the subaltern classes, insofar as this is mass politics and not merely an adventure by groups claiming to represent the masses.[35]

Theory and consciousness are therefore integrated through the medium of class struggle; intellectuals and masses are shaped by the same historical conditions, and therefore struggle against bourgeois domination in unison. The intellectuals articulate a new conception of the world in their role as theorists, educators, and leaders but they do not become the final repository of creative ideas or the main vehicle of socialist construction. Historical subjectivity belongs to the masses who gradually expand their potential for critical thought and subversive action in the very process of transforming bourgeois society.[36] It was from this perspective that Gramsci sometimes referred to socialist revolution as the "modern popular Reformation."

Gramsci, Luxemburg, and Lenin

The theory of mass politics that Gramsci developed in the

Notebooks had much in common with Luxemburg's earlier emphasis on popular consciousness, which entered her work after the Russian Revolution of 1905, and with Sorel's vision of proletarian solidarity formed through a shared myth. In the prewar years, when objectivist Marxism still predominated, Luxemburg and Sorel stood virtually alone in affirming that revolutionary action must be rooted in a system of collective norms, emotive symbols, and language; and they were among the first to question the economistic premises of the orthodoxy. Yet in riding the crest of the postwar neo-Hegelian wave, Gramsci was able to move theoretically well beyond their tentative and incomplete explorations—especially those of Sorel, whose militant and romantic syndicalism soon degenerated into a reactionary populism and therefore lost its relevance for the development of Marxist theory.[37] Above all, Gramsci rejected their deep conviction that the proletariat itself, through its own spontaneous self-activity, could become a revolutionary force. At the same time, he stopped short of accepting the simple vanguardist alternative introduced by Lenin and the Bolsheviks.

Luxemburg started with a notion of the proletariat as subject-object of history, according to which consciousness was understood as moving organically in a socialist direction—as maturing through a long series of crises and political struggles. She perceived each new upsurge of the working class, each new confrontation with bourgeois power, as part of a progressive awakening that would bring revolution closer. Socialism was not, as Lenin had argued, a world-view that would have to be inculcated into the workers from outside the sphere of production; rather, "socialism is simply the historical tendency of the class struggle of the proletariat in capitalist society against the rule of the bourgeoisie."[38] Luxemburg looked with great optimism to the spontaneous life-force of the workers, citing the 1905 Russian Revolution as an example of large-scale direct mass action that surged ahead of the conservative party bureaucracies. To the extent that leadership had always oscillated between prudent moderation and Blanquism, its political impact was to repress conscious popular involvement; it could never get beyond the elitist view of human beings as manipulated objects. In her classic critique of the Leninist model of political organization, which she described as a return to nineteenth century Jacobinism, she wrote;

> Blanquism was not based on the immediate class consciousness of the working masses. Therefore, it did not

need a mass organization. On the contrary. The great mass of the people were to appear in the arena only in the moment of revolution. The preparatory action for the revolutionary coup was the work of a small minority. Consequently, in order to succeed, the sharp separation of those persons executing this mission from the masses of the people was directly necessary. This was possible and practicable because there was absolutely no inner connection between the conspiratorial activity of a Blanquist organization and the daily life of the masses.[39]

In the spirit of combating opportunism and revisionism, Lenin had set out to build an "organizational kernel" largely set off from its surrounding milieu, with all initiative reserved to a small nucleus of elites. Strategy and tactics would be formulated outside the realm of mass struggles, since only experienced leaders can possess the ability to respond creatively and rapidly to new situations. Luxemburg believed that such an undialectical politics was the disastrous result of a weakly developed proletarian consciousness in Russia, where centralism could easily prevail over the democratic-popular element. The Bolsheviks came naturally to consider revolution as an *event* rather than a *process*, as a tactic of the "first blow" rather that a long phase of class struggle within civil society. Under these conditions "Lenin's concern is essentially the control of the activity of the party and not its fruition, the narrowing and not the development, the harrassment and not the unification of the movement."[40] For Luxemburg, the idea of substituting vanguard leadership for mass self-activity was a Jacobin delusion which in the end denied the authenticity of socialist objectives. In contrast to Lenin, she viewed Marxism not simply as a (scientific) theory but as the broad *critical consciousness* of a popular movement "which, in all its moments, *in its entire course*, reckons on the organization and the independent direct action of the masses."[41]

Luxemburg was really the first theorist to raise these issues within a framework that transcended a limited anarchistic spontaneism. Her sophisticated analysis of capitalist development, her uncompromising attack on anarchism and her scattered positive references to the role of a revolutionary party, workers' councils, and soviets is enough to show that her celebrated "spontaneism" must be strongly qualified.[42] If the "socialization of society" should only be realized through the "tireless struggle" of the working masses, it was nonetheless true that organized leadership (the

Social Democrats, the Spartacus League) would still have to be created out of "the most conscious, purposeful part of the proletariat."[43]

Yet her theory failed to avoid some of the most debilitating classical Marxist assumptions: a boundless revolutionary faith in the proletariat, a vision of progress tied to a unilinear concept of historical development, and a strong reliance upon crisis theory. In her rejection of both the SPD's narrow reformism and Leninist Jacobinism she found refuge in the "masses" who would counter the powerful authoritarian currents at work within Marxism. But her vision of the mass strike, as well as her desire for a "dialectic" between leaders and followers—furnished no tangible solution to the problem of building a sustained democratic socialist movement. Whatever significant insights her work generated, it was largely devoid of new and original *concepts*. Luxemburg's great attachment to the mass strike resembled more than anything else a Sorelian myth that enabled her to sidestep the intricate problem of the relationship between consciousness and organization; it also permitted her to avoid taking up the issue of democracy in its *concreteness*, as part of the movement to create popular, non-bureaucratic structures of authority.[44]

Luxemburg was thus ultimately forced to rely exclusively on the masses themselves, with their properties of innate rationality and free self-determination—a schema not too far removed from the anarchism she had rejected. But such an outlook became increasingly less defensible by the mid-1920s, when the reconsolidation of capitalism and the rise of fascism placed the whole issue of mass consciousness in a new light. It was in Germany, ironically, where material conditions seemed most mature and the systemic crisis most acute, that Luxemburg's spontaneism failed to meet its clearest test. In large part abandoned to its own unmediated struggles, the postwar German working-class movement encountered chaos, division, isolation, and eventually harsh defeat.[45]

The Hegelian Marxism of the early Lukacs could also be defined as "spontaneist" insofar as *History and Class Consciousness* represented a monumental theoretical effort to restore proletarian subjectivity to the revolutionary process. For Lukacs, as for Luxemburg, the exploited position of the working class within capitalist production set it in opposition to the total system, conferring upon it an historical mission; socialism was defined less as a particular theory or world-view than as the culmination of proletarian struggles calling into question the social priorities of capital. Workers gradually develop the capacity to organize as they achieve critical awareness of their collective alienation and impoverishment, so that each proletarian "is driven by the absolutely imperious dictates of his misery—the practical expression of this necessity—to rebel against this inhumanity."[46] Hence there could be no external or universal criteria for evaluating consciousness formation independent of the (imputed) historical definition of the proletariat itself, which meant that there could be no revolutionary "state of the future" outside the concrete, living working-class movements which are "the conscious subject of total social reality."[47] In Lukacs' words: "Consciousness does not lie outside the real process of history. It does not have to be introduced into the world by philosophers."[48]

In his seminal critique of mechanistic Marxism, Lukacs philosophically demolished the pretense of a "scientific" historical knowledge separate from human consciousness, of a theory outside the unfolding of class struggle. Like Luxemburg, he viewed the proletariat as the subject-object of revolutionary change, but he emphasized the role of crisis, breakdown, and cataclysmic upheaval to a lesser extent than she did. For Lukacs, regardless of the specific material conditions of historical forces at work, one thing remained certain: "Only the consciousness of the proletariat can point the way that leads out of the impasse of capitalism."[49] Furthermore, to effectively pose the issue of socialism such consciousness would have to transcend the *economic* categories typical of bourgeois consciousness, or what he called the "crassest form of 'false consciousness.' "[50]

The problem was that Lukacs' theory of the proletariat as universal revolutionary subject permitted few insights into *specific* and *variable* expressions of class consciousness or the conditions required to overcome reification. Divorced from its ever-changing and contradictory psychological elements, class consciousness for Lukacs became little more than the assigned world-historical role of the proletariat, a form of designated collective awareness that justified his revolutionary optimism. The theoretical predicament here stemmed from Lukacs' inability to see the open-ended, problematic, and thus *constructed* nature of class consciousness. Indeed, much later, in his own introduction to *History and Class Consciousness*, Lukacs criticize his conception of an "imputed" consciousness that could never supply the foundations of a transformative politics. No better proof of the young Lukacs' failure to ground a political strategy in his version of spontaneism is to be found than in his own retreat to Leninism as he took up the question of organization [51]

Gramsci shared the disenchantment of Luxemburg and Lukacs with the elitism of social democracy, as well as their dramatic shift in emphasis toward the theme of popular self-activity, but Gramsci was more guarded in his assessment of spontaneity than either of them. During the *Ordine Nuovo* period, of course, Gramsci had flirted with a type of syndicalist localism which seemed close to the spirit of the factory councils and the movement for workers' control. The collapse of the councils forced him to rethink this posture, and over the next several years he gravitated toward a more party-centered communism that owed a good deal to Lenin, the Bolshevik tradition, and the Comintern. So it is hardly shocking to find in the *Notebooks* a sympathetic response to Lenin's earlier critique of spontaneism in *What is to Be Done?* But Gramsci, as we shall see in his treatment of organic intellectuals, drew altogether different theoretical and political conclusions.

Lenin viewed working-class consciousness in its "given" form as essentially the mirror reflection of bourgeois ideology rather than as its negation. It followed that the requirements for theory, innovative leadership, and political vision were not likely to be generated solely or even primarily within proletarian social existence; the workers were so enslaved to a practical survival mentality that they could never, on their own, move beyond immediate material concerns. Lenin had little tolerance for the spontaneists (or "economists") in Russia because they would restrict the labor movement to its most retarded stage of political growth insofar as they automatically equated the "proletariat" with "socialism" regardless of the extent to which the workers themselves were committed to such goals. Of course large numbers of workers would be driven by their exploited position to struggle for change, but left unmediated such struggles would not produce revolutionary consciousness but rather an economistic reformism inevitably confined to the logic of bourgeois ideology. Thus:

> There is much talk of spontaneity. But the *spontaneous* development of the working-class movement leads to its subordination to bourgeois ideology ... for the spontaneous working class movement is trade unionist... (which) means the ideological enslavement of the workers by the bourgeoisie. Hence, our task ... is to *combat spontaneity*, to divert the working class movement from this spontaneous, trade-unionist striving to come under the wing of the bourgeoisie, and to bring it under the wing of revolutionary Social Democracy.[52]

Lenin concluded that only the intervention of an "external" *political* force could reverse the strong pressures toward reformism and opportunism, for "we *shall never be able* to develop the political consciousness of the workers...by keeping within the framework of the economic struggle, for *that framework is too narrow.*'[53] Only a centralized party led by full-time professional cadres could instill revolutionary consciousness in the masses and thus raise the class struggle to the level of socialist politics. Such a party would become the main repository of theory *and* consciousness. Following Kautsky, Lenin argued that Marxism and Social Democracy were the historical expression not of the proletariat but the "educated representatives of the propertied classes", i.e., the intellectuals, who elaborated their theories "altogether independently of the spontaneous growth of the working-class movement."[54] All of this served to theoretically justify Lenin's vanguardism.

The imposing continuity from *What is to be Done?* through the October Revolution and beyond can only be understood as a function of the dialectical relationship between theory and practice that shaped Bolshevik struggles in Russia. Basic to such continuity was Lenin's forging of a cohesive political instrument designed to conquer power at a moment of grave crisis in the traditional order; he brilliantly carried out such a conquest in the absence of broad popular support and without a significant prior transformation of civil society. But if for Lenin seizing state power became the first priority, with socialist construction to follow in a subsequent stage, then the party-state would be superimposed upon an amorphous and even hostile population. Local organizations such as the soviets and factory committees which might have democratized the revolutionary process had little space to flourish, and were ultimately destroyed by the Bolsheviks. Hence the task of reconstituting social and authority relations was left to the vanguard apparatus itself—a contradictory situation in which the gulf between state and civil society typical of pre-1917 Russia would inevitably be reproduced. An ideologically insular stratum of elites became virtually the sole proprietor of new values, resulting in two separate levels of discourse, two spheres of activity: one expressed through the Marxist culture and language of intellectual activists, the other through the largely manipulated responses of the masses.[55]

Gramsci's Marxism can be understood as an implicit effort to transcend the extreme polarities of Luxemburgian spontaneism and Leninist Jacobinism. As indicated in the previous section, Gramsci consistently adhered to the idea of proletarian self-emancipation, even during the depressing years of fascist hege-mony. Yet this understanding was more complicated for Gramsci than it was for Luxemburg and Sorel. Already by 1921, and possibly earlier, Gramsci had endorsed Lenin's view that the transition to socialism would require distinctly *political* forms of intervention.[56] And this outlook assumed a different sense of urgency with the rise of fascism and the growing fragmentation of the Italian left.[57]

In his prison writings, as we have seen, Gramsci looked to a dialectical synthesis of vanguard and masses, theory and con-sciousness: put another way, he sought to "democratize" the external element by giving it popular substance. Above all his concept of ideological hegemony opened up new theoretical space and allowed for transcendence of the spontaneist-Jacobin dualism. On the one hand, the very fact of bourgeois hegemony meant that spontaneous popular struggles would be restricted to bourgeois categories of thought and action; they would be economistic, incapable of challenging the system as a whole. In the wake of the postwar defeats throughout Europe, it would have been a sheer delusion to think that socialism could be the natural outgrowth of a maturing proletariat. The transition had to be seen as a matter of architectonics, as a creative political intervention that could shape emergent movements. In Gramsci's view, the spontaneists had totally ignored the problem of hegemony and, given their irrepres-sible optimism in direct mass action, lost sight of this architectonic dimension.[58] On the other hand, to the degree that the concept of hegemony called attention to the role of ideological contestation—to the necessary conquest of civil society—Leninist vanguardism, with its consuming emphasis on state power, becomes obsolete. For Gramsci, the organized elite sphere (sometimes referred to as the "collective intellectual") would initially carry out largely ideolog-ical or *pedagogical* rather than instrumental functions. Moreover, it would operate more as a *catalyst* in the revolutionary process than as the main locus of consciousness through all phases of the transition.

The concept of hegemony further introduced an *historical* element to the problem of consciousness transformation that was absent from both Luxemburg and Lenin. Their reliance upon essentially a priori criteria—i.e., definitions of class consciousness in advance—negated comprehension of *different* modes of class struggle, different possible outcomes, different strategic impera-tives. Thus spontaneism and vanguardism were equally caught up in an undialectical theory of the role of intellectuals: either the intellectuals were completely marginalized, or they were the sole bearers of revolutionary conscience and vision. Gramsci sought an alternative to the populist anti-intellectualism of the first and the elitist authoritarianism of the latter.

The Theory of Organic Intellectuals

Gramsci's preoccupation with ideological hegemony, mass consciousness and the "*ensemble* of relations" led him to consider the role of intellectuals relative to both their social position in capitalist society and their contribution to socialist politics. It could be argued that Gramsci was really the first Marxist to confront the problem of intellectuals directly, as a theoretical issue.[59] The term "intellectual" did not connote for Gramsci a particular kind of individual—someone from the traditional educated stratum with a claim to social autonomy[60]—but rather a universal set of activities tied to the moral-political dimension of class struggle. Intellectual *activity* in this sense might be understood as furnishing cohesion and "homogeneity" to class formation; as such, it works to either reproduce or undermine the forms of bourgeois hegemony.

In contrast to the Kautsky-Lenin thesis, which conceived of intellectuals as purveyors of scientific knowledge, Gramsci looked upon all human interaction as in some measure "intellectual" to the extent that everyone "contributes to sustain a conception of the world or to modify it, that is, to bring into being new modes of thought."[61] Or, put differently, "the majority of mankind are philosophers insofar as they engage in practical activity and in their practical activity (or in their guiding lines of conduct) there is implicitly contained a conception of the world, or philosophy."[62] The intellectual sphere, therefore, did not involve a specialized type of mental work associated with conventional scholastic or literary traditions but was an integral part of everyday life—culture, social relations, work, politics. Thus: "The mode of being of the new intellectual can no longer consist in eloquence, which is an exterior and momentary mover of feelings and passions, but in active participation in practical life, as constructor, organizer, 'permanent persuader,' and not just a simple orator...."[63] Gramsci further suggested that intellectual activity, at least from a political standpoint, includes not only discovering or creating ideas but also *disseminating* them: "Creating a new culture does not only mean one's own individual 'original' discoveries. It also, and most particularly, means the diffusion in a critical form of truths already discovered, their 'socialization', as it were, and even making them the basis of vital action, an element of coordination and intellectual and moral order."[64]

In general terms, therefore, intellectuals carry forward the most elaborate and mature expression of the prevailing traditions, culture, and moral values; they impart a sense of historical purpose to social activity; and they erect an ideological defense of particular class interests. Here once again Gramsci departed from Croce's idea of an autonomous ethico-political realm by insisting that every intelligentsia is in some way part of a class formation and is necessarily, by virtue of its social role and ideological influence, a creative force in politics. Insofar as cohesive infrastructures (e.g., the state, parties, education) are vital to sustain ruling-class legitimacy, the network of ideological hegemony tends to converge with the "common sense" of popular consciousness. Gramsci's theory was most appropriate to the "Western Front"—to the developed bourgeois societies—where hegemony reduces the gulf between state and civil society through the impact of mass education, the media, and the cultural apparatus.[65] On this basis he thought that an intellectual stratum would be needed to perform mediating tasks which could lend the social immediacy of class self-activity with the global, unifying dimension of politics.

For this reason Gramsci was perfectly aware that, even allowing for the universality of intellectual discourse, all people are not intellectuals in exactly the same way at exactly the same point in time: they differ greatly in terms of social position, levels of education, cultural development, and, above all, their distinct *political role*. It could hardy be otherwise within a capitalist division of labor that routinely separates intellectual and physical activity within the sphere of production; bourgeois society reproduces uneven *intellectual* as well as uneven economic development. The division of labor, moreover, denatures working-class life along with the political movements it generates.

From the viewpoint of the proletariat, Marxism represents a human vision and mode of analysis that clearly sets it apart from common sense and the multitude of hegemonic ideologies; as such it takes hold unevenly throughout bourgeois society as a whole. Gramsci indicated that Marxist intellectuals, of whatever social origins, perform functions that are "advanced" relative to the overall evolution of the working class and other subordinate groups. These functions, perhaps diffuse and unfocused in the early stages, tend with the expansion of mass struggles to cohere within broad counter-hegemonic political formations.

One example of such a transformative process would be the revolutionary party, which in the *Notebooks* Gramsci referred to as the "collective intellectual" or "myth prince" to distinguish it from a "Caesarist" centralized elite. This type of party would be less a vehicle of "scientific truth" than a moral-intellectual force which could lay the groundwork for popular self-activity on a wide scale. Marxism would never gain ascendancy simply because of the logical consistency of its analysis or the body of knowledge it could furnish, nor because of the theoretical innovations of great thinkers—significant as these might be. On the contrary: "The most important element is undoubtedly one whose character is determined not by reason but by faith."[66] "Theory" in this sense achieves its fullest and most dynamic expression in the norms of collective action, where the general level of consciousness is altered to such a degree that the division intellectuals-masses is abolished and everyone becomes an intellectual in the best Marxian (and Gramscian) meaning of the term.

The transformative power of Marxism, therefore, can be actualized only through its critical and dialectical engagement with existing popular ideology, with the daily lives of working people. In pedagogical terms this involves a two-fold dynamic: the various layers of bourgeois hegemony within the *"ensemble* of relations" are gradually stripped away, and the emergent patterns of thought and action are given subversive meaning. Hence at the very outset Marxism

> ...must be a criticism of 'common sense', basing itself initially, however, on common sense in order to demonstrate that 'everyone' is a philosopher and that it is not a question of introducing from scratch a scientific form of thought into everyone's individual life, but of renovating and making 'critical' already existing activity. It must then be a criticism of the philosophy of the intellectuals out of which the history of philosophy developed and which, insofar as it is a phenomenon of individuals...can be considered as marking the 'high points' of the progress made by common sense, or at least the common sense of the more educated strata of society but through them also of the people.[67]

Throughout the ceaseless struggle for hegemony, then, the more "advanced" intellectuals would presumably take on a large number of indispensable ideological-cultural projects: subverting the illusions of conventional ideologies, introducing and disseminating critical views of social reality, presenting an alternative vision of the future, and so forth. Within capitalist society, however, the widely-accepted definition of intellectuals as either technical "experts" or "learned men of culture" restricts ideological struggle to specialized and esoteric forms of discourse. Marxism is equally susceptible to these pressures, often creating its own elitist and even obscurantist language remote from and unintelligible to the general population. And this is not all: Marxist intellectuals, much like the traditional intellectuals which they would replace, are commonly interested in preserving whatever power and privilege they derive from their superior educational credentials, knowledge, cultural sophistication, and status. Given the social division of labor, it is relatively easy for intellectuals to lay claim to the rights of theoretical and political tutelage vis-a-vis the working class or other subordinate groups.[68] This predicament reinforces one of the great dualisms within Marxist parties and movements: a tendency toward elitism and utopianism among intellectuals, and toward pragmatism and anti-intellectualism among workers.

Gramsci himself was acutely aware of such dilemmas. Indeed, he saw in the philosophy of praxis a fundamentally "democratic" enterprise in which the very role of theory and theorists would be decisively transformed. But the actual historical predicament of Marxism belied such pretenses, since in practice "the great intellectuals formed on the terrain of this philosophy, besides being few in number, were not linked with the people, they did not emerge from the people, but were the expression of traditional intermediary classes, to which they returned at the great 'turning points' in history."[69]

Gramsci had an ingenious solution to this chronic dilemma: the theory of an "organic" intellectual formation in which the intellectuals would be simultaneously "leading" and "representative" insofar as they were to constitute an expression of working-class social existence. "Theory" in this sense would eventually be integrated into the entire fabric of proletarian life at the workplace and in the community, giving rise to a new stratum of Marxist *working-class* intellectuals. Only through the mediation of such organic intellectuals could an authentic revolutionary subjectivity be realized; they would provide the dynamic connecting link between theory and practice, the intellectual and the spontaneous, the political and the social. The philosophy of praxis can achieve its fullest meaning only through the intervention of organic intellectuals.

Gramsci did not quarrel with the empirical content of the Kautsky-Lenin proposition that bourgeois intellectuals rather than workers were the original source of socialist consciousness, as far as it went. There could be no arguing with the contention that Marxism had been introduced into the class struggle from outside, from the "educated representatives of the propertied classes." But while Gramsci conceded that intellectual defectors from the bourgeoisie would play a key role in the early stages of revolutionary change, he insisted that the crucial force over the long run would have to be a "new type of intellectual" generated through the class struggle itself.[70] Hence, "One of the most important characteristics of any group that is developing towards dominance is its struggle to assimilate and conquer 'ideologically' the traditional intellectuals, but this assimilation and conquest is made quicker and more efficacious the more the group in question succeeds in simultaneously elaborating its own intellectuals."[71] This "internal" principle (or what might be called the "internalization of the external element") was more than Gramsci's imaginative attempt to escape the Jacobin logic inherent in the vanguardist approach. It was the basis of a more effective socialist strategy in advanced capitalism to the degree that political activity would be grounded in a continuous counter-hegemonic process.[72] While the Kautsky-Lenin thesis might have been historically valid, given the actual role of intellectuals in early capitalist or pre-capitalist development, its anti-democratic implications for any *future* transition to socialism in the West would now have to be faced.

The concept of organic intellectual thus constituted the *sine qua non* of any democratic socialism. It would have dramatic repercussions for the theoretical enterprise itself because "...a new way of conceiving the world and man is born and that this conception is no longer reserved to the great intellectuals, to professional philosophers, but tends to become a popular, 'mass' phenomenon..."[73] Here again we return to a familiar Gramscian theme: all human beings are in some ultimate sense "intellectuals." Short of this, however, we encounter a transitional figure in the form of a democratic philosopher—"the historical realization of a new type of philosopher...in the sense that he is a philosopher convinced that his personality...is an active social relationship of modification of the cultural environment."[74]

For organic intellectuals to become a critical force in class struggle, however, traditional social cleavages, cultural divisions, and political tensions between different strata would have to be broken down. This was of special importance to Gramsci, since the ideological dualisms reproduced by capitalism run very deep:

> The popular element 'feels' but does not always know or understand; the intellectual element 'knows' but does not always understand and in particular does not always feel. The two extremes are therefore pedantry and philistinism on the one hand and blind passion on the other...The intellectual's error consists in believing that one can know without understanding and even more without feeling and being impassioned: in other words that the intellectual can be an intellectual if distinct and separate from the people-nation, i.e., without feeling the elementary passions of the people...One cannot make politics-history without this passion, without this sentimental connection between intellectuals and people-nation.[75]

What, then, would be the distinctly transformative role of the organic intellectuals? Gramsci was not always clear on such matters, so it is necessary for the interpreter to project a set of coherent meanings from literally hundreds of fragmented statements and generalizations contained in the *Notebooks*. These formulations conveyed a thematic unity consistent with Gramsci's general theoretical struggle to overcome the extremes of spontaneism and Jacobinism.

First, it seems evident that the "directive" ideological functions previously reserved for the external political sphere would now be centered in working-class struggles at the point of production. Second, intellectual activity would no longer be confined to specific roles, statuses and institutions but would be incorporated into a larger social totality, into a fluid movement with very imprecise boundaries. Third, the organic intellectuals would become a democratizing agency in their own right insofar as they actively contribute to the diffusion or socialization of knowledge, skills, and vision—that is, give political substance to the dictum that all persons are intellectuals. Finally, the theoretical functions carried out by intellectuals, while never rigorously "scientific" in the Kautskian sense, would require some kind of organizational expression (councils, party), for otherwise theory would be lacking in strategic translation. While Gramsci's thinking on these issues obviously converged with Lenin's at specific points, in its larger meaning the notion of organic intellectual suggests a thorough reformulation of the way intellectual activity had been understood within Marxism.

Here it might be useful to examine Gramsci's original response to the crisis of identity which had surfaced within Marxism after

World War I—reflected in the collapse of the Second International and, later, in the submersion of Comintern parties into the orbit of Soviet political experience. The crisis manifested itself in the intractable dilemma of isolation vs. compromise, sectarianism vs. incorporation. Lenin's solution was centralized political organization, Sorel's was the recovery of ideological passion or "myth", while Luxemburg's was the energy of the masses themselves. Gramsci's solution might be seen as an effort to combine all of these, with the organic intellectuals finally emerging as the most important conduit of socialist values. Yet Gramsci's approach was not without its own dilemmas: the main problem was how to integrate a socialist world-view into the everyday life of the masses—how to create a new leading stratum representative of the "people-nation"—without compromising the revolutionary essence of that world-view. Would not the categories of common sense, or bourgeois hegemony, be so over-powering as to blunt or absorb the work of organic intellectuals before it could reach political maturity? Had not Gramsci himself noted that previous counter-hegemonic struggles (the Reformation, late Christianity, European Socialism) degenerated in the process of expanding as they sought to incorporate diverse and conflicting popular elements?

Gramsci was clearly willing to live with such risks, given his conviction that any vanguardist attempt to impose socialism from above could only be self-defeating; for democratic transformation to have a real chance, there could be no intellectual subcultures—Marxist or otherwise. It was precisely in this spirit that Gramsci the political activist criticized the bureaucratic PSI and CGL leaderships before 1920, embraced the Turin factory councils as prefigurative formations, rejected Bordiga's ultra-centralist and abstentionist programs for the early PCI, and opposed frontist political alliances.

Yet the theoretical and political complexities of this problem could not be so easily set aside. In the end, Gramsci never fully confronted the implications of a Jacobinism which so thoroughly permeated the *Notebooks*, with the result that his approach to the intellectuals too yielded to this seemingly relentless logic. The question he effectively posed—whether, and in what ways, the proletariat could through its self-activity generate its own critical intellectuals—was therefore never resolved. A major problem was that Gramsci did not identify the actual *source* of the organic intellectuals. It would presumably not be the working class itself, since its subordination to bourgeois hegemony clearly blocked the development of a "collective intellectual" needed to carry out socialist transformation. At the same time, to have located the source within the bourgeois intelligentsia would have been contradictory to Gramsci's general analysis as well as his sensibilities. Two difficult issues emerge here, neither of which were really explored in the *Notebooks*. The first concerns the type of social-psychological mediations through which elements of the subaltern strata might become radicalized sufficiently and in such a way as to form a revolutionary intellectual grouping.[76] A second, and more fundamental, problem involves the extent to which there can be enough social autonomy within advanced capitalism to permit the growth of organic intellectuals along lines envisioned by Gramsci, especially since the working class had no real economic base of its own.[77]

Left with this ambiguity—that is, without a concrete historical agent—Gramsci was compelled to revert to the vanguard party, in much the same fashion and for many of the same reasons as Lukacs. We are left with the global presence of a party that would socialize and bring together the organic intellectuals for the purpose of turning them into *political* intellectuals, or leaders in the conventional sense.[78] Gramsci himself was sometimes candid about this Jacobin retreat: "The political party, for all groups, is precisely the mechanism which carries out in civil society the same function as the state carries out...in political society. In other words it is responsible for welding together the organic intellectuals of a given group..."[79] If this was indeed Gramsci's political recipe for consciousness formation, then, despite the novelty of his theory, his commitment to overturn the social division of labor must remain qualified.[80] In advanced capitalist society, where social existence is increasingly fragmented and privatized, and where disparate popular struggles tend towards parochialism and corporatism, the logic of a coordinating party structure may become even more seductive, as Gramsci recognized in the Italian setting. Unfortunately, he never confronted the strategic consequences of this predicament for his otherwise persuasive theory of organic intellectuals.

The Logic of Popular Revolt

Before turning to Gramsci's theory of revolution proper, an additional question remains: how to establish the conceptual linkage between self-conscious class activity and political mobilization directed against the total system. Even assuming that a stratum of organic intellectuals could solidify its presence within civil society and forge new levels of consciousness, through what medium would the various local and sectoral struggles become politicized and unified? An organizational solution alone, as we have seen, would clearly be inadequate. Like Sorel, Gramsci paid great attention to the ideological dimension of popular revolt, to the subjective factors of language, symbols, myths, and cultural traditions. The answer would have to be found in the development of what Gramsci called a "revolutionary historical bloc"—a counter-hegemonic convergence of forces still grounded in civil society but seeking expression on the terrain of state power.

Gramsci's concept of "bloc" is best understood in the context of an escalating crisis of bourgeois hegemony. Such a bloc is actualized through the generalized moment of "catharsis," when collective social forces penetrate the mystifying facade of class domination to achieve a clearer ideological-political sense of their objectives, when structural restraints finally give way to active political groupings. Thus:

> The term 'catharsis' can be employed to indicate the passage from the purely economic...to the ethico-political moment, that is the superior collaboration of the structure into superstructure in the minds of men. This also means the passage from 'objective to subjective' and from 'necessity to freedom.' Structure ceases to be an external force which crushes man, assimilates him to itself and makes him passive; and is transformed into a means of freedom, an instrument to create a new ethico-political form and a source of new initiatives.[81]

In Gramscian terms, therefore, the expansion of social movements presupposes the disintegration of old cultural and linguistic boundaries, with the old definitions of right and wrong, good and bad, possible and impossible yielding to new definitions during "cathartic" phases of upheaval. This disintegration, if it progresses far enough, can precipitate a massive crisis of authority and of the state—the sort which occurred in Russia in 1917 and in Italy during the *Biennio Rosso*. The crisis in turn must be viewed as an outgrowth of many factors, including the character of political mobilization itself; there were no strict "objective" determinants.

The term "bloc" adds conceptual refinement to Gramsci's rather vague treatment of mass consciousness in the *Notebooks*. He actually employed the category in several ways: "ideological bloc," "political bloc," "historical bloc," "moral-intellectual bloc." In each case, however, he referred to an historically crystallized formation of popular groupings or movements built around a common ideology—around a subjective sense of political identity—in contrast to the "objective" sociological categories (class, social position) employed by orthodox Marxism. Gramsci's definition thus encompasses far more than simple alliances, coalitions, or otherwise loose configurations of social forces, and it extended outside the formal sphere of institutions, outside the bourgeois state. "Bloc" connoted a broad merging of struggles, always shifting and changing, which occurred at specific (and usually explosive) historical conjunctures and led to a process whereby "popular feelings became unified" and gave form to mass revolt.[82] In the Italian context, Gramsci anticipated a wide range of possibilities, such as "national blocs," "urban blocs," and "southern rural blocs", where otherwise divergent interests converge as a homogenous bloc around shared visions or objectives.[83]

Rooted in Gramsci's critique of economism, this concept draws attentions to a dialectic of mass mobilization within civil society around themes which transcend an exclusive class basis: nationalism, anti-authoritarianism, anti-clericalism, regional separatism, ethnicity, and so forth. While these supra-class issues might be antagonistic to socialist movements during periods of stability, or in the early stages of mass struggles, they can be sources of radicalization at times of crisis, when strata previously in conflict sometimes join forces to fight a common battle—as in the development of a multi-class alliance around nationalist objectives.[84] In political terms, Gramsci was convinced that the transition to socialism would be something other than a "pure" form of class struggle between wage-labor and capital; more likely, it would be a complex mediated process involving a dynamic constellation of interests and goals perhaps having little pre-defined relationship to specific class structures. He rejected as metaphysics the assumption that particular classes are the necessary historical bearers of a revolutionary consciousness, or that such attributes could be ascertained in advance, on the basis of a universal logic.

The concept of durable solitary social blocs—not to be confused with temporary elite-based alliances or coalitions—was for Gramsci linked to a number of strategic insights: the centrality of ideological struggle, the role of nationalism (inherited from Machiavelli), the need to overcome corporatism and sectoralism, and the vision of a movement in Italy bringing together the struggles of northern workers and southern peasants. From this viewpoint the emergence of a social bloc furnishes the concretely "global", and therefore potentially revolutionary, ingredient of disparate mass struggles which, left to their own partial sphere of activity, would probably drift toward reformism or, even worse, disintegration.[85]

All of this is compatible with Gramsci's earlier advocacy of a "united front" strategy for the PCI—an approach which attempted, with mixed results, to mobilize workers, peasants, and petty bourgeoisie into an anti-capitalist *popular* alliance. With the rise of fascism he vigorously pressed for expansion of the factory and peasants' committees, which still symbolized the *Biennio Rosso* period, and distanced himself from efforts to build either a vanguard party or an electoral coalition with the PSI. Gramsci felt that local forms could accomplish two objectives: resist the Mussolini regime and keep alive the "actuality of revolution." Before Gramsci's arrest in late 1926, the PCI had in fact begun to enact a policy encouraging workers' and peasants' committees throughout the country as a means of building party membership (then only about 30,000), but it was already too late. The Lyons Theses captured the spirit of this Gramscian popular strategy, emphasizing the party's historical role in creating a homogeneous bloc of forces organized at the grassroots rather than through the reformist trade-union bureaucracies.[86] The peculiar weakness of Italian capitalism, along with the "colonial" status of the *Mezzogiorno*, would presumably establish fertile terrain for the growth of such a bloc.

Neither Bordiga's centralism of the 1921-23 period nor Togliatti's later Popular Front tactics were congruent with Gramsci's emphasis on popular mobilization. The Bordighist approach did combat ideological sclerosis, but in the end the price was too costly: mass initiative was stifled, social struggles were instrumentalized, and the prospects for a counter-hegemonic movement were necessarily deferred. Thus the early PCI leadership, according to Gramsci, fought "deviationist" currents by imposing rigid boundaries to party activity; its overriding concern was to "form and prepare cadres" and to elaborate principled and fixed programmatic lines. "As a consequence, the situation of mass movements is only examined in order to check the line which had been deduced on the basis of formalistic and sectarian concerns."[87]

Although Gramsci was in prison and nearing the end of his life in the mid-1930s when the Comintern adopted the Popular Front tactics of entering into anti-fascist coalitions with bourgeois parties, there is compelling evidence that he had earlier opposed

PCI consideration of a similar policy.[88] In any case, the new frontism was clearly antithetical to Gramsci's understanding of the revolutionary process insofar as frontism opted for a defense of bourgeois institutions over a program of mass based anti-capitalist struggles. Even more significantly, he surely would have objected to the way in which this version of frontism became an institutionalized strategy for the post-World War II PCI, whose leaders ironically chose to invoke the legacy of Gramsci in order to legitimate the same parliamentarist, social-democratic strategy which he had found so bankrupt in the PSI. The postwar PCI lost its revolutionary identity largely because it operated almost *exclusively* within the electoral and trade-union arenas, thus gradually submerging itself within the orbit or the bourgeois state, within the logic of the capitalist division of labor, and finally abandoning any real *transformative* presence within civil society. Gramsci would have predicted as much.[89]

The irrepressible continuity in Gramsci from the early Crocean years to the *Prison Notebooks* stems from his consistently dialectical-critical approach to socialist politics. A thematic unity links the concepts revolutionary collective will, organic intellectuals, social bloc, and counter-hegemonic movement (or "war of position"). A fascinating dimension of Gramsci's thought here was its synthetic quality, unique to the early European Marxist tradition: within the same theoretical framework it is easy to detect the influence of Marx and Machiavelli, Croce and Labriola, Sorel and Lenin—another reason Gramsci resists easy classification. The result, though of course fragmentary and incomplete, was a reconstituted vision of revolutionary change which at once transcended the outlook of the classical Marxists, the spontaneists, and the Jacobin vanguardists.

As opposed to the orthodox theorists, Gramsci took consciousness to be a problem rather than a given, affirming what had previously been denied: the role of collective subjectivity. As opposed to the spontaneists, he rejected as naive the assumption that a mature revolutionary movement could emerge organically through class self-activity, without the intervention of an "external element;" here parallels with the transition from feudalism to capitalism were misplaced, since the proletariat (unlike the bourgeoisie) lacked social autonomy. Finally, as opposed to the ultra-centralist Jacobins, Gramsci could never accept the notion of consciousness formation as essentially an elite-inspired phenomenon, the preserve of a party leadership that places itself "above" the masses and distrusts any expression of spontaneity. What differentiated Gramsci from all of these traditions, even as his theory incorporated elements of each, was a conception of socialist transformation that would be both global and popular involving a shifting "ensemble of relations" in the direction of a fundamentally new social totality.

Footnotes

1. On the traditional Marxist fallacy of correlating the ideologies of insurgent movements with a distinct set of class interests, see George Rude, *Ideology and Popular Protest* (New York: Pantheon, 1980), esp. Introduction.

2. This outlook, close to that of E. P. Thompson, can be described as Gramscian only up to a certain point. Clearly Gramsci would not have shared Thompson's political evolutionism nor his seeming indifference to the role of bourgeois hegemony in *distorting* working-class experience. For Thompson's approach, see *The Making of the English Working Class* (New York: Vintage Books, 1963), esp. ch. 16. For a critique of Thompson from a Gramscian perspective, see Tom Nairn, "The English Working Class," in Robin Blackburn, ed., *Ideology in Social Science* (New York: Vintage Books, 1973), pp. 187-206.

3. The linkage between the early Marxian critique of "utopianism" and the failure to confront the issue of class consciousness is stressed by Gouldner, *The Two Marxisms*, p. 346.

4. For an excellent critique of classical Marxism from this viewpoint, see Bertell Ollman, *The Social and Sexual Revolution* (Boston: South End Press, 1979), ch. 2.

5. See Rosa Luxemburg, "Organizational Questions of Russian Social Democracy," in *Selected Political Writings*, pp. 289-95. See the commentary by Jacoby in *The Dialectic of Defeat*, p. 69.

6. Wilhelm Reich, "What is Class Consciousness?" in Lee Baxandall, ed., *Sex-Pol: Essays, 1929-1934* (New York: Vintage Books, 1972), p. 284.

7. *Ibid.*, pp. 288-89.

8. *Ibid.*, pp. 290-91. On the issue of ideology itself, Reich stated that "Any revolutionary who underestimates the material power of ideology is certain to fail. In our period of history, it has proved stronger than the power of material poverty; were this not so, the working class, not Hitler and Thysen, would be in power today." *Ibid.*, p. 310.

9. As early as 1921 Gramsci had written, in a spirit not far removed from Reich's later work: "Fascism had presented itself as the anti-party; had opened its gates to all applicants; has with its promise of impunity enabled a formless multitude to cover over the

233

savage outpouring of passions, hatreds and desires with a varnish of vague and nebulous political ideals. Fascism has thus become a question of social mores; it has become identified with the barbaric and anti-social psychology of certain strata of the Italian people which have not yet been modified by a new tradition, by education, by living together in a well-ordered and administered state." "Elemental Forces." April 26, 1921, in *Political Writings II*, pp. 38-39.

10. On this point see Remo Bodei, "Gramsci: volonta, egemonia, razionalizzazione," in Ferri, ed., *Storia e politica in Gramsci*, pp. 65-66.

11. "Socialism and Culture," in *History, Philosophy and Culture in the Young Gramsci*, p. 21.

12. The bulk of Gramsci's writings after 1920 focused on the decline of PSI-style politics in the context of Mussolini's rise to power. See in particular "Problemi morali e lotta di classe," August 7, 1921, in *Scritti Politici*, pp. 469-71; "I Partiti e la massa," September 25, 1921, in *Ibid.*, pp. 591-94. For a more extensive account of Gramsci's critique of the PSI, see Cammett, *Antonio Gramsci and the Origins of Italian Communism*, chs 3,4.

13. "Marinetti Rivoluzionario?", January 5, 1921, in *Scritti Politici*, pp. 413-14. This interest in futurism was the underlying motive in Gramsci's great preoccupation with the work of Pirandello. While Futurism did not of course disappear after the war, its pronounced rightward drift negated any progressive cultural potential.

14. "Cultura e lotta di classe," May 25, 1918, in *Scritti Politici*, pp. 138-39. See also "Culture and Class Struggle," in *History, Philosophy and Culture*, pp. 109-10.

15. Letter to Tatiana, November 19, 1928, in Lawner, ed. *Letters from Prison*, p. 136.

16. "The Modern Prince," *SPN*, p. 184.

17. "Some Aspects of the Southern Question," in *Political Writings-II*, p. 448.

18. Quoted from "Notes on Machiavelli," *SPN*, p. 187.

19. "State and Civil Society," *SPN*, p. 225.

20. For an analysis of "primitive" or "pre-political" types of rebellion in Italy (and elsewhere), see E. J. Hobsbawm, *Primitive Rebels* (New York: W. W. Norton, 1959). Stressing the dialectical character of such revolt, Hobsbawm referred to many examples of its evolution towards, or incorporation into, more advanced political movements (including the Italian Communist Party).

21. "Problems of Marxism," *SPN*, p. 421. Here Gramsci was

distinguishing his own approach from that of Bukharin. At another point he poked fun at Bukharin's preoccupation with the "great philosophical and scientific systems" to the exclusion of the real problem of mass consciousness: "Reading the *Manual* one has the impression of someone who cannot sleep for the moonlight and who struggles to massacre the fireflies in the belief that by so doing he will make the brightness lessen or disappear." "Problems of Marxism," p. 433.

22. "Problems of Marxism," *SPN*, p. 422.

23. "La volonta delle masse," June 24, 1925, in *Scritti Politici*, pp. 620-21.

24. "Problems of Marxism," *SPN*, p. 423.

25. The close relationship between religion and common sense at the level of everyday life in Italy further complicated this problem. As Gramsci observed: "The principle elements of common sense are provided by religion, and consequently the relationship between common sense and religion is much more intimate than that between common sense and the philosophical systems of the intellectuals [Marxism]." "Problems of Marxism," *SPN*, p. 420.

26. "The Modern Prince," *SPN*, pp. 192-93.

27. "The Modern Prince," *SPN*, p. 199.

28. "State and Civil Society," *SPN*, pp. 272-73. Gramsci's distinction between "generic" or "semi-feudal" and "modern" forms of revolt parallels Hobsbawm's distinction between "primitive" and "modern" rebellion—the former chaotic and pre-political, the latter possessing coherent theory and ideology, leadership and organization, and a particular "target" (e.g., the state). See Hobsbawm, *op. cit.*, introduction.

29. According to Rude, this developmental concept of mass consciousness represents Gramsci's most significant and useful contribution. See *Ideology and Popular Protest*, esp. pp. 22-24.

30. Once again the parallel between Gramsci and Reich is striking, as reflected in this passage: "Everything that contradicts the bourgeois order, everything that contains a germ of rebellion, can be regarded as an element of class consciousness; everything that creates or maintains a bond with the bourgeois order, that supports and reinforces it, is an impediment to class consciousness." See "What is Class Consciousness?," *op. cit.*, p. 295.

31. "The Modern Prince," *SPN*, pp. 181-82. Similarly, at another point Gramsci wrote that "The concept of revolutionary and of internationalist, in the modern sense of the word, is

correlative with the precise concept of state and of class: little understanding of the state means little class consciousness (and understanding of the state exists not only when one defends it, but also when one attacks it in order to overthrow it ...)." "State and Civil Society," *SPN*, p. 275.

32. "The Study of Philosophy," *SPN*, pp. 333-34.

33. It might be argued that this conceptualization—intellectuals as catalysts, masses as subject of revolutionary change in the long run—was close to Marx's, but Marx never really confronted this problem theoretically or devoted much attention to it. On the comparison of Marx and Gramsci here, see Badaloni, "Liberta individuale e uomo collettivo in Antonio Gramsci," in *Politica e storia in Gramsci*, pp. 9-21. Badaloni corectly stresses the uniqueness of Gramsci's effort to show the reciprocal interaction between consciousness and concrete social relations.

34. "The Modern Prince," *SPN*, p. 201.

35. "The Modern Prince," *SPN*, p. 198.

36. To what extent Gramsci anticipated a strict relationship between class position and critical consciousness in the final analysis was never made clear in the *Notebooks*. While popular ideology has no definite class correlates so long as bourgeois hegemony holds sway, a *mature* political consciousness might well be more congruent with specific class interests. Mouffe, for example, argues that Gramsci's anti-economism challenges the notion of a clear-cut class consciousness throughout. See "Hegemony and Ideology in Gramsci," in *Gramsci and Marxist Theory"*, pp. 188-92.

37. The brief relationship between Gramsci and Sorel during the early Turin period, and Sorel's influence upon Ordine Nuovo, was discussed in chapter three. In the *Notebooks* Gramsci's judgment of Sorel took a harshly critical turn: the latter's "mechanical" spontaneism failed to give concrete political form to the collective proletarian will, reducing his conception of myth to a mere "abstraction." See "The Modern Prince," *SPN*, pp. 127-30.

38. Rosa Luxemburg, "Mass Strike, Party, and Trade Unions," in *Selected Political Writings*, pp. 288-89.

40. *Ibid.*, p. 295.

41. *Ibid.*, p. 288. Here it should be emphasized that Luxemburg's commitment to proletarian self-activity was counter-balanced by an underlying economic determinism; mass consciousness, in other words, was ultimately shaped by levels of capitalist development. Thus: "In its action, the proletariat is dependent upon the given degree of ripeness of social development. But social

development does not take place apart from the proletariat. The proletariat is its driving force and its cause as well as its product and its effect. The action of the proletariat is itself a codetermining part of history. And though we can no more skip a period in our historical development than a man can jump over his shadow, it lies within our power to accelerate or to retard it." "The Crisis in German Social Democracy," in *Selected Political Writings*, p. 333.

42. On Luxemburg's endorsement of the workers' councils, see "What Does the Spartacus League Want?," in *Selected Political Writings*, pp. 366-376.

43. *Ibid.*, p. 375.

44. It might be added that Luxemburg further ignored the political (and ideological) role of bourgeois democracy in the development of capitalism. On the one hand, her implicit abstentionism failed to come to grips with the hegemonic presence of bourgeois institutions; on the other, she simply avoided any discussion of the tactical use to which such institutions might be put—i.e., their value as a medium of consciousness transformation. See Norman Geras, "Rosa Luxemburg After 1905," *New Left Review* no. 89, January-February 1975, pp. 13-15.

45. For a brief but excellent critique of Luxemburg's spontaneism, see Lucio Magri, "Problems of the Marxist Theory of the Revolutionary Party," *New Left Review* no. 60, pp. 107-11.

46. Georg Lukacs, *History and Class Consciousness*, p. 20.

47. *Ibid.*, p. 22.

48. *Ibid.*, p. 77.

49. *Ibid.*, p. 76.

50. *Ibid.*, p. 64. Lukacs appropriately noted that "In the class struggle we witness the emergence of all the hidden forces that usually lie concealed behind the facade of economic life, at which the capitalists and their apologists gaze as though transfixed." *Ibid.*, p. 65.

51. For a critique of Lukacs from this viewpoint—and a discussion of his lapse into vanguardism, see Arato and Breines, *The Young Lukacs*, ch. 9. On Lukacs' "Leninism," see *History and Class Consciousness*, pp. 295-342, and *Lenin* (Cambridge: MIT Press, 1971).

52. V. I. Lenin, "What is to be Done?," in Tucker, ed., *The Lenin Anthology*, p. 29. (Italics in the original.)

53. *Ibid.*, p. 49. (Italics in the original.)

54. *Ibid.*, pp. 24-25. The implications of this assumption for the Marxist theory of intellectuals will be taken up in the next section.

55. On the development of a specific Marxist intellectual

culture, see Alvin W. Gouldner, "Prologue to a Theory of Revolutionary Intellectuals," *Telos*, winter 1975-76, pp. 3-36. See also the interesting treatment in Gombin, *The Radical Tradition*, ch. 2, and George Konrad and Ivan Szelenyi, *The Intellectuals on the Road to Class Power* (New York: Harcourt, Brace, Jovanovich, 1979), chs. 12, 13.

56. As early as 1918 Gramsci was praising Lenin's "creative" approach to revolution and cited the Bolshevik success as a possible model; but Gramsci's perception of "Leninism" during those initial post-revolutionary years, as I emphasized in chapters one and two, was hardly vanguardist. Still, Gramsci was attracted to Lenin's critique of spontaneism and orthodox Marxism, as reflected in his "Revolution against *Capital*," *op. cit.* and "Lenin's Work," in *History, Philosophy and Culture*, pp. 134-38. At about the same time Gramsci had begun to articulate his own critique of spontaneism, for example in his "Culture and Class Struggle," *op. cit.*

57. See, for example, "Socialists and Communists," "Parties and Masses," "Masses and Leaders," and "Elements of the Situation," all in *Selected Political Writings-II*.

58. This general orientation towards the spontaneist position had a basis in Gramsci's overall theory rather than in any specific attack on Luxemburg—though, as we have seen, Gramsci did criticize Sorel extensively in the *Notebooks*. While the *Notebooks* contained scattered references to Luxemburg, most were in fact favorable and nowhere did Gramsci really discuss her theory of mass consciousness. He did, however, briefly criticize her notion of "crisis" set forth in *The Mass Strike*, as follows: "It was thus out and out historical mysticism, the awaiting of a sort of miraculous illumination." "State and Civil Society," *SPN*, p. 233.

59. See Giuseppe Vacca, "La Quistione politica degli intellectuali e la teoria marxista dello Stato nello pensiero di Gramsci," in Ferri, *Politica e storia in Gramsci*, pp. 440-41.

60. In adopting this perspective Gramsci diverged from the theory of Karl Mannheim, who formulated the notion of a "socially unattached intelligentsia" which, by virtue of its special educational status, was never firmly anchored in the social order. See *Ideology and Utopia* (New York: Harcourt, Brace and World, 1964), pp. 154-58.

61. "The Intellectuals," *SPN*, p. 9.

62. "The Study of Philosophy," *SPN*, p. 344.

63. "The Intellectuals," *SPN*, p. 10.

64. "The Study of Philosophy," *SPN*, p. 325.

65. Unfortunately this critical insight, which some com-

mentators have viewed as Gramsci's most useful theoretical contribution, was nowhere developed in his work. One reason was that the setting for most of Gramsci's observations (Italy) was a *transitional* one where tendencies at work in the more developed northern European capitalist societies were much less evident. Furthermore, Gramsci's obsession with Fordist rationalization was bound to obscure the *variety* of hegemonic forms in advanced capitalism.

66. "The Study of Philosophy," *SPN*, p. 339.

67. "The Study of Philosophy," *SPN*, pp. 330-31.

68. On the development of a "special order of discourse" among Marxist intellectuals, see Alvin W. Gouldner, "Prologue to a Theory of Revolutionary Intellectuals," *Telos* no. 26, winter 1975-76, pp. 3-36. Gouldner speaks of the emergence of a "cultural bourgeoisie" within Marxism, and traces this phenomenon back to the legacy of Marx himself. (pp. 4-6). For a similar perspective, see Gombin, *The Radical Tradition*, ch. 2. Both Gouldner and Gombin draw heavily upon the work of the early twentieth century Polish theorist Jan Machajski.

69. "Problems of Marxism," *SPN*, p. 397.

70. Gramsci's theory of organic intellectuals, which involved a rather complex set of historical processes, should not be confused with the familiar theme of bourgeois intellectuals merely "defecting" to the proletariat. For an example of such confusion, see Seliger, *The Marxist Conception of Ideology*, p. 115.

71. "The Intellectuals," *SPN*, p. 10.

72. Gramsci was quite aware of the hidden dangers accompanying a counter-hegemonic strategy of this sort. One obvious danger would be the tendency to approach political mobilization simply as a matter of consciousness transformation without considering the imperatives of the struggle for state power. Another might be the adoption of a fatalistic attitude towards change, given the necessarily long-term, molecular transformation Gramsci had in mind. Here the priority of creating a stratum of organic intellectuals around essentially pedagogical functions could be invoked to avoid the dictates of conscious *political* intervention. Yet another and more complex difficulty —one which Gramsci never resolved—concerns the degree to which an emergent hegemony (involving the proliferation of organic intellectuals) could prevail within civil society *before* the final contestation for state power. Gramsci's extensive critique of Croce in the *Notebooks*—most emphatically his rejection of an autonomous ethico-political sphere—can be read as an anticipation of such dangers.

See, for example, the attack on Croce's "political morphinism" in "Notes on Italian History," *SPN*, p. 114.

73. "Problems of Marxism," *SPN*, p. 417.

74. "The Study of Philosophy", *SPN*, p. 350.

75. "Problems of Marxism," *SPN*, p. 418.

76. Gramsci, to be sure, was not alone in falling into this theoretical morass. Among Marxists of the period probably only Reich confronted the social-psychological dimensions of popular mobilization, but Reich, whatever the potential of the sex-pol movement in Germany, had little to say about the role of intellectuals in the transition to socialism. Reich's far-reaching insights did illuminate the flaws of a strictly rationalist psychology shared at the time by virtually all Marxists, including Gramsci. On Gramsci's rationalist assumptions, see Adamson, *Hegemony and Revolution*, p. 154.

77. On this point see Jerome Karabell, "Revolutionary Contradictions: Antonio Gramsci and the Problem of Intellectuals," *Politics and Society*, vol. 6, no. 2, 1976, pp. 154-56. Karabell further notes, correctly, that Gramsci's failure to examine the implications for his theory of the rise of a *technical* intelligentsia in advanced capitalism only complicates this problem.

78. From a slightly different angle, this is the gist of Vacca's observation that the formation of Gramsci's "new type of intellectual" is dependent upon the evolution of new forms of political organization and state power. See "La quistione politica degli intellectuali e la teoria marxista dello Stato nello pensiero di Gramsci," in Ferri, ed., *Politica e storia in Gramsci,* p. 478.

79. "The Intellectuals," *SPN*, p. 15.

80. One could go further and hold Gramsci accountable to a more directly elitist and hierarchical view of intellectual activity, especially in the conventional sphere of education proper. See Harold Entwistle, *Antonio Gramsci: Conservative Schooling for Radical Politics* (London: Routledge and Kegan Paul, 1979), pp. 39-40.

81. "The Study of Philosophy," *SPN*, pp. 366-67.

82. From a methodological perspective Gramsci viewed the concept of "historical bloc" as reflecting the "unity between nature and spirit (structure and superstructure), unity of opposites and of distincts." "The Modern Prince," *SPN*, p. 137. See also "The Study of Philosophy," *SPN*, pp. 366, 377.

83. Here Gramsci contrasted the notion of "homogenous social blocs" with the phenomenon of undisciplined "volunteers" which lacked collective political will. See "The Modern Prince," *SPN*, pp. 203-04.

84. The prospects in Italy of a dynamic "national-popular" bloc of forces incorporating northern workers and southern peasants into a broad-based revolutionary movement fascinated Gramsci just as it did Lenin in the Russian context. See, for example, "Notes on Italian History," *SPN* pp. 98-100, where Gramsci suggested that "The relation between city and countryside is the necessary starting-point for the study of the fundamental motor forces of Italian history." (p. 98). Here Gramsci's concept of "bloc" would harness two sources of political energy that Marxists had commonly overlooked: the unified strength of the industrial proletariat and rural peasantry, which longstanding conflicts between the two classes had precluded, and the mobilizing power of nationalism, which indeed would later play a major catalytic role in all twentieth century revolutions. On the historical difficulties of forging worker-peasant alliances in Europe, see David Mittrany, *Marx Against the Peasant* (New York: Collier Books, 1961), chs. 1-5.

85. "The Modern Prince," *SPN*, pp. 157-58. At the same time, Gramsci recognized certain obstacles to sustaining such a bloc. For example, a party based upon a fragile convergence of very different constituencies might easily collapse from its own centrifugal tendencies, especially when "fundamental" (class) issues come into play.

86. Thus Gramsci wrote that the "anti-fascist and *anti-capitalist* struggle which the communists are striving to create must aim at being an organized united front, i.e., at being based on bodies around which the masses as a whole can regroup and find a form. Such are the representative bodies which the masses themselves are tending to create today, from the factories and on the occasion of every struggle, since the possibilities for the trade unions to function normally began to be limited." "Lyons Theses," in *Political Writings-II], p. 372.

87. *Ibid.*, p. 360.

88. On this point, see Lucio Colletti, "Gramsci and Revolution," *New Left Review* no. 65, January-February 1971. This type of "frontism" should be clearly distinguished from the "united front" which, as previously indicated, looked to the formation of an *anti-capitalist* bloc with explicitly socialist objectives.

89. The distortion of Gramsci's Marxism by Togliatti and other postwar PCI leaders is analyzed in my *The Impasse of European Communism*, pp. 119-137.

7 A Consensual Revolution?

If the major theoretical point of departure for Gramsci was the seemingly hopeless effort to resolve the crisis of Marxism in postwar Europe, leading to his novel concept of ideological hegemony in the *Prison Notebooks*, then his driving political motivation was to help elucidate the imperatives and tasks of revolution in the West. Gramsci was first and foremost a theorist of revolution whose vision was almost hypnotically focused on dialectical change—a rupture in the old system of class and power relations, an overturning of the capitalist division of labor, the realization of a classless society rooted in democratic self-management. Such transformation would occur, not through a mechanical breakdown of the capitalist mode of production, but as part of a sharpening crisis of ruling-class legitimacy.

The great unifying themes, of the *Notebooks*—hegemony, organic intellectuals, historical bloc, war of movement—all derived from Gramsci's fascination with the problem of consciousness and his emphasis on the power of collective revolutionary will. As we have seen, this "critical" orientation situated Gramsci within an emergent Western Marxist tradition which stressed the centrality of ideological and cultural factors in historical change. But there was an undeniably "Leninist" side of Gramsci, as reflected in the Jacobinism of the "Modern Prince", which dwelled upon the autonomy of politics and the task of articulating a coherent Marxist *strategy*. Unlike Sorel or even Luxemburg, for example, Gramsci found it necessary to explore the various modes of organizational intervention which politically define the formation of classes,

243

blocs, and interests. This meant above all confronting the question of the revolutionary party.

Yet, whereas Lenin's vanguardism was a product of the largely pre-industrial, autocratic setting of Tsarist Russia, Gramsci's attention was focused westward, toward Italy and the more industrialized regions of Europe. Gramsci's "Leninism" was therefore highly misleading in a number of respects, as we shall see. The success of the Bolshevik Revolution was not matched anywhere in the West, with the partial exception of the short-lived Hungarian experiment in 1919; moreover, it had become obvious by the late 1920s that the Moscow-centered Comintern parties would not sink very deep roots in a European context separated from Russia by a vast economic and cultural gulf. The historical meaning of Gramsci's contribution becomes apparent here: as a revolutionary influenced deeply by the Bolshevik tradition, he was probably the first Marxist to draw theoretical conclusions from the growing *political* impasse of the European left in the wake of crushing postwar defeats. For him the effort to conceptualize the transition to socialism involved a sustained critical reassessment not only of social democracy and Council Communism, but of Leninism too.[1] A good many of the old assumptions about the nature of the state, the role of the party, the relationship between leaders and masses, and the impact of economic crisis would have to be abandoned—or at least reconstructed. The irony is that Gramsci, from the almost complete isolation of fascist prisons, would be able to contribute so much to this project.

Interestingly enough, Gramsci's theory of revolution owed far more to Machiavelli, an early sixteenth century thinker, than to Marx. The reason for this, of course, was that on matters of political organization and strategy Marx was either silent or rather obscure. Entirely different strategies can be, and have been, derived from Marx's writings; passages supporting a revolutionary spontaneism (proletarian self-emancipation), Jacobinism (the leading role of the vanguard party), and even reformism can be readily located in his work.[2] The significant point is that Marx furnished no rigorous analysis of political movements, much less of the forms and processes that were expected to define socialist transformation.[3] He was almost exclusively preoccupied with early *capitalist* development. Following Marx's death a clear split along strategic lines began to occur: anarchism and syndicalism inherited the spontaneist, democratizing side of the classical tradition while the two main expressions of organized Marxism—social democracy and Leninism —stressed the need for educated leadership, organizational hierarchy, and state power. At the point Gramsci started work on his prison writings in the late 1920s, the contradictions of this elite-centered form of politicized Marxism had already clearly surfaced, in quite different settings. The narrow parliamentarism of social democracy and the bureaucratic centralism of the Bolshevik party were both logically tied to a statism which, from Gramsci's viewpoint, only retarded the prospects for a *democratic socialism*.[4]

The revolutionary process that Gramsci envisioned was therefore qualitatively different from these traditions, in two respects: first, the nature of modern European development required a new conceptual framework and, second, the actual *goals* of that transformation were to be redefined and broadened. For Gramsci, this was not simply a question of translating previously agreed-upon universal principles into specific historical contexts, or even of affirming the thesis of separate national paths to socialism. The transitional logic in the advanced countries would be quite distinct from previous models, East and West. Capitalist rationalization was giving rise to new social contradictions and modes of conflict; a new relationship between state and civil society, between politics and economics, between public and personal life; an increasingly diversified proletariat; and the vast expansion of cultural and ideological infrastructures (e.g., media, education). Under such conditions, the Leninist conjunctural scenario of class polarization, cataclysmic economic crisis, and strategic isolation of the state fortress was obsolete. So too was the comfortable Bernsteinian faith in an evolutionary, peaceful transition from liberal capitalism to a rational, socialized order.

Neither strategy, whatever its popular and democratic objectives, was really compatible with the prefigurative outlook Gramsci adopted during the Turin factory council years; their premises were essentially authoritarian and statist. Gramsci's subsequent theorizing contained the implicit promise of a completely new model of change (a "new era of humanity") that would be *consensual* in the sense that previous revolutions were not. Hence, in contrast with Lenin, the critique of economism and the reappropriation of politics which so deeply permeated Gramsci's thought was inspired by a concern for radical democracy: collective self-activity, workers' control, social renewal, the mass party.[5] Democratization means not only destruction of the bourgeois state—not only the supersession of parliamentary democracy and bureaucratic instruments of repression—but the creation of new local organs of direct popular involvement. This sensibility, which

Lenin too expressed in *State and Revolution* and in certain slogans calling for "all power to the soviets," was in Russia destroyed by the bureaucratic centralism of Bolshevik political practice.

Yet Gramsci's commitment to a new type of democratic politics was hardly unqualified, as the Jacobin strains in the *Notebooks* revealed. In his theory of the party he sought to incorporate Machiavelli and Lenin—both classic Jacobins—while simultaneously going beyond them. Surveying the totality of Gramsci's work, one detects a persistent and unresolved tension between the vanguardist and popular, instrumental and prefigurative, coercive and consensual elements of his theory.

The Rediscovery of Politics

It has sometimes been observed that the nineteenth century was above all a period of general hostility toward politics, of a flight from issues related to public power, the state, and collective action in the aftermath of the French Revolution.[6] Certainly Marxism no less than liberalism and anarchism was a product of this anti-political spirit, which encouraged a certain epiphenomenal interpretation of the political sphere; social and economic forces constituted the deeper, more "basic," determinant level of reality, with politics their offshoot. Insofar as theorists chose to confront politics in any fashion, it was uniformly treated as an expression of larger historical factors, rarely as a total complex of institutions and social relationships with its own logic and causality. In Marxism—despite what Marx said about Feuerbach being "too much concerned with nature and too little with politics"—there was from the outset a theoretical obsession with the economic "structure" to the virtual exclusion of the "superstructure" (including politics, law, and ideology). The fact that Marx himself never really developed a systematic theory of politics and the state—nor of revolution—left a significant void which later theorists and movements, confronted with more urgent political situations, would have to fill *de novo*.

Marx's early writings, with the memory of the Jacobin terror in France still vivid, expressed a strong antagonism to anything resembling the autonomy of politics; he considered the attempt to impose a new political order upon a civil society not yet prepared for qualitative change as something destined either to fail or to bring about new forms of centralized power. Socialism was expected to be the product of a specific phase of socio-economic development rather than of an institutional engineering process based in state initiative—an axiom that the Blanquists, conspiratorial sects, and other "alchemists of revolution" had failed to understand. Marx's distrust of politics was understandable enough, corresponding as it did to spontaneist elements in his theoretical outlook, but the unfortunate absence of a Marxist political theory served to postpone any real strategic discussion until at least the 1890s.[7] The problem was twofold: first, Marx was concerned much less with the transition to socialism than with a critique of the capitalist political economy as such and, second, he apparently thought that socialist transformation would resemble the transition from feudalism to capitalism to the extent that the proletariat would gradually build an autonomous presence within civil society leading up to its conquest of state power.[8] In any case, the strong productivist bias of classical Marxism generated, paradoxically, a theory strong in economic analysis but weak in exploring questions related to social *movements*, political conflict, the dynamics of revolutionary *change*.

But whereas nineteenth century theory stressed the primacy of economics, twentieth century history has given expression to precisely its opposite—the primacy of politics. The rise of fascism, the transformation of competitive capitalism into state corporate capitalism, the emergence of bureaucratic centralism in the USSR, and the proliferation of Third World military dictatorships have all effectively called into question the classical Marxist approach to politics.

It was Lenin, of course, who first reversed this order of priorities within Marxism by emphasizing the role of politics over economics both in his theoretical work and in his leadership of the Bolshevik Party. Lenin departed from the classical formula by insisting that working-class movements confined to economic struggles—to the immediate conflict between wage-labor and capital—could never escape the logic of bourgeois politics. To counter that logic these movements would have to advance to the *political* terrain, which alone can universalize the disparate forms of anti-capitalist opposition. Thus:

> Social-Democracy represents the working class, not in its relation to a given group of employers alone, but in its relation to all classes of modern society and to the state as an organized political force. Hence, it follows that not only must Social-Democrats not confine themselves exclusively to the economic struggle, but that they must not allow the organization of economic exposures to become

the predominant part of their activities. We must take up actively the political education of the working class and the development of its political consciousness.[9]

Lenin saw in economism a narrow, particularistic form of interest-group activity that could never propel class conflict to the level of generalized struggles against the whole system of capitalist domination. Politics was an integrative, global force through which mass mobilization and the seizure of state power would be carried out. The perfect tool for this mission was the vanguard party with an ideological identity and organizational mobility designed to facilitate intervention at the moment of most acute crisis in the traditional order. Leninist strategy, which was criticized as "ultra-politicism" by Paul Axelrod and as "Blanquism" by Rosa Luxemburg, was Jacobin precisely in the sense of urgency it conveyed and in the degree of initiative it gave to a small elite of professional revolutionaries. This was indeed the key to Bolshevik political vitality, and to the success of the October Revolution. No doubt this "minority revolution" variant of Marxist strategy was the predictable outcome of Lenin's rediscovery of politics, which was made necessary for two reasons: the theoretical impasse of classical Marxism and the autocratic nature of Russian society.[10]

Lenin's "rejuvenation" of Marxism made a deep impression upon Gramsci, although he did not take up the primacy of politics as a serious theoretical issue until the lessons from the *Ordine Nuovo* collapse fully took hold—not until the early PCI years and, more substantially, the *Notebooks*. From one angle, Gramsci set out to extend Leninism by adding important new dimensions to it, that is, by "Westernizing" it. The Leninist breakthrough opened up new theoretical (but not political) space in European Marxism, which Gramsci was among the first to grasp and utilize. He readily accepted Lenin's devastating critique of economism and his assumption that politics was the driving force of revolutionary struggle, but, given the different historical conditions in Italy, he looked to incorporate the "popular" element that, as we have seen, stemmed from his theory of ideological hegemony and mass consciousness.

Gramsci's new appreciation of politics coincided with his theoretical shift from the factory councils to the revolutionary party—a shift that was already visible in 1920-21 as the PCI was being founded. Here Gramsci's temporary disillusionment with the council experience, along with the apparent success of the Bolshevik model in Russia, pushed him close to Bordiga's centralism for a short period. In contemplating the political defeat of both the

PSI and the councils, Gramsci seemed to have little choice but to embrace some species of vanguardism.[11] In a context of retreat and repression, this choice may have appeared all the more reasonable: a fragmented left, on the defensive and struggling for survival, was drawn to the need for organizational unity and discipline. Here Gramsci was able to justify the vanguard party from three distinct perspectives: in contrast to PSI reformism, it would furnish the organization and leadership needed to preserve revolutionary identity; as opposed to the councils, it focused strategic attention on the state and the imperatives of overthrowing it; and, against fascism, it recognized that insofar as the Mussolini regime was highly-centralized Communists would be forced to use similar political forms to avoid being crushed.[12]

The result was that Gramsci's earlier fear of Jacobinism gave way, between 1920 and 1924, to a view of the party as "protagonist of history"—a Bolshevik-type structure which "represents the *totality* of the interests and aspirations of the working class",[13] He praised Leninist strategy throughout the period, attacking the institutionalized division of labor between party and trade unions typical of the Second International, which Gramsci thought would only polarize the movement around two equally reformist tendencies: electoralism and economism.[14] In 1925, Gramsci called for the PCI to implement a policy of mass mobilization based upon a network of cells—the small-scale, basic party units that had been introduced by the Bolsheviks under the label "democratic centralism." The Russian experience had conclusively shown that both factory and territorial cells were indispensable to popular struggles against the state. For the Italian party, then, "Bolshevization as it is reflected in the organizational sphere is an imperative necessity. No one will dare to claim that the Leninist criteria for party organization are peculiar to the Russian situation, and that their application to Western Europe is purely mechanical. To oppose the organization of the party by cells means to still be tied to old social-democratic conceptions."[15]

Nowhere in Gramsci's articles of this period was there even the slightest hint that the growing consolidation of fascist power after 1925 had pushed him toward the type of alliance strategy that would later be identified with the Popular Front. Like Bordiga, he remained fully committed to a vanguardist politics and view of organization. This meant not only rejection of the "parliamentary road" to socialism which was still associated with the bankrupt PSI; it further indicated that, for the weakened PCI, *socialist* objectives would remain the first priority. Even in 1925-26 Gramsci argued that the party should be dedicated to an *offensive* struggle against *both* capitalism and fascism since the two targets were politically inseparable:

> The fundamental problem which the Communist Party must set out to resolve in the present situation is that of leading the proletariat back to an autonomous position as a revolutionary class; free from all influence of counter-revolutionary classes, groups and parties; capable of collecting around itself and leading the forces which can be mobilized for the struggle against capitalism. The Communist Party must, therefore, intervene actively in all fields open to its activity, and must take advantage of all movements, all conflicts, all struggles, even of a partial and limited character, in order to mobilize the proletarian masses and transport the resistance and opposition to fascism of the Italian working population onto a class terrain.[16]

At the same time, Gramsci's Leninism—even at this desperate point in Italian political history—was not the sort of narrow, one-dimensional voluntarism normally associated with the Jacobin party. In this respect much of the vanguardist language employed by Gramsci, especially in the turbulent 1924-26 years, is highly misleading. For instance, there was nothing to suggest that Gramsci had turned his back on the positive side of the *Ordine Nuovo* legacy or, for that matter, on his earlier interest in the "ethico-political" sphere taken over from Croce. If the party now assumed a more prominent place in Gramsci's thinking—and he did, after all, become the PCI leader during this period—this fact did not necessarily imply a singular role for it in the transition. On the contrary, the factory councils to be found in the north and the peasant committees in the south remained a vital component of his strategic thinking. In the "Lyons' Theses," he and Togliatti referred to these local structures as a key to the party's "united front" formula: "the workers' and peasants' committees are organs of unity of the working class, whether mobilized for a struggle of an immediate nature or for political actions of a broader scope. The slogan calling for the creation of workers' and peasants' committees is thus a slogan to be implemented immediately...It makes evident and concrete the need for the workers to organize their forces, and counterpose them in practice to those of all groups of bourgeois origin and nature, in order to become the determining and preponderant element in the political situation."[17] Still, Gramsci mentioned the role of local councils and committees only occasionally and, even more troublesome, he never proposed any specific *relationship* between party and committees, between the vanguard and the popular-democratic elements. This lack of clarity was evident in the earlier and later phases of Gramsci's thought as well.

On the requirement for *some* kind of mass party, however, Gramsci was absolutely unequivocal. His debates with Bordiga took place around exactly these issues: whether the PCI was to be the coordinator or prime mover of popular movements, whether organizational centralism should be preserved to the point of electoral abstentionism (Bordiga's position), whether the struggle for state power was the immediate and overriding task of the party (as Bordiga assumed), and so forth. In reacting against Bordiga's mechanistic notion of an ultra-vanguard party, Gramsci returned to the principle of totality, which in the *Notebooks* would lead him to the *doppia prospettiva*, a balanced approach that was meant to counter the Bonapartist dangers inherent in the primacy of politics. The fatal defect of Bordiga's strategy was its underestimation of the party's "social content." The result was an elitist definition of the PCI as "organ" of the working class (a "synthesis of heterogeneous elements") rather than as "part" of the class.[18] This view of the PCI as a "part" or *expression* of the working class was Gramsci's way of stressing the multi-faceted nature of revolutionary change. In 1925 he identified *three* main phases of the struggle against capitalism—the economic, political, and cultural-ideological—with each phase interrelated with the others in a complex totality.[19] The political element itself contained three principal subphases: the effort to impede the exercise of bourgeois power (e.g., within parliament) with the goal of creating a new balance of forces and greater freedom of mass organizing; the struggle to conquer power and establish a new socialist state; and the removal of technical and social obstacles standing in the way of full communism.

All of this anticipated Gramsci's well-known discourses on the "Modern Prince" in the *Notebooks*. More distanced from everyday political concerns, during imprisonment he seemed less interested in carrying forward Leninist orthodoxy than in rescuing the political realm from its dismal fate within classical Marxism and social democracy. Gramsci wanted to correct the productivist bias of Marxism by arguing for a distinctly political framework of communication, mode of analysis, and instrument of revolutionary change.[20] But instead of reversing the traditional schema by substituting a *political* determinism or crude voluntarism of a Blanquist or Gentillian type for economism, he turned to politics largely to the extent of restoring the Marxist totality. In Gramsci's view, Marxism had forgotten the degree to which human beings are ultimately political by nature: "To transform the external world, the general system of relations, is to potentiate oneself and to develop oneself." Hence: "one can say that man is essentially 'political' since it is through the activity of transforming and consciously directing other men that man realized his 'humanity,' his 'human nature'."[21] The difficulty was that in positing a social development governed by "scientific" laws of motion, Marxism had permitted the concept of the state and political action to degenerate; the diverse elements of the "superstructure" were left to themselves, to move spontaneously in the manner of a "haphazard and sporadic germination."[22]

The consequences of economism were not merely theoretical in scope: it also undermined the search for political solutions to the contradictions of bourgeois society. Indeed, while at an earlier point economism represented a certain theoretical advance beyond traditional idealism, as in the work of Marx, ultimately it generated a language that could only lead to theoretical and *practical* immobility:

> Confronted with (historical political) events, economism asks the question: 'who profits directly from the initiative under consideration?' and replies with a line of reasoning which is as simplistic as it is fallacious: the ones who profit directly are a certain fraction of the ruling class ...This sort of infallibility comes very cheaply. It not only has no theoretical significance—it has only minimal implications for practical efficacy. In general, it produces nothing but moralistic sermons, and interminable questions of personality.[23]

It was Gramsci's seemingly un-Marxian fascination with the political sphere that sensitized him to conjunctural events and permitted him to draw strategic conclusions from them. Among Marxists only Lenin, and to a lesser extent Trotsky, possessed this quality. Within such a framework Gramsci could investigate the fragility of the Italian liberal state, explore the politico-ideological component of fascism, and analyze the Bolshevik Revolution as an historical phenomenon. To be sure, he sometimes exaggerated the importance of politics while adopting a rather cavalier attitude toward the economic sphere and the material obstacles that might impede collective political action. Yet he never argued a case for "political autonomy" in the sense that politics could be seen as a "neutral" realm, hovering over class relations, as the "elite" theorists (Michels, Mosca, and Pareto) had claimed. For example, there was nothing resembling the concept of a separate "political class" anywhere in Gramsci's work. It would be more accurate to say that for Gramsci the political sphere was semi-autonomous insofar as it was mediated through a complex social totality but was never "determined" by underlying economic forces.[24]

From Machiavelli to Gramsci

In challenging the productivist legacy of Marxism, Gramsci rejected a time-honored premise that the most decisive human action was always *economic* action, countering with the notion that all action is political and posing the question: "can one not say that the real philosophy of each man is contained in its entirety in his political action?"[25] The primacy of economics had obscured the fact that class struggle ultimately achieves its fullest expression through politics, where, at critical historical moments, "the search for appropriate means to control in practice the overall political strategy will always remain of exclusively political competence."[26] This consuming interest in politics attracted Gramsci to the theory of Machiavelli, whose obsession with Italian unification inspired *The Prince*—a work which saw in the universalizing power of the state a solution to the peninsula's chronic fragmentation.

Gramsci identified Machiavelli as the "first Jacobin" and praised him lavishly in "The Modern Prince" as a thinker who effectively brought together theory and politics, who passionately wanted to combine historical understanding with a strong commitment to "partisanship" and to building human community through political action. Thus: "In his treatment, in his critique of the present, he expressed general concepts...and an original conception of the world. This conception of the world too could be called 'philosophy of praxis', or 'neo-humanism' [which] bases itself entirely on the concrete action of man, who, impelled by historical necessity, works and transforms reality." And Gramsci added: "But what Machiavelli does do is bring everything back to politics—i.e., to the art of governing men, of securing their permanent consent, and hence of founding 'great states.' "[27]

This ability to capture the essence of politics and to recognize its special domain was, in Gramsci's view, Machiavelli's great contribution. The painstaking investigation of historical forces was for Machiavelli a necessary point of departure; but the true "statesman", or prince, never confines his attention to "effective reality" but seeks to understand the present and future as part of the total historical process. He utilizes politics—the only truly "common" realm—to establish a new relation of forces, a new social order. Inevitably, therefore, Machiavelli was much less concerned with the static world of descriptive observations ("objective" conditions) than with the key mechanism for transforming that reality (politics), since whereas the former was always confined to social immediacy the latter provided space for initiative and foresight. In this sense the detached scientific enterprise was innately conservative. Since Machiavelli believed that politics was the only terrain upon which the popular will could be mobilized, he looked to its personification in the prince as the vehicle for establishing unity where before there had been only cleavage and disunity, as in the case of the Italian city-states. Politics was what moved human beings forward to some new ideal, what enabled them to "dominate" reality as part of analyzing it. Gramsci depicted Machiavelli as "...not merely a scientist: he was a partisan, a man of powerful passions, an active politician, who wishes to create a new balance of forces and therefore cannot help concerning himself with what 'ought to be'..." He went on:

The active politician is a creator, an initiator; but he neither creates from nothing nor does he move in the turbid void of his own desires and dreams. He bases himself on effective reality, but what is this effective reality? Is it something static and immobile, or is it not rather a relation of forces in continuous motion and shift of equilibrium? If one applies one's will to the creation of a new equilibrium among the forces which really exist and are operative—basing oneself on the practical force which one believes to be progressive and strengthening it to help it to victory—one still moves on the terrain of effective reality, but does so in order to dominate and transcend (or to contribute to this). What 'ought to be' is therefore concrete; indeed it is the only realistic and historicist interpretation of reality, it alone is history in the making, it alone is politics.[28]

What Marxism lacked, Gramsci argued, was precisely this Machiavellian theory of statecraft which aims not so much at "knowledge of man" or "disinterested scientific activity" as at "connecting seemingly disparate facts" and laying down the "means adequate to particular ends."[29] Politics must be equally as concerned with arousing popular passions, with activating the collective will as with discovering forms of knowledge or presenting categories of logic. *The Prince*, for example, was a "live" theoretical work, combining historical generalizations with the powerful appeal of "myth". Gramsci suggested that "Such a procedure stimulates the artistic imagination of those who have to be convinced, and gives political passions a more concrete form."[30] Not surprisingly, Gramsci drew parallels between Machiavelli's "prince" and Sorel's "myth" insofar as both were viewed as emotive agents of ideological unification. Thus Machiavelli's was neither the "cold theorizing" of Plato's utopia nor the "learned discourse" of Locke's treatises, but rather the creative instrument of social transformation wherein politics functions primarily to *transcend* the given "ensemble of relations." His was "the style of a man of action, of a man urging action, the style of a party manifesto."[31]

Gramsci's ambitious effort to reclaim Machiavelli for the twentieth century—and for Marxism—was hardly fortuitous, since within Machiavelli's thought converged a number of themes that were to permeate the *Notebooks*: the primacy of politics, the role of popular consensus, the struggle for national unification. Indeed this Machiavellian spirit, far more than the Hegelian or Crocean spirit, dominates large sections of the prison writings—an influence that has not generally received sufficient notice in the Gramsci literature.[32] There can be little doubt that the heavily Jacobin orientation of "The Modern Prince" and other parts of the *Notebooks* owed as much to Machiavelli as to Lenin.

From the standpoint of modern Italian history, Gramsci looked to politics as a tool for harnessing mass energies behind the long struggle to create a socialist community out of the myriad divisions of capitalist society. The great "protagonist" of this epochal drama—the concrete embodiment of the "prince," or the "modern prince"—would of course be the Marxist revolutionary party. Only through such a Jacobin force could the parochial interests of sectoral or regional movements be subordinated to the global requirements of socialist transformation. The difficulty with Sorel's myth was that, in relying so heavily on the spontaneous impulse of Bergson's *elan vital*, it left no room for the planned or "conscious" element. At the same time, Croce's vision of a new Italian culture emerging out of changes within the ethico-political sphere was partial in that it denied the importance of *structural* change. Yet Lenin's more extreme variant of Jacobinism amounted to a novel form of bureaucratic centralism insofar as it envisioned the formation of a tightly-disciplined nucleus of professional cadres. What Gramsci wanted was neither a pluralistic assemblage of autonomous mass struggles nor an *elite* party that would be the exclusive repository of politics, but a synthesis of the two poles—an organic linkage between elite and mass, the organized and the spontaneous, the planned element and the vital impulse. While politics would forge a socialist identity by "universalizing" diverse popular struggles, the party would accomplish this task largely by means of "leading," by its moral-intellectual or pedagogical guidance, instead of through the more familiar technique of organizational control.

Gramsci's Jacobinism thus contained a "popular" or consensual dimension that was not usually associated with Leninism. For Gramsci as for Machiavelli, the intervention of skilled leaders necessarily coincided with the emergence of an active citizenry. Thus: "One may therefore suppose that Machiavelli had in mind 'those who are not in the know', and that it was they whom he intended to educate politically." And he continued: "Who therefore is 'not in the know'? The revolutionary class of the time, the Italian 'people' or 'nation', the citizen democracy which gave birth to men like Savonarola and Pier Soderini, rather than to Castruccio or a Valentino."[33] Presumably, it would be the task of organic intellectuals to "democratize" theory—i.e., to disseminate revolutionary ideas to "those not in the know." The authority of leaders would always have to be conditioned by the trust and active engagement of the masses; where the latter become passive, manipulated objects, the leadership itself loses dynamism and becomes politically inert.[34] Here Gramsci introduced the term "Cadornism" (after the Italian general Luigi Cadorna) to refer to the shortsighted attempts of authoritarian leaders to establish political power without winning over the support of the people they seek to lead.[35] It was, of course, this very failure to deal with the imperatives of consent that Gramsci found unacceptable in Bordiga's politics.

The economic, religious, and regional cleavages of Machiavelli's time not only persisted into Gramsci's time but were compounded by the peculiarly uneven development of Italian capitalism. Gramsci brilliantly grasped the importance of this theme for revolutionary politics, especially as it applied to the Southern Question. He further observed that capitalist rationalization in the north was atomizing and dividing the working class along lines of wages, status, and culture, making it likely that an oppositional movement would reproduce those divisions. With local struggles following the logic of their own parochial or "corporatist" interests, a universalizing Jacobin presence was even *more* critical for socialist transformation. In Italy of course this presence would be Gramsci's own Communist Party, which though momentarily on the defensive against fascism, had inherited the historical mission of building a "revolutionary bloc" out of the cleavages and contradictions of bourgeois society.

Gramsci's strategic interest in politics did not so much negate the role of economic struggles as establish a reciprocal relationship between the spheres of politics and economics that was absent from earlier Marxist theories. Still, politics occupied a very special theoretical niche in the overall scheme of things, for two reasons: it constituted a new terrain for the unfolding of capitalist crisis, and it represented the transformative mechanism of class struggle. The implications of this rather dramatic shift away from a labor-defined dialectic would ultimately pose some troublesome questions for the whole Marxist theoretical paradigm. At the same time, Gramsci himself (following Lenin) clearly thought that, by restoring the forgotten element of politics, he was *reconstituting* (and not transcending) Marxism as the most comprehensive and living philosophy of the historical period. He found inspiration in Machiavelli, just as he did in Croce and Sorel at an earlier point, for the purposes of incorporating phenomena that Marxists had previously devalued, with the goal of reconstructing the Marxist totality.[36] How else could he have written that "To maintain that the philosophy of praxis is not a completely autonomous and independent structure of thought, in antagonism to all traditional philosophies and religions, means that one has not severed one's links with the old world...the philosophy of praxis has no need of support from alien sources."[37]

Gramsci's search for a contemporary incarnation of the Jacobin prime-mover thus represented an attack on *productivist* Marxism rather than Marxism *tout court*. Machiavelli's "prince" was a great resource in the theoretical combat waged against economism—an outlook that reflected distinctly capitalist priorities and therefore gave rise to a political strategy which loses any real "capacity for cultural expansion." In other words: "Here we are dealing with a subaltern group which is prevented by this theory (economism) from ever becoming dominant, or from developing beyond the economic-corporate stage and rising to the phase of ethico-political hegemony in civil society, and domination of the state."[38] A Marxism devoid of any creative political theory, any art of statecraft, would be disarmed from the outset.

The crisis of bourgeois hegemony, and with it the emergence of counter-hegemonic movements, was not strictly a matter of *economic* breakdown, for the crisis which Marxists had long predicted was now in Gramscian terms expected to achieve its fullest expression on the political-ideological terrain, where "partial" demands would be translated into "fundamental" ones challenging the entire social system. Such a crisis would require massive cracks in the legitimating apparatus, opening new space for ideological ferment, the development of critical consciousness on a broad scale, and, ultimately, for intervention of a unifying political force. As Gramsci put it:

> One of the commonest totems is the belief about every-thing that exists, that it is 'natural' that it should exist... and that however badly one's attempts to reform may go they will not stop life going on, since the traditional forces will continue to operate and precisely will keep life going on...One may say that no real movement becomes aware of its global character all at once, but only gradually through experience—in other words, when it learns from the facts that nothing which exists is natural...but rather exists because of certain conditions.[39]

Such a "global" force, however was always absent in Italian history—a phenomenon that both Machiavelli and Gramsci recognized. Their conceptualization of this problem, and the frustrating search for a Jacobin agency to fill the void, was the cornerstone of their respective political theories. For Gramsci, there had never been a Jacobinism capable of transcending deep social cleavages and linking a modernizing elite stratum with large sectors of the population, as had occurred in the French Revolution. In Italy, as we have seen, no hegemonic force had stirred the passions of the people enough to create a national community; the bourgeois revolution, presided over by an insular group of Piedmont industrialists, bankers, and intellectuals, never penetrated the old Papal strongholds, the *Mezzogiorno*, Sicily, or Gramsci's native Sardinia. There had evolved no unified system of national beliefs, no nation-state in the full ethico-political sense, whereas in France the emergence of strong "positive elements" made patriotic rejuvenation a realizable goal. If in Italy liberalism never supplied the basis of a strong hegemony, in France the rise of an "audacious, dauntless" Jacobinism expressed not the momentary needs of the masses but the historical vision of a community.[40] In France, as in England and the United States, the modern state attained a nearly universal scope of legitimacy—the kind of ethical and cultural cohesion which Croce thought was central to historical progress. The "impediments" stemming from traditional residues (notably Catholicism) made Italy somewhat unique in this respect.

Yet insofar as a "supremacy of the political moment" never appeared in Italy, this fact offered new opportunities for socialist movements that were not present in other countries, and Gramsci had the foresight to anticipate such a "national" dimension of Marxism in twentieth century Italy. Put simply, Gramsci argued that the failure of the bourgeoisie to achieve Italian unification gave Marxists an historical opening to do so on their own terms, without waiting for capitalism to run its full course. Lenin, of course, invoked his theory of imperialism to make a similar argument for the left in Russia. The weakness of bourgeois hegemony presented a critical advantage to Marxism, or at least a Marxism that was not crippled by scientific determinism. The "second Risorgimento," in Gramsci's view, would be a communist extension of the first—a more global system of hegemony that would overcome class, religious, north-south, and other regional divisions at last. In this fashion the interests of the northern proletariat and the southern peasantry would finally converge, bringing to an end the colonial status of the *Mezzogiorno* and the islands—under a Marxist banner.[41]

These insights generated a remarkably lucid strategic conception for the PCI, based upon three imperatives: the primacy of politics, the "national" function of Marxism, and the construction of a revolutionary bloc. But the key to everything, in Gramscian theory, was resolution of the Southern Question, since "Any formation of a national-popular collective will is impossible unless the great mass of peasant farmers bursts *simultaneously* into political life. That was Machiavelli's intention through the reform of the militia, and it was achieved by the Jacobins in the French Revolution. That Machiavelli understood it reveals a precocious Jacobinism that is the (more of less fertile) germ of his conception of national revolution."[42]

If the orthodox Marxists of the PSI failed to grasp this dialectic, the Italian Communists of the early 1920s were hardly more advanced: they too had been oblivious to the prescriptions of Machiavelli, and thus remained strategically inept. Under Bordiga's leadership the PCI was isolated and immobile, in part because "proletarian internationalism" was defined to exclude any uniquely national road to socialism.[43] From Bordiga's viewpoint the PCI was an extension of the international Communist movement based in Moscow, which meant that as far as theory, strategy, and even tactics were concerned the Italian party was little more than an appendage of the Comintern. Gramsci would observe later that Bordiga's fetishism of Comintern authority was *one* factor which undermined the party's capacity to mobilize significant mass support.[44] Bordiga, for understandable reasons at the time, paid little attention to the dictum that, for Marxism to achieve *popular* or hegemonic status, it must express itself in national terms, through a particular culture and language. Political strategy and tactics could not be imposed by a global center, but would have to be mediated through a set of historically specific conditions. Bordiga had confused the need for international *solidarity* with the uniform application of a single revolutionary model. Or, to put it in different terms:

> In reality, the internal relations of any nation are the result of a combination which is 'original' and (in a certain sense) unique: these relations must be conceived and understood in their originality and uniqueness if one wishes to dominate them and direct them. To be sure, the line of development is towards internationalism, but the point of departure is 'national'—and it is from this point of departure that one must begin. Yet the perspective is international and cannot be otherwise.[45]

In this context Gramsci referred to a deformed Jacobinism ("Bonapartism") where a rigid authoritarian centralism substitutes for local democratic energy rooted in national traditions, leading to political inertia and passivity. For example, even in the case of European Social Democracy after World War I it was possible to speak of a mechanical internationalism to the extent that "nobody believed they ought to make a start—that is to say, they believed that by making a start they would find themselves isolated; they waited for everybody to move together, and nobody in the meantime moved or organized the movement." Similarly, Gramsci attacked the later Stalinist concept of "socialism in one country", which viewed the USSR as the single center of world revolution, as an "anti-natural form of Napoleonism."[46] Moreover, whereas Bordiga argued that national factors could play a role only in colonized, underdeveloped countries like Russia, Gramsci countered that the growing significance of the ideological sphere in the advanced capitalist societies actually opened up new and more explosive possibilities for national mobilization, since "It is in the concept of hegemony that those exigencies which are national in character are knotted together."[47] Thus Gramsci was probably the first Marxist to anticipate a convergence of revolutionary socialist and nationalist aspirations for the European *capitalist* countries.

But in Italy during the 1920s it was neither the PSI nor the PCI which mobilized this "national-popular" energy; the task in fact fell to Mussolini and the fascists, whose political ingenuity tapped the resources of mass patriotism for altogether different aims. Not until the Resistance movement of 1943-1945, when popular upheavals against the defeated fascist regime and the German occupation created a massive revolutionary upsurge, did Italian Marxism finally inherit the role assigned to it by Gramsci in the *Notebooks*. From a distinctly Gramscian viewpoint, the partisan movement of World War II accomplished three historic objectives: it precipitated a crisis of legitimacy in the north; it transformed the PCI into a *mass* party, which had enrolled more than two million members by 1946; and it brought together the interests of northern workers and southern peasants into a single (patriotic) "revolutionary bloc."

The first real glimpse of such a confluence of theory and history, intellectuals and masses that was so vital to the philosophy of praxis would therefore not come to pass in Italy until nearly a decade after Gramsci's death. More than any other movement in Italian history, the Resistance gave substance (however partial and temporary) to the Gramscian synthesis: a convergence of the Machiavellian vision of a unified Italian nation-state, the Crocean promise of cultural rejuvenation, and the Leninist ideal of a vanguard party. The emphasis here must be placed upon *synthesis*. For Gramsci, socialist transformation involved more than simply the dissemination of new belief-systems and values by a visionary intellectual elite, as Croce believed; it also required mass participation, as well as structural definition. And it went deeper than the mere ascent to power by a great leader, as in the case of Machiavelli's "Prince," insofar as it meant full-scale reconstruction of the state through the intervention of a collective entity (the party). Thus: "If one had to translate the notion 'Prince,' as used in Machiavelli's work, into modern political language, one would have to make a series of distinctions: the 'Prince' could be head of state, or leader of a government, but it could also be a political leader whose aim is to conquer a state, or found a new type of state; in this sense, 'prince' could be translated in modern terms as 'political party'."[48] Finally, the Gramscian version of the "myth prince," or "collective intellectual," differed from Leninist vanguardism because it incorporated the *consensual* focus of classical and Italian idealist thought.

Beyond Leninism

That Gramsci's model of revolutionary change departed emphatically from Lenin's could be seen in his preoccupation with ideological hegemony and the "national" role of Marxist theory and practice. At the core of this divergence was Gramsci's famous "dual perspective," which revolved around the key distinction between force and consent in politics—and which he conceptualized in terms of the dichotomy "organic" vs. "conjunctural".[49] By conjunctural Gramsci meant the passing and often momentary phase of crisis during which contesting political forces struggle for state power—a period roughly equivalent to the strategic concept "war of position" or "war of maneuver". This was the realm of historical contingency and unpredictability (*fortuna* in Machiavelli's language), tactical decision-making, and of course military combat. And it was the arena of political activity for which Lenin's cadre party was essentially designed.

The "organic" side of politics, on the other hand, referred to the gradual, long-term struggle for hegemony within civil society, to the decisive shift in the balance of social forces that must precede and accompany the conjunctural moment. Gramsci called this the "war of position." During this phase the Jacobin party would carry out largely "moral-intellectual" or pedagogical tasks, downplaying the more narrowly organizational functions of the Leninist model. Gramsci's strategic outlook integrated *both* the organic and conjunctural phases within a dialectical totality: the Marxist party assumes the character of both "collective intellectual" and "modern Prince," allowing for a more reciprocal interaction between party organization and the larger complex of social relations than the conventional notion (and reality) of Jacobinism permitted. In other words, the Gramscian schema advanced the theoretical possibility of a *democratic* reconstruction of both civil society and the state in advanced capitalism.

Gramsci fiercely resisted ultra-centralist formulas which reduced virtually all political action to the conjectural phase.

However, in both his party writings and the *Notebooks* it was actually his arch-rival Bordiga rather than Lenin who presented the main target of Gramsci's assault on mechanical vanguardism. For several reasons, as I have suggested, Gramsci steadfastly avoided any direct confrontation with the heroic figure of Lenin. Yet one is immediately struck by the degree to which Gramsci's attack on Bordiga can equally apply to the living, historical Lenin— or at least what the "Leninism" of the Bolshevik Party had become in Russia already during Gramsci's lifetime. The point is that for Lenin, as for Bordiga, the conjunctural side was virtually all-consuming: revolution seemed to be a one-dimensional process, geared almost exclusively to the realm of military-political combat, large-scale organization, professional elites, and the seizure of state power. What was political "success" likely to mean for such a strategy? The answer for Gramsci was the probability of "Bonapartism"—a bureaucratically-imposed regime that, lacking in hegemonic vitality, would rapidly degenerate into a new form of statist domination.[50]

Of course it might be argued that Lenin too was fearful of such authoritarian deformation, as his frequent attacks against "Blanquism" indicate, and that, furthermore, he was actually quite sensitive to the themes of ideological hegemony (in *What is to be Done?*) and democratic participation (in *State and Revolution*). Some observers have insisted, moreover, that one cannot identify any single "Leninism", since Lenin himself changed theoretical and strategic positions in his own writings from time to time, in response to new situations and events.[51] That Lenin was very adaptable on some issues and even inconsistent is beyond doubt. Yet, at the most general political level, what emerged out of the theory and *practice* of the Bolsheviks under Lenin's guidance— from the RSDLP split in 1903 to the struggle with the Mensheviks, to the October Revolution and the post-revolutionary consolidation of power—was a vanguardist politics *sui generis* that possessed a continuity dwarfing in significance the variations in Lenin's theoretical and policy statements.

If we accept the idea of a rather *historically* uniform Lenin, at least as far as political strategy is concerned, the unique version of Gramsci's "Leninism" becomes apparent. The dual perspective suggested far more than a straightforward translation of Bolshevism into the Italian situation, for it pointed to an entirely different model of political action—not to mention a quite dissimilar vision of Marxism itself. Instead of an affirmation of politics over the social sphere typical of Lenin, one finds in Gramsci a more reciprocal interaction between the two levels: "The history of a party, in other words, can only be the history of a particular social group. But this group is not isolated; it has friends, kindred groups, opponents, enemies. The history of any given party can only emerge from the complex portrayal of society and state."[53] From this angle, the dual perspective was another way of locating politics as a mediating force between structure and consciousness, as suggested in chapter six.[54] For Gramsci, then, politics was deeply-embedded in all phases of movement formation, not simply in the struggle for state power; as such, it was neither an epiphenomenon reducible to class relations (as Marx assumed) nor an all-powerful prime mover (as Lenin contended). The "war of position" dictated that the Machiavellian-Leninist fixation on the conquest of governmental power must be supplemented by a prior expansion of "dual power" networks of authority throughout civil society.[55]

What distinguished Gramsci's theory of the revolutionary party from Lenin's was its dual role as both the *expression* and the *mobilizer* of popular struggles. Its leadership activities would be largely "indirect," structured around the tasks of guiding and educating in the broadest counter-hegemonic sense; spontaneity would be redirected through ideological as well as organizational methods. The arch-typical Gramscian political actor (e.g., the organic intellectual) would be fully immersed in the larger social milieu, in the cultural norms of civil society—in contrast to the full-time professional revolutionary of Lenin's cadre party.

Hence, during the organic phase it is probable that distinctly extra-party formations (e.g., factory and neighborhood committees, councils, civic associations, educational and media groups) would be more directly involved in popular mobilization than the party itself. While Gramsci never formulated a theory of "dual power" in the *Notebooks*, the very notion of "spontaneous forms of state life" seems implicit in his organic "war of position" strategy and would of course be consistent with his general pre-prison strategic outlook.[56]

Against this dualistic framework Leninism appeared one-sided in its fetishism of the "external" political element over civil society. Here Gramsci wrote of a tendency he called "volunteer action"—an impatient military strategy oriented to rapid success but which in the end opens the door to the aforementioned Bonapartism, which is a "surrogate for popular intervention" and indulges the passivity of the masses. The strictly "conjunctural" focus was far too crisis-bound, too prone to look for organizational solutions where the issue of mass consciousness had yet to be posed. The result would likely be a form of detached vanguardism:

...there is a voluntarism or Garibaldism as the initial moment of an organic period which must be prepared and developed; a period in which the organic collectivity, as a social bloc, will participate fully. 'Vanguards' without armies to back them up, 'commandos' without infantry or artillery, these too are transpositions from the language of rhetorical heroism—though vanguards and commandos as specialized functions within complex and regular organisms are quite another thing. The same distinction can be made between the notion of intellectual *elites* separated from the masses, and that of intellectuals who are conscious of being linked organically to a national-popular mass. In reality, one has to struggle against the above-mentioned degenerations, the false heroisms and pseudo-aristocracies, and stimulate the formation of homogeneous, compact social blocs, which will give birth to their own intellectuals, their own commandos, their own vanguard—who in turn will react upon those blocs in order to develop them and not merely so as to perpetuate their gypsy domination.[57]

In the absence of a fully-evolved organic phase of social transformation, Marxist parties which did manage to conquer state power would confront insoluble contradictions: their "socialism" would likely become a ritualized, "rhetorical" ideology employed by a new elite stratum to perpetuate its domination. This extreme form of Jacobin *power* amounted to what Gramsci labelled "bureaucratic centralism"—as distinguished from "organic centralism". Thus: "When the party is progressive it functions 'democratically'; when the party is regressive it functions 'bureaucratically.' The party in this second case is a simple, unthinking executor. It is then technically a policing organism, and its name of 'political party' is simply a metaphor of a mythological character."[58] Lacking "organicity," bureaucratic centralism ignored the need for "a continual adaptation of the organization to the real movement, a matching of thrusts from below with orders from above, a continuous insertion of elements thrown up from the depths of the rank and file into the solid framework of the leadership apparatus which ensures continuity and the regular accumulation of experience."[59] Here Gramsci no doubt had in mind a more complex relationship between party and state than the Leninist primacy of the vanguard party *over* the state. Of course the party would still carry out a wide range of tasks in both the "organic" and "conjunctural" moments of contestation,[60] but with the transfer of power it would possess no higher legitimacy or monopoly of force but would simply be one *expression* of a newly-unfolding state system grounded in civil society.[61]

There can be no denying Lenin's powerful influence upon Gramsci's theoretical development, even if that influence was sometimes ambiguous or refracted, as I argued in the introduction to this volume. Gramsci's Marxism was always *in some measure* the Marxism of the Comintern, however critical and eclectic it might have been. Yet if Gramsci initially seized upon the Leninist breakthrough to mount his own critique of orthodox Marxism, he ultimately outgrew Lenin as he began to grapple with the imperatives of political struggle in the conditions of advanced capitalism. The result was a unique Gramscian "breakthrough" identified conceptually with the theory of hegemony and normatively with a vision of democratization that held out the possibility of a consensual revolution. Gramsci, however, was not permitted to leave long enough to expand upon his seminal but still fragmentary and unfinished contributions.

The implication of Gramsci's synthesis for revolutionary strategy has become more visible with the passing of time. The Bolshevik Revolution, which Gramsci himself praised as the "decisive turning point in history," had already lost its revolutionary promise while Gramsci was still alive; the regime it gave birth to stands today as a new type of authoritarian regime which fits precisely the bureaucratic centralism Gramsci had feared—and would have predicted. The developmental pattern of the Soviet party-state cannot be attributed to leadership "betrayal" or to bureaucratic deformation alone, for even though the general features of the system cannot be traced back to the October Revolution, the main authoritarian and socially-repressive structures did originate in the Jacobin strategy authored by Lenin.[62] If Gramsci himself was never in a position to fully analyze this phenomenon, then his theoretical orientation in the *Notebooks* at least suggests such a critique.

Bureaucratic centralism was therefore neither a deviant historical formation nor a simple expression of Stalin's personality, but was the outgrowth of what Gramsci defined as detached vanguardism. The impetus toward "modernization" and a totally-administered society was predictable enough once the original (Leninist) path was chosen. A heavy reliance upon state initiative in an economically undeveloped society where regime support was narrow and fragile—i.e., where "consensus" was lacking—guaranteed a bureaucratic course of evolution. True, the Bolshevik leadership counted upon insurgency in Europe to consolidate its international position, but Jacobinism by its very nature presupposed a large element of risk and even isolation. Post-revolutionary conditions—economic chaos, civil war, left opposition—*reinforced* a centralist direction but in no way *caused* it, since Leninist strategy was meant to anticipate and confront such conditions. The historical situation did not contradict the assumptions of Jacobin politics.[63]

If Marxism was originally an anti-statist theory, Soviet development after Lenin had generated what Stojanovic calls the "statist myth of socialism."[64] From the standpoint of the Bolshevik model, "socialism" became inseparable from the idea of state activity: control, ownership, planning, capital accumulation, social mobilization. Statism subjugated the working class to a new ruling bureaucratic stratum that perpetuates its hegemony under the banner of Marxism, or "Marxism-Leninism".[65] The long-term impact of statism in the USSR, and in other countries where this type of strategy has been successful, has been the *extension* of the system of domination and destruction of autonomous forms of popular activity within civil society.[66] Under these conditions the transition to socialism can only assume a kind of mystical quality, wherein the forms of consciousness, social relations, and political involvement required for an egalitarian order would be negated at every turn. The bureaucratic penetration of civil society has reduced the concepts of "advanced democracy," "state of the whole people," and "withering away of the state" to illusory, ritualized dogmas. The Soviet experience suggests that the very ideal of socialist transformation remains a myth so long as the structure of state domination remains its primary embodiment—that is, so long as there is no political theory (and practice) or revolutionary democracy to give substance to it.

The Jacobin Predicament

One of Gramsci's enduring contributions was to theoretically pose an alternative to detached vanguardism and bureaucratic centralism without at the same time lapsing into the common Marxist inclination to abandon politics altogether. This dual perspective countered a mechanical Jacobinism by inserting the popular, democratic, and counter-hegemonic element into the revolutionary process—by balancing prefigurative against instrumental, organic against conjunctural phases of struggle.

To what extent, then, might Gramsci's political strategy be understood as a clear departure from the Leninist tradition? While at times his transcendence of classical vanguardism was rather bold, at other times it seemed ambiguous, compromising, and even tortured. Two persistent issues enter the picture: first, despite the coexistence of prefigurative and instrumental or even statist elements in Gramsci, this coexistence was vague and haphazard, with the Jacobin imposition ultimately predominating and, second, the prefigurative dimension itself lacked any coherent structural-political expression. In the totality of Gramsci's writing, we encounter vacillations from one sphere to the other but never a systematic fusion of the two. Thus, when Gramsci embraced the Machiavellian primacy of politics in the *Notebooks* he essentially dropped any mention of the Turin factory council experience. He did, however, establish the philosophical and theoretical basis of a synthesis in the *Notebooks* but once again he specified no concrete mediations (beyond the party) to concretize it. The compelling vision of a counter-hegemonic movement, guided by organic intellectuals comitted to a new "integrated culture," lacked strategic immediacy—until the vanguard party appeared on the scene, paving the way to a triumph of Jacobinism by default.

From a political (and not strictly theoretical) viewpoint, therefore, the Gramscian alternative represents (like the Lukacsian one) a certain unavoidable lapse back into Leninism. The theoretical breakthrough could never achieve full political articulation. Despite an elaborate attempt to merge the vanguardist and prefigurative sides into a new synthesis, the former was clearly supreme: the party-state would in the end assume a primary role, with "democratization" coming largely from above. In contrast, a fundamentally new Marxian strategy would reverse this relationship by asserting the prefigurative sphere over the Jacobin-instrumental. For the party by definition is primarily an *instrumental* mechanism designed for concrete political tasks rather than the cultural objectives of reshaping civil society and abolishing the bourgeois division of labor; it tends naturally to be an agency of domination rather than of popular self-emancipation. Since the prefigurative function can be fully carried out only through local structures of "dual power," it is these which must emerge as the primary locus of revolutionary change. According to such a synthesis the party would no longer constitute itself as the prime-mover of mass struggles but would express itself *through* these struggles as a coordinating vehicle—an insight which Gramsci was probably the first to grasp *theoretically* but which he was never able to formulate in clear strategic terms.

Footnotes

1. As Badaloni notes, already by 1920-21 Gramsci was beginning his search for a strategic alternative to both Jacobinism and syndicalism, which were the twin responses to the breakdown of reformist orthodoxy. See "Gramsci and the Problem of Revolution," in Mouffe, ed., *Gramsci and Marxist Theory*, pp. 90-91.

2. The divergent strategic outlooks contained in Marx are explored by Stanley Moore, *Three Tactics: the Background in Marx* (New York: Monthly Review, 1963), and Magri, "Problems of the Marxist Theory of the Revolutionary Party," *op. cit.*

3. See my "Revolutionary Process, Political Strategy and the Dilemma of Power," *op. cit.*, pp. 359-64.

4. Gramsci never criticized Bolshevism, or Lenin, directly in any of his writings. Even during the prison years he still remained attached to the PCI and the Comintern, despite policy differences with other leaders. Yet his sustained critique of Bordiga's ultra-centralism (especially in the 1924-26 period), along with his general treatment of revolution in the *Notebooks*, suggests a fundamental departure from what is generally defined as "Leninism." It is worth noting here that, aside from the issue of electoral abstentionism, Bordiga's theory was consistent with what Leninism became in practice in the USSR after 1918.

5. While it is true that such themes also appeared in Lenin's work—notably *State and Revolution*—they were overwhelmed by the theoretical and practical hegemony of a manipulative organizational structure. On this point, see Frederic and Lou Jean Fleron, "Administrative Theory as Repressive Political Theory: The Communist Experience," *Telos*, Summer 1972.

6. See in particular Sheldon Wolin, *Politics and Vision* (Boston: Little, Brown and Company, 1961), ch. 9.

7. Colletti explains this absence of a political focus in Marx by noting that Marx believed communism on a world scale would appear organically and also quite rapidly. As Colletti further notes: "The result was that the sphere of political structures remained little examined or explored. One could formulate this paradoxically by saying that the political movement inspired by Marxism had been virtually innocent of political theory." "Interview with Lucio Colletti," *New Left Review*, no. 86, July-August 1974, p. 15.

8. Marx never actually drew explicit parallels between the bourgeois and socialist revolutions, but such an interpretation can be derived from the general analysis of capitalist development contained in *Capital* and other writings, and from his response to the Paris Commune. See Avineri, *The Social and Political Thought of Karl Marx*, ch. 7.

9. "What is to be Done?" in Tucker, ed., *The Lenin Anthology*, pp. 35-36.

10. The concept "minority revolution" is employed by Moore in *Three Tactics*, p. 110.

11. On Gramsci's early transition from councilism to vanguardism, see Davidson, *Antonio Gramsci*, pp. 150-56.

12. Gramsci's strongest advocacy of the vanguard party during the PCI period was expressed in the following articles: "Insegnamenti," May 5, 1922, in *Scritti Politici*, pp. 530-31; "The Communist Party," September 4 and 9, 1920, in *Political Writings-I*; "The Livorno Congress," January 13, 1921, *op.cit.;* "Socialists and Communists," March 12, 1921, *op. cit.*; "Parties and Masses," September 25, 1921; "The Italian Crisis", September 1, 1924, *op. cit.*; "Democracy and Fascism," November 1, 1924, *op. cit.*; and "Elements of the Situation," November 24, 1925, *op. cit.*

13. "The Italian Crisis", *op. cit.*, p. 266. Also "La Crisi italiana," in *Scritti Politici*, p. 580. (Italics mine)

14. "The Internal Situation of our Party and the Tasks of the Forthcoming Congress," July 3, 1925, in *Political Writings-II*, p. 294.

15. *Ibid.*, pp. 296-97. See also "L'Organizzazione del base del Partito," August 15, 1925, in *Scritti Politici*, pp. 642-44. Whether this "Bolshevization" of the PCI actually was designed to *replace* the councils or local committees with the cellular network was never made clear by Gramsci, but his general theoretical outlook indicates that this would have been extremely unlikely. For an interesting discussion of these issues, see Rosa Alcara, *La formazione e i primi anni del Partito Comunista Italiano nella storiagrafia marxista* (Milan: Jaca Book, 1970), pp. 19-54.

16. "Elements of the Situation," November 24, 1925, in *Political Writings-II*, p. 308.

17. "Lyons Theses," *op. cit.,* pp. 372-73.

18. *Ibid.*, pp. 359-60. For Bordiga's concept of the party—and his critique of Gramsci—see Franco Livorno, ed., *Amadeo Bordiga: Scritti scelti* (Milan: Feltrinelli, 1975), pp. 183-86.

19. "Necessita di una preparazione ideologica di massa," May 16, 1925, in *Scritti Politici*, p. 600-601.

20. On the function of political discourse in Gramsci's thought, see Umberto Cerroni, "Universalita e politica," in Ferri, ed., *Politica e storia in Gramsci*, esp. pp. 134-57.

21. "The Study of Philosophy," *SPN*, p. 360.

22. "State and Civil Society," *SPN*, p. 247.

23. "The Modern Prince," *SPN*, p. 166.

24. Despite certain superficial parallels between Gramsci and the "elite" theorists, their basic points of divergence were so great—as Gramsci himself noted in his prison writings—that it would be grossly misleading to consider them as part of the same tendency. See the discussion in Adamson, *Hegemony and Revolution*, pp.204-206. Of course it is precisely Gramsci's *Marxism* which creates the unbridgeable gulf here, as Adamson observes.

25. "The Study of Philosophy," *SPN*, p. 326.

26. "State and Civil Society," *SPN*, p. 250-51.

27. "State and Civil Society," *SPN*, p. 248-49. For a discussion of this aspect of Machiavelli's thought from a similar perspective, see Wolin, *Politics and Vision*, ch. 6.

28. "The Modern Prince", *SPN*, p. 172.

29. "State and Civil Society", *SPN*, p. 252.

30. "The Modern Prince", *SPN*, p. 125.

31. "The Modern Prince", *SPN*, p. 134.

32. A refreshing exception to this tendency of minimizing the influence of Machiavelli on Gramsci can be found in Matthew F. Stolz, "Gramsci's Machiavelli," *op. cit.* Stolz argues that "The Machiavellian moment survives and flourishes in the political thought of Gramsci." (p. 70) However, Stolz pushes his contention too far in suggesting that Machiavelli was *the* key to Gramsci's whole theoretical identity (p. 70). Interestingly enough, Stolz' overemphasis of the Machiavellian side of Gramsci reveals precisely why most Marxist commentators have overlooked this dimension: for Stolz, Machiavelli's primacy of politics was what enabled Gramsci to go beyond the boundaries even of Hegelian Marxism. (pp. 71, 85) This question will be taken up later.

33. "The Modern Prince," *SPN*, p. 135.

34. For a comparison of Machiavelli and Gramsci on their respective approaches to mass participation, see Stolz, "Gramsci's Machiavelli," *op. cit.*, pp. 83-85.

35. Gramsci's critique of this sterile, heavy-handed form of authoritarianism can be found in "The Modern Prince," p. 130-33.

36. This view of Gramsci's relationship to Machiavelli differs from Stolz' contention that "Machiavelli's entrance into Gramsci's theoretical project challenges the foundations of Marxism itself.

The giant figure of Machiavelli, at once the political scientist and heroic actor, threatens to reduce the influence of Marx on Gramsci to a shadow." "Gramsci's Machiavelli," *op. cit.*, p. 70. Not only does this argument reduce Marxism to the scientific materialism and one-sided economism of its orthodox variant, it also ignores the multiple theoretical influences which shaped Gramsci's thought and which, *for him*, contributed to a revitalized Marxism.

37. "Problems of Marxism," *SPN*, p. 462.

38. "The Modern Prince," *SPN*, p. 160.

39. "The Modern Prince," *SPN*, pp. 157-58.

40. "Notes on Italian History", *SPN*, pp. 78-80.

41. This "national" function of Italian Marxism was first outlined by Gramsci (and Togliatti) at the Lyons' Congress of the PCI in 1926. See the "Lyons Theses," in *Political Writings-II*, pp. 340-75. The alliance between workers and peasants, with the goal of breaking the colonial relationship between north and south, was precisely the definition Gramsci gave to the "united front" tactics in Italy. See *Ibid.*, pp. 372-73.

42. "The Modern Prince," *SPN*, p. 132.

43. Bordiga's position on nationalism was, in the historical context, explicable enough. After all, it had been a canon of European Marxism that the categories "nation" and "class" were mutually antagonistic for working-class movements in the advanced countries. Moreover, with Mussolini on the rise in Italy, the very concept of a "national" socialism was obviously tainted with fascist ideology.

44. One electoral measure of the PSI's early success at outreach: in the elections of May 1921 the PSI won 1,600,000 votes (with 123 deputies), while the PCI received only 300,000 (with 15 deputies). This impasse was never overcome before the party was forced underground in 1926.

45. "State and Civil Society," *SPN*, p. 240.

46. "State and Civil Society," *SPN*, p. 241.

47. *Ibid.*

48. *Ibid.*, pp. 253-54. Or: "the protagonist of the new Prince could not in the modern epoch be an individual hero, but only the political party." "The Modern Prince," *SPN*, p. 147.

49. On the distinction between the "organic" and "conjunctural" dimensions of revolutionary transformation, see "The Modern Prince," *SPN*, p. 177-80.

50. Again, Gramsci for understandable reasons never criticized the Bolshevik experience *directly* on those grounds. His discussion of "Bonapartism" or "Caesarism" was in fact largely directed

against the Italian liberal "dictatorships of Depretis, Crispi, and Giolitti." Referring to the authoritarian phase *of transformism*, Gramsci noted that "the bureaucracy became estranged from the country, and via its administrative positions became a true political party, the worst of all, because the bureaucratic hierarchy replaced the intellectual and political hierarchy. The bureaucracy became precisely the state/Bonapartist party." "State and Civil Society", *SPN*, pp. 227-28.

51. On the thesis of many "Lenins", see Antonio Carlo, "Lenin on the Party," *Telos*, no. 17, Fall 1973.

52. Thus Piccone stresses the gulf between Lenin's "scientific" Marxism and Gramsci's "critical" or Hegelian Marxism. See Paul Piccone, "Gramsci and Leninism," *Theory and Society* (forthcoming). This distinction is correct up to a point, but it ignores the profound anti-positivist theoretical *influence* which Lenin and the Bolshevik Revolution initially had upon the Marxist tradition—a phenomenon which Gramsci himself emphasized in "The Revolution against *Capital*."

53. "The Modern Prince," *SPN*, p. 151.

54. From a political standpoint, this reciprocal interaction between structure and consciousness once again contradicts a familiar myth that Gramsci's theory embraces a primacy of "ideology" over "institutions." See Bobbio, "Gramsci and the Conception of Civil Society," in Mouffe, ed., *Gramsci and Marxist Theory*, p. 36 for an example of this idealist reading of Gramsci.

55. As Perry Anderson observes, this schema poses some additional problems. For example, any tendency to simply equate the "war of position" with the consensual moment of struggle—or to assume that the consensual phase can simply precede the coercive or the "war of movement" phase—necessarily ignores the powerful role of coercion within civil society, with disastrous consequences for strategy. See "The Antinomies of Antonio Gramsci," *op. cit.*, pp. 70-72.

56. The phrase "spontaneous forms of state life" is from Vacca, who detects in Gramsci's Marxism the logic of a "dual power" approach. See Giuseppe Vacca, "La 'questione politica degli intellectuali'," in Ferri, ed., *Politica e storica* in Gramsci,' pp. 467-68. Unfortunately, one can only speculate about any real shifts in Gramsci's thinking after 1926, since nowhere in the *Notebooks* did he chose to analyze the council experience or specify a possible relationship between party and councils.

58. "The Modern Prince," *SPN*, p. 155.

59. "The Modern Prince," *SPN*, pp. 188-89.

60. Even within the "conjunctural" or "war of movement" phase, Gramsci further identified three "relations of forces" that must be strategically taken into account—the social, political, and military—each with its own dynamic, yet comprehended as part of a whole process. See "The Modern Prince," *SPN*, pp. 180-82.

61. Once again, this distinction between Gramsci and Lenin is more or less deduced from Gramsci's general theory of revolution, since it was nowhere elaborated in the *Notebooks*. For a discussion of this point, see Bagio de Giovanni, "Lenin and Gramsci: state, politics, and party," in Mouffe, ed., *Gramsci and Marxist Theory*, esp. p. 273.

62. Nowhere in his writings did Gramsci support Trotsky's position in the Bolshevik Party as an alternative to bureaucratization. Indeed, if anything Trotsky was even more of a centralist, and Gramsci's frequent criticisms of "Bronstein" in the *Notebooks* were unequivocal. Thus, in referring to the labor program Trotsky initiated at the IXth CPSU Congress, Gramsci observed that "the military model had become a pernicious prejudice and the militarization of labor was a failure." See "Americanism and Fordism", *SPN*, p. 301. Trotsky appeared to be even more enamored of capitalist rationalization methods than Lenin, as Gramsci noted.

63. Boggs, "Revolutionary Process, Political Strategy, and the Dilemma of Power," *op. cit.*, p. 367.

64. Svetozar Stojanovic, *Between Ideals and Reality* (New York: Oxford University Press, 1973), ch. 3.

65. This argument is perhaps most fully developed in George Konrad and Ivan Szelenyi, *The Intellectuals on The Road to Class Power*.

66. Bahro suggests that this form of statism, which bears a certain kinship to Marx's "Asiatic Mode of Production," has actually produced multiple and overlapping structures of domination in Soviet-type societies. See Rudolf Bahro, *The Alternative in Eastern Europe* (London: New Left Books, 1978), ch. 6.

8 The Conflicted Legacy

In his preface to "The Study of Philosophy" in the *Prison Notebooks*, Gramsci commented that "Philosophy cannot be separated from the history of philosophy, nor can culture from the history of culture. In the most immediate and relevant sense, one cannot be a philosopher, by which I mean have a critical and coherent conception of the world, without having a consciousness of its historicity, of the phase of development which it represents and of the fact that it contradicts other conceptions or elements of other conceptions."[1] This passage could just as well have applied to the evolution of Marxism in general, and to Gramsci's own theoretical role in particular. Viewed in the context of the European radical tradition, Gramsci's Marxism must be located within its own peculiar *historicity*, within the dialectical flow and rhythm not only of the Marxist tradition but of capitalism itself. In this sense the real "Leitmotif" of Gramsci's thought can only be understood as the expression of a transitional and therefore contradictory historical phase—which accounts for the "three faces" of his theory discussed in the introduction, and which further explains so much of the ambiguous and conflicted Gramscian legacy.

The truly prodigious theoretical, journalistic, and programmatic writings that Gramsci was able to complete before his prison-induced death in 1937, over a span of barely two decades, constitutes one of the most remarkable achievements in European intellectual history. Although the *Notebooks* did not reach a very large audience even in Italy before the 1960s, and were scarcely known elsewhere before the early 1970s, they have become general-

275

ly recognized—both within and outside of the Marxist tradition—as a unique contribution to twentieth century thought, with an impact beyond Italy and Western Europe. From the perspective of the 1970s and 1980s, in the wake of the new radicalism (extra-parliamentary opposition, youth and student movements, feminism, ecology and anti-war struggles) that erupted in many advanced capitalist societies, Gramsci's thought takes on added meaning because it was part of the "underground" current that kept alive a critical-dialectical Marxism through the deformations of Stalinism, the Popular Front, and the postwar deradicalization of mass Communist parties.[2] Along with Korsch, Luxemburg, Lukacs, Reich, the Council Communists, Marcuse and the Frankfurt School, Gramsci laid the theoretical basis of an alternative to the bureaucratic social-democratic and Leninist models, but with a more distinctly *political* bias than these other theorists. Gramsci's philosophy of praxis, his original concept of hegemony and his sensitivity to the hidden dimension of mass consciousness, his early attachment to the factory councils, dual power, and pre-figurative struggle, and his expansive approach to revolution—all of this amounted to a novel vision of democratic socialism which, unfortunately, was never conceptually deepened in his work of the 1920s and 1930s.

The belated "discovery" of Gramsci by Marxist intellectuals in Western Europe and North America is understandable given the number of striking parallels between Gramscian theory and various themes incorporated by social movements in advanced capitalism.[3] At the same time, Gramscian motifs have begun to penetrate a number of academic disciplines—notably history, political science, sociology, and education but also literature, film and anthropology—and have since the mid-1970s become rather fashionable. The hundreds of English-language books and articles on Gramsci, and the many others influenced strongly by his work, have concentrated on three broad topics: ideological hegemony, the role of intellectuals, and political strategy. Other more specialized studies have dealt with Gramsci in the context of Italian historiography, his leadership of the PCI, his study of Pirandello and other cultural figures, and his theories of education—to name some. And of course there have been the anticipated intellectual and political biographies.[4] Gramsci has even provided the inspiration for a novel (*Daniel Martin*, by John Fowles) and a dramatic play (*Occupations*, by Trevor Griffiths). His work has been taken up not only by Marxists but also by new leftists, libertarian communists, Third World nationalists, and even liberals. Politically, he has been praised as the architect of an "open," rejuvenated Communist tradition and of the extraparliamentary left; of a "modified" Leninism and of Eurocommunism; of the dictatorship of the proletariat, of the parliamentary road to socialism, and of council or "soviet" democracy. Apparently the list of possibilities, and contradictory possibilities, is endless in what Davidson has referred to as "the varying seasons of Gramscian studies."[5]

This brief but multidimensional and divided legacy has its origins in the very transitional character of Gramsci's Marxism. Gramsci can now be situated more clearly in a definite period of European political and intellectual development, spanning the phases of orthodox Marxism and Leninism which prevailed on the left between 1890 and 1930 as well as the later struggle for a post-Leninist critical Marxism more appropriate to the period of bureaucratic state capitalism. That Gramsci was never able to escape the predicament imposed by this transitional character of his period—best symbolized by his active yet always ambivalent leadership role in the Italian Communist Party—goes far to explain the various pulls and strains within his theory. Thus Gramsci was one of the first Marxists to arrive at fresh concepts and generalizations on the basis of (expected) profound social transformations within bourgeois society; in this respect he was a Western Marxist. Still, he remained the product of an historical experience shaped by the Bolshevik Revolution and the Comintern, the failure of working-class insurgency in the West, and the rise of fascism and Stalinism. Living in Italy, moreover, his Western Marxism was limited insofar as he could only dimly foresee the outlines of a rationalized capitalism that would reshape post-World War II European societies.

Disenchanted with the economistic formulas of conventional Marxism, Gramsci instinctively looked to the Leninist model as a solution to the impasse. Then, after capitalist consolidation in Europe and the triumph of bureaucratic centralism in the Soviet Union, he began to explore some theoretical alternatives—except that, *politically* speaking, he still took for granted many original Bolshevik and, more suprisingly, even some distinctly orthodox premises. It is therefore no wonder that, aside from the harsh obstacles imposed by years of prison confinement, Gramsci was never in a position to fully develop the vast implications of his own thought, and indeed he seemed to be quite modest about its possible universality.

If Gramsci's *intention* was to construct a new Marxist totality for a completely novel phase of capitalism, his "Leitmotif" in reality straddled two distinct sides of the theoretical question on at least three fronts: the role of production and class forces, the issue of revolutionary democracy, and the conceptual meaning of ideological hegemony. On each of these fronts Gramsci was able to pose new questions and present a vision of new possibilities, yet on each too he carried over abundant residues from the past.

Many commentators have observed, correctly, that Gramsci was not really a serious theorist of "political economy" and that from this viewpoint he deviated significantly from conventional Marxian concerns. It is true that Gramsci devoted relatively little attention to economics as such, at least in comparison with his analysis of more specifically historical, political, or even cultural themes: like other Western Marxists, he de-emphasized the sphere of material forces, production, accumulation, wages and prices, and so forth. While this departure is commonly seen as a defect or "void" in his thought, the point is that Gramsci himself was clearly aware of what he was doing; he was resolved to leave behind the classical Marxian framework which, as he argued throughout the *Notebooks*, was theoretically confining and politically useless. Hence the downplaying of economics was no mere oversight or lapse on Gramsci's part but was rather a conscious effort to escape, on the conceptual level, the seemingly relentless logic of capital itself.[6] Indeed, this is the only way one can begin to comprehend the "Leitmotif" of his theory: the sustained critique of economism, the primacy of politics, the concept of hegemony, and the dynamic role of the organic intellectuals, culture, and popular consciousness. For Gramsci, the philosophy of praxis expressed a subjectivity that could never be compromised by the power of historical "necessity"; revolution was above all a human, active, political phenomenon that energetically bursts through whatever material boundaries and obstacles stand in the way.

Yet Gramsci remained uncritically wedded to certain orthodox productivist assumptions. He fully accepted the Enlightenment faith in progress through industrial growth, and shared the view of both Kautsky and Lenin that the transition to socialism would require a developed scientific and technological infrastructure inherited from the bourgeoisie. If Gramsci was less enthusiastic than Lenin about simply taking over capitalist production and administrative techniques and using them for socialist purposes, he nonetheless looked to administrative forms of industrial mobilization (state control, centralized planning, labor discipline) as a means of modernizing a semi-developed Italy. True, Gramsci did describe the brutal and depoliticizing effects of capitalist rationalization in "Americanism and Fordism," but he never questioned in theoretical terms the presumed "neutrality" of such techniques.[7] An even more telling residue of orthodoxy was his consuming emphasis on the point of production, the factory, and above all, the industrial proletariat as universal revolutionary subject. His formative experience in the factory council movement, in which a homogeneous, militant, and unified working class appeared capable of making history by itself, no doubt exerted a strong influence on his thinking until the end. Beneath his attachment to the concept "social bloc" in the *Notebooks* persisted a certain Marxian (and also Sorelian) moral superiority of the producers linked to the privileged status of the factory.[8]

This productivist framework originally corresponded to the early competitive capitalist stage which Marx studied in Victorian England, and which in part applied to pre-fascist Italy, but this framework would become increasingly obsolete as rationalization began to create a new working-class structure, more diversified in its social composition and less centered in the traditional manufacturing sectors and the factory. Gramsci obviously anticipated such a transformation, which helps to explain his theoretical shift in emphasis from sphere of production to civil society in the *Notebooks*—a shift consonant with his evolving Western Marxism. Still, one can detect an underlying tension between these two approaches throughout Gramsci's work or, to put it another way, the productivist categories were never entirely purged from the theory.

A further dualism, involving a pervasive conflict between the Jacobin and democratic sides of Gramsci discussed in earlier chapters, has given rise to similar theoretical ambiguities and, in turn, to a good deal of confusion. Here again Gramsci posed a range of new questions within Marxism but was never able to draw out the full extent of their political implications. That Gramsci was committed throughout his life to the ideal of democratic socialism—to a society organized around the principles of self-management, workers' control, direct mass involvement—is beyond doubt. Despite his recurrent Jacobinism in the *Notebooks*, the strategic conception "war of position" seemed calculated to add a theoretical dimension to the council democracy associated with *Ordine Nuovo*. If so, however, Gramsci made no effort to define "war of position" in concrete *structural* terms, and thus wound up ceding the political-institutional sphere to the centralized party (and party-state) apparatus. In this respect he failed to articulate a new strategy either for transforming civil society or for capturing state power in the advanced countries.[9] Following Luxemburg and Lukacs, Gramsci was compelled to retreat to the easy solutions of Leninism despite a general theory which pointed well beyond it. In the end, Gramsci was stranded between two worlds, so that his attachment to the Bolshevik Revolution, the PCI, and the Comintern (cemented by his deep respect for Lenin) inevitably closed off avenues leading to a more sharply-defined democratic socialism.

The abstract character of Gramsci's democratic vision was best reflected in his surprisingly weak analysis of the capitalist state and his near-silence on the issue of bureaucracy; his richly-suggestive analysis of political organization in the *Ordine Nuovo* literature was scarcely even mentioned, much less developed, in the *Notebooks*.[10] Thus after 1920 he made scant reference to the dual-power model of revolution—one based in the councils (and in the more mature soviets)—having apparently dismissed the idea that democratization could proceed through local forms of civil insurrection. Yet in his intense reaction to the council defeat he never swung to the vanguardist extreme identified with Bordiga. His Jacobinism, both before and during prison, was anchored to a popular or consensual foundation, which contrasted with the imputed (and authoritarian) Leninist equation of "democracy" with "dictatorship of the proletariat." But while Gramsci's earlier hostility toward bourgeois democracy—and the parliamentary road to socialism—was well known, he more or less dropped this theme from his later writings, including the *Notebooks*. The presence of fascist dictatorship in Italy during the 1920s and 1930s allowed him to sidestep such a critique almost entirely, so that unfortunately he was left with little to say about the complexities of an expanding bourgeois-democratic *state* in advanced capitalism. The result was that Gramsci could not possibly have formulated a theoretical or strategic conception of democracy (or socialist democracy), or an alternative to bureaucratic centralism.[11]

In practical-historical terms, therefore, Gramscian theory could not have signified anything more than a political refinement of Leninism to meet Italian conditions—that is, the commitment to a vague frontal strategy against the state made possible by the "actuality of the revolution" and given shape by a mounting crisis of ideological hegemony. This neo-Leninism corresponded to Gramsci's efforts to "Bolshevize" the PCI after 1924, which in effect meant suspension of any *concrete* debate around the issue of democracy. And, as we have seen, there was nothing in the *Notebooks* to fundamentally reverse this pattern.

The third area of tension in Gramsci's Marxism involves his

dual usage of the term ideological hegemony: sometimes this concept was given a strict class definition, but more often it referred to independent or universalistic ideological forms of expression. There is little doubt that Gramsci's understanding was quite different from that of Lenin and the Comintern, where hegemony was viewed strictly as the ideological reflection of particular class interests and where, in any case, it applied to the phenomenon of working-class organization and alliances rather than to the dynamics of ruling-class domination. In this latter sense, Gramsci most often conceived of hegemony as an historically-defined system of beliefs and values—nationalism, Catholicism, liberalism, cultural traditions, and so forth—which *mediate* the class struggle in various ways. He located these ideologies less within the sphere of production (though of course this was a factor) than within the larger realm of civil society, which meant that the dialectic of hegemony and counter-hegemony could in principle unfold outside the factory (or capital-labor relations in general), in the larger societal arena of schools, churches, the family, mass media, and the neighborhoods as well as the workplace. According to this rather diffuse schema hegemony was more often linked to a bloc of social forces than to singular class formations. The very notion of *non-class* sources of ideological mobilization represents a dramatic break with Marxist orthodoxy.[12]

But Gramsci's break was hardly complete, as I have suggested. The carry-over of productivism mentioned above at times pushed him toward a more class-based analysis of hegemony—his interpretation of Fordist development in the U.S. being one such example. Another was his inclination to define the Southern Question as the outgrowth primarily of uneven capitalist expansion and northern economic colonization of the south while downplaying the role of the Church and other historical or cultural factors peculiar to Italy. Moreover, in the case of the advanced countries Gramsci seemed to be setting forth two distinct and contradictory arguments: on the one hand, hegemony was becoming more monolithic and depoliticizing with the emergence of rationalized production, while at the same time *counter*-hegemony took on greater significance with the growing complexity of civil society. He may well have been oblivious to this unresolvable tension in the *Notebooks*, at least judging from his failure to specify the *forms* of ideological domination (and resistance) and their relationship to particular structures in the economy, state, and civil society. In other words, the concept of hegemony required much greater operational articulation than it received (and perhaps could have received) in the *Notebooks*.[13]

Of course Gramsci's sometimes confusing treatment of these problems was probably unavoidable given the residual impact of orthodox Marxist (and Leninist) categories on his thinking. It must be remembered too that the social conditions Gramsci was able to observe first-hand in postwar Italy bore little resemblance to those of the more mature industrial societies around which so much of Gramsci's *general* theory was formulated. This explains why his insights into capitalist rationalization—based largely upon secondary literature and speculation—were so sketchy and limited, and why he could not have grasped the critical impact of new hegemonic forces (the culture industry, consumerism) which had begun to preoccupy the Frankfurt School theorists in Germany. In this context (and allowing further for his long period of incarceration), it would be unrealistic to demand of Gramsci a fuller elaboration of what was already a remarkably original theoretical framework. Still, the frustrating lack of specificity—itself a mark of Gramsci's transitional place within European Marxism—effectively undercut for that period any non-Leninist, non-economistic strategic application of the concepts hegemony, counter-hegemony, social bloc, and "war of position."

The critique of Gramsci must be understood within an historical context that simultaneously opened new paths of discovery and closed off further explorations. Despite its contradictions and ambiguities, Gramscian Marxism by the 1970s enjoyed a certain theoretical prominence in the West and even in some Third World countries (e.g., in Latin America). Above all, the concept of ideological hegemony has pointed to exciting new areas of research and political activity that Marxists had previously ignored or downplayed: culture, social relations, consciousness formation, the role of intellectuals. Gramsci's popularity derives in part from the peculiar *elasticity* of his concepts; what from a methodological standpoint was a weakness can indeed be translated into a durable theoretical strength.[14] Thus the notion of hegemony, for all of its diffuseness and lack of operational specificity, had been reappropriated more regularly than any of the presumed "scientific" concepts found in orthodox Marxism and Leninism. This kind of elasticity has given more recent theorists and observers the space to isolate Gramscian ideas from their orthodox residues and incorporate them into new paradigms, including some non-Marxian paradigms.[15] For this reason it was not the particular answers Gramsci was able to supply that made his theory so fruitful, but rather his capacity to pose fresh questions within a critical-dialectical framework.

In the *Notebooks* Gramsci had concluded that, with the shifting relationship between state and civil society in advanced capitalism, the theme of hegemony would be so decisive a factor as to rule out catastrophist strategies built around economic crisis or a vanguard seizure of state power. It was precisely this historical situation that separated the West (Italy included) from Russia. The old dichotomies base vs. superstructure and state vs. civil society were being gradually dissolved into a broad "ensemble of relations," creating the need for a complete rethinking of the methods, strategies, and even goals of socialist transformation in Europe. Central to this rethinking process for Gramsci were two imposing challenges: to theorize the role of organic intellectuals, and to redefine the scope of politics itself.

Contemporary capitalism has given rise to all of those features that Gramsci envisioned in "Americanism and Fordism," and much more: the technological revolution, bureaucratized methods of production and work, the vast expansion of education, mass media, and popular culture, a depoliticized working class—all part of the colonization of civil society by the state in which the distinction between public and private has progressively broken down.[16] Hegemonic patterns of thought and behavior are systematically reproduced by an enlarged intellectual stratum functioning within the sphere of government, corporations, the military, universities and schools, advertising, the culture industry, and research foundations. The breadth of these functions dwarfs anything known to previous class societies. It follows that the socialization process through which the general population (imperfectly) internalizes dominant values—e.g., possessive individualism, the work ethic, patriotism, racism, sexism—is more and more *universal*. And of course the concomitant atomization, alienation, and depoliticization is likewise increasingly universal. Hence the "one-dimensionality" of an advanced corporate capitalism legitimated by technocratic intellectuals presents new obstacles to the growth of oppositional struggles and movements.[17] Yet this very totalization of bourgeois hegemony creates novel opportunities for subversive politics, illuminated by what might be called the "ecological" dimension of crisis and resistance, which makes the system more vulnerable than before.[18]

The intellectual and mass revolt against this universalized system of hegemony—a driving force of the new radicalism in the 1960s—is Gramscian insofar as it generates a new approach to the relationship between politics and social life, politics and culture. Since the ideological underpinnings of domination are so deeply embedded in social and cultural life, so expressive of the seemingly most innocent and trivial manifestations of daily existence ("common sense"), surely popular resistance must pass through these same realms, transforming them in the very process of politicizing them. The formation of counter-hegemonic movements, or an "emergent" hegemony, therefore evolves less as a discrete system of beliefs, ideas and values (or *Weltanschauung*)than as a comprehensive pattern of "lived social relations."[19]

From this standpoint, Gramscian theory necessarily moves towards a more immediately social and even psychological level: the problem is to conceptualize the dialectic whereby repressive consciousness is transformed into its opposite—that is, into an emancipatory consciousness which gives meaning to socialist politics within the sphere of "lived social relations." Gramsci glimpsed the general outlines of this problem but little else. Clearly, it suggests a revolutionary process more complex and multi-dimensional than anything envisioned by previous Marxist parties and movements.[20] If an "emergent" hegemony requires such a profound shift in collective consciousness, then people will have to "discover" the oppressor in their own minds so that they can become subjects of their own destiny, capable of "seeing the world through new eyes." Only when the traditional ideologies come under serious challenge, so that time-honored myths, fears, and distortions are finally put to rest on a large scale, does critical consciousness become actualized in a truly political sense.[21] Since bourgeois hegemony encourages the displacement or sublimation of human resentment, or simply confines it to the personal realm, any politicization of everyday life issues is inevitably counter-hegemonic. But in confronting this problem we are immediately brought face-to-face with the strategic tasks of the organic intellectuals.

If for Gramsci intellectual activity provided the thinking and organizing element of class consciousness, the foundations of revolutionary change, and the cohesive "integrated culture" of a new order, then the problem of linking the social immediacy of popular struggles with the transformative potential of political action takes on a new urgency. Gramsci was the first Marxist to seriously raise the question of how and under what conditions the working class could give expression to its own critical intelligentsia; in the absence of such a formation, he believed it would be impossible to avoid the pitfalls of either spontaneism or vanguardism. His concept of organic intellectuals, which questioned the separation of mental and physical activity intrinsic to the bourgeois division of labor, coincided with the imperatives of counter-hegemonic politics in advanced capitalism, since now the intellectuals (broadly defined) would play a large and *decisive* role.

In modern capitalist society both the *social position* and the potential *critical function* of intellectuals has rendered obsolete most earlier forms of Marxist class analysis. Conventional theories counterposed a small, traditional intelligentsia to a massive, proletarianized work force, which seemed valid enough for the initial phases of capitalist industrialization. In advanced capitalism, however, this situation had qualitatively changed: the expanded role of science and technology, the massive impact of education, culture, and media, and the bureaucratization of public life have all led to the remarkable growth (and redefinition) of intellectual activity. Rather than occupying a realm peripheral to the social relations of production, or carrying out strictly ideological tasks within them, the intellectuals—as technicians, managers, professionals, academics, cultural workers, and top-level bureaucrats—now carry out a *variety* of *necessary* tasks within the economy, political system, and culture. The new intelligentsia assumes a hegemonic position within the rationalized division of labor, and, while its autonomy is limited, its transformative capacity as a *stratum for itself* is greater than anticipated by Marx, Lenin, Kautsky, and even Gramsci. The failure of Marxism, theoretically and politically, to grasp the historical meaning of social movements emerging from within this stratum since the 1960s is simply one reflection of this conceptual paralysis.

The inadequacy of earlier frameworks has given rise to a plethora of theories, which can be grouped into three basic approaches. The first of these situates the intellectuals within a broadened and educated proletariat—a "new working class"—typical of a new phase of class struggle in a period when production depends increasingly upon scientific and technical knowledge.[22] Given its concern for autonomy, professional norms, and "qualitative" social and cultural issues, this stratum can be expected to press for a variety of radical demands: workers' control, participatory democracy, cultural transformation. If intellectuals enjoy a privileged status (in terms of income, social standing, education, skills) within the workforce as a whole, their role is nonetheless defined by the wage-labor they perform. One variant of this theory sees in the proletarianization of mental work the basis of a convergence between intellectual and manual activities, skilled and unskilled tasks.[23]

A second perspective focuses upon intellectuals as an emergent class (or stratum) possessing its own independence and inner dialectic no longer strictly reducible to the conflict between capital and wage labor. The argument follows two sharply divergent paths: one which sees the new formation as hegemonic within the bourgeois division of labor, and attached to a technocratic ideology and lifestyle that reinforces capitalist domination,[24] and another which views it as a potentially revolutionary class on its own terms, the locus of an unfolding critical consciousness.[25]

The hegemonic view suggests that intellectuals in advanced capitalism have become part of a "professional-managerial class" of salaried mental workers that is economically and culturally distinct from both the bourgeoisie and working class. Despite its seeming "autonomy," however, and despite its occasional flirtations with radical politics, this grouping is dependent upon the ruling class insofar as it lacks the capacity to provide an organizing principle for society as a whole. Its primary function, therefore, is the reproduction of capitalist culture and class relations. Following Marcuse, this approach stresses the decisive role of technocratic intellectuals in legitimating the rationalizing impulses of advanced industrialism.[26] The "critical" orientation, on the other hand, sees this technocratic side of intellectual work but insists that it is (or can be) part of a subversive, emancipatory discourse with revolutionary implications. Alienated from power and denied real creativity, the intellectuals—as a "flawed universal class"—are often compromised by their privileged social position and their statist, bureaucratic ideology. In the final analysis, as Gouldner emphasizes, "the New Class is the most progressive force in modern society and is the center of whatever human emancipation is possible in the foreseeable future."[27]

Finally, a third schema views intellectuals as occupying "contradictory class locations" in capitalist society to the degree that their social character is shaped by multiple and conflicting class identities rather than by a single unified class formation.[28] The objective here is to show how simplistic class dichotomies grounded in economic contradictions cannot be adequate for a theory of intellectuals, and therefore must be superseded by an account that focuses upon both the complexity and the simultaneous ideological and economic dimensions of class relations. Framed somewhat differently, the intellectuals occupy a contradictory class location between workers and petty bourgeoisie at the economic level, and between workers and the bourgeoisie at the ideological level.[29] Hence the intellectuals share interests and outlooks in common with the two main conflicting social classes; they are, in other words, "objectively torn between two classes;" and thereby also torn between hegemonic and subversive, technocratic and critical roles.

This third approach seems to offer the most useful point of departure, and also happens to converge best with Gramsci's theory of organic intellectuals. Its great advantage is that it integrates the best insights of the "new working class" and "new universal class" theories while also borrowing from the otherwise one-sided "hegemonic" conception. But the "contradictory locations" theory needs to be modified. In material terms, it would make more sense to define intellectuals as a particular stratum within the working class for, however privileged they are within the social division of labor, they still perform wage labor and experience the alienation of a bureaucratic workplace.[30] In ideological terms, while it is necessary to retain a sense of dynamic social contradictions, these can be more fruitfully defined around the *political* division (in Gramscian language) between hegemonic and counter-hegemonic or subversive functions instead of the abstract sociological division between working class and bourgeoisie, insofar as no strict correlation between social location and consciousness can be assumed *a priori*. These contradictions, moreover, are in no way aberrant but are rooted in the division of labor and must be seen as a normal expression of working-class development in advanced capitalism.

From a neo-Gramscian perspective, then, it is possible to analyze the political role of intellectuals within the changing ensemble of relations of working-class social existence itself. Politics accordingly takes the form of struggles around the division of labor—between critical, subversive, counter-hegemonic forces seeking ascendancy and technocratic or hegemonic elements striving to preserve the system of bureaucratic capitalism. These struggles are simultaneously economic, political, and ideological in scope; with widening proletarianization, the conflicts generated by the new contradictions become more acute and popular revolt (around "control" issues, the fiscal crisis of the state, definitions of cultural life) is more explosive even where it is not directly radicalized.

At this juncture the situation of the intellectuals is contradictory too. On the one hand, they have a privileged status along with commitments (however ambivalent) to a more rationalized economy. On the other hand, they value the kind of creativity, open discourse, and occupational autonomy generally associated with high levels of education. As capitalist rationalization advances, it is this latter (critical) side which inevitably clashes with the dehumanizing effects of proletarianization and, in posing anew the issue of bourgeois hegemony, indicates the possible emergence of a stratum of organic intellectuals. A dynamic of this sort has been at work in some advanced countries—for example, France and Italy—where the prospects of a radicalized "new middle strata" have been debated for some time (within and outside of the Communist parties).[31] Recent investigation of class struggles and consciousness among highly-educated technical and scientific workers in Italy supports this analysis. To the extent that the familiar separation between manual and non-manual jobs is declining with the proletarianization of mental work, the increasing concern of technicians with issues of self-management and social change can be explained as a response to workplace bureaucratization which blocks creativity and mobility. Moreover, it appears that the goal of upward mobility among intellectual workers does not necessarily erode militancy or even radicalism but instead inspires new demands and expectations that cannot be met within capitalist production.[32]

If the intellectual function is degraded by rationalization, its political side is ironically sharpened as it assumes an increasing *strategic* importance in social transformation. Concretely, this suggests that intellectuals as an expanding force have a larger potential to assert control over technocratic norms, popular control over bureaucratization, and social equality over all forms of domination. Such an emergent hegemony is compatible with those theories which anticipated an organic convergence between mental and physical work, between new and traditional strata or the labor force, between the "intellectual" and "popular" element typical of advanced capitalism itself. The material conditions which could furnish substance to Gramsci's dictum that "all persons are intellectuals" could thus be realized in a way Gramsci himself never imagined. At the same time, the social-psychological process whereby this convergence of forces might achieve a unified *subjective* (cultural and political) expression is not very well understood.

All of this further solidifies the assumption that an enlarged intellectual formation might struggle to change its own ensemble of relations and, in he process of self-transformation, merge with the kindred forces at the workplace and in daily life to form a new kind of subversive movement. Put another way, its struggle for autonomy and self-management would be "organic" precisely insofar as it becomes part of the general struggle for democratization and social equality. Second, the drive to create public space for open, imaginative communication places intellectuals in direct opposition to the new forms of technocratic domination and social control which serve to mystify class and power relations. This (potential) confrontation allows intellectuals to carry out an indispensable activity: the translation of economic crises into a generalized crisis of legitimation.[33] Thirdly, while popular struggles require the unifying intervention of larger movements, this is no longer the specialized task of intellectuals but grows out of the gradual merger of separate groups that have incorporated critical objectives within their own spheres of activity. The Jacobinism inherent in the Kautsky-Lenin thesis therefore effectively loses its rationale. Finally, in any sustained challenge to bourgeois hegemony, intellectuals will carry out essential *cultural* functions—for example, those of subverting the dominant forms of commodified culture, of creating shared art forms—but this integrative process too can be seen within the new social context as a fusion of disparate local struggles rather than the imposition of elite subcultures.[34]

Having reconstituted the material and social foundations of intellectual activity, capitalist rationalization has thus produced the conditions of a progressive *diffusion*—not an elitist *specialization*—of intellectual praxis. The role itself remains more or less distinct but no longer as an imported "external element" from the ranks of the bourgeois (or petty-bourgeois) intelligentsia. Paradoxically enough, this new possibility captures the spirit of Gramsci's organic intellectuals more faithfully than Gramsci's own formulation in the *Notebooks*—that is, it gives substance to the ideal of new (collective, prefigurative) forms of cultural and political "direction" generated from within the system of capitalist production, but extending beyond the factory into other spheres of work and social activity.

From the standpoint of political strategy, however, this visionary outlook has been obscured by the weight of official and semi-official interpretations of Gramscian Marxism since the late 1950s. The revolutionary cutting-edge of Gramsci's work has only rarely pierced the surface of this legacy. His image as a founding father of one of the largest Communist parties in the world—indeed, the most "successful" non-ruling party—has easily overwhelmed the subtleties of his critical and eclectic theory. The social-democratization of the postwar PCI, whose leadership claimed Gramsci as its original and most heroic inspiration, has only further obscured his real contributions.[35]

In Italy (and to some extent elsewhere in Western Europe), Gramsci's close historical association with the PCI has given rise to a simultaneous Leninist and Togliattian (or structural reformist) understanding of Gramsci's politics. In each interpretation Gramsci stood as the symbol of a revitalized Communist tradition which, at least in the advanced countries, had been politically impotent. While still organizationally centralized, socially conservative, and in many ways attached to the Soviet myth, the Western European parties sought desperately to present an "open," liberal, pluralistic face to their electorates while at the same time clinging to the Bolshevik tradition as a source of political identity. The Leninist side of Gramsci made him a perfect legitimating figure for the party leaderships, which could define "wars of position" and "social bloc" in both vanguardist and electoralist terms. However, the plain fact that Gramsci never really developed a theory of structural reforms (this was always a Kautskian tradition) nor endorsed the parliamentary road to socialism reveals the superficiality of such linkages.

Yet there is a certain logic to this type of cooptative effort.[36] Beneath the rhetorical gulf separating Leninism and structural reformism lies a shared focus on institutional engineering that coincides with a de-emphasis of the ideological and prefigurative dimensions of change.[37] Insofar as both affirm the primary role of organizational elites, accept the premises of social hierarchy, downplay non-productivist goals, and stress the conquest of the existing state machinery, they both pursue (in quite different ways) a statist and instrumentalist strategy. Politics, in the narrow sense of Gramsci's "conjunctural" moment, revolve around the immediate exchange of favors and services for votes or organizational support; it is largely a *tactical* process wherein the masses are dealt with as constituencies to be manipulated and administered. It was by no means coincidental, therefore, that both Kautsky (the inspiration behind European Social Democracy) and Lenin (the architect of the Bolshevik Revolution) held in common an elitist-authoritarian definition of Marxism, and that both managed to dodge the issue of socialist democracy. This explains how PCI theorists, in presenting their "third road" as a convergence of Lenin and Togliatti, could borrow Gramsci's concepts (e.g., hegemony, social bloc, war of position) and then proceed to instrumentalize them within the bourgeois political sphere.

One result of this misappropriation of Gramsci by the PCI has been a certain disinterest in his thought within the European radical left—with some exceptions.[38] In the U.S., on the other hand, with its considerable political distance from the Gramsci-PCI connection, there has been less of a tendency to ignore the radical or critical substance in Gramsci's writings (council democracy, prefigurative struggle, cultural transformation, etc.). While this radical side of Gramsci has often been obscured not only by Eurocommunist distortions but by the survivals of orthodoxy and vanguardism in his own work, my consistent aim in this volume has been to explore the radical dimensions of his critical Marxism without losing sight of the many tensions and contradictions that permeate his theory. While it would be futile to try to identify any single historical Gramsci, it is surely possible to locate specific transformative concepts which possess an elasticity and universality that goes far beyond their point of origin.

Gramsci was more than anything else a theorist of *revolution*, not only by virtue of the concepts he introduced but through his life as a political activist; his spirit of revolutionary optimism in the midst of defeat, fascism, and prison; his uncompromising hostility to bourgeois institutions; and his deep involvement in the social and political world of the Turin workers. This was hardly the mark of a traditional idealist, or of a social democrat, or of a detached intellectual. Moreover, while Gramsci had the same revolutionary impatience as Lenin, his outlook contained a democratic sensibility and cultural breadth that was absent from Leninism. In spirit, if not in theory, Gramsci was perhaps closest to Rosa Luxemburg of all the major Marxist theorists of the period. In the advanced capitalist countries today, where statism has triumphed over civil society, where industrial civilization has created a depoliticized and alienated public sphere, where new forms of hegemony operate to absorb or neutralize popular revolt, this Gramscian vision—and with it a remaking of politics itself—is more relevant than ever.

Footnotes

1. "The Study of Philosophy", *SPN*, p. 324.

2. See Karl E. Klare, "The Critique of Everyday Life, the New Left, and the Unrecognizable Marxism," in Dick Howard and Karl E. Klare, eds., *The Unknown Dimension: European Marxism Since Lenin* (New York: Basic Books, 1972), pp. 3-33.

3. Gramsci has also been favorably received by Marxist intellectuals in Latin America, Japan, and elsewhere, but the thematic nature of his popularity in these different contexts lies outside the range of the present commentary.

4. For a comprehensive and annotated bibliography of English-language works on Gramsci, see Harvey J. Kaye, "Antonio Gramsci: An Annotated Bibliography of Studies in English," *Politics and Society* 10, no. 3, 1981, pp. 335-53.

5. Alastair Davidson, "The Varying Seasons of Gramscian Studies," *Political Studies*, December 1972, pp. 448-61.

6. That Gramsci understood productivism as an outgrowth of classical Marxist political economy, rather than merely as a deformed theoretical tendency within the Second International, is evident from a reading of his early essay, "The Revolution against *Capital*", in *Political Writings-II*. The depth of this critique distinguished it from Lenin's own (more limited and strategically focused) critique of economism in *What is to be Done?*

7. In "Americanism and Fordism," for example, Gramsci wrote as part of his critique of Trotsky's militarization of industry policy that "the principle of coercion, direct or indirect, in the ordering of production and work, is correct: but the form which it assumed was mistaken." *SPN*, p. 301.

8. There is an interesting dualism here in Gramsci. On the one hand, his concept of hegemony indicated that with capitalist expansion ideological and cultural forces would increasingly come to the fore; on the other hand, his analysis of rationalization in the American context suggested that social life would revolve more and more around production as industry penetrated all areas of civil society. Thus: "Hegemony here is born in the factory and requires for its exercise only a minute quantity of professional political and ideological intermediaries." "Americanism and Fordism," *SPN*, p. 285.

9. It would not be fair to argue here, however, as Poulantzas does, that Gramsci's problems stemmed from his definition of "war of position" as *exclusively* an application of the Leninist model to Western conditions, which led him into a number of "blind alleys." See Nicos Poulantzas, *State, Power, Socialism* (London: New Left Books, 1978), p. 256.

10. Gramsci did devote a brief section of the *Notebooks* to the problem of bureaucracy, but, aside from its sketchy quality, it contained no analysis of the bureaucratic phenomenon in the capitalist countries or in relationship to working-class movements. See "The Modern Prince," *SPN*, pp. 185-90.

11. Aside from some infrequent references to Trotsky and Stalin in the *Notebooks*, Gramsci wrote nothing about Soviet development or the rise of Stalinism during his prison years. His commentary on the CPSU between 1923 and 1926 was largely favorable, and nowhere was there a hint at a critique of *Soviet* bureaucratic centralism of the sort presented by Luxemburg, Kautsky, Pannekoek, and Korsch well *before* 1926. The following passage reveals Gramsci's orientation toward the USSR as late as 1926: "Not just the working masses in general, but even the mass of members within our parties see, and wish to see, in the Republic of the Soviets and in the party which is in power there, a single combat unit that is working in the general perspective of socialism. Only insofar as the Western European masses see Russia and the Russian party from this point of view, do they accept freely and as a historically necessary fact that the CPSU should be the leading party in the International; only for that reason are the Republic of the Soviets and the CPSU today a formidable element of revolutionary organization and propulsion." "On the Situation in the Bolshevik Party" (letter to Togliatti), October 1926, in *Political Writings-II*, p. 428.

12. For a theoretical elaboration of this point, relying upon Gramscian inspiration, see Rude, *Ideology and Popular Protest*, ch. 1.

13. On this point, though developed from a slightly different angle, see Adamson, *Hegemony and Revolution*, p. 241.

14. The ability to formulate such elastic, historicized concepts was also a key factor in Marx's durable theoretical influence, and indeed is vital to the renewable *appeals* of any theory. On the theme of elasticity, see E.P. Thompson, *The Poverty of Theory* (New York: Monthly Review, 1978), pp. 110-11. Thompson notes that conceptual elasticity is incompatible with a fixed theoretical system attached to the logic of historical necessity—a contention that Gramsci would have shared fully.

15. Once again, Stolz's argument that Gramsci's theory of politics derived from Machiavelli actually points *beyond* Marxism reveals this explosive dimension of Gramsci's thought. See "Gramsci's Machiavelli", *op. cit.*, pp. 70-71, 85.

16. On the increasing penetration of the state (and bureaucratic forms in general) into civil society in the advanced countries, see Henry Jacoby, *The Bureaucratization of the World* (Berkeley: University of California, 1973), chs. 6, 7 and 12.

17. See Herbert Marcuse's classic *One-Dimensional Man* (Boston: Beacon Press, 1964), chs. 5-7. A more specific application of this thesis is contained in Stuart Ewen, *Captains of Consciousness* (New York: McGraw-Hill, 1976).

18. On potential new sources of insurgency, viewed from this theoretical lense, see Marcuse, *Counterrevolution and Revolt* (Boston: Beacon Press, 1971), ch. 1, and Andre Gorz, *Ecology as Politics* (Boston: South End Press, 1980).

19. This approach has received its most lucid expression in the work of Raymond Williams, which owes a great deal to Gramsci. See *Marxism and Literature* (London: Oxford University Press, 1977), pp. 123-25.

20. Among Marxists writing during the 1920s and 1930s only Wilhelm Reich fully grasped the significance of the social-psychological dimension. See especially his "What is Class Consciousness?", in Baxandall, ed., *Sex-Pol Essays*, pp. 275-358.

21. See Paulo Freire, *The Pedagogy of the Oppressed* (New York: Seabury, 1971), pp. 36-47.

22. See, for example, Andre Gorz, *Strategy for Labor* (Boston: Beacon Press, 1967); Serge Mallet, *Essays on the New Working Class* (St. Louis: Telos Press, 1977); and Alain Touraine, *The New Industrial Society* (New York: Random House, 1971).

23. Harry Braverman, *Labor and Monopoly Capital* (New York: Monthly Review, 1976).

24. The most elaborate statement of this thesis is Barbara and John Ehrenreich, "The Professional-Managerial Class," in Pat Walker, ed., *Between Labor and Capital* (Boston: South end Press, 1979).

25. Alvin W. Gouldner, *The Future of the Intellectuals and the Rise of the New Class* (New York: Seabury, 1979).

26. Poulantzas' framework, in which the intellectuals are characterized as the "new petty bourgeoisie", can be subsumed under this thesis. Although the Ehrenreichs and Poulantzas differ on many points, they agree that the intellectuals constitute a new formation, that their position in bourgeois society cannot be

understood through conventional Marxist class categories, and that their ideological domination over the working class generally pits them *against* workers in the class struggle. For Poulantzas' argument, see "The New Petty Bourgeoisie," in Alan Hunt, ed., *Class and Class Structure* (London: Lawrence and Wishart, 1977).

27. Gouldner, *The Future of the Intellectuals*, p. 68.

28. Erik Olin Wright, "Intellectuals and the Class Structure of Capitalist Society," in Walker, ed., *Between Labor and Capital.*

29. Wright, *op. cit.*, p. 204.

30. On this point, see Gorz's discussion in "Technology, Technicians, and the Class Struggle", in Andre Gorz, ed., *The Social Division of Labor* (Atlantic Highlands, N.J.: The Humanities Press, 1976).

31. On France, see George Ross, "Marxism and the New Middle Classes," *Theory and Society*, March 1978; Andrew Feenberg, "France: The New Middle Strata and the Legacy of the May Events," in Boggs and Plotke, eds., *The Politics of Eurocommunism*; Nicos Poulantzas, *State, Power, Socialism*, part II; and Arthur Hirsh, *The French New Left* (Boston: South End Press, 1981). On Italy, see John Low-Beer, *Protest and Participation: the New Working Class in Italy* (Cambridge: Cambridge University Press, 1978); Marcello Lelli, *Tecnici e lotta di classe* (Bari: De Donato, 1971); and Carl Boggs, *The Impasse of European Communism*, ch. 4.

32. Low-Beer, *Protest and Participation*, ch. 4.

33. See Jurgen Habermas, *Legitimation Crisis* (Boston: Beacon Press, 1973), pp. 68-75. The convergence between Habermas' concept and the Gramscian theme crisis of hegemony is quite striking, except that Habermas succeeded in constructing the kind of non-economistic theory of crisis which Gramsci, as we have seen, never quite achieved.

34. An earlier formulation of this argument is contained in my "Marxism and the Role of Intellectuals," *New Political Science*, fall-winter 1979-1980, pp. 7-23.

35. For a more extensive discussion of Gramsci's misappropriation at the hands of the PCI, see my *The Impasse of European Communism*, pp. 119-37; Paul Piccone, "Beyond Lenin and Togliatti: Gramsci's Marxism," *op. cit.*,; and Jonas Pontusson, "Gramsci and Eurocommunism," *op. cit.*, esp. pp. 216-32.

36. This Gramscian "convergence" was already present in Togliatti's seminal interpretation in the late 1950s, and has been widely accepted by PCI theorists since that time. See *On Gramsci and Other Writings*, chs. 6-8. A more recent statement of the same thesis can be found in Gruppi, *Il concetto di egemonia in Gramsci.*

See also Buci-Glucksmann, *Gramsci and the State*, for a general assessment which fits this pattern.

37. On the differing conception of the political—more specifically the relationship between the political and social—see Claudio Pavone, "Togliatti, la 'neutralita' dello Stato e delle istituzioni," in Il Manifesto, *Da Togliatti alla nuova sinistra* (Rome: Alfani Editore, 1975), pp. 138-39.

38. For example, in Italy the *Il Manifesto* group, which broke away form the PCI in 1969, published a lengthy "Theses" which relied heavily upon Gramsci's concepts and language, entitled *Per il Comunismo* (1970). An English translation of the "Theses" is contained in *Politics and Society*, Fall 1971.

39. The contemporary movement which perhaps most closely approximates this Gramscian "model" is Polish Solidarity—a paradoxical reality given that new forms of class struggle in Poland are directed against the system of bureaucratic centralism rather than against the type of capitalist structures Gramsci was analyzing. Before it was repressed by martial law in December 1981, Solidarity successfully posed—on a *mass* level—a variety of Gramscian themes: counter-hegemony, war of position, dual power, social struggle, historical bloc. In the most generic sense, this movement could be understood as part of a larger historical pattern of struggles in Poland to recapture civil society from the state. See, for example, Stanislaus Starski, *Class Struggles in Classless Poland* (Boston: South End Press, 1982), part 3, and Andrew Arato, "Civil Society Against the State," *Telos* no. 47, spring 1981, pp. 23-47.

Glossary of Theorists

Eduard Bernstein (1850-1932) was born in Berlin. He was editor of the influential *Social Democrat* from 1880 to 1890 and co-authored (with Karl Kautsky) the Erfurt Programme in 1891, which laid the theoretical foundations of the German Social Democratic Party (SPD). He lived in England for many years and was convinced, on the basis of what he observed there, that the Marxist assumption of an imminent capitalist crisis was illusory and that the only viable strategy would be one of gradual reforms. His controversial views were stated in a series of articles and essays which appeared in the late 1890s, and which were later assembled in a volume that would be entitled *Evolutionary Socialism* (1900). He was denounced by Kautsky, Lenin, and Luxemburg for his "un-Marxian" theories, but his influence within the SPD grew after 1900, especially within the pragmatic trade-union movement. He was a deputy in the Reichstag (German parliament) from 1902 to 1918 and 1920 to 1928. He is generally considered to be the founding father of social-democratic ideology.

Amadeo Bordiga (1889-1970) was born in Naples. An engineer by profession, he joined the Italian Socialist Party (PSI) in 1910 and became one of the leaders of the left faction within the party. He founded the theoretical journal *Il Soviet* in 1918 and argued in its pages for a strongly disciplined vanguard party that would abstain from electoral politics. One of the founders of the Italian Communist Party (PCI), he engaged in a series of debates with Gramsci around the issue of the factory councils and the role of the party—Bordiga favoring a more centralized structure closely tied to the Comintern, Gramsci stressing local structures, direct democracy, and a mass party. Bordiga was leader of the PCI until 1924, when he was replaced by Gramsci. Arrested by the fascists in 1926, he was tried for anti-state activity in 1928 and acquitted. He was expelled from the PCI in 1930. For the remaining years of his life he was active in small Bordighist groups which continued to push the vanguardist politics he had always championed.

Nikolai Bukharin (1888-1938) was born in Moscow. He joined the Bolshevik party in 1906 at the age of 18, carrying out propaganda work. He was among the leading party figures at the time of the October Revolution, and in 1918 became editor-in-chief of *Pravda*. He was associated with the left wing of the Bolsheviks in 1918, but then soon moved toward the centrist position of Lenin and later was identified as a leader of the "right" opposition. He was respected as one of the most brilliant Marxist theoreticians in the party, mainly on the basis of his *Imperialism and World Economy* (1918) and *The Economics of the Transition Period* (1920). He also authored two "manuals" for party cadres: *The ABCs of Communism* (1919) and *The Theory of Historical Materialism* (1921), which were systematic expositions of the party's general philosophy based upon a strict scientific interpretation of Marxism. It was *Historical Materialism* which Gramsci attacked in the *Notebooks* for its crude determinism and political fatalism. Initially an advocate of centralized economic planning, he switched to a defense of the New Economic Policy in 1921; from that point on he anticipated a long phase of coexistence between the party-state and small-scale private industry, a peasant economy, and free trade. He came to reject the policy of rapid industrialization and forced collectivization which Stalin introduced in his first five-year plan. He came under fire for being a "right" deviationist in the 1930s and was executed for "conspiracy" by Stalin in 1938.

Benedetto Croce (1866-1954) was born in Apulia and attended the University of Rome. A philosopher and theorist of Italian history, he carried forward the Italian idealist tradition, helped to translate Hegelianism into a national intellectual tradition, and emerged by the turn of the century as probably the country's leading intellectual figure—a kind of "lay pope," to use Gramsci's language. He had a powerful influence upon the young Gramsci during 1915-1918, and the *Notebooks* are filled with references to his work. His theories are most fully expressed in *What is Living and What is Dead of the Philosophy of Hegel* (1915) and *A History of Italy* (1929). In politics a liberal and an anti-fascist, he served as Minister of Education in the Giolitti government in 1920-1921. Following Mussolini's rise to power he went into retirement and exercised a waning influence on the Italian scene.

The Frankfurt School was founded in 1923 by small group of radical intellectuals as the Institute for Social Research in Frankfurt. Its early members included Friedrich Pollack, Theodor Adorno, Max Horkheimer, and Leo Lowenthal; they were joined later by Herbert Marcuse, Eric Fromm, and others. The Institute was disbanded in 1933 after Hitler's rise to power, and its members went into exile—either to other European countries or the United States. Though intellectuals associated with the tradition comprised a very diverse group, they shared a commitment to developing a "critical" theory inspired in part by Hegelianism, in part by a return to the early Marx. The overall focus was one that was hostile to scientific Marxism and to the bureaucratic politics of Social Democracy and Leninism. Their theoretical concerns revolved around philosophy, culture and aesthetics, social life, psychology and psychoanalysis—all themes which were anathema to orthodox Marxism. Ironically, while the tradition lost much of its cohesiveness after the 1930s, the collective influence of its theoretical proponents actually grew in the postwar period.

Giovanni Gentile (1875-1944) was an Italian philosopher and collaborator of Croce, with whom he edited the important liberal periodical *La Critica*. He was influenced largely by Hegel and Croce and only marginally by Marx, and thus fits squarely into the Italian idealist current. Known for his celebration of the role of active human will in history, he became disillusioned with both socialism and liberalism and, after World War I, moved rapidly in the direction of fascism. He became Minister of Education under Mussolini and was later the chief theoretician of Italian fascism. He was arrested and executed by partisans of the Italian Resistance in 1944.

Karl Kautsky (1854-1938) was born in Prague and spent much of his early life in Vienna. In 1883 he founded *Die Neue Zeit*, the most important Marxist journal in Europe, which he edited until 1917. Through it he did much to popularize Marxism, and for his efforts he became widely known as the leading figure, or "dean," of European Marxism and the major proponent of its orthodox current. He was co-author (with Bernstein) of the SPD's Erfurt Programme in 1891, and was a staunch defender of the Second International—a perspective from which he launched attacks against both Bernstein's "revisionism" and Lenin's vanguardism. In return he was branded a traitor by Lenin, in part because he rejected the insurrectionary model of revolution, in part because he supported the SPD's decision to go along with the German war effort in 1914. His theoretical output was huge, and touched upon an immense variety of topics and debates. The most important of his writings include: *The Social Revolution* (1907), *The Road to Power* (1909), *The Dictatorship of the Proletariat* (1918), *Terrorism and Communism* (1919), and *The Materialist Conception of History* (1927).

Karl Korsch (1886-1961) was born in Hamburg, received a law degree at the University of Jena in 1910, and went to London in 1912. While in England he was influenced by British Fabian

Socialism. In World War I he served as an officer in the German army and was disciplined for his anti-war sentiments. After the war he taught at Jena, where he remained until 1933. A member of the German Communist Party (KPD), but critical of its leadership, he was Reichstag deputy from 1924 to 1933 and edited the party's theoretical journal *The International*. In the early 1920s he was regarded as an "ultra leftist" and was personally attacked at the Fifth Comintern Congress in 1924. He wrote a series of essays which culminated in his most significant work, *Marxism and Philosophy* (1923). His reservations about Lenin and the Comintern grew in the late 1920s and 1930s, when he emerged as a strong critic of the Soviet regime. In 1936 he went to the U.S., where he spent the rest of his life and where, in 1938, he wrote what is generally considered to be one of the best biographies of Marx (*Karl Marx*).

Georg Lukacs (1885-1971) was born in Budapest and, during his university years there, became involved in a number of socialist groups associated with the left social democrat Ervin Szabo. While not yet a Marxist, he was attracted to Hegelianism and syndicalism. His early work was devoted largely to cultural issues, and in 1916 he published *The Theory of the Novel*. He joined the Hungarian Communist Party in 1918 and participated in the short-lived Hungarian Soviet republic in 1919 under Bela Kun. After the overthrow of Kun he fled to Vienna where he became identified with the left Communist tendency. During these years he produced his most comprehensive statement of Marxist philosophy, *History and Class Consciousness* (1923); shaped by a pervasive Hegelian outlook, this volume became an important link between classical Marxism and the emergence of Western Marxism. Though attacked by the Comintern for his philosophical views, he supported Lenin and wrote a book, *Lenin* (1929), praising Bolshevik strategy. He went to the USSR in 1933 and, despite a tense relationship with the Stalinist regime, remained there until the end of the war. He was briefly Minister of Culture in the Nagy government in Hungary in 1956, after which he was driven from the Communist Party. Readmitted to the party in 1967, he continued his work throughout the 1950s and 60s, focusing mostly on issues related to culture and philosophy. A 14-volume edition of his works appeared after his death.

Rosa Luxemburg (1870-1919) was born at Zamosc in Poland and, although she was instrumental in the founding of the Polish Socialist Party, her political and intellectual life was shaped within the German socialist movement. Within the SPD in the 1890s she became a leading figure in the radical left and wrote a pamphlet,

Social Reform or Revolution? (1900) which attacked Bernstein and stated her own leftist views. After 1905 she adopted a "mass strike" strategy which favored the role of working-class spontaneity over that of vanguard leadership. In 1912 she wrote her most important book, *The Accumulation of Capital*, and four years later she wrote her famous *The Crisis of Social Democracy* (The "Junius Pamphlet") which became the theoretical basis for the Spartacus League—a radical group formed after the war and a prelude to the KPD. She spent a good deal of the war years in German prisons. In 1919 she participated in a Spartacus League uprising in Berlin, which resulted in the murder of both herself and Karl Liebknecht at the hands of the Freikorps.

Antonio Labriola (1843-1904) was born in Cassino and went to the University of Naples where he was deeply influenced by Hegelian philosophy and Mazzinian Liberalism. He became a schoolteacher in Naples, where he lived until 1874. He began work in the area of philosophy and history, and wrote an anti-clerical volume *Morality and Religion* in 1873. During the 1880s he gradually moved from liberalism to Marxism, a shift which is reflected in his *On Socialism* (1889). He was a key figure in establishing the Marx-Hegel connection in Italy. His most well-known work was *Essays on the Materialist Conception of History* (1896), which apparently had a strong impact on the young Gramsci. While he integrated Marx into his writings he did not consider himself a Marxist in any strict sense, and always managed to keep his distance from the politics of the Second International.

Niccolo Machiavelli (1469-1527) was born in Florence where, in the domain of the Medicis, he lived most of his life. At the age of 29 he got a job working in the Chancery which lasted for 14 years, during which time he was able to observe the workings of the power structure first-hand. He saw a Florentine apparatus that was corrupt, incompetent, and lacking in political purpose. *The Prince* represented an attempt to apply the lessons of these observations, to specify the conditions under which political power could be used to overcome the fragmentation of the city-states and create an Italian national unity for the first time. Because of his mildly anti-Medici views, he was fired from his job in 1512, after which he retreated to a small farm near Florence and continued his writing. In addition to his *The History of Florence*, he wrote a number of plays, including the comedy *Mandragola*. His work was an important inspiration for Gramsci's "The Modern Prince."

George Plekhanov (1856-1918) was born in the Russian province of Tambov and in 1873 enrolled in the Constantine Military

Academy in St. Petersburg, which he left for the Mining Institute in 1874. Expelled after two years, he took up radical politics and founded the Land and Freedom group in 1876. He soon fled to Berlin to avoid arrest and adopted the life of a professional revolutionary. Settling in Geneva, he became a Marxist and in 1883 helped to found the emigre Emancipation of Labor group, which laid the theoretical foundations for Russian Social Democracy. He rejected both populism and anarchism, insisting upon the centrality of class analysis and the (future) role of the proletariat. Throughout the 1890s and later he was associated with the orthodox tradition, in which Marxism was viewed as a scientific theory grounded in historical necessity—i.e., as dialectical materialism. He exerted a strong influence on the young Lenin. His most important works include: *In Defense of Materialism* (1894), *Fundamental Problems of Marxism* (1908), and *The Role of the Individual in History* (1898).

Romain Rolland (1866-1944) was a French poet, novelist, and dramatist who was quoted often by Gramsci. His phrase "Pessimism of the intellect, optimism of the will" was carried on the masthead of the journal *Ordine Nuovo*. He played an important role in the international campaign to free Gramsci from jail in the 1930s, during which time he wrote a pamphlet entitled: "Antonio Gramsci: Those Who Are Dying in Mussolini's Prisons." Though not a Marxist, he was influenced by Hegelianism and French syndicalism.

Wilhelm Reich (1897-1957) was born in Austrian Galicia, studied psychology, and came to Vienna after World War I to practice psychoanalysis. He was influenced by Freud but soon rebelled against strict Freudianism because it ignored the role of social factors. In the early 1920s he became a Marxist and in 1927 he joined the Austrian Socialist Party. During his "Marxist" period (roughly 1927 to 1936) he sought to integrate the concerns of Marx and Freud, devoting attention to themes—social psychology, mass consciousness, sexuality—which Marxists had largely ignored. In 1930 he founded the Sex-Pol movement in Berlin under the auspices of the KPD, which he joined the same year. He was expelled from the KPD in 1933 and from the International Psychoanalytic Association in 1934. He later moved to the U.S. where his interests changed from politics and Marxist theory to biology. His most significant writings include: *The Imposition of Sexual Morality* (1932), *The Sexual Struggle of Youth* (1932), *What is Class Consciousness?* (1934), *The Mass Psychology of Fascism* (1933), and *Character Analysis* (1934).

Gaetano Salvemini (1873-1961) was born in Naples and, as an historian whose work focused mainly on the development of southern Italy, had a deep influence on Gramsci's understanding of Italian history. In 1917 he took up a professorship at the University of Florence. A critic of PSI, he was editor of the liberal newpaper *L'Unita* and was later (in 1919-1921) a liberal deputy in parliament. He was arrested by the fascists in 1925, soon released, and left for the U.S. where he became a professor of history at Harvard. His most well-known book is *Under the Axe of Fascism* (1936).

Georges Sorel (1847-1922) was born in Cherbourg, studied at the Ecole Polytechnique, and became an engineer for the French government, where he worked until 1892. He then became interested in Marx and later in Proudhon, who supplied the theoretical basis of the syndicalism he developed after 1895. He argued for a movement rooted in the spontaneous energy of the working class directed against the centers of economic power and outside of the trade unions and political parties. He emerged as one of the most severe critics of parliamentary democracy. His impact upon Gramsci and *Ordine Nuovo*, notably in the emphasis upon direct activity at the point of production, was profound. Not long after the appearance of his important works, *Reflections on Violence, The Illusions of Progress,* and *The Disintegration of Marxism* (all 1908), he drifted away from syndicalism and toward nationalism. By the time of his death he had long since detached himself from the life of any political movement.

Angelo Tasca (1892-1960) was born in Turin, attended the University of Turin, and founded the youth section of the PSI in 1909. He was responsible for initiating Gramsci into the PSI in 1911 and was one of Gramsci's early political mentors. His main early interest, which remained with him for years, was in the trade unions. He was a founder (along with Gramsci, Palmiro Togliatti, and Umberto Terracini) of the *Ordine Nuovo* group in 1919. Already by 1920, however, he was at odds with Gramsci over the latter's great faith in the councils. He was one of the founders of the PCI in 1921. After Gramsci's arrest, he and Togliatti shared the leadership of the party for a short period. In 1930 he was expelled from the PCI for "right wing" tendencies. In exile, he wrote as a political sociologist under the name A. Rossi.

Palmiro Togliatti (1893-1964) was born in Genoa and attended the University of Turin at the same time as Gramsci. He joined Tasca's youth section of the PSI in 1914, and in 1919 he was co-founder of *Ordine Nuovo*. In 1922 he became a member of the Central Committee of the PCI and threw his weight behind

Gramsci in the debate with Bordiga. In 1927 he shared the leadership of the party with Tasca, and by 1930 he was a major figure in the Comintern (serving as one of its secretaries after 1935). After spending the war years in the USSR, he returned to Italy in 1944 and steered the PCI toward the "Salerno turn"—toward a parliamentarist strategy. He served as a minister in several postwar governments, was secretary-general of the PCI until his death, and was a strong force (in the late 1950s and early 1960s) behind the move toward "polycentrism" within International Communism. He sought to present a continuity from Gramsci to his own structural reformist theories within the PCI, in articles and party statements which are contained in three anthologies: *The Party* and *The Italian Road to Socialism* (both published in 1964), and the English-language collection *On Gramsci and Other Writings*.

Index

abstentionism, 9, 70, 226, 251.
Action Party, 173, 177
"actuality of revolution," 230
Adamson, Walter, 32n, 240n, 271n, 293n.
Adler, Franklin, 116n.
Adorno, Theodor, 150n.
Agazzi, Emilio, 61n.
Agnelli, Giovanni, 97, 98.
Alcara, Rosa, 270n.
alienation, 3, 44, 47, 69, 169, 216.
Althusser, Louis, 146n.
"Americanism," 178, 179, 180, 185.
Anarchism, 5, 73, 208, 215, 244, 246.
Anderson, Perry, 33n, 35n, 145n, 191n, 198n, 273n.
Arato, Andrew, 34n, 194n.
aristocracy, 173, 178.
"aristocracy of labor," 154
Auciello, Nicola, 35n, 193n.
Avineri, Shlomo, 146n, 270n.
Axelrod, Paul, 248
Badoloni, Nicola, 145n, 194n, 236n, 269n.
Bahro, Rudolf, 274n.
Balibar, Etienne, 146n.
Barbusse, Henri, 44, 63, 74.
base-superstructure model, 24, 41, 123, 140, 156, 158, 186, 246.
Baxandall, Lee, 233n.
Bergson, Henri, 5, 255.
Bernstein, Edward, viii, 26, 146, 153, 155, 245, 297.
Biennio Rosso, 8, 15, 16, 18, 21, 53, 70-72, 76, 79, 82, 88, 95, 99-102, 105, 117, 228, 230.
Blanquism, 213, 247-48, 252, 263.
Bobbio, Norberto, 32n, 149n, 273n.
Bodei, Remo, 234n.

Boggs, Carl, 32n, 241n, 274n, 295n.
Bologna, Sergio, 113n.
Bolshevik party, 5, 19, 20, 46, 67, 83, 218, 249, 263, 272, 274.
Bolshevik Revolution, x, 1, 7, 20, 27, 54-58, 67, 70, 74, 75, 126, 244, 248, 252, 263, 266, 273, 277, 280, 290.
"Bonapartism," 260, 263, 264, 272.
Bordiga, Amadeo, 9, 16, 19, 70, 90-95, 102-05, 109n, 114-116n, 205, 226, 230, 244, 260, 263, 269n, 270n, 272n, 280, 297.
bourgeois democracy, 226, 258, 283, 284, 288-89.
bourgeois revolution, 258.
Braverman, Harry, 294n.
Breines, Paul, 34n, 194n.
Bricaner, Serge, 67n.
Buci-Glucksmann, Christine, 32n, 63n, 191n, 296n.
Bukharin, Nikolai, 122, 126, 131-136, 148n, 159, 235n, 297.
bureaucracy, 82, 84, 89, 148, 154, 160, 181-85, 267, 280, 285.
bureaucratic centralism, ix, 20, 24, 245-47, 256, 265, 266, 277, 280, 293.
Cadorna, Luigi, 256.
"Caesarism," 165, 222.
Cammet, John, 31n, 116n, 234.
Carlo, Antonio, 273n.
Cappillo, Santiago, 35n.
"catharsis," 228.
Catholicism, x, 11, 28, 50-54, 122, 130, 142, 149, 172, 175-176, 180, 195, 259, 281.
Cavalcanti, Pedro, 30n.
Cavour, 177.
cells, 249.
Cerroni, Umberto, 271n.

305